THE STORY OF WELSH BOXING

THE STORY OF WELSH BOXING

PRIZE FIGHTERS OF WALES

LAWRENCE DAVIES

pitch

First published by Pitch Publishing, 2019

Pitch Publishing
A2 Yeoman Gate
Yeoman Way
Worthing
Sussex
BN13 3QZ
www.pitchpublishing.co.uk
info@pitchpublishing.co.uk

A CIP catalogue record is available for this book from the British Library.

ISBN 978-1-78531-503-9

Typesetting and origination by Pitch Publishing

Printed and bound in India by Replika Press Pvt. Ltd.

Contents

Dedication

This book is dedicated to the memory of my late father, who never stopped fighting.

Foreword

It is a privilege and an honour to be asked to write the foreword to such a well-researched book as Lawrence Davies has produced in the following pages, bringing to light the deeds of the early Welsh bare knuckle fighters, whose accomplishments have long been lost in the mists of time. What makes this book even more impressive is the fact that Wales, with its strong chapel background, was very reluctant to publish any news pertaining to bare knuckle prize fights, or information on the men who took part in them, unless, of course, a death occurred, or a pugilist got into trouble with the law, or was arrested for drunkenness, assault, etc.

The Cambrian was the only Welsh newspaper reluctantly giving any real sort of coverage to the early days of the bare knuckle art (and that was poor to say the least), but it by far outdid any other Welsh newspapers of the day in its coverage of the sport. This was a trend that was to recur as regards boxing in Wales, both with bare knuckle prize fighting and with the gloves (Marquess of Queensbury rules), right up to until the First World War of 1914–1918 (and even after that) with but few exceptions. But in the following pages, Lawrence Davies brings to life not only the more famous men of Welsh origin (and those who claimed to be) in the very early days of bare knuckle prize fighting and its heyday, such as Ned Turner and 'Paddington' Jones, but also sheds light on men such as Jack Rasher, Edward Morgan ('The Welch Boy'), James Francis ('The Terrible Welchman'), Ellis Pannwr, Ned Davis of Wrexham, Ned and William Savage, William Charles, Bob Parry, John Thomas of Merthyr, plus many more.

In fact, this book could be said to excel the author's previous excellent book *Mountain Fighters, Lost Tales of Welsh Boxing*, which covered the later bare knuckle prize fighters of Wales. What really impressed me in this book was the inclusion of early 'prize fights', with the broadsword and quarterstaff etc, besides those with bare fists, as it gives the reader a glimpse of when bare knuckle prize fighting (with the fists) broke away from being bracketed with the broadsword and the quarterstaff, in the days of James Figg and Ned Sutton.

Yes, this is a truly well-researched book on a very difficult subject. I am sure that Lawrence will one day join the prize ring historian Tony Gee in the 'Bare Knuckle Boxing Hall of Fame'. After producing such a remarkable book, and to have done so when there is so little to go on, is a feat in itself that deserves recognition, which I am sure it will receive.

Harold Alderman MBE
Boxing Historian, Aylesham, Kent

Acknowledgements

Over the course of many years researching Welsh boxing and prize fighting history, I must acknowledge the assistance of staff at a number of libraries within Wales, including those at Cardiff, Merthyr, Newport, Pontypridd, and Swansea amongst others, in addition to staff at the National Library of Wales, Aberystwyth. The author is also grateful for the help given by British Library staff over the course of long hours spent researching at the British Library newspaper archive at Colindale, London, which has sadly now closed. Thanks must also be given to April Schupmann of Austin, Texas, who digitally restored a large number of the rare images and portraiture taken from the author's personal collection that appear within this book, many for the first time. I am also grateful to the History of Parliament Trust for allowing me to reproduce the portrait of Sir Watkin Williams Wynn by Albin Roberts Burt included in this volume, the copyright of which is owned by the Trust.

I am grateful for the kindness of Harold Alderman MBE, the pioneering British boxing historian, of Aylesham, Kent, who wrote the Foreword for this book. Mr Alderman's historical work on boxing and the early glove period has paved the way for much that is understood about British boxing history today. Without the many years that Mr Alderman devoted to documenting the records of boxers of the past, it is unlikely that a large number of books on boxing history would have been written.

I am thankful for the support of the prolific award-winning author and boxing authority Graeme Kent, whose superbly written book *A Welshman in The Bronx: Tommy Farr vs. Joe Louis* (Llandysul: Gomer Press, 2009) was a treasured present from my late father. The author is indebted to Mr Kent's kindness following the publication of my first book *Mountain Fighters, Lost Tales of*

Welsh Boxing (2011), and his support of my second book on Welsh boxing, *Jack Scarrott's Prize Fighters, Memoirs of a Welsh Boxing Booth Showman* (2016). Without Mr Kent's kind encouragement and his appreciation of my original research, it is unlikely that this book would have been written.

I must also credit the assistance of the prize ring historian Tony Gee, whose book *Up To Scratch: Bareknuckle Fighting and Heroes of the Prize-ring* (Harpenden: Queen Anne Press, 1994) remains one of the most keenly researched and accurate books on British prize fighting to date. Tony Gee is an expert on the prize ring, and has assisted the British Museum, the National Portrait Gallery and the Jewish Museum of London. Tony Gee has also written a number of articles on early pugilists and pugilism for the Oxford Dictionary of National Biography, which must be viewed as essential reading for the boxing historian seeking to understand this frequently inaccurately recorded period of early pugilism. The author wishes to thank Tony Gee for his assistance in documenting the early period of boxing history relating to some of the early prize fighters or 'weapons exponents'. It must be stated that any errors found within are entirely the author's own. Finally, I must also thank Paul and Jane Camillin of Pitch Publishing for supporting this book.

Introduction

Boxing has always played an important role in the sporting and social history of Wales, and was responsible for the rise of some of the most familiar Welsh sporting heroes in the early years of the 20th century. Men such as Freddie Welsh, Jim Driscoll and Jimmy Wilde are remembered as boxing legends that put Wales on the map as a country capable of producing fighters whose names are ranked alongside some of the greatest British fighters ever to have pulled on the gloves. For most sports historians, this is where the story of Welsh boxing begins, with the rise of nationally acknowledged champions such as Tom Thomas of Penygraig, who lifted the British middleweight crown in 1908. It seems logical to conclude, though, that for a champion to have travelled the path towards such fame, he must have beaten those challengers that are often forgotten. The greatest part of the early story of Welsh glove boxing has never been written. This being the case, it is perhaps understandable that the story of Welsh prize fighting, or bare knuckle boxing, has never been told.

Before the widespread adoption of boxing gloves, rules and regulations, there was another fighting breed – the 'mountain fighters'. These Welsh bare knuckle fighters found that the only way to hold contests without the interference of the police was to climb up on to the lonely mountains above the towns and villages of South Wales.

At these notorious 'bloody spots' or 'blood hollows', brutal open-ended fights that sometimes lasted as many as 80 rounds would be fought, and the injuries sustained by the combatants often resulted in death. Until recent times, only the briefest of details were recorded alongside the names of these men. Names of mountain fighters that were once whispered with reverence or fear, such as John Jones of Treorchy, better known as 'Shoni Engineer', and Redmond Coleman, the 'Iron Man' of Merthyr, had slipped into the mists of time.

The author's first book, *Mountain Fighters, Lost Tales of Welsh Boxing* (2011), attempted to tell some part of the untold story of these later bare knuckle Welsh pugilists, who influenced the development of gloved boxing in Wales in ways that had previously been unexplored, for the first time. It was through the influence of later travelling fairground boxing booth owners, such as the showman William Samuels, Robert Dunbar, Patsy Perkins and the legendary Jack Scarrott, whose life was outlined in the author's second book, *Jack Scarrott's Prize Fighters, Memoirs of a Welsh Boxing Booth Showman* (2016), that gloved boxing started to become accepted as a legitimate entertainment within Wales, even if some of the promoters (in the case of William Samuels and Robert Dunbar) had previously been bare knuckle fighters themselves.

But what of those bare knuckle Welshmen who fought even prior to this time, in the days when the careers of English prize fighters were eagerly followed by the working man and gentry alike? When men such as Tom Spring and Jem Belcher were celebrated throughout the land as symbols of manliness and bravery, irrespective of the humble backgrounds from which they were frequently drawn? Even amongst boxing historians, it would be truthful to say that only two prominent Welsh fighters of the prize ring are now even vaguely recalled. Dan Thomas, better known in his native land as 'Dan Pontypridd', started his fighting career over 150 years ago, and by the time he had finished fighting, Thomas was a nationally celebrated champion of the lightweights. Soon after his retirement, Dan Thomas shunned his previous career as a prize fighter and turned to God, burning his championship belt and becoming a Baptist Deacon of a Welsh chapel. In the years after his death, the fistic achievements of Dan Pontypridd were gradually all but forgotten, and if his story was remembered at all, it was usually as little more than a folk tale told by those who came later.

Two hundred years ago, the Welsh knuckle fighter Ned Turner, known by the cognomen of the 'Out-and-Outer', was kicking his heels in Newgate prison after being imprisoned for manslaughter following the death of Jack Curtis, his first opponent in the London prize ring. It was a tragic start to what would be an impressive fighting career, and in the years that followed the name of Ned Turner was second only to that of Jack Randall, the champion of the lightweights. Ned Turner, born in Southwark, London to Welsh parents, was undoubtedly the greatest Welsh prize fighter of the period, although there were many more Welsh pugilists both before and after his time that battled for glory in the ring within Wales, as well as further abroad.

So when does the story of Welsh boxing begin? This book attempts to answer that question for the very first time, and records the deeds of those Welsh prize fighters who fought in the earliest days of British boxing. Sadly, there were no Welsh boxing enthusiasts, authors, or journalists to have recorded the achievements of their fighting countrymen alongside their English counterparts, whose fighting careers were documented to some degree by early scribes such as Captain Barclay, William Oxberry and, most notably, the gifted pen of Pierce Egan. Newspapers, ordinarily viewed as being the most accurate source of historical information, did not come into being in Wales until the early part of the 19th century. Most Welsh newspaper editors saw little merit in reporting on a sport that was frequently viewed by moral guardians as being as indefensibly barbaric as a dog fight, with money wagered on the destruction of one man by the fists of another. Even if the newspapers recognised that there was an interest in prize fighting amongst their readership, they rarely dared risk stirring the powerful wrath and public condemnation of the Welsh preachers and church folk by reporting on important local contests.

The story of Welsh boxing or fist fighting (pugilism) stretches back over 250 years, the first recorded prize fighting Welshmen having raised their fists in the days of Jack Broughton, now remembered as the father of British boxing. Their gladiatorial predecessors had fought with swords, shields, sticks and staffs in the days of James Figg, considered the first pugilistic champion of England. The vast majority of the early Welsh prize fighters and pugilists presented within this book have never been recorded in any previous book of boxing history. It is hoped that this volume, based on the extensive original research of the author, succeeds in recording the deeds of a number of forgotten fighting men of Wales, and revives the memory of a few who should not have been forgotten.

Lawrence Davies

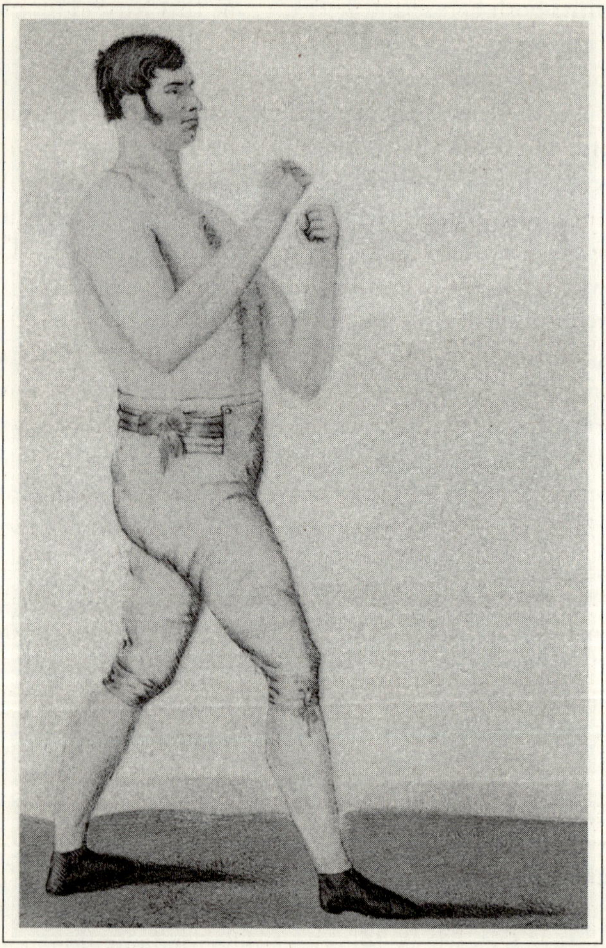

Chapter 1

The Bold Welshmen and the Master of Montgomeryshire

In the first year of the 18th century, Mr Jones of North Wales ventured from his mountainous homeland to the city of London to demonstrate his ability as a 'prize fighter'. Shortly afterwards, the *True Protestant Mercury* newspaper of 24–26 April 1700 contained the following notice:

> On Wednesday in the afternoon (24 April) a tryal of skill was performed between Joseph Thomas, Master of the noble science of self defence, and one Mr Jones, a gentleman that came out of North-Wales on purpose to fight him, at the Theater in Dorset Gardens, where were abundance of the nobility and gentry; and between each bout was a very fine consort of musick; but in the conclusion Mr Jones gained the day, with great applause.[1]

It is possible that Mr Jones might be the earliest Welsh prize fighter to be recorded in print. Although the term 'prize fighter' is now more closely associated with fist fighting as opposed to any other form of combat, in the days of Mr Jones, these 'original' prize fighters were commonly what might be better termed as 'weapons exponents'. Prior to the above contest, held at the Dorset

1 This record of the prizefight between Mr Jones and Joseph Thomas was also recorded in *Anecdotes of the Manners and Customs of London During the Eighteenth Century*, Volume 2, by James Peller Malcolm, F.S.A (London: Longman, Hurst, Rees and Orme, 1810) and in *La Belle Assemblée Or, Bell's Court and Fashionable Magazine*, Volume 5, (London: J. Bell, 1808).

Gardens Theatre, at Whitefriars, prize fighting with weapons in gladiatorial contests had long been an entertainment that was patronised by the good and the great alike.

Samuel Pepys would record in his Diary[2] that he had attended one such 'prize' fought between 'Mathews' and 'Westwicke' on 1 June 1662, at the New Theatre near the Strand May-pole. The combatants 'fought at eight weapons, three boutes at each weapon'. Mathews was victorious, and Westwicke was 'soundly cut several times both in the head and legs, that he was all over blood; and other deadly blows they did give and take in the very good earnest, till Westwicke was in a sad pickle'. Perhaps expecting an element of trickery, Pepys examined one of the swords used, and 'found it to be very little, if at all blunter on the edge than the common swords are'. The diarist also recorded that he had been surprised by the large amount of money thrown upon the stage by the spectators between each bout.

A decade later, Monsieur Lorevin de Rocheford would recount that he had witnessed a bloody prize fight in his book *An Account of a Journey to the British Isles* (1672), which was held at the Bear Garden in Southwark. Rocheford found that these prize fights were fought without chicanery, and frequently resulted in considerable personal injuries to the combatants.

'We went to see the "Bergiardin" where combats are fought by all sorts of animals, and sometimes men, as we once saw. Commonly, when any fencing-masters are desirous of showing their courage and great skill, they issue mutual challenges, and before they engage, parade the town with drums and trumpets sounding, to inform the public there is a challenge between two brave masters of the science of defence, and that the battle will be fought on such a day.

'We went to see such a combat, which was performed on a stage in the middle of an amphitheatre, when, on the flourish of trumpets and the beats of drums, the combatants entered, stripped to their shirts. On a signal from the drum, they drew their swords and immediately began to fight, skirmishing a long time without wounds. They were both very skilful and courageous.

---

2 *Diary and Correspondence of Samuel Pepys*, Volume 2, by Samuel Pepys (Philadelphia: J.B. Lippincott & Co., 1866).

The tallest had the advantage over the smallest, for, according to the English fashion of fencing, they endeavoured rather to cut than to thrust in the French manner, so that by his height he had the advantage of being able to strike his antagonist on the head, against which the little one was on his guard. He had in his turn one advantage over the tall man in being able to give him the Jarnac stroke, by cutting him on the right ham, which he left in a manner quite unguarded. So that, all things considered, they were equally matched. Nevertheless, the tall one struck the little one on the wrist, which he almost cut off, but this did not prevent him from continuing the fight, after he had been dressed, and taken a glass or two of wine to give him courage, when he took ample vengeance for his wound; for a little afterwards, making a feint at the ham, the tall man stooping in order to parry it, laid his whole head open, when the little one gave him a stroke which took off a slice of his head and almost all his ear. For my part, I think there is a barbarity and inhumanity in permitting men to kill each other for diversion. The surgeons immediately dressed them and bound up their wounds; which being done, they renewed the combat, and both being sensible of their respective disadvantages, they therefore were a long time without receiving or giving a wound, which was the cause that the little one, failing to parry so exactly, being tired with his long battle, received another stroke on his wounded wrist, which, dividing the sinews, he remained vanquished, and the tall conqueror received the applause of the spectators.[3]'

While these stage fights benefitted the gladiators financially, with the men receiving the stakes deposited on the outcome of a contest, and often a share of the gate money, they also publicised the ability of a 'prize' fighter. Public demonstration of skill encouraged spectators to engage the services of the prize fighters as teachers if they had developed sufficient skill with weaponry to have earned the honourable title of 'Master of the Noble Science of Defence'. The title of 'Master' had official status and was only awarded to a weapons exponent of the highest rank, and might be thought of as being somewhat akin to a black belt awarded

3 As quoted in *Schools and Masters of Fencing From the Middle Ages to the Eighteenth Century*, Egerton Castle, (London: G. Bell & Sons, 1885) and *London in the Time of the Stuarts*, Volume 6, by Sir Walter Besant (London: A & C. Black, 1903).

to experienced martial artists. At another notorious London amphitheatre where such contests took place, the Bear Garden, located at Hockley in the Hole, the *True Protestant Mercury* of 21 June 1700 recorded a well-contested battle as having taken place between two Welshmen.

'Yesterday, a prize was fought at the Bear-garden, between one King and another, said to be both Welshmen: they no way counterfeited, but cut each other to that degree that they both jump'd off together, and gave great satisfaction to the company.'

It seems possible that the unnamed combatant who engaged Mr King may have been Mr Jones himself, and that Mr Jones of North Wales might have studied the use of weaponry as a 'scholar' under a particularly well-regarded Master named James Harris from Herefordshire. A later advertisement printed in the *Post man* on 29 October announced a contest between James Harris, 'a Herefordshire man, master of the noble science of defence (who hath fought fourscore and seventeen prizes, and was never worsted…' and his opponent, Francis Gorman, 'who lately cut down 3 famous men, master of the said science'. The advert also draws attention to Harris's status as the 'master to Mr Jones, the bold Welshman, and Mr King.[4]'

James Harris had fought 97 battles by this time, and was a 'Master' of standing, following a long career in which he met many skilled weapons exponents. Harris, like a number of early prize fighters, had prior experience in the use of weaponry due to his military background, in addition to having studied under a 'Master', as Harris's later response to a challenge issued by George Gray of Norwich in 1709 suggests.[5] By this time, Harris claimed...

---

4 The Mr King referred to in this advert is unlikely to be the 'Welsh' King referenced in the *Protestant Mercury* of 21 June 21 1700. It seems more likely that this is William King of 'Tidbury' (Tetbury) in Gloucestershire.

5 The famous Scottish prize fighter Donald McBane and Captain James Miller are two examples of prominent weapons exponents who came from a military background. McBane wrote a highly regarded and detailed manual of swordsmanship entitled *The Expert Sword-Man's Companion* (Glasgow: J. Duncan, 1728), and claimed to have fought 37 prize fights. The skill of Captain James Miller was liberally praised by Captain John Godfrey, and Miller also authored an illustrated album entitled *A Treatise on backsword, sword, buckler, sword and dagger, sword and great gauntlet, falchon, quarterstaff* (London: 1738).

to have 'fought a hundred and ten prizes' and stated that he had 'formerly rid in the horse-guards'.

> At the Bear-garden in Hockley-in-the-hole, near Clerkenwell Green, a trial of skill shall be performed between two masters of the noble science on Wednesday next, at two of the clock precisely.
>
> I GEORGE GRAY, born in the city of *Norwich*, who have fought in most past of the *West Indies*, namely, *Jamaica* and *Barbadoes*, and several other parts of the world, in all twenty-five times, and upon a stage, and never yet was worsted, and being now lately come to *London*, to invite James Harris to meet and exercise at these following weapons, namely, back-sword, sword and dagger, sword and buckler, single falchion, and case of falchions.
>
> I JAMES HARRIS, master of the said noble science of defence, who formerly rid in the horse-guards, and hath fought a hundred and ten prizes, and never left a stage to any man, will not fail, God willing to meet this brave and bold inviter at the time and place appointed: desiring sharps swords and from him no favor. No person to be upon the stage but the seconds. VIVAT REGINA![6]

The fame of James Harris ensured that he was 'well known throughout England', according to the *Daily Courant*, by 1709[7]. Harris's proven ability with weapons meant that his services as a teacher were much in demand into his later years. An advert published in the *Ipswich Journal* in 1729 is especially intriguing, given his tuition of Welsh scholars, and notes that as 'one of the best Swords-Men in England', Harris had 'the Honour to Teach Dukes and Lords, and abundance of Nobility in England, Ireland, Wales and Holland'.[8] It might be imagined that James Harris may have been asked to teach the use of weaponry to the 'Nobility' in Wales by special invitation, given that at the time the largest

6 This challenge, issued by George Gray to James Harris is taken from a show bill, dated 13 July 1709.

7 As recorded in the *Daily Courant*, 30 August 1709.

8 As recorded in the *Ipswich Journal*, 2–9 August 1729.

financial rewards for a 'Master of the Noble Science of Defence' lay in teaching their art in the thriving towns and cities of England.

That Mr Jones of North Wales was a more than capable prize fighter with a variety of weapons appears certain given his defeat of the well-regarded prizefighter Joseph Thomas at the Dorset Gardens Theatre. Joseph Thomas is notable for having fought the skilful Master John Terrewest of Oundle in Northamptonshire, in 1701,[9] and was also advertised to meet the accomplished Thomas Cook, and could therefore be considered to have been a prize fighter of some standing. An advert published in the *Post Man* in September of 1700 also draws attention to 'Jones the bold Welshman' having recently fought a 'Tryal of Skill' against the well-known weapons exponent William King, of 'Tidbury' (Tetbury) in Gloucestershire, at the 'Play house'.[10]

Sadly, of Mr Jones 'the bold Welshman' and Mr King, there does not appear to be any further information recorded. It seems likely that there may well have been other Welsh weapons exponents who regularly competed in the amphitheatres at this time, as Thomas Soon, another 'Bold Welshman' of 'Rixham', [11]Denbyshire, was advertised to meet John Terrewest, in August of 1711.[12] Soon was apparently viewed as having been of sufficient skill as to warrant a second meeting with Terrewest in May of 1712,[13] with both fights billed to take place at the Bear Garden in Hockley in the Hole.

---

9 Joseph Thomas was stated to have recently fought John Terrewest in the *Post Man* of 5–8 July 1701. The *Post Boy* of the same date records that Thomas had fought William King. If the *Post Boy* is correct, it would not be as significant as Thomas fighting Terrewest, although King was a very capable fighter.

10 As recorded in the *Post Man* of 7–9 September 1700.

11 Thomas Soon is recorded as having come from 'Rixham', 'Wraxham', and 'Wrixham' in the *Daily Courant*. At this time, spelling had not yet been standardised.

12 As recorded in the *Daily Courant*, 29 August 1711. An earlier advertisement that appeared in the *Daily Courant,* 18 August 1711, confirms the reputation of the bear-garden as often having attracted an unruly crowd, stating that 'A peculiar Care will be taken towards the Suppression of the Mobb in the Gallerys that no Gentleman shall be molested'.

13 As recorded in the *Daily Courant,* 21 May 1712, the contest was to take place on the same day, at the Bear Garden in Hockley in the Hole.

Thomas Soon was then matched to fight against George Gray of Norwich a few months afterwards at the George Inn in the Borough of Southwark.[14] Gray could be considered an opponent of some standing, albeit one of lesser reputation than John Terrewest.[15]

Thomas Soon was apparently proficient with a host of weapons, perhaps demonstrating enough ability to have attained the status of a 'Master of the Noble Science of Defence'. Certainly, he is remembered as such by John Lucas, the 18th century schoolmaster of Leeds, in his *Memoranda Book*.[16] Thomas Soon exhibited his skills in the town in the company of one 'Thomas Pidgeon, the 'Champion of the West', in 1713:

> *Page* 14: *Memoranda* 1713
>
> Wednesday 19 August, Thomas Soon, the bold Welshman, and Thomas Pidgeon, Champion of the West, two masters of defence, fought with six or seven sorts of weapons in the Queen's Arms and the spectators paid 12s. & 6d.

Lucas was apparently not greatly impressed by the display, stating that 'the performers proved to the satisfaction of very few'.[17] It

---

14 As recorded in the *Daily Courant*, 14 July 1712, the contest was to take place on the same day, at the George Inn in the Borough of Southwark.

15 Master John Terrewest of Oundle, in Northamptonshire, was advertised to meet such accomplished weapons exponents as Timothy Buck, George Gray, James Harris, John Parkes, Adam Wood and Thomas Hesgate. Terrewest was included in a footnote in Egerton Castle's highly regarded *Schools and Masters of Fencing From the Middle Ages to the Eighteenth Century*, which names John Terrewest at the top of the list amongst the following 'well-known prize-fighters in the heyday of back-sword fighting' – John Terrewest, John Stokes, William Gill, Perkins and (*Michael*) Butler (both Irishmen), (*Ned*) Sutton, Mr. Johnson, Mr. (*William*) Sherlock and John Delforce. Captain Godfrey would record that the skill of Delforce ensured that he was 'a rival to Fig's memory' although 'he fought with the Cudgell only'.

16 *The Memoranda Book of John Lucas 1712–1750*, Vol. 16 by John Lucas, edited by Jonathan Oates, (Leeds: The Thoresby Society, 2006).

17 There appears to be little information recorded on Thomas Pidgeon, the 'Champion of the West'. Prior to this date, in the first decade of the 18th century, the title of 'Champion of the West' had been assumed by a prize fighter named John Davis.

seems plausible that this was a performance given as part of a tour undertaken by Thomas Soon, as the *Archaeologia Aeliana,* published by the Society of Antiquaries of Newcastle upon Tyne in 1860, records that in 1713, 'two profound masters of the noble science of Defence, Thomas Soon of London, known as the "Bold Welshman" and William Emerson, the "Norfolk Champion" who lately fought the "Bold Indian" at Bridge-Town, Barbadoes', appeared at the Nag's Head public house in Gateshead. Perhaps the spectators were more impressed than John Lucas with the display that followed as, 'there was convenience made for gentlemen and ladies,' and the 'heroes exhibited their skill with back-sword, sword-and-dagger, sword-and-buckler, single-falchion, case-of-falchions, and quarter-staff'.[18] The 'Bold Welshman' and the 'Norfolk Champion' afterwards concluded their performance with a fight for ten guineas aside.[19]

The most famous of the early prize fighters was the celebrated James Figg, who was said to have been born in Thame, Oxfordshire, and is generally considered to have been the first pugilistic champion of England, although he was better known in his time for his expertise as a weapons exponent. By 1714, Figg was living in London and was learning the use of weaponry as a scholar under the notable Master, Timothy Buck of Clare Market, attaining such skill as to be given the title of Master later that year.[20] Timothy Buck's ability with weaponry was commented upon by Captain John Godfrey in his book, *A Treatise Upon the Useful Science of Defence*,

---

18 The 'back-sword' is a short, light, single-edged sword with a single-handed grip. The 'buckler' was a small round shield up to 18 inches in diameter used as a companion weapon to deflect the blow of an opponent's sword. There are many variations of the 'falchion'. The falchion pictured in Captain James Miller's album *A Treatise on backsword, sword, buckler, sword and dagger, sword and great gauntlet, falchon, quarterstaff*, is a short one-handed sword with a curved single-edged blade featuring an integral knuckle guard. To fight with a 'case-of-falchions' appears to mean to fight with a falchion in either hand. The 'quarterstaff' was a hardwood pole measuring anywhere between 6 and 9ft long that was used as a striking weapon.

19 William Emmerson would appear to have been a man of considerable skill and some renown, having been advertised to meet Timothy Buck, the Master who taught James Figg, in the *Daily Courant* on 14 August 1711.

20 James Figg was frequently described as a 'scholar' of Timothy Buck, as can be seen in one example published in the *Daily Courant* on 16 October 1714.

in which Godfrey tells his readers that, 'Timothy Buck was a most solid Master, it was apparent in his Performances, even when grown decrepid, and his old age could not hide his uncommon Judgement, He was the Pillar of the Art, and all his Followers, who excelled, built upon him.'

James Figg afterwards opened his own amphitheatre, which adjoined his house in Oxford Road, where he taught the various 'manly arts' to interested gentlemen. In time, Figg's Amphitheatre would become London's principal venue for sporting entertainments, featuring not only 'trials of skill' (involving weapons), but also 'trials of manhood' (using fists). Some of the most celebrated boxers of the day appeared at Figg's, including the Lincolnshire drover John Whitacre (Whitaker), a Westminster cabinet-maker by the name of John Gretton (Gretting), and a pipe maker from St Giles named Thomas Allen, better known as 'Pipes'. Despite Figg now being regarded as having been the first pugilistic champion, his own achievements as regards boxing seem to have been mostly confined to his appearances on his booth at Southwark Fair. James Figg is recorded by Pierce Egan in *Boxiana* as having exhibited 'his knowledge in various Combats – with the Foil, Back-sword, Cudgel and Fist' at the Fair for the entertainment of the crowds.

James Figg, considered the first pugilistic champion of England.

Pierce Egan would maintain that James Figg was 'indebted to strength and courage' for his success in battle, stating that if 'Figg's method of fighting was subject to the criticism of the present day, he would be denominated more of a *slaughterer* than that of a neat, finished pugilist'. Egan attributes Figg's expertise with the foil and cudgel to having given him a 'decidedly superior advantage over the other boxers of that day by his thorough acquaintance with *time* and *measure*'.

The author of *A Treatise Upon the Useful Science of Defence*, Captain John Godfrey, is perhaps better placed to speak of James Figg's skill with weaponry, having trained under him as his pupil.

AT

FIG'S GREAT TIL'D BOOTH,
On the Bowling-Green, Southwark,
During the time of the *FAIR*,
(Which begins on SATURDAY, the 18th of SEPTEMBER,)
The TOWN will be entertained with the
MANLY ARTS OF
Foil-play, Back-sword, Cudgelling, and Boxing,
in which

The noted PARKS, from Coventry, and the celebrated gentleman prize-fighter, Mr. MILLAR, will display their skill in a tilting-bout, showing the advantages of *Time* and *Measure*.

ALSO,

Mr. JOHNSON, the great Swordsman, superior to any man in the World for his unrivalled display of the *hanging-guard*, in a grand attack of SELF-DEFENCE, against the all-powerful arm of the renowned SUTTON.

DELFORCE, the finished Cudgeller, will likewise exhibit his uncommon feats with the *single-stick;* and who challenges any man in the kingdom to enter the lists with him for a *broken-head*, or a *belly-full!*

BUCKHORSE, and several other *Pugilists*, will show the Art of Boxing.

To conclude

With a GRAND PARADE by the Valiant FIG, who will exhibit his knowledge in various Combats—with the Foil, Back-sword, Cudgel, and Fist.

To begin each Day at Twelve o'Clock, and close at Ten.

Vivat Rex.

N. B. The Booth is fitted up in a most commodious manner, for the better reception of Gentlemen, &c. &c.

A handbill advertising Figg's booth at Southwark Fair (taken from Boxiana*). Weapons exponents including John Parkes, Ned Sutton and the cudgeller, John Delforce, headline the bill. Unnamed pugilists other than 'Buckhorse' (John Smith) appear as a secondary entertainment.*

> I have purchased my Knowledge in the BACK-SWORD with many a broken Head, and Bruise in every Part of me. I chose to go mostly to FIG, and exercise with him; partly, as I knew him to be the ablest Master, and partly, as he was of a rugged Temper, and would spare no Man, high or low, who took up a Stick against him. I bore his rough

> Treatment with determined Patience, and followed him so long, that FIG, at last, finding he could not have the beating of me at so cheap a Rate as usual, did not shew such Fonndess for my Company.

Despite the hardness of his tuition at the hands of James Figg, or perhaps because of it, Godfrey remained convinced of Figg's superiority over the other weapons exponents of the time, stating that:

> FIG was the Atlas of the Sword ... In him, Strength, Resolution, and unparallel'd Judgement conspired to form a matchless Master ... He was just as much a greater MASTER, than any other I ever saw, and he was a greater Judge of *Time* and *Measure.*

It can be imagined that those who chose to challenge James Figg were sorely treated, as the Irishman William Holmes would no doubt agree. Holmes was the unfortunate opponent of James Figg on the occasion of his 271st battle on 14 October 1730. It was the third time that they had met in two months and would be the last, the contest having terminated when the wrist of Holmes was cut to the bone. In *The Memoirs and Adventures of the Marquis De Bretagne and Duc D'Harcourt*, a graphic account of a sword fight between James Figg and an Irish Sergeant is described.[21] This trial of skill had headlined a comprehensive bill of entertainments, with a number of 'diversions' consisting of cudgelling, boxing and wrestling amusing the spectators prior to the main event.

'The first Trial of skill was with Sticks, which the English call Cudgels. They use them after the Manner of Hangers (*swords*), and the Strokes are given with so good Will, that I cannot conceive how they can give each other so many without breaking Arms or Heads, for they fight quite naked. Whoever draws Blood from his Antagonist's Head first, is Conqueror.'

21 *The Memoirs and Adventures of the Marquis De Bretagne and Duc D'Harcourt*, Volume 2 by Antoine François Prévost d'Exiles, Translated from the Original French By Mr. Erskine, (London: T. Cooper at the Globe, 1743).

After having witnessed his first cudgelling match, the Marquis was then treated to a boxing contest, which proved to be a shocking spectacle for the uninitiated.

'After cudgelling, comes boxing. The two Combatants strip, and are naked to the Belt, and the Strokes they give to one another are so violent, that they make the Blood sometimes spout out from the Mouth. I have seen some of them fall, and remain some Moments immoveable, but they soon recovered by the help of Vinegar put to their Nose. Upon which they get up, embrace their Adversary, and fall to Blows, till one or other has quite lost Strength, and sometimes Life itself. This Exercise seemed to me the most violent and dangerous.'

A wrestling bout followed the boxing contest, and was the final match prior to the main event between Figg and the Irish Sergeant.

'You see two lusty well made Fellows approach one another softly, and with Precaution observing one another carefully for a few Minutes, turning round, as it were to discover the weak Part; touching Hough to Hough, and at last grapling, they squeeze and shake one another with a suprizing Force and Agility; and sometimes it is a considerable Time before any Inequality is observed; at length, when Victory has declared itself in Favour of one, he lends a helping Hand to raise the vanquished, and then they fall to it anew, 'till one or other is quite spent.'

If the violence of the boxing match had shocked the Marquis, he must have been quite unprepared for the bloodshed that marked the sword fight between James Figg and the Irish Sergeant, who shortly afterwards appeared on the stage ready for battle.

'Figg offered the Serjeant the Choice of Swords, of several that were brought upon the Stage, about two Inches in breadth, and the Points ground off. I had the Curiosity to take one of them in my Hand, and found that it was sharp edged enough to cut off an Arm or a Leg. The Combatants, after shaking Hands, as a Mark of Friendship and Esteem, put themselves in a Posture of Defence, crossed their Weapons, and began a furious Attack. We must not imagine that there was any foul play in the Case, or that they were not serious, they let fly at one another so heartily, and with such Vigour and Rapidity, that the Spectacle became terrible, and the whole Assembly was in a profound Silence. The Serjeant made a Blow at Figg, which cut a pretty large Piece of his Stocking, without touching the Leg. Figg, whose Coolness and Judgement were suprizing, felt the Stroke; ho, ho! said he, I see thou hast a Mind to my Leg, but take Care of thy own, and with the same Breath whipped off a large Piece of the Calf of his Adversary's Leg, which fell upon the Stage; the general Applause was given to this clean Slash by clapping of Hands, and crying bravo, bravo, encora, encora, which is a sort of Approbation that they have learned from the Italians. The Serjeant, not able to support himself, sat down and looked at his Blood, which ran in Streams.'

Following the bloody outcome of this contest, the Marquis de Bretagne was convinced that Figg handled 'a broad Sword with the greatest Dexterity of any Man alive'. James Figg's greatest rival for prize fighting honours was Edward Sutton, the Gravesend pipe maker known as the 'Champion of Kent'. Figg and Sutton fought two matches with alternate success, and a third match was organised to decide which combatant could claim superiority over the other. Despite having been recorded by many as having been a boxing match, the contest between Figg and Sutton held on 14 April 1725, was a fight involving swords and quarterstaffs. Figg attacked first with such vigour that it was thought that he might have succeeded in cleaving Sutton's head clean off, had his sword not been artfully deflected by the pipe maker. So powerful was Figg's attack that his sword broke in two, although Figg fought on with his broken weapon until Sutton's blade was also seen to 'run away from its hilt'. Figg and Sutton continued to do battle with their damaged weapons, until it was noticed that Figg had sustained an injury to his side from which 'hot blood spouted out'.

In a brief halt in proceedings, Figg appealed to the spectators, pointing out that his wound had been due to the broken blade of his own sword. The combatants then resumed the battle until Figg cut Sutton's right arm. Evenly matched, the crowd called for a trial of skill using the quarterstaff to settle the affair. In the first bout, Ned Sutton was seen to good advantage, and his forceful blows were thought likely to have downed a lesser man than James Figg.

The second bout brought the issue of whether Sutton or Figg was the better man to a swift and decisive conclusion when Figg hit Sutton a blow to the knee of such force that it disabled the pipe maker, resulting in Figg's victory. After a long and celebrated career in which the name of James Figg became famous throughout the land, Figg died on 8 December 1734, at the house attached to his famous amphitheatre, and was buried three days later at the parish church of St Marylebone.

At around the same time as James Figg had been opening his amphitheatre in 1719, another Welsh weapons exponent by the name of Henry Davis, billed as having come from 'Rixham' in Wales, was advertised to meet opponents of proven ability at the Bear Garden in Hockley in the Hole.[22] On 9 June 1719, Henry Davis was advertised to fight the London prize fighter, Robert Waldron.[23] The following month would see two further contests advertised in the *Daily Courant,* with Davis having been billed to pit his skills on both occasions against Irish opponent Thomas Barrett of Dublin.[24] That Henry Davis was obviously an accomplished prize fighter can be seen from the fact that both of his opponents tangled with some of the most prominent weapons exponents of the period. Robert Waldron was advertised to fight such notable figures as James Figg, James Miller, and the prolific gladiator John Parkes of Coventry, while the Irishman Thomas Barrett also contested against such skilled men as Michael Butler, Felix MacGuire and James Stokes.

While there appear to be no records of any Welsh weapons exponents having performed at the celebrated amphitheatre of James Figg, another 'Bold Welshman' and Welsh 'Master of the Noble Art of Defence' from Montgomeryshire was engaged to fight at the amphitheatre of one of his rivals. James Stokes was the proprietor of Stokes' Amphitheatre, which adjoined his house on Islington Road, near Sadler's Wells. A contest was advertised to take place at the amphitheatre on 13 March 1727, featuring

---

22 It seems likely that Henry Davis of 'Rixham' actually came from Wrexham, as well as Thomas Soon.

23 The advertisement for the trial of skill between Henry Davis and Robert Waldron appeared in the *Daily Courant* on 9 July 1719, and was scheduled for the same day.

24 The advertisements for the two trials of skill between Henry Davis and Thomas Barrett appeared in the *Daily Courant* on 6 July 1719, and 28 July 1719, and both contests were scheduled for the following day.

another Welsh weapons exponent. What is most surprising about the contest is that the Welshman, a Master from Montgomeryshire by the name of John Crumpton, challenged such a formidable opponent as the arch rival of James Figg, the pipe maker Ned Sutton. The following advert was published in the *Weekly Journal or the British Gazetteer* a couple of days previously:

ADVERTISEMENT

At Mr. Stokes's Amphitheatre joining to his House in Islington Road, on Monday next, being the 13th of March, will be performed a Trial of Skill by the following Masters.

I John Crumpton, from Montgomeryshire in Wales, Master of the Noble Science of Defence, about 6 Years past, fought three Battles in London, with good Success, and since, the best Masters in the Kingdom of Ireland, and North of England, and most parts of Great Britain: In my long Absence there are some Upstarts and Pretenders of the Sword, who feed themselves full of Vanity. I do invite Mr Sutton, who, I understand, makes it his Business to fight such Persons that does not know the Hilt from the Point, to gain a Character, at the usual Weapons practis'd on the Stage, desiring him to be Smart in Time of Action, and to use his utmost Skill, and the best judgement he is Master of, with the most Severity.

I Edward Sutton, from Gravesend, in the County of Kent, Master of the said Science, making no Apology, will not fail meeting this bold Welshman at the place above specified: where I believe I shall learn him to take Care how he deals with such Pretenders and Upstarts, which shall be my utmost Care, to please the Gentlemen with intire Satisfaction, as my usual Custom is.

The Boxes will be set at Three, and the Masters mount at Five.

N.B. There will be the Diversion of Cudgel playing before the Masters mount.

No person to be admitted under one shilling.

* * * *

There can be no doubt that John Crumpton must have been an accomplished weapons exponent to have challenged a Master of such standing as Sutton, less than two years after Sutton's famous battle with James Figg. That Crumpton also routinely fought his fellow Masters throughout the British Isles over the course of six years after having met challengers in London would suggest that John Crumpton was a man of considerable skill. Surprisingly, given the dangerous nature of fighting with bladed weapons and the high risk of personal injury, some prize fighters fought large numbers of battles over the course of their long careers. Few could probably rival the record of the famous gladiator John Parkes of Coventry, who, in a 25-year career, was remembered as having fought an astonishing 350 contests.[25] Sadly, reports on the outcomes of advertised prize fights between weapons exponents are few and far between, and the outcome of John Crumpton's meeting with Edward Sutton (or even if it took place) remains a mystery.

Perhaps the mysterious Mr Jones of North Wales, the obscure Mr King, Thomas Soon and Henry Davis of 'Rixham', along with the 'Master of Montgomeryshire', John Crumpton, are the only traces now remaining that 'Bold Welshmen' once fought and battled with the sword and staff alongside other weapons exponents in the days of James Figg. Of those who may have had the temerity to swap fists in boxing contests in the days of Figg, it appears that there is no trace left at all. The first Welshman who appears to have been recorded as having fought competitively with the fists emerged in the days of Jack Broughton, commonly known as the 'father of British Boxing', on the booth of his great rival, George Taylor.

---

25 John Parkes is buried in St Michael's churchyard, Coventry. His epitaph reads: 'To the memory of Mr John Parkes, a native of this city. He was a man of a mild disposition, A gladiator by profession, Who, after having fought 350 battles, In the principal parts of Europe, with honour and applause, At length quitted the stage, sheathed his sword, And with Christian resignation, Submitted to the Grand Victor, In the 52nd year of his life. Anno 1733.'

Chapter 2

The Terrible Welchman and the Welch Boy

After the death of James Figg, a barber and wig maker named George Taylor, known as 'George the Barber', was considered second only to Jack Broughton as the best boxer of the age. As with Figg, George Taylor's abilities as a pugilist were built on a sound foundation in swordsmanship. *Boxiana* states that Taylor was 'rated as a strong, able pugilist, possessing a most extraordinary skill, and aided by his knowledge of the small and back sword, and a remarkable judgement in the cross-buttock-fall' and that he was thought 'able to contend for victory with any one'. Based on his skill with sword and fist, Taylor thought himself to be 'a proper person to succeed the late Figg in his amphitheatre, and lost no time in becoming its proprietor'. George Taylor invited the most celebrated men of the various branches of self-defence to display their skills at the amphitheatre. As the takings at these events often amounted to as much as £150, it meant that the pugilists were not slow in recognising the benefit of putting themselves under Taylor's management. The pugilists were enabled to increase their earnings to a quite unprecedented degree by the terms of the division of the door takings. One third of the takings went to the proprietor, with the remaining funds being divided between the 'champions', the victor receiving two-thirds and the loser receiving the remaining third.

A band of famous fighters soon came under George Taylor's banner, and after Jack Broughton himself, the best of these was undoubtedly Thomas Allen ('Pipes') and John Gretton (Gretting), followed by Jack James, James Field, John Smith ('Buckhorse') and a particularly intriguing figure in these early days of pugilism known as Prince (Benjamin) Boswell. Boswell is said to have come from a gypsy encampment on Finchley Common. Pugnus in his *History of the Prize Ring* and Oxberry's *Pancratia* record Boswell as being the son of the king of the English Romanies, while other sources claim that he was the nephew of the ruler of the Yorkshire clan. Regardless of the nature of his position amongst his people, it must have been a great surprise to them when Benjamin Boswell renounced his status and decided, after a short period of time where he appears to have been a highwayman, to become a professional pugilist. At some point he caught the eye of George Taylor, and he afterwards became a popular performer on the 'Great Booth at Tottenham Court', where Taylor was the proprietor.

The main source on which we can draw evidence of Boswell's fistic abilities is Godfrey's *A Treatise upon the Useful Science of Defence*. Godfrey was particularly impressed with the force with which Boswell was able to throw a decisive blow with the left hand, commenting, 'He had a particular Blow with his left Hand at the Jaw, which comes almost as hard as a little Horse kicks', and which was extremely successful in fracturing the jaws of multiple opponents. Also noteworthy was Prince Boswell's 'Power of Fighting, his excellent Choice of Time and Measure, his superior Judgement, dispatching forth his executing Arm!'

Given his recognition of Boswell's skill as a boxer, it is perhaps surprising to read that the author of *A Treatise upon the Useful Science of Defence* believed that Boswell lacked the courage (or 'Bottom') to 'qualify him for a compleat Boxer', and even wished to see him defeated.

'...fye upon his dastard Heart, that mars it all! As I knew that Fellow's Abilities, and his worm dread Soul, I never saw him beat, but I wished him to be beaten. Though I am charmed with the Idea of his Power and Manner of Fighting, I am sick at the Thoughts of his Nurse-wanting Courage.'

Godfrey alleged that had Boswell been equipped with sufficient courage or 'true *English* Bottom (the best fitting Epithet for a Man of Spirit)', Boswell would be likely to 'carry all before him, and be a Match for even BROUGHTON himself'. It seems curious that having so openly praised Boswell's fistic skills, Godfrey proves to be quite so harsh in his judgement of Boswell's character. It seems plausible that as Boswell was a gypsy, Captain

Godfrey may well have been quicker to seek evidence of a lack of 'English' courage than he might have perceived amongst Boswell's contemporaries.

Jack Broughton, the father of British boxing.

Although Godfrey's viewpoint has to be respected, having been an accomplished amateur sportsman, perhaps it is best taken with a pinch of salt. In Boswell's defence, he possessed sufficient courage to meet George Taylor in battle, although the contest that is usually referenced by ring historians is one which occurred on 16 June 1741, of which *Pugilistica* states that Boswell 'lost heart at finding Taylor so difficult to get at, and surrendered after a few sharp rounds'. As research undertaken by the prize ring historian Tony Gee in his book *Up To Scratch, Bareknuckle Fighting and Heroes of the Prize-ring* shows, it is fair to say that to record Boswell's career in such a perfunctory manner does not do him justice. An earlier fight between Boswell and Taylor was reported in the *Daily Advertiser* on 6 October 1739. On this occasion, George Taylor was defeated 'after a stout Engagement, which lasted sixteen Minutes'. Through having uncovered newspaper advertisements in which both Boswell and Taylor were advertised to meet, Gee suggests that they may have fought on up to five occasions between 1737 and 1743.

As Boswell's fame grew, numerous contests against potential opponents would be advertised, although only a few reports of these battles were recorded in the press, and the outcome of many contests in which Boswell participated are unknown to us. What is intriguing is that one of these challengers was a pugilist from Flintshire who was familiar enough to those spectators crowded around the 'Great Booth' to have earned himself the cognomen of the 'Terrible Welchman'. The following advert appeared amongst the pages of the *Daily Advertiser* on Friday, 26 December 1740:

> At the Great Booth at Tottenham Court on Tuesday 30th. I, James Francis, known by the name of the Terrible Welchman, from Flintshire, do challenge the noted

> Benjamin Boswell to box him for thirty pounds and show him his deficiency in the Art.
>
> James Francis
>
> I, Benjamin Boswell, will not fail meeting Mr Francis at his desire, and fight him for the sum mention'd, and will be sure to give him some of my usual Likers.
>
> Benjamin Boswell

Somewhat inevitably, there are no records in the annals of the prize ring to tell us any more about James Francis. That Francis was a pugilist of some ability can only be imagined by the fact that he was thought a worthy challenger for Boswell, and that he must have had some support to do so, as the 'Terrible Welchman' was challenging for the not insignificant sum of £30. It seems conceivable that there may have been other Welshmen fighting with fists in the various booths and rings dotted about the city of London, although more likely at an inferior level. In the years that followed, pugilists of merit were most often found performing at Broughton's amphitheatre.

Jack Broughton was the greatest boxer of the age. While James Figg could perhaps be said to have brought the fledgling sport to wider public attention, it is Broughton who is largely credited as having been the founder of boxing. Jack Broughton was a powerhouse of a fighter, broad chested and muscular, standing an inch short of 6ft and weighing under 14st. His eyes were quick to perceive the weaknesses of his adversaries, and he was skilled at stopping his opponent's blows and knocking them away with such ease that he astonished rivals and spectators alike. Broughton would often catch blows aimed at his head with an open hand. While Broughton commonly utilised a blow to the stomach that frequently terminated contests in his favour, he was also well known for a 'lunge' that he sought to land under the left ear, and which resulted in 'terrible consequences'. At the disabling cross-buttocks throw, Broughton was also masterful. As the first scientific boxer of note, Jack Broughton was always improving his technique. Pierce Egan would say of him that,

> BROUGHTON, like all great masters, generally exhibited something NEW in every performance; and

> those pugilists who had witnessed his contests, and afterwards entered the lists with him, expecting to find that he would fight upon the *old suit*, were most terribly deceived; as, contrast to most other boxers, he did not depend upon any *particular* blow, although he was distinguished for giving some remarkable hits, which were scarcely ever *forgotten*.

Those opponents unlikely to have forgotten Broughton's tremendous blows over the course of his long pugilistic career included Thomas Allen ('Pipes'), John Gretton (Gretting), Thomas Edwards and Charles Raventon (Reventon). Jack Broughton laid waste to any pretensions that George Taylor might have had as to being the 'Champion' in May of 1737. The coachman, George Stephenson (Stevenson), was also defeated the following year. When it was suggested to Broughton by his ever-growing circle of sporting friends that they had grown weary of the Spartan facilities offered by Taylor's booth, Broughton was quick to see the advantages of striking out on his own, and he drafted a proposal for another London-based amphitheatre to showcase the art of boxing. Contributions from well-heeled admirers amongst the gentry and nobility were not slow in coming. Many were no doubt eager to do so in order to attend Broughton's academy of boxing, where gentlemen could learn to box with mufflers intended to protect them from the 'Inconveniency of *black Eyes*, *broken Jaws*, and *bloody Noses*.' Broughton's 'New Amphitheatre' would open its doors a few months later on 10 March 1743, on the Oxford Road.

It was the beginning of the end for George Taylor's establishment. While Taylor was quick to engage Broughton in a war of words, the barber soon realised that the writing was on the wall. Taylor ended up closing his doors and threw in his lot with Broughton, bringing a number of the pugilists who had appeared on his booth with him. Broughton's New Amphitheatre was well furnished, with both boxes and a gallery for those gentlemen desiring a greater degree of comfort, and a pit for the masses that crowded around the stage. Broughton's amphitheatre quickly became the leading sporting venue in London, where spectators could witness the skills of the foremost pugilists of the day. Its popularity was aided by the fact that while its interior provided comfortable accommodation for the gentry, the cheaper entrance fees also attracted large numbers of the general public.

In the same year, 1743, Jack Broughton drafted his most long-lasting contribution to the sport of boxing when he penned his rules of boxing, enabling a greater degree of order in competition that the ring had previously seen. Originally drawn solely for the better management of his amphitheatre, the rules would be almost universally adopted outside of it, as they outlined the best practices in use at that time. That these regulations were a sound innovation can be seen by the fact that they remained the main guidelines for pugilistic combat for almost a century afterwards. Broughton's amphitheatre would also set the stage for one grandly advertised 'trial of manhood' between one Edward Morgan, known as the 'Welch Boy', and John James in January of 1745:

Daily Advertiser, 9 January 1745

AT Broughton's New Amphitheatre, in Oxford, the back of the late Mr Figg's, on Wednesday the 23rd, instant, will be exhibited a severe trial of manhood between the following champions, viz.

I Edward Morgan, commonly call'd the Welch Boy, which same about ten years ago was a terror to the most celebrated boxers now in vogue, especially to the famous Thomas Smalwood, and the noted Bellows, both which I beat with ease in one day, being lately returned from _____ hearing of the gallant behaviour of the illustrious Mr John James, in order to revive my reputation, and increase my honour, do invite him to fight me for ten pounds, when I doubt not but to put a stop to his conquests, and convince the spectators, that the superiority of mankind belongs to

"EDWARD MORGAN"

I JOHN JAMES accept the above challenge, and will not fail to meet and fight him for his sum, hoping to continue the character gentlemen have been pleased hitherto to favour me with

"JOHN JAMES"

> There will be several bye battles as usual. The doors will be open'd at ten, and the champions mount at twelve.

* * * *

The appearance of the 'Welch Boy' on the stage at Broughton's Amphitheatre is intriguing for a number of reasons. Firstly, the contest was obviously of considerable interest to the sporting men of the time, with Edward Morgan's battle against John James receiving top billing, above the minor (bye) battles that were to be contested prior to the main event. This can be attributed in part to the high regard in which John James was held. James came from a well-known fighting family, and his father 'old Jockey James' of Newmarket had been billed at one time as 'the bravest of his Age in the manly Art of Boxing'. Captain John Godfrey would be particularly complimentary of John James's accomplishments, stating,

> JAMES I proclaim a most charming Boxer. He is delicate in his Blows, and has a Wrist as delightful to those who see him fight, as it is sickly to those who fight against him. I acknowledge him to have the best Spring of the Arm of all the modern Boxers; he is a compleat Master of the Art, and, as I do not know he wants a Bottom, I think it a great Pity he should be beat for want of Strength to stand his Man.

If any further reference to John James's status as a top-level competitor were needed, the fact that he once fought Jack Broughton, albeit unsuccessfully, would confirm his reputation as a pugilist of the first rank. James is also recorded as having fought and beaten a notable pugilist named Dick Harris, better known as 'Chicken' Harris, by virtue of his having been a poulterer, in a 'severe though short battle' on 19 July 1741, at George Taylor's booth.

It would appear that Edward Morgan was a seasoned performer, with some credentials to rightfully claim to have been a 'terror' amongst the boxers performing in London some ten years previously. It was certainly no small boast to have beaten the 'famous Thomas Smalwood' as well as the 'noted Bellows' on the same day 'with ease'. Thomas Smallwood stands tall amongst the fighting men of the period. Captain Godfrey would state that he believed the courage of Smallwood along with that of the coachman, George Stevenson, made them the 'best Bottom Men of the modern Boxers'. Expanding upon the attributes of Smallwood, Godfrey would write that,

> SMALLWOOD is thorough game, with Judgement equal to any, and superior to most. I know nothing SMALLWOOD wants but Weight, to stand against any Man; and I never knew him beaten since his fighting DIMMOCK (which was in his Infancy of Boxing, and when he was a perfect Stripling in Years) but by a Force so superior, that to have resisted longer would not have been Courage but Madness. If I were to chuse a Boxer for my Money, and could but purchase him Strength equal to his Resolution, SMALLWOOD should be the Man.

According to *Fistiana*, this fight against Dimmock occurred on Taylor's Great Booth in May of 1741. There would appear to be no shame in the defeat, as Dimmock was a fighter of great strength and considerable skill. Smallwood's next battle, against Dick Harris on 23 November 1741, was also commented upon by Pierce Egan in *Boxiana*, and apparently vindicated any doubts as to his ability following his loss to Dimmock.

> SMALLWOOD proved himself fully entitled to the high opinion which had been held of him respecting his science and bottom, in a desperate conflict with one DICK HARRIS, a proper piece of hardihood. It was a most obstinate battle indeed, continuing above an hour, and was considered as *game* a one as had been witnessed for many years. HARRIS, knowing that he had got a trump to deal with, showed out with all the courage of a hero; and SMALLWOOD, to recover from his former defeat with Dimmock, endeavoured to place himself on an eminence with the first-rate pugilists of the day, by the science and intrepidity which he displayed: the fight was primely contested, and victory, for a long time, appeared doubtful

> – but DICK, not being so thoroughly acquainted with the advantages of the art to relieve himself when distressed for wind, was reluctantly compelled to acknowledge the superiority of SMALLWOOD.

Thomas Smallwood was also a great favourite of Jack Broughton himself, who witnessed the fight, and was reportedly 'much pleased with the set-to of SMALLWOOD, and his method all through the contest'. At the end of the fight, Broughton slapped him on the back and exclaimed, 'Well done, TOM! Such courage and science ought not to go unrewarded!'

It is interesting to note that as regards John James and Thomas Smallwood, both were regarded as boxers of vital importance to the takings of George Taylor's booth when Taylor's establishment was under threat following the opening of Broughton's amphitheatre. *The Gentleman's and London Magazine* would record that the 'undertaking of Mr Broughton justly gave alarm to the proprietor of the Tottenham Court Booth' and that 'Stevenson, James and Smallwood' were immediately engaged 'under articles, like regular performers, not to fight on any stage but his'.[26]

Of the 'noted Bellows' who Edward Morgan claimed to have beaten on the same day, there is very little to record other than that it seems likely he was Richard Bellows, who fought a 'bye' (or minor) battle in March of 1745, and who was also referred to as 'the noted Bellows'. Perhaps more significantly, Bellows was advertised to meet the prolific Dublin fighter Patrick Henley in December the previous year. Assuming that the defeat of both Smallwood and Bellows occurred roughly around the year 1735, (five years prior to the challenge issued by James Francis to Benjamin Boswell), Edward Morgan, the 'Welch Boy', might well be the first Welsh pugilist of prominence who fought in the London Prize Ring to be recorded in print.

Edward Morgan would not be the only Welshman recorded as having appeared at Broughton's amphitheatre. Despite having founded his establishment principally to further the sport

26 As recorded in *'Modern History of Boxing'* within *The Gentleman's and London Magazine or Monthly Chronologer, 1741–1794* (Dublin: John Exshaw).

of boxing, Broughton saw profit in continuing to publicise occasional 'tryals of skill' with weapons. One of these contests was advertised in *The Penny London Post or, The Morning Advertiser* in July of 1746, although it was incorrectly announced as being a 'Tryial of Manhood' (meaning with fists). The headlining contest was between the celebrated John Needs, the 'Green Knight' from Frome in Somersetshire, against Thomas Hodgkins. Prior to the main event, William Gwinn of Cardiganshire in South Wales announced he wished to meet any willing 'Boxing Heroes' prior to the Masters mounting the stage:

The Penny London Post, or, the Morning Advertiser
Monday 14 July to Wednesday 16 July, 1746
By particular Desire,

AT BROUGHTON's New Amphitheatre in Oxford Street, this Day, the 16th instant, will be a severe Tryial of Manhood between the following Persons.

I John Needs from Frome in Somersetshire, known by the Name of the *Green Knight*, which Name I was first invested with by the chief Nobility of this Realm, on Account of that Gallantry that I always shewed, whenever I faced an Enemy; do hereby invite this Terrifermo, who seems to carry Death's Head at his Main-Top-Mast, hoping to lower his Top-Sail, and I doubt not but I shall give him a thorough Taste of his Error, both in Falchion, Staff and Steel; which shall be the utmost Endeavour of,

Your most humble Servant,
John Needs.

I Thomas Hodgkins, will not fail meeting this notified Mr Needs at Staff and Flachion, which he has so very much boasted of: I will meet him at single and double Faulchion, besides all the other Weapons fought on the stage; and I don't in the least fear but I shall make him repent his Challenge, and give this Mr Needs his Bellyful of Falchion and Staff, which shall be the chief Ambition of, Gentlemen, Your humble Servant,

Thomas Hodgkins.

The Doors will be opened at Four o'Clock, and the Masters will mount the Stage at Six precisely.

N.B. Thomas Flowers, who fought the noted Chitam such a severe Battle last Wednesday, fights the noted Dunny Boy for five Pounds.

☞ I William Gwinn, from South-Wales, Cardiganshire, do invite any of the Boxing Heroes to face and fight me to divert the Company, till the Masters mount.

William Gwinn.

❖ Mr. Hodgins is fully resolved to maintain his School Gratis, to all Well-Wishers of King George and Duke William, that they may know how to maintain their Cutlas against their Enemies. Your humble Servant,

THOMAS HODGKINS.

Sadly, there is no way of knowing whether William Gwinn actually appeared on the stage at Broughton's Amphitheatre, as he was only challenging the pugilists present to meet him prior to the main event. Perhaps if nothing else, this surviving entry for William Gwinn at least suggests the strong possibility that there may have been other Welsh pugilists of lesser distinction featuring in bye-battles around the booths and amphitheatres of London at this time.

Following the ignominious defeat of Broughton by Jack Slack in March of 1750, which was apparently the only battle that Broughton lost in over 20 years, support for prize fighting went into a steep decline. After a few years struggling on, Broughton's New Amphitheatre closed its doors for good. As pugilism became subject to further legal interference, the press sided with the authorities against the perceived barbarism of the ring. Inevitably, the majority of prize fights after this time went unrecorded, and what records do exist give a fractured picture of pugilistic activity. It wasn't until the late 1780s that boxing started to show signs of recovery, partly due to the interest and influence of the Prince of Wales, the future King George IV. The newspapers afterwards began to report on boxing in greater detail, and it seems likely that that there would have been Welsh pugilists engaging in contests throughout this time.

AT BROUGHTON'S NEW AMPHITHEATRE,
OXFORD-ROAD,
The back of the late Mr. FIG's,
On TUESDAY next, the 13th instant,
Will be exhibited

THE TRUE ART OF BOXING,

By the *eight famed* following men, viz.

ABRAHAM EVANS,	——— ROGER,
——— SWEEP,	——— ALLEN,
——— BELAS,	ROBERT SPIKES, and
——— GLOVER,	HARRY GRAY, the clog-maker.

The above eight men are to be brought on the stage, andto be matched according to the approbation of the gentlemen who shall be pleased to honour them with their company.

N.B. There will be a BATTLE ROYAL between the
NOTED BUCKHORSE,
and SEVEN or EIGHT more; after which there will be several BY-BATTLES by others.

Gentlemen are therefore desired to come by times. The doors will be open at nine; the champions mount at eleven; and no person is to pay more than A SHILLING.

A notice advertising the opening of Broughton's New Amphitheatre which opened on 10 March, 1743 (taken from Boxiana*). Note that boxing contests appear as the main entertainment, and that weapons exponents do not feature on the billing.*

On 20 January, 1774, the *Morning Chronicle, and London Advertiser* alerted its readers to a fight that had taken place four days previously 'behind the Duke of Bedford's garden, near the British Museum', which had seen 'Black Jemmy, a very noted Welsh chairman', engage a bargeman named Mathew Kelling, with a reputation as a 'very noted bruiser in Berkshire', for ten guineas. After a 'very obstinate battle of twenty-two minutes', Black Jemmy was decisively beaten by Kelling. The Welshman presented a sad spectacle at the end of the contest and was 'carried off by his friends with the loss of one of his eyes', and was 'otherwise bruised in a terrible manner'.

One encounter with an unnamed pugilistic Welshman can be found in the career of the lightweight phenomenon Bill Perdue. Despite standing barely 5ft tall and weighing just 8st 12lbs, Perdue routinely beat men considerably larger and heavier than himself.

After having served as a sailor, Perdue set up in business as a butcher in Fleet Market, and it was there, outside of his organised fights, that he recorded a number of victories over those brave enough to test his skills in impromptu 'turn-ups'. One of these undated meetings, which probably occurred around the early 1780s, was against a 'hardy Welchman of Herculean strength' as *Boxiana* relates:

> A hardy Welchman, of Herculean strength, abused PERDUE at his own shop door, in Fleet Market, on a Saturday evening, on account of his selling his meat so dear, threatening, at the same time, to give such a little fellow a thrashing – 'You can't do it!' said BILL. A fight immediately commenced, when the *nob* of the Welchman, in the course of a few rounds, was beaten as black as the ace of spades; however, the violence of the Welshman was so great, that he had not only bit a piece out of PERDUE'S cheek, but also dislodged *four* of his teeth. The Welchman, not satisfied, brought a charge against PERDUE, before an Alderman; but the latter person was so convinced of the propriety of PERDUE'S conduct, that the Welchman had to pay all expenses.

Despite the seemingly dangerous nature of continuing his trade in Fleet Market, Perdue was still to be found there at the age of 64 in 1821, having become a respected master butcher. According to Pierce Egan, in the 'skirmishes, rows, turn-ups and battles' in which Perdue had engaged, which numbered at least a hundred, the 'Little Fighting Butcher' was never once defeated. A Welshman named Lloyd was more successful in a battle that occurred in 1787 at Ongar, in Essex, against a local man named John Smith. On 17 October 1787, the *World, Fashionable Advertiser* reported that at 'the beginning of last week, a dreadful pitched battle was fought at Ongar, between Lloyd, a Welchman, and John Smith, of Ongar'. Lloyd secured the victory in 16 rounds, despite Smith's pugilistic skills having been highly regarded in the area.

Another unnamed fist-fighting 'Welchman' was recorded as having fought a 'Tinman' on the same stage following the second battle between Tom Johnson (real name Jackling) and the Irish champion Michael Ryan on 11 February 1789, at Cashioberry Park in Hertfordshire, in which Ryan was soundly defeated in 33 minutes.[27] Although this battle between the Welshman and the tinman would appear to have gone unrecorded in the newspapers of the time, *Pugilistica* suggests that the unnamed Welshman's opponent might well have been the celebrated Bill Hooper of Bristol.[28]

These minor references to early bare knuckle Welsh pugilists aside, it wouldn't be until 1785 that a young Welshman named Thomas Jones made his first steps towards prominence in the London Prize Ring. In time, his sound reputation as a fighting man of considerable ability would lead him to become more familiar to all as 'Paddington' Jones.

---

27 As recorded in *Pancratia, or a History of Pugilism* (London: W. Oxberry, 1812).

28 Tom Johnson famously defeated the Herculean Birmingham champion Isaac Perrins in 62 rounds on 22 October 1789 at Banbury. It is intriguing to record that a pugilist named 'Thomas Perrings' of Birmingham offered to fight 'any man in London or elsewhere' for £500 in the *Hampshire Chronicle* of 28 January 1788, having heard that Johnson 'and several others' wished to fight him. The *Hampshire Chronicle* of 4 February 1788 records that the challenge was accepted by a 'gentleman from North Wales' who was a 'dexterous boxer' and was 'supposed to exceed any man in England' in strength and agility. The Welsh challenger stated that if he beat Perrings he would give all the money to a 'Welch charity school'. The *Hampshire Chronicle* comments, 'Thus, we shall see a Welchman coming forward with all the intrepidity of a lion, not actuated by any pecuniary motive, but to convince the world, that the Ancient Britons are still unconquerable in this country'. It must be wondered, given the details supplied within the challenge issued by 'Thomas Perrings' whether he was actually Isaac Perrins. Sadly, the identity of the Welsh challenger remains a mystery. It seems likely that there would have been few Welshmen at this time that could be physically compared with Perrins, or were considered a 'dexterous boxer'.

Chapter 3

Otherwise 'Paddington'

'PADDINGTON JONES – This is the best lot of the "old 'uns," and would be a credit to any stables in the Kingdom. He was got by *Taffy*, a Montgomeryshire horse, out of *Leekina*; but, while yet a foal, was brought up to Paddington, where he took root and flourished with great luxuriance. He has been within the ropes of the Race Course 138 times, either as principal or a trial horse, and was never known to go the wrong side of the post, or to call forth the displeasure of his owner.'

Bell's Life in London and Sporting Chronicle, 24 February 1828. (Taken from *Affairs of the Fancy*, which describes pugilists in equestrian terms)

Thomas Jones was little more than a boy when he first raised his fists and stepped up to do battle. That he was particularly skilled at fighting can be guessed from the fact that he afterwards never stopped, and was said to have had 'more battles than any man of his day', with the possible exception of Caleb Baldwin. Jones was born to Welsh parents in Montgomeryshire on 18 November 1771,[29] and was brought to London as a child. His parents settled in the area of Paddington, which later earned the youngster the cognomen of 'Paddington' Jones as he rose through the pugilistic ranks. Jones began boxing when he was a youth, and was engaged in a number of skirmishes prior to his first contest of note,

29 This is the birth date and year of birth given in Paddington Jones's obituary in *Bell's Life in London and Sporting Chronicle*, 11 August 1833. *Boxiana* records the same date as *Bell's Life*. *Fistiana* gives no birth date, but states his year of birth to be 1769. *Pugilistica* also gives no date, but states his year of birth to be 'about' 1766.

which occurred around 1785,[30] against an opponent named Ned Holmes[31] at Paddington Fields. Although the contest was said to have been fought for just half-a-crown, those present recollected that the fight was 'as well contested as if one hundred pounds had been the stakes'. Young Paddington found that he had bitten off more than he could chew and failed to seize the laurels of victory. It had been an ambitious decision to engage Holmes in battle, as Paddington had been a youthful novice, while his opponent was a 'full-grown' and experienced man.

With the hope of building his pugilistic reputation, Jones engaged a one-eyed sailor in battle in February of 1786[32] for ten guineas a-side in the Ring at Hyde Park. The sailor was considered one of the ugliest customers who ever stood up to fight, and yet he was decisively licked by the young Welshman after a desperate battle. Not satisfied that Jones had proved his superiority, the bold sailor challenged again, and was defeated for a second time. Valiantly, the twice-vanquished pugilist pressed for a third contest,

30 *Boxiana* records that the first contest against Holmes was fought 'about' 1785. *Pugilistica* records this first contest as occurring 'about' 1786. *Fistiana* does not list the first contest against Holmes at all, and records the three fights against the one-eyed sailor in Hyde Park as having been the first entries on Paddington Jones's record. The *Sportsman's Magazine* records Holmes as 'Ned Holmes (the Barber)' and gives the date of the contest as having been 1 March 1784 in its Ring Chronology, featured in *The History of British Boxing from Fig and Broughton to the Modern Time*.

31 *Boxiana* records Jones's opponent as 'Ned' Holmes. *The Sportsman's Magazine* records him as 'Ned Holmes (the Barber)' in its Ring Chronology, featured in *The History of British Boxing from Fig and Broughton to the Modern Time*. *Fistiana* and *Pugilistica* record him as 'Jack' Holmes.

32 *Fistiana* records all three contests with the one-eyed sailor as taking place in February 1786, stating them as having been fought for ten guineas, five guineas and seven guineas. *Pugilistica* records the first contest as having taken place in February 1786 for ten guineas, with the second contest occurring 'soon afterwards' for the same amount. *Pugilistica* makes no indication of the time elapsed between the second and third contests, and does not say how much money the third contest was fought for. The *Sportsman's Magazine* seemingly records all three contests against the one-eyed sailor as having taken place on the same day, 13 February 1786, in its Ring Chronology, featured in *The History of British Boxing from Fig and Broughton to the Modern Time*. It is also noted that the 'three hard battles' were for '10, 5 and 7 guineas each'.

and although he showed great courage in the fight that followed, he was severely punished and was forced to give in.

Having had plenty of time to consider his previous defeat at the hands of Ned Holmes, Jones challenged Holmes to a rematch in December[33] of the same year for a guinea and a half at Harley Fields, by which time Jones's abilities had improved dramatically, and he 'obtained an easy conquest'. Due to his 'intuitive science' that was already very much in evidence, Paddington attracted the notice of the champion Tom Johnson (Jackling), who was quick to perceive that he had had the good fortune to have stumbled across a future pugilistic star.

A Life Guardsman by the name of Jack Aldridge[34] had been boasting of his pugilistic prowess at Tom Johnson's public house, near Lincoln's Inn Fields. Having tired of Aldridge endlessly recounting his numerous brave deeds, the pugilist Joe Ward commented that he knew a boy who would prove to be his Master. Refusing to believe that a mere boy might bring about his downfall, Aldridge consented to a match being made against Paddington for two guineas against his watch. The venue for the fight was at Marylebone,[35] and excited a great deal of interest amongst the pugilists of the day, after hearing Joe Ward say that he would be seconding a 'stripling' against a man. Jack Aldridge, being of superior age, size and strength, laughed with contempt after Jones had pulled off his shirt to do battle. Enjoying a significant reach advantage, the Life Guardsman had the better of Jones to begin with, and severely punished the fledgling fighter. It was only in

33 *Pugilistica* records this second fight against Holmes as having taking place on 19 December 1786. *Fistiana* only records one contest for Paddington Jones against Holmes, which appears to be the occasion of this second fight (placing it after the contest with the one-eyed sailor in February 1786), and giving the date of the battle against Holmes as having taken place on 12 December, at Harley Fields.

34 *Boxiana* records 'Jack Aldridge' as having been the Life Guardsman's name, and claims Paddington Jones fought him a second time prior to his fight with the baker Dick Horton, although this second contest against Aldridge is not recorded either in *Fistiana* or *Pugilistica*.

35 *Fistiana* records this fight as having taken place on 19 December 1787. There appears to be some confusion or error in recording the date of this contest, as *Pugilistica* records the second Holmes fight as having occurred on the exact same date the previous year in 1786.

the second half of their encounter that the courage of the youthful Welshman proved too much for the boastful Guardsman, and he was soundly beaten in 15 minutes.[36] That 'Paddington' Jones had 'arrived' was shown by the astonishment of those pugilists that witnessed the victory, having been greatly impressed by the ferocity of Paddington's spirit. Jones pocketed his handsome new timepiece shortly afterwards.

Encouraged by his victory over Aldridge, Paddington Jones shortly afterwards fought a lime-burner by the name of Jack Blackwell,[37] with a reputation for 'ruffianism', on the same turf for the princely sum of ten shillings, and although Blackwell fought ungallantly, the lime-burner was easily beaten by Jones. One of Blackwell's companions, Tom Burley, was so annoyed by Blackwell's defeat that he had the temerity to enter the ring at the end of the fight, challenging Paddington for a similar sum. Burley proved to be as much a 'ruffian' as his defeated associate, but quickly found that his attacks were easily warded off by Jones, and he was overwhelmed by the scientific skill of Paddington, who landed at will, forcing Burley to concede his defeat. By this stage, Jones's star was in ascendancy, as can be seen by the fact that the celebrated Major Hanger (later Lord Coleraine) and his black servant stood in as the second and bottle holder of Paddington Jones.

Tom (Otherwise 'Paddington') Jones, as pictured in Boxiana.

---

36 *Boxiana* records this fight as only having been of 'about 15 minutes' duration. Inexplicably, both *Fistiana* and *Pugilistica* record the fight as having been 60 rounds in duration, which seems highly unlikely.

37 The *Sportsman's Magazine* records the contests against Jack Blackwell and Tom Burley as having taken place in 1785 in its Ring Chronology, featured in *The History of British Boxing from Fig and Broughton to the Modern Time*. *Boxiana* and *Pugilistica* both state that the contest occurred 'shortly after' the fight with Aldridge. *Fistiana* does not record the contest at all, but seems to suggest that Paddington Jones's record is incomplete, adding the footnote 'Jones fought a vast number of minor battles'.

The next contest of Paddington Jones brought his name before an even wider audience, having been fought on the same stage prior to the fight between the celebrated Daniel Mendoza and Bill Warr of Bristol on 14 May 1792. The fight took place at Smitham Bottom, near Croydon. Tom 'Paddington' Jones battled valiantly against Caleb Stephen Ramsbottom, better known as Caleb Baldwin, the 'Pride of Westminster', for 47 minutes.[38] Although 'severe blows were given and received',[39] Baldwin was the stronger man and knocked Jones down with greater frequency. The battle was fought for a purse of £20. Owing to a dispute between the two parties, Baldwin claimed the victory, although it was afterwards declared a draw by the referee.

At this point, an old adversary stepped into the breach in the form of Jack Aldridge, the Life Guardsman. Aldridge's challenge would prove to be in vain, as after a 'good battle' for six guineas a-side at Paddington Fields, the Life Guardsman was 'severely beaten'.[40] Shortly after this contest, Paddington Jones was again testing the strength of his arm at the Ring in Hyde Park, which was the setting for so many of his early conquests, with Paddington having been said to have fought there 19 times.[41] On this occasion, Paddington's opponent was Dick Horton, a baker by trade, for 20 guineas. Although the baker had some knowledge of pugilism, the Welshman hit him so hard and fast that Horton soon cried 'Enough!'

Paddington Jones was not only a constant presence as a combatant in the ring at this time, but was also willing to lace up his boots and walk considerable distances to watch a particularly good 'mill' as a spectator. One contest that engaged Paddington's interest enough for him to take to the road was one between Bill

38 As recorded in *Diary; or Woodfall's Register*, 15 May 1792.

39 As recorded in *Public Advertiser*, 15 May 1792.

40 *Boxiana* records this second (undated) contest against Aldridge. The *Bell's Life in London and Sporting Chronicle* obituary for Paddington Jones states that he fought 'in succession', Jack Aldridge, Dick Horton, and then Keely Lyons (twice). Although it records the impromptu 'turn-up' against Abraham Challice, it does not record this battle as taking place after Dick Horton in the list of fights fought 'in succession'.

41 As recorded in *Bell's Life in London and Sporting Chronicle* obituary for Paddington Jones on 11 August 1833.

Hooper, the tin-man, and an opponent named Bunner, which was held at Bentley Green, a few miles from Colchester on 4 September 1792. On the following day, a man by the name of Abraham Challice,[42] who had earned considerable fame for himself as a bully and a terror to the inhabitants of Bentley Green, would cross paths and then fists with Paddington Jones. On seeing Jones standing on the raceground, Challice picked the smaller Welshman as an easy target. After tripping the unsuspecting pugilist, Abraham Challice proceeded to give Paddington a great deal of verbal abuse, threatening him with a good hiding. Undaunted by the fact that his antagonist was a strapping six-footer of great strength, Paddington, perhaps showing more pluck than prudence, decided to teach the bully a lesson, and pulled off his shirt to make ready for battle. The spectators were alarmed at the youthful appearance of Jones, who weighed just 10st 5lbs, and feared for his safety. At first, Abraham Challice had the advantage, his tremendous strength ensuring that the Bentley terror took the first three rounds. In the fourth round, the tables turned after Jones landed a telling blow under the ear, which knocked Challice to the ground. Perceiving that Paddington was starting to outshine the bully, Tom Johnson immediately offered to back Jones for £100.

Once Abraham Challice had found his feet, he appeared groggy on his pins and more than a little confused. Seeing his advantage, Jones tore into Challice and pummelled him at will until he could barely move. The Bentley Green bully was forced to concede his defeat after 15 minutes, having never received such a sound thrashing before.[43] Paddington Jones secured a fairly decent payday on that occasion as the local farmers were so pleased to witness Challice's downfall that they made a quick collection amongst themselves and presented Paddington with 30 guineas for his trouble.

---

42 The *Sportsman's Magazine* records Abraham Challice as 'Andrew Challis' in its Ring Chronology, featured in *The History of British Boxing from Fig and Broughton to the Modern Time*, and claims the fight was of 15 minutes duration. *Boxiana* and *Pugilistica* agree on Abraham Challice having been the name of Paddington Jones's opponent.

43 *Fistiana* records the fight as having been 15 minutes in duration.

The next day, a countryman, well known at Bentley Green by the curious name of 'Leather Jacket', leapt upon the stage, and with considerable boastfulness, challenged any Londoner to dare to fight him. These words had barely passed his lips when Jones jumped up from the crowd, paying no attention to the bruising his hands had sustained the previous day after demolishing Abraham Challice, and made ready for battle. Leather Jacket was thunderstruck with astonishment, and quickly withdrew his challenge, exclaiming 'Na! na! You be the man that beat Ab. Challice yesterday – I mean ony one but thee!' and quickly scuttled from the stage, amidst a loud chorus of laughter and jeers from the bemused spectators.

Keely Lyons was the next to fall as a result of the clenched fist of Paddington Jones, although Lyons fought bravely over the course of their well-contested, albeit brief, ten-minute battle.[44] It took place on 10 May 1794, at Blackheath, for a purse of 20 guineas. The faithful Tom Johnson seconded Paddington and Lyons was left 'severely beaten' by the end of the encounter.[45] Paddington Jones and Lyons would cross paths again the following year on a stage at Hounslow on 22 June 1795. It was a good fight, and the 'bottom' or courage of Lyons was much in evidence once more. The contest lasted a little longer, but Jones emerged victorious after nine rounds and 16 minutes.

It was a little under two months later that a curious event occurred in August,[46] after Paddington travelled from London to Lansdown Fair to do battle with one 'Spaniard' Harris, a collier from Kingswood in Bristol, accompanied by Tom Johnson and

---

44 *Fistiana* records the fight as having been ten minutes in duration.

45 *Fistiana* and *Pugilistica* both agree on the first fight between Jones and Lyons having taken place at Blackheath on this date, for 20 guineas, with the second contest against Lyons having taken place on a 'stage' at Hounslow on 22 June 1795. *Fistiana* records that the second fight at Hounslow was fought for the sum of ten guineas, as does the *Sportsman's Magazine* in its Ring Chronology, featured in *The History of British Boxing from Fig and Broughton to the Modern Time*. *Boxiana* reverses the order of these fights, giving the Hounslow contest as having been their first meeting and the Blackheath fight as their second, although both are undated.

46 *Fistiana* records that the contest against Spaniard Harris took place on 12 August 1795, as does the *Sportsman's Magazine* in its Ring Chronology, featured in *The History of British Boxing from Fig and Broughton to the Modern Time*.

other pugilists of note. After 20 minutes of fighting, a dispute took place, and the unscrupulous Harris got hold of the purse and bolted with it, much to the surprise of all. The next recorded contest of Paddington Jones took place on 6 April 1797, against the 'Chaffcutter' for a purse of four guineas at Two Waters, Hertfordshire. The game Welshman had his fist raised in victory after a battle of 22 rounds, lasting 38 minutes.

The following year,[47] Paddington was matched against the Bristol fighter George Nicholls, who afterwards became a pugilist of celebrity following his famous defeat of the great Tom Cribb. Daniel Mendoza and Tom Johnson accompanied Paddington to Lansdown, near Bath, to engage Nicholls for what was anticipated to be a keenly fought contest. After stripping for battle, and just before commencing the fight, Nicholls cried out 'Stop!', and observed that Jones was his superior in height, and promptly announced that he would not fight, leaving the battleground without further explanation, much to the surprise and the disappointment of the spectators. Having claimed victory over every challenger who had opposed him since after his first contest, and his only defeat having come from the hands of Ned Holmes in the days on his youth, Paddington Jones was riding high. The Welshman could not have imagined the storm clouds that were gathering on the horizon in the form of an astonishing pugilistic marvel whose skills would soon be known to all. Paddington Jones would shortly hear of a miraculous young pugilist from Bristol by the name of Jem Belcher.

Jem Belcher stands tall as the greatest fighter the British prize ring ever produced up to this time. While the appearance of Jack Broughton, Tom Jackson, and in particular Daniel Mendoza, all marked the beginning of new stages in the development of boxing as a science, all those who came before James Belcher would have recognised the genius of the in-built fighting instincts that were evident in young Jem from his earliest days. Belcher's methods so completely revolutionised pugilism that all theories and thoughts on the sport were exploded by the appearance of the boy from Bristol. Born at St James Churchyard, Bristol, on 15 April

47 *Pugilistica* records the year of this aborted contest between Paddington Jones and Nicholls as having occurred in 1798.

1781,[48] Jem came from solid fighting stock, as his grandfather on his mother's side was the famous John Slack, the only man to have beaten Jack Broughton. When Jem was little more than a toddler, Bob Watson, perhaps one of the best men in England at his weight, was courting Jem's eldest sister. In later years, after becoming Jem's brother-in-law, Watson would often recall how a chubby-faced Jem Belcher had once stood between his knees and doubled up his fists, imploring Bob to spar with him.

Jem Belcher, the 'Napoleon of the Ring'.

The contest that made Jem famous throughout Bristol was his fight with Bob Britton, which was due to a dispute at Lansdown Fair, when Belcher was 16 years of age. Jem is said to have soundly beaten a young cabinet maker from Bath with the mittens in a hasty set-to, and his opponent, having been enraged by the defeat, pulled off his gloves and demanded a bare-knuckle battle. The two went at it in furious fashion, until Bob Britton, well known as a fighter around Bristol and Bath, caught wind of the fight. Fearing for the safety of the youthful cabinet maker, Britton pulled his acquaintance away. Resentful at having been denied his victory, Jem challenged Britton, and told him that if he wouldn't allow his friend to fight, he should step up himself. Britton told the impudent upstart that he had a good mind to hand him a beating, before taking the battered cabinet maker away.

Some later sources relate that two days after the initial confrontation, Bob Britton turned up at the Guildhall Tavern and, seeing Belcher's brother-in-law Bob Watson there, asked if young Jem was ready to take a hiding. Bob Watson was quick to reply that he was; but answered that he thought that it would take a better man to hand it to him. Suitably enraged, Britton wanted to fight Belcher on the spot, so Watson rose and left the premises, and went to his own butcher's shop, where Jem served as his apprentice, and brought Jem back to the public house a

48 As recorded in *Boxiana*.

short time later. Bob Watson suggested that they fight it out in a fortnight's time for ten guineas a-side, to which Britton rather sulkily consented.

On the day of 6 March 1798, Belcher and Britton met at the little village of Hanham, to settle the matter once and for all.[49] No one would have given young Jem Belcher a chance of success. Slim and supple, but not yet 17, it seemed like madness to pit the youth against such a powerful and experienced opponent. From the outset, Jem dodged, ducked and defied all his adversary's attempts to strike him, but made no attempt to land any blows of his own. The spectators hissed and booed, thinking Belcher to be nothing more than a cowardly trickster who was reluctant to engage in battle. Just as they were coming to the conclusion that it was to be a theatrical performance and little more, Jem shot in like lightning, and landed with both fists on Britton's face, and then got away from the return. He immediately reappeared within range, and slashed away in a flurry of fists. The blood ran in streams from half-a-dozen cuts on Britton's forehead soon after.

The nature of the fight had changed in an instant. Jem hit his opponent as he pleased, while Britton launched his attacks in vain. Jem's style bore no comparison to anything that had ever been seen, and everything he did seemed to be done right, and at the right moment. For 33 minutes, Jem showed Britton that he was his master. As Britton grimly fought on, it became apparent that he was being soundly beaten by a boy who he thought he could thrash with consummate ease. His eyes closing rapidly and having been severely cut about the face, Britton sullenly gave in. Jem Belcher was then credited with his first astonishing victory in the prize ring.

It was after this victory that Jem decided that he was destined to become a prize fighter. After a long consultation with Bob Watson, Jem told his mother and father that he wanted to travel to London to seek his fortune as a pugilist, and made his way to the city the following year. On arriving in London, Belcher was introduced to the celebrated Bill Warr (Ward), who had famously

49 *Fistiana* records the Jem Belcher vs. Bob Britton fight as having taken place on 6 March 1798, and gives the duration as having been 33 minutes in total.

battled against Daniel Mendoza at Smitham Bottom when Paddington Jones had met Caleb Baldwin back in 1792. By this time, Bill Warr was the landlord of the One Tun in Jermyn Street. Warr, anxious to see what Jem was made of, asked the youngster to demonstrate his skills before a few acquaintances from the sporting world who were dining that evening at the One Tun, and elected to take on the youngster himself, as related in *Boxiana*.

'On his coming to London, *Bill Ward* invited BELCHER to his house, and a private sparring-match (with the gloves on) took place in *Ward's* dining-room, when the veteran was so astonished at JEM'S superior knowledge of the art, that he exclaimed, in falling over a table from one of BELCHER'S *touches* – "By G-d! JEM, I am perfectly satisfied that you can beat any man in the kingdom." In conversation with *Ward*, after dinner, BELCHER observed, "*I could have done a great deal better, Sir, but I was afraid I might hit you too hard, and you should be affronted.*" – "Come along, my boy," replied the Veteran, "we'll have no gloves on now, and you shall do your best; I am not, nor ever was afraid of a blow!" The *set-to* instantly commenced, when the GUEST (out of pure friendship) *levelled* his HOST several times. *Ward* wanted no further *convincing* proofs of his talents. They sat down, and spent the remainder of the evening very harmoniously, and *Ward* immediately offered to back JEM against any man in the country.'

The toffs of Warr's acquaintance roundly agreed with his judgement, so Jem was matched against Paddington Jones for 25 guineas. The spot chosen for the contest was Old Oak Common, a wild and somewhat desolate spot a little beyond Wormwood Scrubs. On 12 April 1799, just three days before Jem Belcher's 18th birthday, hundreds gathered to witness the fight between the unknown novice, Jem Belcher, and Paddington Jones.

Paddington Jones was by now approaching his 30th year, and was a veteran pugilist of proven worth, while his youthful adversary had not yet developed the full strength of his arm. Jones was not as tall as Belcher, giving away some 3in in height, and there was a significant difference in weight as Belcher outweighed Paddington by over 2st, having scaled about 12st 6lbs to the Welshman's 10st 5lbs. The odds were 6/4 on Belcher, the spectators having been influenced by Bill Warr, who had waxed lyrically about the abilities of the Bristol boy. Warr stood in Belcher's corner along with Bill Gibbons, waiting to see if his pupil would live up to his expectations. Facing a veteran of so many fights might well have fazed any other youth of his age, but Jem showed no nervousness at the task in front of him.

Jem Belcher at once flew into action, although his rapid assaults were met with a coolness and steadiness from Paddington that delighted the spectators. If, however, Jem could not get at Paddington, it was equally true that the experienced Welshman could also not get at him. Jem's astonishing rapidity in recovering his guard after delivering a blow was continually displayed. His quick two-handed hitting was much in evidence, and yet he made no impression on his resolute and wary foe. Jem Belcher's failure to make a dent in his opponent's defence frustrated him, and for a moment he lost his temper and his head. Seizing the opportunity, Paddington shot in his right, landing heavily on Jem's face and knocking him clean off his feet. As the second and third rounds commenced, Jem regained his composure, and the exchanges of the combatants became more of a give-and-take fashion. It was in the fourth round that Jem Belcher showed his quality and fought with tremendous skill, finally levelling Paddington Jones and again succeeding in doing so in the following round. Paddington was by no means a man to be beaten off-hand, and in the sixth and seventh rounds, he stepped up in spectacular style, the spectators witnessing one of the 'finest displays of the art' with stopping and hitting being the order of the day. The odds were now 5/4 on Jones, although no one gathered about the ring seemed to notice a growing confidence in the Bristol youth, who battled on with a steely eye.

The eighth and ninth rounds were contested with mutual courage, but it was in the tenth that Jem attacked his man with extraordinary fierceness, and put in punch after punch with the rapidity of lightning. This would turn out to be the turning point of the fight, the boy becoming the favourite, and the veteran becoming the underdog, and the odds now changed in Jem's favour. Paddington Jones fought on with heroic courage for several more rounds, and tried everything in his power to pull the fight out of the fire, but all his efforts were in vain. Jem appeared to be able to do as he pleased with the ailing Welshman, and floored him time after time. Seeing that the battle was lost, Joe Ward,

Paddington's second, stepped forward and threw up the sponge in recognition that his man had been beaten, so after 33 minutes of hard and determined fighting, Jem Belcher was hailed as the winner of his first battle in the London Prize Ring.

It was the first time that Paddington Jones had been forced to hang his head in defeat since his loss to Ned Holmes so many years before. There was no shame in the loss, as the Welsh veteran had engaged a youthful pugilistic star of unparalleled quality never before seen in the prize ring. In an arduous and lengthy contest against such a fresh and strong fighter, Paddington had undoubtedly suffered as a result of the vast disparity in weight, as related by Pierce Egan in *Boxiana*.

'JONES nobly contested for victory for the space of thirty-three minutes, before he gave in. Jem weight twelve stone six pounds; and TOM JONES but ten stone six five pounds weight.'

In his defence, Paddington Jones had also entered the ring in less than perfect health. The battle-worn veteran had been ill advised to have engaged such a difficult customer as Jem Belcher, as the Welshman had been suffering from prolonged sickness prior to the contest, as recounted by Egan.

'It was completely premature on his part to have engaged in such a contest – as he was by no means in sound health, or in possession of that strength and firmness which so characteristically had hitherto marked his combats. From labouring under a long confinement, the system of JONES had lost its tone, and sufficient time had not been allowed to recruit its power, much more restore it to that pristine excellence which he formerly had enjoyed. Three weeks only had elapsed since his recovery, when he had to contend with a HERO, (who afterwards was truly distinguished among all the heroes of the pugilistic schools,) and who was then in the full vigour of youth, health, strength, and every requisite to stamp his character as the first of pugilists. Notwithstanding the evident disadvantages that JONES had to contend against – the disparagement of his having been severely beat in numerous battles, and the hurts from street skirmishes, contrasted with *Belcher*, who had scarcely been pinked, and blooming from the country, TOM'S conduct was far above mediocrity and ought not to be forgotten.'

Chapter 4

The Mahogany Mug and the Stone Mason

'It appears that *Paddington* JONES has fought more battles than any other pugilist now in existence, excepting *Caleb Baldwin*, and for seven years VICTORY crowned all his attempts.'

(*Boxiana*)

Paddington Jones received a great deal of credit for the manner in which he had unsuccessfully stood up to Jem Belcher. Indeed, it would long be remembered that Paddington had stood against the attacks of the 'Napoleon of the Ring' considerably longer than any other of his foes (prior to Belcher having been blinded in one eye following a game of rackets in 1803) ever did. Following their pitched battle, Paddington Jones and Jem Belcher became the best of friends.

After Jem Belcher defeated Jack Bartholomew and seized the Championship of England in 1800, he set his heart upon fighting Daniel Mendoza, wishing to crown his laurels with a victory over the famous Jewish fighter, who had long been acknowledged as the greatest living master of the art of self-defence. Time and again, Jem challenged Mendoza to fight, but as Dan had become proprietor of a public house, and had a wife and children to support, he refused to re-enter the ring.

Nevertheless, Jem Belcher was forever trying to goad Mendoza into making a match, and would frequently saunter down to the East End of London when there were sparring exhibitions at Mendoza's rooms, with the intention of irritating the great pugilist and drawing him into a contest.

On one of these occasions, Belcher took himself off to the East End with a group of pals, amongst whom Paddington Jones featured prominently, to watch a boxing exhibition at Mendoza's place in Capel Court. Dan had recently discovered a new pupil, a fellow Jew of whom he was particularly proud, named Isaac Bitton (Bittoon). Rumours of Bitton's cleverness with the gloves had already spread abroad, even reaching the ears of some of the swells of the West End. Paddington Jones had heard these whispers and decided to join Jem Belcher in his journey to Mendoza's place to see whether Bitton's skills matched his growing reputation. After arriving at Mendoza's school, 'Ould Paddington', as his friends had now taken to calling him, his long record by now having given him the status of an elder of the ring, expressed his wish to pull on the gloves against Bitton. Mendoza was only too pleased to have an opportunity to exhibit the skills of his gifted pupil, and gladly consented, so the Welsh veteran and the Jewish novice promptly donned the 'mufflers' and set to.

It quickly became apparent that the rumours that had circulated of the young Hebrew's ability had not been exaggerated. Crafty strategist though Paddington was, he could not make much impact when pitted against Bitton with the gloves. Mendoza was delighted, and with the extravagant praise he heaped upon his 'boy', he irritated Jem Belcher and his friends a great deal. Paddington was as annoyed as anyone, remarking as he pulled off his gloves that Bitton might think himself lucky that they were not fighting with bare knuckles, as he would have found himself laughing out of the other side of his mouth. Bitton nonchalantly remarked in reply that Paddington might be better off going home to seek out his bed, as he was far too old to fight.

'Ould' Paddington was so enraged, he could have struck Bitton. Had it not been for Mendoza stepping forward and saying that he wouldn't allow any fighting in his rooms, there might have been an ugly scene. Confident in his pupil's abilities, Mendoza announced that he would be happy to back young Bitton against Jones or any other challenger for any sum he liked. Paddington Jones hesitated to accept, he had been out of the ring for over two years, and he didn't know if he was in a position to accept the challenge, as he was unsure whether he might be able to find backers willing to support him.

The insult had pricked the Welshman's pride, and his irritation increased as Jem Belcher and his associates fell into heated discussion on their way home as to the possibility of finding a fighter capable of crushing the vanity of Isaac Bitton. Although 'Ould' Paddington was only now approaching his 30th year, none of his companions seemed to think he was the candidate best suited to thrashing Bitton. The Welsh warhorse had fought more battles than most in living memory, and although no one seemingly counted those contests, it was believed that the number of men he had defeated exceeded three figures. Paddington Jones thought that he should be the man to deal out a beating to Bitton.

While he had been forced to yield to Jem Belcher, a fighter like Belcher was something only seen once in a blue moon, and Paddington could not believe that Bitton was a pugilist of such quality. With these thoughts growing in his mind, Paddington unburdened himself the following day to Jem Belcher, expressing his hope that if he could only find a backer he could fight the boastful Jew and pummel him into submission. Paddington was so anxious to fight Bitton that Jem promised to find him backers. Belcher was as good as his word, and soon afterwards Ould Jones was matched against Bitton for 25 guineas.

It is perhaps worth saying a little more of Isaac Haim Bitton, known by the cognomen as the 'Mahogany Mug'. Although possessed of great strength, Bitton's physique had always been marked by a tendency to run to flabbiness and corpulence, which led some to underestimate his pugilistic ability. Isaac Bitton was not only a skillful boxer, but was also adept at fencing, singlestick, and broadsword. After his fighting career had ended, Bitton could be found teaching pupils at his own sparring school at Gulston Street, Whitechapel, and became a licensed victualler. By this time, 'Old Ikey', as he was known, had grown quite immense, scaling nearly 17 stone. His girth caused a great deal of amusement when he appeared at boxing exhibitions held at the Fives Court, the Tennis Court and Jackson's rooms, even though the activity with which Bitton conducted himself was extraordinary for a man of his size, and he could hold his own with the gloves.

Isaac Bitton's rotundity was commemorated by the Yorkshire comedian Robert Emery, who frequently appeared at the Covent Garden Theatre, in a comic verse that celebrated the Jewish fighter's 'bottom' or courage, while also paying homage to his gargantuan frame:

Bittoon then came, a champion bold,
And dealt with some hard and sly knocks;
But yet, when all the truth is told,
Some ranked him with the shy cocks.
Still, prate like this we must not mind,
A Dutchman true begot 'im;
Who'er has seen Bittoon *behind*,
Will ne'er dispute his *bottom*.

These details aside, to return to the rivalry between Paddington Jones and Bitton, as both Jem Belcher and Dan Mendoza shared a common interest in the outcome of the fight, the public were excited to see whether the Welshman or the Jew would triumph. A large group of sportsmen gathered at Wimbledon Common on the afternoon of 13 July 1801,[50] hoping to witness what promised to be a well-fought battle. Notable amongst their number was Lord Camelford, accompanied by his black servant Bill Richmond, soon to become a famous boxer in his own right. The crowd also contained a large number of Jewish spectators, who laid substantial bets on the 'Mahogany Mug', trusting in Master Mendoza's assurances that his pupil was sure to win. Mendoza himself could be seen in the corner of his pupil, Isaac Bitton. In the other corner, Jem Belcher appeared in support of his friend, Paddington Jones.

50 *Pugilistica* strongly asserts that Paddington Jones's opponent in this fight was not Isaac Bitton, but Samuel Elias, better known as 'Dutch Sam'. The author of *Pugilistica*, Henry Downes Miles, makes this claim on the basis of some newspaper reports that appear to have mistakenly confused the presence of 'Elias Spray', or Spree, who served as Bitton's bottle holder, with Dutch Sam. *Fistiana* and *Boxiana* record Bitton as having been the opponent of Jones in this contest. Henry Downes Miles seems to present this theory principally in one of his many attempts to undermine the author of *Boxiana*, Pierce Egan, of whom Miles can be seen to be especially critical, although he consistently relies upon Egan for source material. According to some later sources, Isaac Bitton would state in later life that he had been the opponent of Paddington Jones, and not Dutch Sam.

Tom (Otherwise 'Paddington') Jones, as pictured in the Sportsman's Magazine of Life in London and the Country *Vol. 1 (1845).*

The contrast in bulk, stature and perceived athleticism between the two combatants caused astonishment at ringside. Paddington was a lightweight, being 5ft 8in tall, and weighing between 10 and 11st. Bitton appeared at least 2in taller, and at least a stone and a half heavier. His prominent paunch disguised the fact that he was exceedingly agile for a man of his size, and there was no hint of the prodigious reserves of strength concealed within his plump physique. While there was not an ounce of flesh to be seen on the frame of the hard and wiry veteran, the experienced eye might have wondered whether the Welshman might have looked a trifle stale by close comparison with his fresh and youthful opponent.

Any doubts as to the Ould one's ability swiftly vanished at the start of the fight. His guard was both firm and stubborn, and Isaac Bitton failed to get past it, or beat it down, try as he might. The young Hebrew had been well advised by Master Mendoza to try to rush Jones, and knock him out of time, before Paddington could bring his ring craft to the fore and his strategy into play. The advice did him little good, and the end of the first round saw Bitton red faced, and blowing from his efforts, while Jones returned to his corner, seemingly unaffected by his exertions. The blistering heat of the day proved troublesome for the portly Jewish fighter, and the sweat poured from his body in streams. Bitton continued to exert all his energy, but Jones remained cool and wary, and he foiled every attack. Seeing his chance, Paddington landed with left and right under each eye, and Bitton's eyes started to swell.

For the first five rounds, everything went in Paddington Jones's favour. The blows of Bitton were parried with great skill, and Jones kept nailing his flabby foe in the face until his blood and sweat ran together down his features. At the close of the sixth round, all the betting was in favour of Jones and the Jewish spectators were beside themselves, having risked such large sums on the rapidly failing novice due to the advice of Daniel Mendoza.

Mendoza was a man of shrewd resources, however, and was quick to employ a secret weapon. The wily Master had brought with him a huge piece of ice, wrapped in a flannel, and by applying this to the back and neck of Isaac Bitton, he kept his pupil fresh, before turning to a bottle of rum to strengthen his fighter's resolve. The dark spirits had a remarkable affect upon Bitton, who seemed 'invigorated and reanimated' after swallowing them. With a tremendous punch to the body, he succeeded in knocking Jones to the ground. In the next round Bitton also landed severely, and for the first time, over Paddington's guard. These two heavy blows changed the outlook for Paddington Jones considerably, and his resolve wavered as the fight progressed. At this point, Paddington could perhaps have hoped to benefit from the assistance of an experienced second, but in this hope he would be disappointed. Brilliant fighter though he was, Jem Belcher was quite lacking in this capacity, and in this respect Bitton had the advantage, as Daniel Mendoza had been in the game for some 20 years.

Paddington Jones battled on, and in the ninth round he taught his opponent that he had not won the fight just yet. Bitton neglected to guard his face, and received a damaging punch that closed his left eye completely. As the other eye was also noticeably puffy, this caused a considerable level of alarm amongst his followers, who saw that another blow upon his right optic might well close his 'shutters' altogether. If Bitton was blinded, he would be as helpless as a child in the hands of Paddington, who devoted all his energies to that aim. On two occasions, Paddington landed very near the target, being just above and then below, but his bony knuckles only served to cut a gash in the flesh of the Mahogany Mug, and by letting out the Hebrew's blood, the Welshman saved him from being rendered completely blind.

Isaac Bitton's situation now looked utterly hopeless and, with Paddington Jones appearing both strong and fresh, it seemed likely that the stout Jewish fighter would be dealt a blow that would bring about his downfall before long. It was during this stage of the battle that there was a brief halt to the contest, which caused some amusement after Bitton had become alarmed at having mislaid some pocket change he had placed in his drawers for safe-keeping, as recalled by Pierce Egan.

'During the time BITTON was fighting with *Paddington Jones*, and at that precise period when the latter had the best of the battle, while sitting upon his second's knee, BITTON felt for 1*s.* 6*d.* that he had put into his drawers, previously to the battle, but not finding it there he refused to continue the *mill* till he had searched for the same. *Mendoza* was quite enraged at this stupid conduct, and urged that the time was expired, but all entreaties were vain, till BITTON felt the money near one of his knees.'[51]

Isaac Bittton, known as the 'Mahogany Mug'.

Despite his growing exhaustion, on resuming the battle it was clear that Isaac Bitton still showed fight, and continued to cover his vulnerable points well, countering with stinging attacks of his own, although the strength of hitting still favoured the canny Welshman. The Jewish contingent was utterly gripped by the spectacle that was unfolding before them and they became tremendously excited, and it proved difficult to keep some of the rougher elements outside the ring.

One person who made himself particularly obnoxious

51 As recorded in *Boxiana*.

by his efforts to force his way into the ring was a brawny drunken butcher from Woolwich who thought that he could do as he pleased. It took the combined efforts of Andrew Gamble along with Symonds, the 'Old Ruffian', to eject him from the ring on two separate occasions. The butcher tried for a third time, and made for Paddington Jones, as if to prevent him from striking Bitton. At this point, Jem Belcher lost all patience and gave the drunken interloper a mighty shove, sending him flying through the ropes. The butcher, undimmed in his rage, attacked a fellow spectator, and a free-for-all ensued. After some scenes of chaos, the butcher was thrown out of the enclosure, but not before he had dealt a few heavy blows upon his assailants.

During this unforeseen interruption, Paddington Jones and Isaac Bitton fought on, with both men trying all they knew to knock the other out of time. The heat of the afternoon sun was now affecting both men. Although Bitton appeared distressed to a greater degree, it might be wondered whether the Welsh veteran was feeling the strength of the blazing sun more keenly. The battle continued at length until at last Paddington Jones landed his bony fist upon the one good eye of his opponent. Daniel Mendoza came to Bitton's aid once more, and at the end of the round, Mendoza made a slight incision in his pupil's swollen eyelid with a lancet, enabling the Mahogany Mug to fight on. Isaac understood the pressing need to step up his efforts, and fought with a greater degree of caution, waiting to deliver a telling blow to some vulnerable part of Paddington's anatomy.

Isaac Bitton was facing a man every bit as wily as himself, and for a minute or two they jockeyed for position, moving here and there, each watching for the opportunity to bring the contest to a close. Suddenly, by a dextrous and agile movement, Bitton moved his foe so that the sun blazed into Paddington's eyes. It was the work of a matter of seconds, but seconds that proved fatal to the Welshman. Seeing his advantage, Isaac delivered a finishing sledgehammer blow that landed on the ear of the Ould one, which felled him with terrible force. Jem Belcher was quick to take Paddington into his arms, and though he and Paddington's bottle holder did all they could to revive him, their efforts proved to be in vain. Not until seven minutes later, and after the Mahogany Mug had been proclaimed the victor did Paddington Jones regain consciousness. The battle had lasted 22 minutes, and was a fight long remembered by those who had had the good fortune to witness it. None of the spectators could have denied that if fortune had not smiled so sweetly upon Isaac Bitton, the result would have been likely to go the other way.

To the great delight of the crowd, an unscheduled second bout then took place in a turn-up between the belligerent butcher, who turned out to be the well-known pugilist Joe Bourke, (Berks or Burke), and Jem Belcher. In the 19-minute tear-up that followed, Jem Belcher got the better of the cantankerous 'knight of the cleaver', and knocked him to the floor, sending blood gushing from his upper lip and nose.

Perhaps at this point it would have been wiser if Paddington Jones had bowed out and left the prize ring to younger men. As it was, he elected to fight on, his next battle of consequence occurring in March of 1802, after the same George Nicholls who had refused to fight him four years before at Lansdown arrived in London. The match came off at Norwood Common for 40 guineas, and while a good contest was hoped for, it ended in scenes of disarray. The first three rounds came off without a hitch and were well contested, with considerable skill demonstrated by both combatants, but in the fourth round a curious incident occurred. Nicholls dashed in with furious intent, and got his head between Paddington's legs. He seized both ankles and threw the astonished Welshman with considerable violence. With Nicholls having completely deviated from the rules of pugilism, a lengthy interruption and dispute took place. Paddington demanded the stakes, but Bill Warr, who had seconded Nicholls, refused to give them up.

The fight thus terminated with it having been impossible to come to a decision, although it appears to have been afterwards accepted as a victory for Paddington.[52] Making his way home after the contest, Paddington had a skirmish with a man named Carter, who poured scorn on him about a challenge from a pugilist named 'Simpson', who was a promising pupil of Tom Johnson. 'Ould' Paddington was not greatly hurt from his contest with Nicholls, and set about Carter in a spirited fashion, and soon

---

52 This fight, against George Nicolls, is recorded as having been a 'Win' for Paddington Jones in *Fistiana*.

Tom 'Paddington' Jones vs. Isaac Bitton.

convinced him that he was in the wrong. Paddington Jones would afterwards meet Simpson for ten guineas a-side on the Edgware Road in June of 1804. It was deemed to have been a good fight, and Jones emerged victorious in ten rounds.[53] The following year, on 6 August 1805, Paddington fought another opponent by the name of Lyons, 'the Yokel Jew', for ten guineas a-side at Hounslow.[54] By this time he was perhaps too long in the tooth to engage in arduous contests, and the fight was said to have been one of the most disappointing battles that Paddington Jones ever fought. The Welshman suffered severely in the fight, as Lyons was a 'desperate punisher'. Nevertheless, the Yokel Jew finally gave in. Although this would appear to be the last prize fight 'officially' recorded for Paddington Jones, he fought legions more over the course of his 20-odd years as a fixture within the prize ring.[55]

---

53 This fight against 'Simpson' is recorded as taking place in June 1804, on the Edgware Road, in *Fistiana*. It is recorded as having taken place on the Green, near Putney, in June, 1804, in *Pugilistica*.

54 *Bell's Life in London and Sporting Chronicle,* 24 February 1828, claims that this fight took place 'on Blackheath'.

55 The record of Paddington Jones is clearly far from complete given the large number of contests that he is remembered as having taken part in, and the lengthy gaps between those contests recorded above. *Bell's Life in London and Sporting Chronicle,* 24 February 1828, contains a summary of the career of Paddington Jones that largely corresponds with the contests detailed within this book. Two intriguing (but unverified) additions are that 'In August, 1788, he was beaten by Bob Watson over Brighton Race Course' and 'that he was invariably the trial horse of Jack Randall'.

Throughout the Borough of Paddington, Tom Jones was long remembered for his distinguished career as a prize fighter, and had collected many 'trophies of victory from the guardsmen' who had, 'in the neighbourhood of Paddington, at various times endeavoured to serve him out because he was considered as a scientific pugilist'. These mementoes of his victories 'would not prove far short in furnishing half a company'.[56] Others remembered his many battles at his old stomping grounds at Paddington Fields, where he had vanquished George Stringer, who had challenged the Welshman for five guineas a-side, and although Stringer fought with conviction, he fell, like so many others, at the hands of Paddington Jones.[57] A carpenter with some pugilistic experience named Jem Smith was also said to have battled Jones at Lisson Green in Paddington. Smith was left so beaten that he was scarcely able to leave the scene of battle, but proved to be a worthy competitor, displaying fine skill and demonstrating considerable courage.[58]

After his fighting days were over, Paddington Jones remained a familiar figure in prize fighting circles. His long experience within the ring, and his sage advice, ensured that his service as a second, bottle holder and adviser were strongly in demand following his retirement. Jones appeared in the corner of many of the best-regarded fighting men years after his retirement, and was a favourite second of both Jack Randall and Jem Ward. At a later date, *Bell's Life* would state that as far as their records could tell, Paddington Jones entered the ring as a fighter, second or bottle holder on no less than 140 occasions. Paddington also proved to be a good teacher, turning out a number of gifted pupils, and remained as keen as ever to pull on the gloves at benefit events to compete against his fellow pugilists.

His last fight took place on 5 March 1823, by which time 'Ould' Paddington was of sufficient age to finally warrant his cognomen. It came about in the following circumstances. A number of workmen had been employed to put the finishing touches to a new church, St Pancras at Battle Bridge, when one

---

56 As recorded in *Boxiana*.

57 As recorded in *Boxiana*.

58 As recorded in *Boxiana*.

of their number, a 'great gaunt fellow', who was a stone mason, thought that someone had been meddling with his stone barrels during his absence. Aggravated by the discovery, the mason looked about for someone to take his annoyance out on. His gaze fell upon a 'little old gouty man' leaning heavily on the shoulder of his son, and the stone mason decided the boy was as good a target as any, and promptly struck the youth. Outraged, the old man cried, 'Who gave you free toleration to strike that there boy? Why, you curst wretch, was it not for my poor pins, you should not go unpaid, that you sho_____'. The old man's words were cut short by the powerful blow that was thrown at his head, but the blow never landed. The 'little old gouty man' was Paddington Jones, who had seen the punch coming and shifted whilst simultaneously throwing a right hand of his own, which landed on the mason's mug. Paddington reeled and after taking a return blow to the body, he went down. The first round thus ended in surprise for the mason and indignation on the part of Jones. The rest of the account of the fight, as published in *The Annals of Sporting and Fancy Gazette* from April of that year (1823), is transcribed below:

> **Second** – At this moment the gout left him, and his appetite returned: the mason waxed wroth, and threatened chastisement, aloud: he grumbled curses deep and vengeance high, so the assembled guests, though "unbidden to the feast," expected to see the Paddingtonian reduced to *mince meat* at the next *chop*. He did indeed salute the gravel this second round, but much more was requisite to make him "bite the dust".
>
> **Third** – The big-one rushed in, and dashed the old-one to earth: he had, however, a good second, in a passenger by Smith's stage, which just before drew up, the driver-owner "standing responsible" that Tom should have *time*, – that surety against manslaughter.
>
> **Fourth** – Jones, lively upon his pins, retreated from the big one's rush, planting two upon the nob, but catching several bodiers. The mason, however, hit round, his blows making a show and a rattle on the ribs of poor old Tom: the big-one slipped down, and shouts rent the air from the

> Paddington coach boxes, five or six stages having pulled up in the mean time. "Go it, Tom!"
>
> **Fifth** – The mason's rushing was over: he pretended to spar, – good faith: this was the moment for *work*. Jones caught the opportunity, and planted a flush right-hander between the eyes! It was a flabbergaster for the compo-stone-mason and he dropped in the spot as he stood! This was truly the triumph of science; all hands joined the shout that greeted or lamented the fall of this modern Dagon. Bellows to mend.
>
> **Sixth** – Hearkening to the joint advice of his co-workmen, the compo-mason stood still, slashing away from his body, Jones now and then dealing out little services about the old spot for three rounds more, reducing his man, but being *down* each time.
>
> **In the ninth round**, Jones attempting to plant another hard one across the *proboscis* of his big adversary, was hit off with great force by a breast-cut, that sent him spinning away to a great distance, and he fell rudely.

* * * *

The blow itself did not damage the Welshman to any great degree, but rather unluckily for 'Ould' Paddington, he fell upon his open hand, and broke two of the small bones of his wrist, and the battle terminated.

In his final fight, Paddington Jones demonstrated his evergreen courage once more:

> Thus terminated a battle of the moment, in which all the strength, youth, health and training lay on one side, with a method of attack by no means to be *sneezed* at; on the other, nothing but the art of manual defence was discernable, with the knowledge when to seize the favourable moment for "*returning compliments*," and of the place where these would please – least.
>
> It is very seldom we hear of ten stone odd, getting rid of nearly 14 stone! Yet these were the weights by computation, of the two men (or rather *man and a half*) on this day.

After this battle, it was hoped that the stone mason had learned his lesson and would think twice before picking a fight with a stranger again, being wary of finding a future adversary to be something more than an 'old gouty man' once his fighting spirit was enflamed. Paddington took his shattered wrist to an amateur surgeon, who did his best to fix the Welshman up, although it was said that he suffered for a long time afterwards as a result of the fracture.

Paddington Jones remained a key figure in the pugilistic world, taking up the position of Master of Ceremonies at the famous Fives Court situated in Little St Martin's Street, Leicester Fields, London, following the death of the previous Master of Ceremonies, old Joe Norton, in 1822. Poor Joe Norton had died at Harry Harmer's tavern a day or two after having been assaulted by Tom Hickman, the 'Gas-Man', who had lost his temper with the old pugilist. Paddington Jones took over Norton's role with the same vigour that had marked his career in the prize ring, and he officiated over many contests, exhibitions and benefits held at the Fives Court. In August of 1825, a benefit event was held at the Fives Court for the hardy Welsh warhorse, and was attended by a few of the most prominent pugilists of the day, including such notables as Harry Jones 'the Sailor Boy', Peace Inglis 'the Phenomenon', Young Dutch Sam and Jonathan Bissell, better known as 'Young Gas'. The *Morning Advertiser* was quick to recognise that the retirement of Paddington Jones signified the end of a golden age:

> In the days of Paddington Jones, men never scrupled to fight until they weighed their antagonist in fact to a scruple. Money was not thought so much of as fame, and where no money could be produced as a stimulant, the men, like the Shamrockshire heroes, fought *for love*... Paddington Jones was recollected by the Amateurs as one of the most respectable Veterans of the "Old School". His gallant fight with the renowned Jem Belcher, established his fame, though he was defeated. Latterly Jones, as he is now advanced in years, has only interested himself in the prize ring, by occasionally administering his sage advice to combatants in the ring, and attending to proper decorum being observed at sparring

> exhibitions. In fact, he is the Cato and Petronius (arbiter elegantiarum) of the prize ring.[59]

The author of *Boxiana* would later recollect in a footnote within his book, *Pierce Egan's Book of Sports, and Mirror of Life* (London: Thomas Tegg and Son, 1836), that it was while acting in his capacity of Master of Ceremonies that Paddington Jones had been responsible for renaming the future pugilistic champion Tom Winter on his first appearance at the Fives Court. Tom Winter was afterwards forever known as by his fellow pugilists as Tom 'Spring'.

> To the best of our recollection, Old Paddington Jones was Tom's godfather. On Winter's first appearance at the Fives Court, and the spectators crying out "Name, name?" Jones, seeing Winter a fine looking young man, and without enquiring his name, in the impulse of the moment, exclaimed, *"Young Spring!"* which designation Winter has held ever since; and it is most likely the appellation of Spring will continue with him until the day of his death.

Ould Paddington was occasionally somewhat dismayed by the younger generation of pugilists he sometimes encountered who refused to fight for less than £100, and was quick to tell them that they were 'regular chaff cutters,' and he would have happily polished off half a dozen of them in his younger days for a fraction of the sum. Remembering the Welshman's past days of prize ring glory, *Bell's Life* would say of the fighting abilities of Paddington Jones that,

> He was perfect master of the science... his guard was formidable and commanding; his left well out before him, and his right ready for the return. He was a tremendous hitter, and could use left and right with equal effect. He was what is properly termed 'a fair stand-up fighter;' [*and*] went to the head of his antagonist, steady and firm – brave as a lion, and without a hint of 'flinch' about him.

59 As recorded in the *Morning Advertiser*, 10 August 1825.

Tom 'Paddington' Jones died on 2 August 1833, at his lodgings in Stephen Court, Stephen Street, Lisson Grove, Paddington, having been nursed on his death bed by his wife. Even though he had fought so many contests, he remained poor 'to the hour of his death'. Despite his circumstances, he was never known to ask for contributions to aid his poverty, although he always gratefully received the assistance that was occasionally offered to him by those who remembered his prize fighting career. *Bell's Life* would print a lengthy obituary which did ample justice to the memory of the masterful Welsh fighter.[60] It was with some sadness that *Bell's Life* also issued a request to his admirers that should they wish to pay tribute to the memory of Paddington Jones, that they might feel obliged to send money to assist with paying his burial expenses to his grieving widow, or to his fellow pugilist Tom Spring, who would forward on any funds received. The editor would appear to been greatly saddened by the end of 'one of the very best of the old school of pugilists – a man who although always poor, maintained a character for unimpeachable honesty and unquestioned game – and whose good conduct, on all occasions... gained him universal esteem'.

Perhaps the last words on the subject of the brave Welshman, Tom 'Otherwise Paddington' Jones, are best left to the pen of Pierce Egan, who would say of him in *Boxiana* that,

> It is impossible that we can take our leave of PADDINGTON JONES without characterising him as a BRAVE and *distinguished* PUGILIST and who is well deserving to occupy a *niche* in the temple of fame.[61]

60 The obituary of Tom 'Paddington' Jones was published in *Bell's Life in London and Sporting Chronicle,* 11 August 1833.

61 Paddington Jones was inducted into the International Boxing Hall of Fame in the 'Pioneer' category in 2010, although is currently incorrectly recorded as having been born in Paddington, London. The other 5 Welsh inductees of the IBHOF to date are; John Graham Chambers (who drafted the Marquess of Queensbury Rules), Jim Driscoll, Freddie Welsh, Jimmy Wilde and Joe Calzaghe.

Chapter 5

The Wrexham Champion and the Champion of Wales

Both before and after the arrival of Edward Morgan, the 'Welch Boy' on the pugilistic stage, there can be no doubt that aside from those Welshmen contending with their rivals in London, there were many more engaging in organised contests in Wales itself.

While these early Welsh pugilists had no amphitheatres in which to hold their contests and there were no Welsh newspapers yet in existence to record their victories and defeats, there is some evidence that fist fighting was an organised sport that enjoyed widespread popularity throughout the country.

One intriguing story of a fighting Welshman of antiquity occurs in the reign of Henry III (1216–1272) when Dyserth Castle in Denbighshire had been a stronghold belonging to Sir Robert Pounderling, a knight of the realm who was also the constable of Rhuddlan castle.

Pounderling was 'celebrated for his prowess at tournaments, not only in handling a lance, or brandishing a sword, but as an adept in the pugilistic art'. Sir Robert is said to have accepted a challenge from a Welshman named Theodore at a local fete called the 'Tytles for Justes'. In the course of their combat, Theodore knocked out one of Pounderling's eyes.

Theodore afterwards attended the court when another fete had been scheduled, to challenge Pounderling to a second contest of 'feates of armes', but Pounderling quickly rejected the challenge, with the justifiable remark that he felt no desire, nor inclination, for Theodore to knock out his other eye.[62] Folktales aside, it is clear that prize fighting was an activity practised in Wales from the earliest times, and that these early fighting Welshmen contested for 'love' and presumably also for 'honour'. *Mist's Weekly Journal* of 17 August 1728 recorded a contest in which a 'young lad' named Samuel Pye caused the death of an opponent at Monmouth, stating, 'At Monmouth, Samuel Pye, a young Lad, was indicted for murthering [sic] another at Boxing; they were at Play together and quarrell'd, and thereupon was found not guilty...'

Intriguingly, one of the first substantial documented reports to be uncovered of an important contest between Welsh pugilists within Wales is of even greater interest as it reveals the name of the first pugilist who appears to have been recorded as having been bestowed with the title of 'The Champion of Wales'. *The Star* newspaper of Saturday 6 August 1791 contained the following report of a severely fought battle which had taken place the previous week on 29 July 1791.[63]

> *Boxing.*
>
> Yesterday se'nnight was fought, at Dolgelly, Merionethshire, the hardest fought battle ever remembered in that part of Wales. The competitors were the well-known Ellis Pannwr, and Roderick Lewis; the former, for several years, was looked upon as the champion of that country. Such display of gymnastic ability has not perhaps been exceeded by Johnson and Big Ben. The hard blows (without falling) re-echoed for thirty minutes and upwards; but to shorten the combat, the former hit his antagonist his favourite blow, under the left ear, which terminated the battle, and brought him to the stage apparently dead; and the umpires REES MEREDITH, and ROWLANDS WEMDU, Esqrs. Pronounced him the conqueror; and notwithstanding he

62 *The Beauties of England and Wales: Or Delineations, Topographical, Historical, and Descriptive, of Each County,* Reverend Joh Evans (London: Longman and Co., 1812) quoting Leland's Itinerary Vol. Volume 1, p21.

63 This contest was deemed of sufficient interest to have also been recorded in the *Kentish Gazette*, 9 August 1791, and in the *Hereford Journal*, 10 August 1791.

> had fought seven pitched battles, the bets were five to two against him.
>
> We are sorry to add, that Roderick Lewes has but little hopes from Dr. DOWTAN of that town, of ever recovering his left sight.
>
> The wager was seventy guineas, seventeen pounds entrance-money was equally shared to these athletic pugilists.

This account, although brief, is significant in that it establishes that pugilism had been a widespread practice in Wales for a long period of time prior to this contest, as Ellis Pannwr had fought seven 'pitched battles' and had been looked upon as the 'Champion' of Wales for several years. Even more tellingly, this brutal contest between Ellis Pannwr and Roderick Lewis, in which Lewis apparently lost the sight in his left eye, was deemed by witnesses to have been the hardest fought battle 'ever remembered in that part of Wales', confirming that pugilistic contests had been taking place long before this time. That entrance money was charged, and the large sum of 70 guineas had been wagered on the fight, would reinforce the suggestion that pugilistic contests attracted a widespread public following by this time, with Welsh prize fighting also having developed a semi-organised structure.[64]

Perhaps one of the most interesting, although undocumented, references to a previous 'Champion of Wales', comes courtesy of another well-remembered tale regarding the inhabitant of an old house called Ty Du (The Black House) located about a mile and a half from Dolbadarn Castle between Caernarfon and Snowdonia. Foulke Jones was celebrated throughout the principality for his muscular prowess, which was in evidence from a very early age. When he was about three years old, Foulke was sitting in front of

---

64 It can be established that boxing within Wales had developed to the point where locally celebrated pugilistic 'champions' in addition to Ellis Pannwr and Lewis Roderick had emerged from a pool of lesser skilled Welsh pugilists before this time. A contest between 'Bloody', a butcher from Montgomery, against another 'noted' unnamed prize fighter held at Ludlow in 1784 was deemed to be of sufficient interest as to be reported in the London newspapers. In 1790, Bloody was matched against the celebrated Bill Warr (Ward) – see *Chapter 21 – Songs of Blood and Glory*.

the door of Ty Du when he was attacked by a gander whose female and brood he had been chasing. Fearing for his safety, the toddler seized the furious bird by the neck and tore him 'into a thousand pieces.'[65] The strength of Foulke Jones multiplied dramatically in the years that followed until at length it exceeded any other man in the principality.

On one occasion, two men were fighting at a public house in Caernarfon, and on entering the house, Foulke Jones was requested to separate them, so he seized them in either hand and bashed their heads together before letting them slide to the floor. Jones was also engaged in another conflict at Caernafon, and had been standing on a bridge when he was approached by a drunken rogue, who insulted him and induced him to fight after striking Foulke in the face. Jones grabbed the man in one hand and lifted him over the wall of the bridge, holding him suspended over the water. The drunk cried loudly for mercy, and after holding the man in this unpleasant situation for some time, Jones lifted him back again, and dismissed his attacker with a stout kick up the backside.

Despite his Herculean strength, it was said that the 'disposition of Jones inclined him at all time to live on the most peaceable terms with his neighbours, seldom exerting his uncommon powers but in acts of utility; or for their amusement'.[66] On one occasion, three workmen were building a wall near his house, and found one stone which their combined efforts could not lift. Foulke told them to leave it and go into the house and eat dinner, suggesting that a hearty meal might help them in their endeavours. During their absence, Jones lifted the stone into place himself, and the men were astonished to find on their return that one man had done what three had attempted in vain. Foulke Jones's strength is also said to have once aided him in carrying a

65 *North Wales: Including Its Scenery, Antiquities, Customs, and Some Sketches of Its Natural History, Delineated from Two Excursions Through All the Interesting Parts of that Country, During the Summers of 1798 and 1801: Illustrated with a Map, Frontispieces, and Music; in Two Volumes, Volume 1*, Rev. William Bingley, (London: T. N. Longman and O. Rees, 1804).

66 *North Wales: Including Its Scenery, Antiquities, Customs, and Some Sketches of Its Natural History, etc.*, Volume 1, Rev. William Bingley, (London: T. N. Longman and O. Rees, 1804).

young calf home on his back, and on another occasion he carried a tree home which he had felled, which had proved impossible to carry by several men.[67]

The most intriguing story regarding Foulke Jones is about his having been visited by the 'Champion of Wales' after tales of the uncommon strength of Jones had spread far and wide, as recounted in *A Tour Through Part of North Wales* by Reverend John Evans.

'Foulke Jones...was noted for his prodigious strength. The esteemed Champion of Wales for boxing, wrestling, &c. came to see him from Denbighshire, for the sole purpose of trying their relative strength. When the stranger arrived, Foulke was mowing hay in the field, near to his house. The stranger went up to him, and inquired, if he knew one Foulke, not supposing from his size and appearance this could be the person he sought. Foulke answered, that his master was in the house, or not far distant, at the same time begged to know what his business was? I have heard, the stranger replied, that he is accounted the strongest man in the Principality, and am come to try out strength together.

'If that be all, Foulke observed, I can soon inform you, whether it be worth your while to see my master, for I am a tolerably strong man myself, but *nothing* in his hands; as I have often experienced to my cost, when I have had the temerity to contend with him; therefore I would have you try, what you can do with me first. They immediately engaged, when Foulke, by his superior strength, flung his antagonist over a high wall into the road. Fully satisfied, he exclaimed, if this be the *man*, what must the master be! And mounting his horse rode home, fully convinced of his superiority.'

Foulke Jones was said to have died in the early 1790s at the age of 75,[68] which would suggest that this tale regarding his meeting with the 'Champion of Wales' occurred many years before, and long before the fighting days of Ellis Pannwr, recorded as having been widely regarded as being the Welsh Champion by this time.

---

67 *A Tour Through Part of North Wales: In the Year 1798, Principally Undertaken with a View to Botanical Researches In that Alpine Country: Interspersed with Observations on Its Scenery, Agriculture, Manufactures, Customs, History, and Antiquities,* Reverend John Evans, (London: J. White, 1800).

68 *A Tour Through Part of North Wales,* by Reverend John Evans, published in 1800, states that Foulke Jones died 'about seven years ago'.

With few pugilistic Welshmen having been recorded outside the small number who had contended for victory in the London prize ring in these days, there are few indications of any other named Welsh fighters of note. One Welsh fighter who had developed enough of a reputation as a fighting man to have been deemed worthy of inclusion within Pierce Egan's *Boxiana* was Ned Davis, despite having never contested within the organised prize ring. Davis was considered to have been the 'Wrexham Champion' in the 1790s, and was a master butcher and a grazier in the town, but was more widely known for his fighting abilities. The Welsh 'knight of the cleaver' fought many battles, and his 'talents for boxing were not only well known, but had been *felt* for miles round *Wrexham*'. Despite his reputation as a fighter, Davis had 'the manners of a gentleman' and was also 'much respected by all his neighbours'. Standing about 6ft tall, and of athletic appearance, Davis was well known for his interest in sporting matters, being a cockfighting enthusiast, and 'an excellent jumper, and a first-rate player at fives'. At the game of fives, Davis was so proficient that he was said to have beaten the boxer, Joe Bourke (Burke), and four others for £100 to £50. This match attracted so much interest that people flocked from Chester and Shrewsbury to witness it. Davis won the match with such style that his victory was crowned with a peal of bells by the church bell ringers at Wrexham.

One story that is told of Ned Davis is that he was in attendance at Chester racecourse when the notable personage, Sir Watkin Williams Wynn,[69] was insulted by a group of ruffians. The situation was very perilous to the baronet, and Ned Davis was quick to defend his personal safety. Oblivious to danger, Davis

69 Sir Watkin Williams Wynn, the 5th Baronet of Wynnstay in Denbighshire was one of the most prominent Welsh patrons of the Prize Ring. Sir Watkin was the Member of Parliament for Beaumaris between 1794 and 1796. Exceedingly rich, the Baronet had a long-standing interest in pugilism, and was present at the fight between Daniel Mendoza and Harry Lee in 1806 (*Pugilistica*). Sir Watkin would later become a member of the Pugilistic Club, founded by 'Gentleman' John Jackson in 1814. The main purpose of the Pugilistic Club was to stamp out fixed fights and ensure fighters were guaranteed purses of between ten and 50 guineas out of money gathered through its annual subscription. Members wore blue coats with lapel buttons engraved PC, over yellow kerseymere waistcoats and top hats.

Sir Watkin Williams Wynn, Welsh patron of pugilism, and member of the Pugilistic Club, © History of Parliament Trust.

forced his way in amongst the crowd, and without ceremony, '*floored*' several of those who had threatened Sir Watkin. The great courage of Davis astonished the crowd, and he was applauded for the 'manly conduct he had exhibited'. Although his pugilistic ability was held in high regard, Ned Davis did not embark on a career as a professional pugilist, although curiously, Pierce Egan also records in *Boxiana* that both '*Mendoza* and *Burke*...refused to enter the lists with him'.

Ned Davis sadly lost his life in tragic circumstances; he was travelling on an errand to purchase some cattle and stopped at a public house within a mile of Wrexham to slake his thirst. Davis was unaware that two brothers who had taken offence to some slight but unintentional remark he had previously made were lying in wait for him. The two brothers attacked the Wrexham Champion, but were quickly flattened by Davis, who resumed his journey. On his return home that evening, Davis unwisely called at the same public house to take some refreshment. He found that the brothers had called on the assistance of three other siblings, besides 56 other people, mostly comprised of workmen in their employment. Davis was forced to fight his way out of the public house and onto a grassy plot at the rear, where he challenged the brothers to fight in succession. Three of the brothers were beaten off-hand, and the other two fell upon him. While Davis was engaged in punishing them for their cowardly attack, one of the workmen planted a terrible blow on his kidneys, which Davis was unable to defend against. As a result of this dastardly and treacherous attack, Davis ultimately lost his life. Prior to his death at the age of 38, *Boxiana* records of Ned Davis, the Wrexham Champion, that 'no individual ever had any *chance* with him; and he defeated, before he died, all the *rough-cast ones*, for miles round Wrexham'.

There are a few other references to pugilistic Welshmen around this time, which would suggest that pugilism was widespread within Wales, but that prior to the establishment of the Welsh newspapers, few of their deeds would go recorded. Amongst the early battles of George Nicholls of Bristol, who famously conquered Tom Cribb, the 'Black Diamond', in 1805, is a mention of a butcher from Chepstow. Nicholls is said to have started his pugilistic career around the year 1792, when 17 years old. Of his early victories, recorded in list form in *Boxiana*, Pierce Egan records that, '*Bill Thomas*, a butcher, of Chepstow, had so good an opinion of his milling qualities, that he sent a public challenge to Bristol to fight the best man in that city'. Sadly, Egan does not record the details of the fight which followed, but merely records that 'NICHOLLS accepted the challenge without delay, and he also won it off-hand'.

That boxing was firmly established as a pastime and an entertainment of note in Wales by the end of the 1790s can be drawn from the memoirs of Daniel Mendoza, who went on a lucrative tour in 1796 to exhibit his fistic skills at towns and cities around the country.[70]

After appearing for one night at Penryn in Cornwall, Mendoza decided that he should visit Wales, and travelled to Cardiff. On reaching the city, he found that there had been other pugilists 'of real reputation' already entertaining the public for a number of nights prior to his appearance.

'On quitting Penryn, I proceeded in the beginning of the year 1797 into Wales, and I exhibited with great success at the town of Cardiff, notwithstanding some pugilists of real reputation, as they styled themselves, had previous to my arrival, been amusing the town, for several evenings, with the same type of entertainment. I remained at Cardiff about a fortnight, and from thence went to other places in Wales, where I experienced considerable success. Having made a tour of four months in this country, I returned to England, and in May 1797 performed at Hereford.'[71]

Sadly, there appear to be no further sources that record the scope of Mendoza's travels within Wales, although the Welsh Wesleyan minister, Reverend John Wood, would later recount that he had met the famous fighter when travelling through Kington in Herefordshire, just two miles from the Welsh border, and had failed in his attempts to get the Jewish pugilist to convert to Christianity.

'...the Rev. John Wood, Wesleyan preacher, used to pass regularly through or near the town when taking his circuit. He has stated that on one occasion when so travelling through it, and hearing that 'Mendoza,' a celebrated pugilist, was in the town

70 Daniel Mendoza records that his tour started in Exeter and he afterwards performed at Teignmouth. Wanting to appear at Plymouth, Mendoza wrote to a theatre owner at Plymouth offering his services, and received a reply on 11 October 1796, although owing to a dispute with the proprietor, Mendoza did not appear there. It must be said that these dates should be viewed with a pinch of salt; Mendoza was not always entirely accurate in the dates that he records in his memoirs.

71 *The Memoirs of the Life of Daniel Mendoza*, Edited by Paul Magriel, (London: B.T. Batsford Ltd. 1951).

teaching some young gentlemen his art, he was moved to desire and attempt his conversion, and for this end waited upon him at the Sun or Swann Inn, and spoke to him of Jesus. Mendoza, who was by profession a Jew, answered, "The Christians say that Messiah is come, the Jews that he is yet to come – but for my part I do not believe he is come or ever will come." Mr Wood, finding his argument of no avail, proceeded on his journey...'[72]

That Daniel Mendoza enjoyed 'considerable success' in his travels within Wales, and that members of the public had developed a strong interest in pugilism, would be underlined by printed accounts of pugilistic contests that were starting to appear in Wales a few years later, when *The Cambrian*, the first weekly newspaper of Wales, was published. Early references to prize fighting give a clear indication of the popularity of pugilism to those 'Game Welchmen' engaging in battles to prove their fistic superiority. It is perhaps also interesting to note that Mendoza's principal backer was a notable sporting gentleman of Welsh descent, named Sir Thomas Hussey Apreece.[73] Sir Thomas was made a baronet by the Prince of Wales in 1782, possibly due in part to their shared sporting interests, not least of which was pugilism[74]. Sir Thomas claimed descent from Gruffydd ap Rhys (d. 1201), the prince of Deheubarth in south-west Wales. Daniel Mendoza prepared for his second fight against Richard Humphries at the home of Apreece at Upminster in Essex. Apreece also served as Mendoza's chosen umpire in his second and third contests against Humphries, and helped finance Mendoza's boxing academy at the Lyceum in the Strand.

---

72 *The History of Kington, by a member of the Mechanics institute of Kington*, by Richard Parry (of Kington), (Kington: Charles Humphreys, 1845).

73 Sir Thomas Apreece is recorded in *The Memoirs of the Life of Daniel Mendoza* as Sir Thomas A. Price. In other instances, he is also recorded using the original Welsh variation of his name as Sir Thomas Ap Rhys.

74 *Pancratia* records that Sir Thomas Apreece was already closely associated with pugilism by the time of the battle between Johnson and Ryan in December 1787, commenting that 'boxing now was again at the zenith of its glory, being patronised and supported by some of the first sporting characters in the country, particularly by the Prince of Wales, Duke of Hamilton, Lord Barrymore, Sir Thomas Appreece, Alderman Coombe, &c.'

Sir Thomas Apreece was not only a spectator and supporter of boxing, but was known as a great amateur boxer in his own right, proving as much on 8 June 1795, when he thrashed a robber that he encountered on the streets of London. The incident was recorded in *Pancratia*, where it is stated that the 'celebrated patron of pugilism, Sir Thomas Appreece, who so frequently adorns the list of visitors on those occasions, had a pugilistic contest with a bruising ruffian in the street, a fellow who went about threatening to strike a woman who accompanied him, in order to excite the interference of the passengers, who generally got well thrashed, and eased of their watch, &c. into the bargain. Sir Thomas, very much to his honour, proved a match for him, and after a severe contest came off victorious, though without much covering'.[75]

The Welsh baronet was known as a long-standing supporter of the prize ring, and was listed in *Fancy-Ana; or A History of Pugilism* (London: W. Lewis, 1824) by Jon Bee as having been one of the principal patrons of the sport in the year 1800.[76] Apreece retained an interest in pugilism and a fondness for Daniel Mendoza into his old age, and the 'white-haired old Welsh baronet' appeared at the battleground for Mendoza's penultimate battle against Harry Lee in 1806, nearly 16 years after he had served as Dan's umpire in his third fight against Humphries.[77]

Sir Thomas Apreece also served as an umpire in the disgraceful contest between the champion, Tom Cribb, and the black challenger Tom Molineaux in 1810. After Cribb had been knocked unconscious by Molineaux and dragged back to his second's knee, it had been Apreece who had yelled 'Time!' after 30 seconds had expired. Sir Thomas yelled it twice more, and Cribb would almost certainly have been disqualified if Molineaux's second, Bill

---

75 The *Sportsman's magazine of life in London and the Country, The History of British Boxing, from Fig and Broughton to the Present Time, Chronology of the Period 1797-1798*, also recorded this street fight, giving the date of the event as 8 June 1795, stating 'Sir Thomas Apreece beat a street-robber, for justice, London streets'.

76 *Fancy-Ana* also lists the Welsh baronet, Sir Watkin Williams Wynn, as having been one of the main patrons of the prize ring in 1805.

77 According to *Pancratia*, Sir Watkin Williams Wynn was also present at this fight.

'The Battle between Crib and Molineaux', by Walker & Knight (1811). From left to right: Sir Thomas Apreece (Appreece/Ap Rhys), 'Paddington' Jones, Bill Richmond, Tom Molineaux, Tom Cribb, John Gully and Joe Ward.

Richmond, had not been distracted by Cribb's second, Joe Ward, allowing Cribb enough recovery time to continue the battle.

The Prince of Wales, who would be crowned King George IV in 1821, had been an ardent supporter of pugilism in his youth, along with his brothers the Duke of York, and the Duke of Clarence. In his support of prize fighting, the Prince had followed in the footsteps of his great uncle, the Duke of Cumberland, who had backed Jack Broughton. The Prince attended a number of fights between 1786 and 1788, and there have even been suggestions that he may have surreptitiously organised matches himself and backed his chairman, Tom Tring, in his pugilistic endeavours.[78] His Royal Highness was said to have been a strong supporter of Daniel Mendoza, and Mendoza would claim in his memoirs that the Prince had organised the fight between him and Sam Martin of Bath at Shepperd's Bush in 1787. The contest was prevented by a magistrate who ordered the 10th Regiment of Dragoons to break it up, and they afterwards smashed up the stage and dispersed the crowd. When the fight did come off between Martin and Mendoza, on 17 April 1787, on a specially built stage at Barnet racecourse, the Prince was amongst the crowd of 5,000 who witnessed the event, in the company of his brother, the Duke of York. The Prince's

78 Tom Tring was reportedly employed by the Prince of Wales for 15 years as a 'chairman' – having been employed to carry the Prince's sedan chair.

chairman, Tom Tring, also acted as a second in Mendoza's corner in this contest, alongside Tom Johnson. The Prince of Wales was also present at the contest between the tailor, Tom Tyne, and a pugilist named Earl, in August of 1788, at Brighton raceground, which proved fatal to Earl. After this event, the Prince is said to have withdrawn his public support from prize fighting in order to avoid damaging publicity after his elevation to the position of Prince Regent. Privately, he would appear to have maintained an interest in the ring, and was reported in *The Times* newspaper as having been present at a contest between a bruiser named Chapman and a 'noted' Jew, less than two years after the death of Earl.[79]

An indication that the Prince's interest in pugilism continued well into the next century can be seen by the fact that at his coronation, on 19 July 1821, he engaged 18 of the leading pugilists of the day to guard the external avenues of Westminster Hall from unauthorised visitors, including such notable prize fighters as Tom Cribb, Tom Spring, Tom Belcher, Josh Hudson and Dick Curtis.[80] The pugilists had been dressed as pages, and Cribb and Spring had stood either side of the main entrance as the chief bouncers. The appearance of the pugilists at the ceremony had been organised by 'Gentleman' John Jackson, after Jackson had been requested to engage their services by another prominent Welsh patron of pugilism, Peter Drummond Burrell, better known as Lord Gwydyr, who also served as Deputy Lord Great Chamberlain.[81]

---

79 As recorded in *Up to Scratch, Bareknuckle Fighting and Heroes of the Prize-ring*, by Tony Gee, (Harpenden: Queen Anne Press, 1998).

80 The 18 pugilists who were engaged to appear at the coronation of George IV were Tom Cribb, Tom Spring, Tom Belcher, Jack Carter, Ben Burn, Harry Harmer, Harry Lee, Tom Owen, Joshua Hudson, Tom Oliver, Harry Holt, Peter Crawley, Dick Curtis, Ben Medley, Bob Purcell, Phillip Sampson, Bill Eales, and Bill Richmond.

81 Peter Robert Drummond-Burrell, 2nd Baron Gwydyr, 22nd Baron Willoughby de Eresby, was the son of the 1st Baron Gwydyr, Peter Burrell, and Priscilla Barbara Elizabeth Bertie, 21st Baroness Willoughby de Eresby. The title, Baron Gwydyr, in the County of Carnarvon, had been created in 1796. Priscilla Bertie was an heir to the Aberffraw claim to the Principality of Gwynedd and Wales through her grandmother, Mary Wynn, who was directly descended from Owain ap Gruffudd (Owain the Great), the King of Gwynedd, North Wales (c. 1100 – 1170).

After the coronation, Lord Gwydyr had sent individual letters of thanks to the pugilists on the behalf of their new Monarch:

> "GREAT CHAMBERLAIN'S OFFICE,
> *July the 22nd*, 1821.
>
> SIR, – Having received His Majesty's commands, through the Secretary of State for the Home Department, to communicate to you, sir, His Majesty's gracious approbation of the manner in which you discharged your duty on the 19th of July, I know no way so effectual of executing these most gratifying instructions, as by inclosing you a copy of the original document. Permit me at the same time to add, how sensible am of your attention to the very imperfect directions I was enabled to furnish you with, and that the arrangements, which have been with so much condescension noticed by your King, are in a great degree to be attributed to the loyalty, judgment, and temper, exhibited by you at His Majesty's coronation.
>
> "I remain, sir,
>
> "Your faithful and obedient servant,
>
> "GWYDYR."
>
> *"To Mr. Thomas Cribb, etc."*

The letter that Lord Gwydyr had received from the Home Secretary, Lord Sidmouth, which Gwydyr duplicated and forwarded on to the pugilists, reads as follows:

> "WHITEHALL, "21*st July*, 1821.
>
> "MY LORD, – I am commanded by His Majesty, to express to your Lordship His Majesty's high approbation of the arrangements made by your Lordship in the department of the Great Chamberlain of England, for the august ceremony of His Majesty's coronation, and of the correctness and regularity with which they were carried into effect.
>
> To the exemplary manner in which these duties were performed by your Lordship, and by those officers who acted under your Lordship's authority, His Majesty is graciously pleased to consider that the order and dignity,

> which so peculiarly distinguished the ceremony, are in a great degree to be ascribed; and I have to request that your Lordship will communicate to the persons referred to the sense which His Majesty has condescended to express of their services.
>
> "I have the honour to be, my Lord,
>
> "Your Lordship's most obedient, humble servant,
>
> "SIDMOUTH."
>
> *"The Lord Gwydyr,*
> *Deputy Great Chamberlain of England."*

As a mark of appreciation, Lord Gwydyr also presented a single gold coronation medal, which he supposedly received directly 'from the hands of his majesty expressly for the boxers'. As the medal could not be split between the pugilists, it was afterwards raffled at a dinner held at Tom Cribb's, which was also paid for by Gwydyr. Tom Belcher won the raffle, and declared that he would not part with the medal until 'death forces him to leave all his worldly goods behind.'[82]

That Lord Gwydyr was an enthusiastic follower of the prize ring can be seen by the fact that the Deputy Great Chamberlain was also, like Sir Watkin Williams Wynn, a member of the Pugilistic Club.[83]

While there were undoubtedly other Welsh pugilists competing in the London Prize Ring, as well as on home turf in organised contests in Wales long before the end of the 18th century, it also seems that there was at least one Welsh woman who was not unacquainted with the practice of pugilism, and who proved to be more than willing to raise her fists given sufficient provocation to do so. An account published within the *Star Daily Evening Advertiser* in 1799 reports of a heated battle between a 'Welch woman' and a male milk seller, which took place in the early hours one Saturday morning in October on the streets of Shoreditch.

---

82 As recorded in *Fistiana*.

83 In the *Lincolnshire Archives*, amongst the manuscripts relating to the Earl of Ancaster, there is a reminder dated 26 April 1823, that 'Lord Gwydyr's subscription to the Pugilistic Club is overdue' (*Reference: 3ANC7/23/94*).

> MONOPOLY OF MILE – On Saturday morning about fiv o'clock, a man employed to retail milk in a caravan about the City Road and Shoreditch, for a cow keeper, whose custom, from the regular carriers, had declined in consequence of his raising them 4d. per gallon, being set upon by a number of women, in Old Street Road, upon whose walks he had intruded to undersell them, one of them, a Welch woman, challenging him to a fair boxing match, he came down, and fought several rounds with her to an evident disadvantage; when, giving her what was deemed to be a foul blow on the breast, the rest of them interfered, and would most probably have killed him, had he not been rescued from them by a number of carpenters going to work.[84]

There are few reports of the spread of pugilism in the early 1800s in Wales itself, but that fighting was widespread and that the rise of organised pugilism was a matter of great concern to the guardians of law and order might be deduced from an entry in *The Cambrian* newspaper of 1805, a year after its foundation. On 2 September 1805, Mr Justice Hardinge spoke before the Grand Jury at Cardiff with regard to a forthcoming manslaughter trial. Speaking in general terms, Hardinge was quick to condemn the cause of such outrages, naming pugilism as having been one of the main causes of death.

'These *manslaughters* are disgraceful to the Welsh, and (I must add with concern) to this part of that whole Principality the most. They arise either from the habit of tippling to excess, (a most prevalent impulse of the Welsh), from a taste of miscalculated sense of honour and spirit, or from the rage for what is called *pugilism*, converted into an article or *taste* – and a *science*.'[85]

That fist fighting had developed into an organised activity of public concern that frequently resulted in fatality would be repeated endlessly throughout the course of the next century. Curiously, however, the first published lengthy account of a stubbornly fought prize fight in Wales to be uncovered would

84 As recorded in *Star Daily Evening Advertiser*, 25 October 1799.

85 As recorded in *The Cambrian*, 7 September 1805.

not concern two native fighters, and was not fought in South Wales, but upon the 'wild mountains of Wales, a few miles from Dynasmouthy, in Merionethshire'.

The 'long expected contest' concerned a 'celebrated Cornish man' named Cavallin and a Cheshire blacksmith named Burkitt, and took place on 2 January 1805.[86] The fight was arranged for 20 guineas, with both men having entered into training the previous month. Snow had to be swept from the battleground before the fight could start.

On removing their shirts, the odds favoured Cavallin, who lived up to expectations, having been a 'fine made man', and standing about 5ft 11in. By comparison Burkitt, the Cheshire man, was 'ill-made, except in his arms and in his chest, which were prodigious', the blacksmith having no doubt developed the musculature of his upper body in long hours striking hammer against anvil. Burkitt was the shorter of the two men, being about 5ft 7in tall. Cavallin appeared to have the advantage for the first six rounds, and the Cheshire and North Wales farmers were said to have trembled at the thought of losing the money they had staked on Burkitt.

They worried needlessly, as it soon transpired that the wily Burkitt had faked the appearance of being beaten in the hope that the Cornishman would attack with his utmost strength and fatigue himself. Burkitt sought the grass in every round at the beginning, but just when those who did not understand his strategy thought him beaten, he rallied and struck Cavallin a terrible blow in the throat. Following it up, Burkitt threw a tremendous punch to Cavallin's ribs, which landed with such force that it nearly lifted him off the ground.

By the 18th round, both men fell into wrestling, but in this activity, Burkitt failed to make an impression. Hard hitting was seen on both sides over the next few rounds, but in the 24th round a decisive turning point was reached. While Cavallin was running in with a hard blow, Burkitt successfully evaded him and struck him two severe hits, one of which landed on the kidneys. He then

86 *Sporting Magazine: Or, Monthly Calendar of the Transactions of the Turf, the Chase and Every Other Diversion Interesting to the Man of Pleasure, Enterprize, and Spirit, Volume 25*, (London: J. Wheble, 1805). The contest between Cavallin and Burkitt was also deemed of sufficient interest as to be recorded in *Pancratia*.

seized Cavallin by the waist, dashed him to the ground and fell on top of his opponent. In the succeeding rounds, Burkitt knocked his man down every time with ease. It was in the 42nd round that Burkitt landed such a smashing blow on Cavallin's ribs that the Cornishman was forced to yield, with the pain of the blow making him unable to continue. Burkitt, by comparison, was very little hurt, except for some minor damage to his face. Exalted by his victory, Burkitt immediately issued a challenge to fight for 50 guineas to any man of the six western counties, Cornwall, Devonshire, Dorset, Gloucester, Monmouth and Somerset; the inhabitants of Bath and Bristol excepted. Burkitt was seconded by 'Cheshire Williams', who even Burkitt readily conceded was his superior.

The outcome of the fight between Burkitt and Cavallin would appear to have been keenly followed by those involved in pugilistic contests in Wales. Soon afterwards, Burkitt's challenge was accepted by a combative Welsh native of some renown, one Evan Price of Monmouth, known by the cognomen of the 'Big Man of Monmouth'. The fight was scheduled to take place three months later, with Burkitt's impressive performance against Cavallin ensuring that bets were taken at 7/1 on his victory. Sadly, no record appears to have been made as to whether the proposed contest between Burkitt and the 'Big Man' ever took place.

A rare account of a fight, which was no doubt of the variety that had so concerned Mr Justice Hardinge in speaking about the pugilistic propensities of the natives of South Wales, took place on 4 January 1811, at Llandaff in Cardiff, and was fought for 100 guineas in front of an estimated 500 spectators.[87] A great deal of money was wagered on the outcome, and large sums of money were won and lost. The principals were 'Stephens, of the White Lion, in Landaff' and 'James, of Ely Mill'. Stephens was seconded by a brazier by the name of Jones, and James was supported by a wheelwright named John Jonas. As the fight began, the betting was even until the fifth round when Stephens was knocked down, and the odds shifted 6/4 on James. By the tenth round, it was James who was showing 'superior science', although his fortunes

87 As recorded in *The Cambrian*, 12 January 1811, and in *The Globe*, 15 January 1811.

changed by the 14th and the superior strength of Stephens came into play. In the 21st round, James rallied and once again turned the tables, landing a violent blow to the stomach, which greatly injured the Llandaff man. Stephens, exhausted at the end of 27 rounds, lasting over 32 minutes, finally gave in, and James of Ely Mill was declared the winner. At the conclusion of the fight, John Jonas, gratified by the victory of his man, challenged any man in Glamorganshire for another 100 guineas.

In February of the following year, *The Cambrian* would also draw attention to a prize fight that had taken place at Newport in Monmouthshire, where a Welshman known as 'George the Sailor' had engaged an English collier for 80 guineas. A large crowd estimated at 3,000 to 4,000 spectators witnessed George the Sailor's defeat in 13 rounds.[88] Another brief account of a 'pitched battle' between two travelling Jews, Abraham Platt and Solomon Moseley at Haverfordwest, was recorded in the *Carmarthen Journal and South Wales Weekly Advertiser* a few months later in June of 1812.

Both combatants appear to have had some experience as pugilists as the battle lasted 37½ minutes, and was reportedly 'well contested' and a 'considerable degree of science' was exhibited. After a busy first round, Platt appeared to be the superior man, although by the sixth, Moseley had rallied, and after some desperate hits that sent Platt to the turf, odds of 5/4 were offered on Moseley.

With Solomon Moseley having been wearied by his endeavours, Abraham Platt afterwards punished Moseley at will, putting in a right-hander in the tenth round that staggered Moseley to the degree that his second, a well-known Irish drover named Michael Armstrong, conceded the battle on Solomon Moseley's behalf as Moseley was so weak that he could not be brought up to the scratch at the call of time.[89]

That there are so few accounts of prize fights taking place in Wales recorded in the press of this time can largely be ascribed to the contempt with which prize fighting was greeted by wider

---

88 As recorded in *The Cambrian*, 15 February 1812, and in *The Globe*, 18 February 1812, as well as in the *Hereford Journal*, 19 February 1812.

89 As recorded in the *Carmarthen Journal and South Wales Weekly Advertiser*, 20 June 1812.

society. The Welsh press viewed the growing tendency of men to settle their differences or indulge in organised contests on which significant sums had been wagered with such negativity that it ensured prize fighting remained a far more underground undertaking in Wales than in the city of London. In 1813, the distaste of the newspaper editor of *The Cambrian* newspaper of reporting on pugilistic matters can be seen by the minimal coverage given to a fatal pugilistic contest at Wrexham. It gave no details of the fight or even the name of the unfortunate combatant, merely commenting that 'A man was killed in a pugilistic contest at Wrexham, on Saturday night last'.[90] *The Cambrian* newspaper did, however, consider the death of an elderly pugilist named John Williams from Clodia, near Welshpool, to be sufficiently newsworthy as to be recorded in the newspaper in 1811. Mr Williams had at one time been better known as '*Jack of the Wern*', and *The Cambrian* would record that 'In his youthful days he practised, with so great success, the *art* of pugilism, that the renowned Glan Brace, and several Cambrian heroes, yielded to his superior strength and dexterity'.[91]

With pugilists having been considered mostly unproven prior to having appeared in the London prize ring, no matter how many battles they may have fought, it will be no surprise to find that the next Welsh pugilist to have achieved widespread national fame first came to light in the city of London. In time, the 'Out-and-Outer', as he became known, would develop such finely honed pugilistic skills that he would be considered one of the most scientific fighters of the period. His name was Edward Turner.

---

90 As recorded in *The Cambrian*, 3 July 1813.

91 As recorded in *The Cambrian*, 11 May 1811.

Chapter 6
The Out-and-Outer

The *game* Ned Turner once a toast,
No better man alive!
He was 'the Fancy's' pride and boast,
On victory did thrive.

(*Pierce Egan's Book of Sports, and Mirror of Life: Embracing the Turf, the Chase, the Ring and the Stage Interspersed with Original Memoirs of Sporting Men, etc*, by Pierce Egan, (London: Thomas Tegg & Son, 1836).

Edward Turner, better known as Ned, was, after the days of Paddington Jones, the greatest fighting Welshman of the age. Turner was born on 8 November 1791 in the borough of Southwark, in Crucifix Lane, London. His parents were both Welsh natives, hailing from Newtown in Montgomeryshire, where many of his relations still lived, and for this reason he was more closely identified with Wales than his birthplace and would see all his endeavours in the prize ring supported by his loyal countrymen.

Ned Turner, the 'Out-and-Outer'.

Ned had shown a talent for fighting since he was a boy, but his pugilistic skills first drew attention when Ned was an apprentice skinman or skin-dresser at a large tanning yard in Bermondsey, an area well known for its prominence in the leather

Ned Turner defeats John Balch.

trade in Turner's day. At the age of 19, Ned Turner took his first pugilistic scalp after battling against John Balch from Bristol, the foreman of the yard and its boxing champion. Despite having been much taller and heavier than Turner, after a determined fight lasting an hour Ned forced his opponent to concede, and Balch was led from the ring 'totally blind'.[92]

92 *Boxiana* gives the age of Ned Turner as 19 years old at the time he fought Balch, which means that this fight has been recorded as having occurred in 1810 in later sources. *Fistiana* records the fight as having taken place in 1810, and records Turner's opponent's name as 'Balche' rather than 'Balch', with the contest having lasted 50 minutes rather than an hour.

It was after this time that a publican named Keating of the Black Horse near St Giles brought forward a large Irishman to fight Ned Turner at the Cockpit located at the Huntsman and Hounds in Lock's Fields for five guineas a-side. For the first three rounds, Turner had the worst of it. The Irishman bored in on the Welshman with the utmost fury, and Ned fell upon his back across the short stakes of the pit. The injuries that he sustained were so severe that he did not recover for several rounds afterwards. Ned Turner rallied in the rounds that followed, and after 25 minutes, the Irishman was beaten left and right and was blinded to the extent that by the end of the fight he 'could not tell whether he was living at that moment either in England or Ireland'.[93]

Shortly after this fight, Turner left London to fulfil an engagement he had made at a skin yard in Glasgow. It was here that Turner's path crossed a pupil of Jack Carter's, a spirit dealer named M'Neil. Prior to the arrival of Ned Turner, M'Neil had stated his desire to defeat all the Englishmen in Glasgow. M'Neil appears to have been perceived as the champion of the city, and stood 5ft 11in tall and weighed 13st. After his arrival at Glasgow, news of Turner's prowess quickly reached M'Neil's ears, and he was quick to seek a contest against the young Welshman. A contest between the two men was made for five guineas a-side to be held in a private room. It took Turner half an hour to comprehensively defeat M'Neil. Unsatisfied by the outcome, M'Neil pushed for a rematch and £5 a-side were deposited to secure another fight for larger stakes. M'Neil apparently afterwards had a change of heart and forfeited rather than meet Turner for the second time.

After leaving Glasgow, Turner made his way to Newcastle, where a new opponent, a slater named Blacket, challenged him. Blacket was well known as a pugilist in the area, and was an

---

93 This fight against the unnamed Irishman is unrecorded in *Fistiana*. *Pugilistica* records this contest as having occurred in 1813, although on what basis it is difficult to establish, but probably does so for convenience as *Boxiana* relates that Turner's fight against M'Neil occurred 'soon after' his fight against the Irishman. *Fistiana* records Turner's next fight against M'Neil as having occurred in 1814. It appears as though *Pugilistica* relies on the years given in *Fistiana* for Turner's other early contests prior to his fight against Jack Curtis, and the author has 'inserted' the year of the contest against the Irishman.

imposingly built man standing an inch over 6ft and weighing over 14st. Thousands of spectators witnessed the contest between the two men, which was held on the racecourse. Blacket was severely thrashed over the course of 45 minutes, after which time he refused to fight, infuriated that 'TURNER was not a fair fighter, and that he did nothing but make hits, and then jump away!' This would appear to be the first contest in which Ned Turner won himself a measure of fame, and he was universally applauded for beating a man so much heavier than himself. A collection was afterwards made amongst the amateurs and presented to Ned as an award for his bravery.[94]

Turner afterwards returned to London, and his next minor battle was fought at St George's Fields against one Youler ('Davenport's Jew'), who was a rough-and-tumble fighter. After 35 minutes, Youler was forced to retire after having received terrible punishment to his body. After this fight, Ned was set upon one evening at the Cottage of Content in Lock's Fields by five watermen. Turner quickly disposed of the first four with complete nonchalance. The fifth had some ability in boxing, and attempted to make a stand against Turner, although his efforts amounted to nothing and the waterman fled with the marks of Ned's fists upon him. By this time, Turner's growing fame had spread, and his capabilities as a pugilist were well known in the neighbourhood of Bermondsey. Talk of Ned's growing skills soon reached Jack Curtis, the elder brother of Dick Curtis, the celebrated 'Pet of the Fancy'. Jack had himself earned some renown following his victories over Westcountry Dick, Tom Rowe, and Lazarus the Jew, and felt such envy at Turner's growing reputation that he repeatedly challenged Turner until he could get him to agree to meet him in combat.

At length, a match was made between Jack Curtis and Ned Turner for 100 guineas, with Curtis's supporters refusing to believe that Turner could stand up for 30 minutes against their man. The two men met in a 20ft ring at Moulsey Hurst on Tuesday, 22 October 1816. Curtis was attended to by Oliver and Clark, while Turner was accompanied by his good friend Tom Owen and

94 *Fistiana* and also *Pugilistica* both record this contest as having taken place in 1816.

Jacobs. Those who had predicted an easy win for Jack Curtis were surprised by Turner's actions right from the beginning. After a cautious start, the Welshman launched an assault, striking Curtis twice before sending him down. Many seemed astonished that the 'novice', as Turner had been termed, had commenced in such style. Turner continued to attack Curtis with noticeable superiority, and again sent him down in the second. Curtis was bleeding as early as the third round. Evidently confused by a fighter who fought with his right foot foremost and one who was so lightning-quick with his left, Curtis began fighting on the retreat. He failed to make any impression on Turner and received such a tremendous blow for his pains in the sixth round that blood streamed down his face, and another sharp punch from the novice sent him out of the ring.

Ned Turner sends Jack Curtis to the turf.

There was no doubt that Ned Turner was the superior boxer, and he continually followed Curtis, who hit short, but had some success in throwing Ned when the fighting closed to short range. It was in the throwing alone that Jack Curtis might have been deemed Turner's master. Ned continually landed over the guard of Curtis with his left hand, and while his game opponent tried to return fire, many of his blows fell short. By the 14th round, Turner's superiority was undeniable, and Curtis was hit 'in all directions' until he was reeling about the ring like a 'man intoxicated' and fell to the turf once more. Jack Curtis was continually punished in the rounds that followed, and he received a tremendous thrashing in the 20th, and was hit out of the ring in the following round. His desperation was in evidence by the 23rd round, and Curtis was again seen to hit short, and he seized hold of Turner's hands in desperation.

As the rounds mounted, Jack Curtis continued to struggle to find his range, and was always on the receiving end of Turner's left, with the marks of severe damage beginning to show on his face. The only way in which Curtis seemed to be able to land a blow was after boring in to close range, and every time he did, he found Turner's left in his face. Curtis put all his hopes on victory in throwing his opponent, which he did with great cleverness but to little effect. Blood covered his face and he was pushed all over the ring by Ned, and by the 37th round Jack Curtis was desperately scrabbling to hold Ned Turner's hands once more. As Turner continued to attack his opponent with the greatest of ease, Curtis forced his way to close range in the 41st round and again seized Turner by the wrists in a tight hold. Unable to break his grip, the Welshman slung Curtis to and fro until his wrists finally slipped from Curtis's grasp. Jack Curtis was sent to the turf again and again, and although it seemed he did not have the slightest chance of winning, his courage compelled him to fight on. By the 50th round, his supporters were pleading with him to concede his defeat, but Curtis refused to give in.

The appearance of Curtis's head was now 'frightful'; he was covered with blood and his sight was rapidly failing him. He struck out in vain when he was out of distance, and when he fought his way to close range, he was severely punished by Turner. Exhaustion now setting in, Jack Curtis went down in the following rounds almost as soon as they had begun. By the 62nd round, he was almost completely blind. He ran past Turner in his desperation to attack, and on turning round to resume the assault he was floored once more. Despite the terrible condition of Curtis, he again struggled with the Welshman in the following round, and threw him forcefully, showing an astonishing level of courage so late in the fight. He again tried to seize Turner's hands, and was hit down once more. Seeing the terrible state of his opponent, Turner stepped back from Curtis and avoided punishing his game antagonist, who fought on in a state of stupor.

The contest finally ended in the 68th round, after one hour 25 minutes. Jack Curtis slumped on to the knee of his second and his head lolled to one side. He was now in a state of absolute darkness, and was completely deaf to the call of 'Time'. Curtis was carried from the ring a short time afterwards, and put to bed at the Red Lion Inn at Hampton. Medical assistance was quickly procured, but proved to be in vain, and the brave Jack Curtis breathed his last at the stroke of midnight.

The inquisition on the death of Jack Curtis was held at the same inn three days later on Friday, 25 October 1816, before Thomas Stirling, the Coroner of Middlesex. John Griffinhoof, a surgeon from Hampton, had been called after Jack Curtis had been brought to the inn, and gave evidence that the beaten man had been in a 'state of perfect insensibility' when he had arrived. Although Curtis's body had been discoloured from the waist upwards, none of these injuries had been of sufficient severity to cause his death. His head was in a dreadful state and Griffinhoof believed the blows that Curtis had sustained to his head were responsible for his demise. Jack Curtis had been bled from the arm, and leeches applied to his temples, but an attempt to get him to swallow a medicinal draught had failed, as the surgeon could not get it down the dying pugilist's throat. Griffinhoof's thoughts were supported by Morris Jones, a surgeon and apothecary, who stated that the pugilist's head was a 'complete mass of blood' and that 'not a single feature' of Jack Curtis's face was distinguishable. Dr Jones was also of the opinion that the blows to the head of Curtis had caused his death, due to a blood vessel having burst. The only hope that Dr Jones had entertained of recovery prior to Curtis's death was by bleeding him profusely.

It emerged that prior to the battle with Edward Turner that Jack Curtis had been suffering from an unnamed disease over the course of the previous month and had been under the care of two physicians of St Thomas's Hospital. His supporters had thought that he had not been in sound physical health, and had begged him not to fight, but Curtis had been determined to see the contest go ahead. A Hampton fishmonger, Richard Coombs, then testified that he had been present at the fight and recalled that after an hour of fighting, Ned Turner had approached Jack Curtis and had advised him to give in. By this time Curtis appeared in a dreadful state, 'blood poured from every pore in his head' and his 'eyes, nose, and mouth were running with blood in streams'. Three rounds later, Curtis had been unable to stand up and the battle had been called in favour of Turner.

A second witness claimed that about 12 rounds prior to the end of the contest, he had personally approached Jack Curtis and told him that he had no chance of winning, and advised him to give in. Jack Curtis's second, Tom Oliver, had also told him to admit defeat long before the battle was over, although Curtis had believed that he could win until the end. In Ned Turner's defence, it was underlined that in the latter part of the fight he had refused to take advantage of the declining state of Curtis when he had him at his mercy on the ropes, and he was thought to have shown a great deal of fair play in his refusal to punish Curtis at will.

Ultimately, the coroner's inquest address stated that the fight had been unlawful, and despite their agreement to fight, Ned Turner had no right to beat Jack Curtis to the point that he died. In Turner's defence, it was thought that by not punishing Curtis when he had the opportunity, Ned had behaved with honour. After summing up the matter before the jury, the judge considered the evidence for 20 minutes before a verdict of manslaughter was returned. After the coroner's warrant was obtained, Jack Curtis's body was taken by hearse to London. The plate affixed to the side of the coffin stated that Curtis was 28 years old at the time of his death. On 1 November 1816, at the Old Bailey, Edward Turner was indicted for the wilful murder of John Curtis with his fists. John Griffinhoof, and the surgeon, Richard Coombs, repeated the statements they had given at the inquest, and after the evidence had been given on the part of the Crown, Edward Turner's written defence was read before the Court:

> My Lords and Gentlemen of the Jury, -
>
> Deeply impressed with the great peril to which I am exposed by the present heavy charge made against me, and with the difficulty I necessarily experience in substantiating my innocence, owing to the danger to which most competent witnesses of the transaction would be exposed, were they to be examined, I must solicit your most serious attention to such facts as I shall

> be enabled to lay before you, by which I trust not only my natural disposition will appear, but that on the occasion of the sad catastrophe imputed to me, I was goaded into a contest to fight the deceased, who was himself a prize-fighter, and with the greatest reluctance I entered the ring, after being assaulted and pursued with the most unremitting vigilance; and when I did so, as soon as I ascertained my superiority over my antagonist, I forbore, on very many occasions, to avail myself of the advantages that presented themselves to me, and with the greatest reluctance I continued the contest until the circumstances occurred which led to the unfortunate event which I must ever deplore, and which has placed me in my present awful situation. I beg to state, that my pursuits in life are honest, and my aversion to prize-fighting great, never having before fought a pitched battle; nor should I on this occasion, but for the great aggravation which will be proved I received. I assure your Lordships and Gentlemen of the Jury, that I am totally innocent of any intention to seriously injure the deceased, and that there never existed in my mind the smallest particle of malice towards him. I trust, therefore, that my character for humanity and forbearance will have its due weight on this occasion.

As the statement was being read before the jury by the clerk of the Arraigns, Ned Turner began to shed tears and appeared to be greatly affected by the words that were read on his behalf. Turner's counsel, Mr Andrews, afterwards called multiple witnesses who repeatedly spoke of the Welshman's good character and mild disposition. Some echoed Turner's own statement that he had never fought a 'pitched battle' prior to that against Jack Curtis and had been repeatedly pressed to fight by the deceased man. Baron Graham then made a statement agreeing that the unfortunate circumstances that had befallen Ned Turner were not due to any previous malice. Turner had been viewed as a young man of fistic prowess over whom a victory would increase the fame of his opponent, and it was under these circumstances that he had been urged, if not goaded, to fight Curtis. Ned Turner and Jack Curtis had both agreed to fight without weapons in a display of manhood and courage, and under normal circumstances it was not thought that such a trial would result in death. While Baron Graham did not wish to speak ill of the deceased, he felt that it might be established that by repeatedly confronting Turner and imploring him to fight, an angry feeling might be imputed on the part of the late Jack Curtis.

Additionally, in Baron Graham's view, Turner had 'cautiously and humanely avoided using, to the extent he might have done, the decided advantage and superiority which he had over the deceased' throughout the duration of the contest. There was nothing in Ned Turner's conduct that had demonstrated cruelty or a desire to injure Jack Curtis beyond the hope of proving that he was the better man in a pugilistic contest. Baron Graham concluded that as a result of these factors, the charge of murder appeared out of the question, although there was no doubt that Curtis had been killed due to having decided to fight Turner. Ned Turner had previously endured a great many insults on the part of Jack Curtis without any desire for retaliation and Baron Graham pointed towards his standing as a man of honour, which had been revealed by the patience with which he had refused to be drawn by these insults.

After a short duration, the jury returned a verdict of manslaughter against Edward Turner, but recommended his merciful treatment at the hands of the court, due to his humanity and forbearance. Baron Graham observed that the feelings of the jury were reflected by the thoughts of the court, and at the end of the Sessions, Ned Turner was sentenced to two months imprisonment at Newgate gaol for the manslaughter of John Curtis.

Chapter 7
Scroggy's Challenge

After his confinement at Newgate, Ned Turner conducted himself with such civility and decorum that he was treated kindly by his jailers, who showed him every courtesy possible. Many of the prominent patrons of pugilism also visited Ned in an attempt to rally his spirits throughout the time of his sentence. Shortly after his release from gaol, Turner took a benefit event at the Minerva Rooms in Leadenhall Street to collect funds to cover the heavy expenses he had sustained throughout his trial and subsequent imprisonment, and the Welshman's fellow pugilists rallied round him in gratifying numbers. At this time, there had been a great deal of talk about making a match between Jack Scroggins and Ned Turner, but the friends of Turner had insisted that Scroggins should not exceed 10st 7lbs coming into the ring. Debate continued until a disagreement between Scroggins and Turner brought them together after all previous attempts to do so had failed.

Jack 'Scroggins', or 'Scroggy' as he was affectionately known, was not the pugilist's real name. Scroggins had been born John Palmer on 31 December near New Cross, Deptford in 1787.[95] As a young boy, he had shown early promise in childhood scraps with other youngsters, and it was while employed on a farm at Kilburn belonging to the great butcher of Bond Street, Mr Giblett, that he first earned his unusual nickname. In 1804, Scroggins demolished Billy Lee, the gypsy, and won a number of minor victories prior to becoming a sailor as a crewmember of the Argo. In short time, Scroggins was considered the champion of the Argo, defeating a

95 As recorded in *Boxiana*.

large number of would-be pugilists who dared to challenge him. On his return to land, Scroggins destroyed Jack Boots of Wilford at Wilsden Green in 1814, and defeated Dolly Smith at Coombe Warren in 1815. Bill Nosworthy had been thrashed in 18 rounds and 15 minutes at Mousley Hurst, while Bill Eales had lasted a little longer, it being 22 minutes and 23 rounds before Scroggins achieved victory. Whittaker, an oilman from Denby in Yorkshire, had criticised the abilities of Scroggins and fought the pugnacious sailor in 1816.

He lasted longer than anyone but conceded after 49 rounds lasting 76 minutes, by which time Scroggins had blinded Whittaker and the Yorkshireman was unable to fight on. In his previous fight against one J. Church of Gloucester, Scroggins had floored his opponent in 58 minutes in the 50th round, and Church was led away by his supporters, having been 'dreadfully beaten'. As a result of his having never been defeated in a prize fight, the fame of Scroggy had grown, and many of the Fancy thought him almost invulnerable to defeat.

The dispute as to whether Ned Turner or Jack Scroggins was the better man was ignited on the evening of Wednesday, 26 February 1817, at a sporting dinner held at the Castle Tavern public house in Holborn. As the deputy chairman was absent, Scroggins filled the vacancy. Scroggy was in a celebratory mood, having returned from the Fives Court after a set-to with Tom Belcher in which his performance had been greatly applauded. After having decided to drink more liberally from his bottle than was entirely wise, Scroggins fell asleep in a drunken stupor. On awakening, the sailor became quarrelsome and picked a fight with the veteran pugilist, Joe Norton, threatening to give him a beating. In an attempt to pacify the war-like Scroggy, Ned Turner commented that Norton's time as a pugilist had long since passed and that Norton was an old man. These remarks angered Scroggins a great deal and he was quick to cast aspersions upon Turner's own ability as a fighter, sharply observing on the death of Jack Curtis that Turner had only ever 'licked a man who was dead before he entered the ring'. Understandably sensitive about the subject, Turner made a disparaging retort that further enflamed the fury of Scroggins, who dealt the Welshman a slap in the face just as he was sitting down.

Ned Turner and Jack Scroggins were quickly separated.

Jack Scroggins and Ned Turner immediately began fighting, but scarcely a blow had passed before they were both on the floor, with Scroggins on top of Turner. They were quickly separated, but Scroggy was incandescent and he immediately challenged Turner to fight him for £100 to £50. Turner rejected the notion outright, believing that this was empty boasting on the part of Scroggins. The feeling amongst the onlookers was that Scroggins had treated the Welshman most unfairly, and as a consequence a deposit of five guineas was made on Ned's behalf to fix a contest for a month's time. On 12 March 1817, the supporters of both men met at the Castle Tavern and the stakes were made good. Few thought that Turner stood a chance against Scroggins as the list of the men defeated by the sailor was uppermost in their minds. Scroggins had the utmost confidence in his superiority over Ned, and asserted that he would win with ease, viewing Turner as little more than an upstart and a pretender.

On the day of the battle, Wednesday, 26 March 1817, large groups of pedestrians took to the Uxbridge Road. Within a few hours, approximately 20,000 people had assembled on the battleground, a field near Hayes, about ten miles from the Tyburn turnpike. Ned Turner was the first to enter the ring and he was immediately followed by Jack Scroggins. Tom Cribb, the champion of England, and Harry Harmer attended Turner, while Tom Oliver and Clarke served as Scroggins's seconds. Lord Yarmouth and Colonel Burton acted as timekeepers. Scroggins was the favourite, the betting stood at 3/1 against Turner, and many thousands of pounds had been laid on the outcome.

At the start of the fight, despite his confidence, Scroggins showed a great deal more caution than was expected. He did not adopt his usual method of 'boring in' on the Welshman to take the fight out of him. Trifling blows passed between them until at length, Turner went down lightly. Scroggins held up his hands in a gesture of superiority, indicating what little regard he held for the skills of his antagonist. In the second, Scroggins appeared a little more on the alert, although he failed to deliver punches of any real consequence. Although Turner went down for the second time, it was not seen to be as a result of effective punching on the part of Scroggins. The mood of the crowd was turning, and many called out, 'Now where's your three to one?' having been unimpressed by the sailor's performance. Slowly getting the measure of his man, Ned Turner fought 'manfully' in the following round, landing a severe punch under the left eye of Scroggins. Although Ned went down at the end of the round, his abilities as a boxer were now starting to reveal themselves, to great encouragement from the spectators.

The fourth round was fiercely contested, and both men went to work in earnest. Scroggins was hurled to the ground by a hard cross-buttocks throw by Turner at the close. The crowd, excited by this unexpected turn of events, pushed against the outer ring on all sides, and the ropes were broken as the masses surged forward. After a few more rounds, the inner ring was then broken into and the ropes trodden underfoot, and the combatants fought with scarcely a yard of space between them. Despite the close proximity of Jack Scroggins to Ned Turner, he was not seen to be getting any the better of his courageous opponent. The ring-keepers tried in vain to push back the crowds, laying about them with horsewhips, but they could not be repelled. As a result, 'Gentleman' John Jackson was forced to declare all bets null and void. By this time the crowds, numbering an estimated 30,000, could not be managed sufficiently for the fight to continue, and after a two-hour delay Jackson announced that the contest would be adjourned to a future date.

There was a great deal of discussion following the aborted contest. Ned Turner, it was thought, had proved himself to be a far more competent fighter than was expected. The Welshman had been seen to stand up against the assaults of Scroggins without intimidation. Both pugilists wore marks of the battle; Scroggins had a black eye, while one of Turner's eyes had also been damaged by the sailor's fists. Opinions differed wildly as to which man had been performing better prior to the ring having been broken into. Many believed that Jack Scroggins was not punished in the slightest, and stated their opinion that Ned Turner had shown the first signs of physical weakness after leaving the ring. With the matter completely unresolved, a meeting was held at the Castle Tavern in Holborn the following Monday, and the following articles were agreed to:

> Castle Tavern, Holborn
> March 31, 1817
>
> John Scroggins agrees to fight Edward Turner, 120 guineas to 80 on the 27th May. Ten pounds on each side are deposited; to fight in a twenty-four feet ring, half-minute time: one-half of the remainder of the money to be deposited at Scroggins's on the 15th of April. The whole to be made good on the 20th of May at Tom Belcher's. The fight to take place not within twenty-five miles from London. To be a fair, stand-up fight. Mr. Jackson to name the place of fighting, and to receive the money, till all is made good. The money, upon the first failure of deposit, to be forfeited, and the other half if not made good. To meet in the ring between twelve and one.
>
> J. SCROGGINS (his X mark)
> E. TURNER
>
> Witness, J.W

Due to the fact that Ascot race week fell at the same time as the time appointed in the articles (27 May), the battle was postponed until 10 June 1817, by mutual consent. The venue that had originally been chosen for the fight was at Matching Green, but on the day of the contest the contest was stopped by the interference of the Essex magistrates. After a short deliberation, it was decided that the battle should come off in Hertfordshire, in a paddock near Sawbridgeworth. Edward Turner was already in the locality, having stayed at the White Lion Inn in Sawbridgeworth the previous evening, after arriving from Newtown in Wales, where he had trained under the care of his uncle. Turner entered the ring in the company of his brother-in-law, Mr Baxter. He had been trained with a great deal of care and was in better condition than in the previously abandoned contest against Scroggins, and at 12.30pm he entered the ring, accompanied by Tom Owen and Jacobs. Scroggins followed soon afterwards, attended by Harry Harmer and Clark. Tom Owen tied the yellow colours of Turner upon the stakes, and Harmer covered it with the blue handkerchief of Scroggins. There was a small contingent of spectators present, barely one deep around the ring, with few people having been able to cover the 30 mile distance to the venue in time. The betting stood at 2/1 on Scroggins. At one o'clock, both men shook hands and the fight commenced.

Ned Turner and Jack Scroggins both appeared to be wary of engaging each other for the first couple of minutes at the start of the fight as they tried to feel each other out. Scroggins appeared at a loss as to how to open up against the Welshman, no doubt bothered by the awkward position of Turner, who stood in his usual unorthodox stance with his right leg forward. At last Scroggins rushed in, and after a scuffling close, Turner went down from a light blow to the head. Pleased by his success, Scroggins dashed in to close quarters again in the second round, but was stopped by Turner's straight right. A rally followed, and although Ned landed artfully on the ribs of Scroggins, the sailor's superior strength prevailed and Turner was thrown to the turf.

Scroggins looked upon his opponent in a new light, realising that he was facing a much more dangerous adversary than he had first realised. The sailor now showed unusual caution, and heavy exchanges took place at long range before Turner was thrown once more. Turner became the aggressor in the following round, feinting cleverly at the body of Scroggins with his left to pull down his guard before smashing a right hand into his throat. Jack again tried some rushing blows, although Ned was too clever in his defence, and Scroggins resorted to a heavy cross-buttocks throw to bring about the end of the round. The fifth round was tremendously fought, and while Scroggins rushed to close range, he was punished by Turner on the retreat, drawing first blood from the face of Scroggy. Undeterred, Scroggins again forced his way to close quarters, and seized Turner in his powerful arms, throwing him with ease. From the sixth round onwards, Ned steadily worked his way to the front, landing severe blows when presented with an opportunity and stopping the continued rushes of Jack while hitting with precision and judgement. He was, however, continually thrown, and it was clear that by this means Scroggins hoped to weaken Turner's resolve. Turner was the first to launch an assault in the 11th round, opening with a heavy left to the cheek of Scroggins. Scroggins launched a tremendous blow at Turner's stomach which, had it landed, might well have changed the complexion of the battle altogether, but he missed. Seizing his opportunity, Jack grabbed Ned about the waist, and with a gigantic effort threw him clean out of the ring. 'Well done Scroggins! He'll tire out Turner', was the cry at ringside.

Jack Scroggins, commonly known as 'Scroggy'.

The 12th round saw both men rallying in grand style, but in closing Turner punished Scroggins terribly, and wound up throwing the sailor to end the round. It was evident at the start of the 13th round that Scroggins had not fully recovered from being thrown at the finish of the previous round, and he retreated from the advance of Turner all over the ring. The spectators, not at all pleased with this strategy, began hissing to express their dissatisfaction at the sailor's timidity. Hearing their disapproval, Scroggins pulled himself together and dashed in with his old vigour, but was met with a smash on the jaw that spun him completely round. Showing remarkable powers of recovery, Jack regained his equilibrium and again dashed at Ned. In the close, both men came down side by side. The tide had turned, and there was no doubt that Turner was now the favourite.

The 22nd round was the best of the fight, and opened with a desperate rally, and the sounds of the blows of both combatants were heard all over the ring. After the break, Scroggins dashed in to try and smother Turner's efforts. Ned was prepared for the assault, and hit upwards just as the sailor was coming in, landing full on the throat. At the close, both went down, with Turner under. At the end of the round, Scroggins looked a sorry sight and sat on his second's knee, and gasped for air before vomiting a large quantity of blood.

The fight was now turning in Turner's favour with every round, and by the 24th round 5/1 and 6/1 were being offered on the victory of Ned. Turner threw a terrific left hand to the face of Scroggins and followed it with a stunning blow to the ribs with his right, which staggered Scroggins to the degree that he could not launch any blow with certainty so he turned to his desperate boring-in tactics once more. After both men had gone down, the combatants sat on the knees of their seconds near each other, and Turner took hold of the sailor's hand and gave it a friendly shake.

In the 26th round, Ned Turner led off with a dreadful punch that landed full on the chin of Jack Scroggins, and then landed a tremendous shot to his ribs, sending him clean off his feet. Odds of 7/1 were now being offered on Turner and it was clear that Scroggins was all but finished by this combination, and he took a long pull on a flask of brandy to enable him to drag himself up to the scratch for the 27th round. From this point onwards, Scroggins was hit down every time he came up in the following three rounds; his condition was now deteriorating so quickly that 10/1 was being offered against him, although there were no takers.

Turner showed his skill in the 31st round, and he weaved in cleverly, feinted, broke ground, and then advanced again to plant a smashing right lead to Scroggins's head, which sent him reeling across the ring. Ned was after him in an instant and as Jack rebounded from the ropes, Turner sent in a tremendous blow to the ribs, and Scroggins collapsed. It was evidently the end for Scroggins, and although he came up for the 32nd time, it was apparent from the shambolic way that he brought himself up to the scratch that he had suffered greatly as a result of the hard blows of Turner and was fast losing his senses. Turner punished him at some length until finally Scroggins dropped to cries of, 'Well done, Turner.'

The 33rd proved to be the last round for Jack Scroggins, who had been the toast of the prize ring for the last three years. He had perhaps taken too much notice of those who had proclaimed his invincibility and he had flattered himself into believing his supporters. It had been seen in the last ten rounds that Scroggins had no chance of victory, although he had fought bravely. The sailor had tried in vain to turn the tide, but it was too late and the punches he landed were insufficient to stem the punishment delivered by Ned Turner and he fell for the final time under the Welshman's fist. On being placed on his second's knee, and after one hour and 12 minutes of hard fighting, Scroggins finally gave in. Harry Harmer hoisted his handkerchief as a token of his defeat. None of the spectators could quite believe it, and seemed stunned by the sailor's defeat, crying, 'What, Scroggins given in? Impossible!' Jack Scroggins was carried out of the ring and put into a post-chaise, and despite the length of their great battle, Ned Turner stepped out of the ring unaided, having received barely a scratch.

Although Jack Scroggins had been defeated, he was not disgraced. Many of those supporters who thought him unbeatable now blamed Scroggins for his reckless confidence, although it was clear he had finally been beaten by a man whose skills were superior to his own. Although fearless and courageous in battle, Scroggins had never been considered a scientific fighter, and the truth of this assertion was proved in this battle against Turner. The judgement and science of Ned Turner had been marked throughout; he never expended his energy in resisting the throws of Jack Scroggins, and had fought defensively, only striking out first when the opportunity was undeniable. The guard of Turner had been so tight that Scroggins could not overcome it without putting himself in grave danger. When faced with the ferocity of the rushes of Scroggins, Turner had engaged him with the greatest coolness. The desperation of Jack Scroggins to enter the fray had previously terrified his opponents. He had been a smashing resolute fighter, but he had no answer to the calculated strategy of Turner. Although Ned appeared visibly unharmed at the end of the contest, he would afterwards acknowledge that in the course of the fight, he had received such a violent blow from Scroggins that he could not open his mouth for a month afterwards without feeling a great deal of pain.

Despite this injury, Ned Turner was considered so fresh that he might have been able to fight another battle, and walked around the ring to watch the contest following his own before retiring from the battleground. He drove back to London unassisted, with Jack Scroggins having been taken back to the city at about one o'clock in the morning. Hundreds of people gathered around his public house in Westminster, waiting to see Scroggins with their own eyes before they could believe that he had been defeated. The whole of the stakes, amounting to £120, were presented to Turner at the Castle Tavern in Holborn on the Friday evening. The night before, Ned Turner had paid a friendly visit to Jack Scroggins, who was quite disheartened by his defeat, which he attributed to having caught one of his feet in a small hole in the ground, throwing him off balance, and leaving him open to a blow to the throat that had made breathing difficult throughout the contest. Scroggins was eager to overturn the defeat and asked Turner to agree to a new contest for £100 a-side. Turner, having decisively beaten Scroggins, was reluctant to meet him again, but as a matter of courtesy said that he could not fight him for less than £200.

After this notable victory, the fame of Edward Turner spread far and wide and he returned to Wales, where he was given a triumphant reception by his countrymen, as recorded by Pierce Egan in *Boxiana*:

> PUGLISTIC HONOURS CONFERRED ON TURNER IN WALES – Ned, it seems, upon his return to New Town,...where he had recently been in training, and which is the birth-place of his parents and the whole of his relatives, was hailed with all the respect due to a hero in a more important cause. The companions of his youth, and the admirers of pugilism among the Ancient Britons, caused a congratulatory peal to be rung upon the bells, in honour of his victory. A feast was held at the first inn in the place, and two roasted fat sheep, with *gilded* horns, were served up with *et ceteras*, including plenty of *game*. The evening was conducted with the utmost conviviality, and

> the Welsh bards who were mustered upon this occasion composed and sang some extempore verses in praise of the brave and the exploits of the ring.

On Ned Turner's return to London, the stakes were made good for a rematch between Turner and Jack Scroggins for 300 guineas, and Scroggins was so eager to fight Turner that he disposed of his public house to concentrate on his training. The opinion of the sporting world did not reflect his confidence, and the betting was 7/4 on a victory for Turner. It was clear that the aura of invincibility around Scroggins had been broken as a result of his previous defeat at the hands of Turner. On the morning of 7 October 1818, large numbers of the Fancy took to the road and headed for Shepperton, which had been appointed as the battleground. They were told on arrival that the location had been changed to Moulsey. Great scenes of confusion and chaos followed as the masses took flight from Shepperton to Walton, where they met a crowd galloping from Hampton to Shepperton.

Having heard the news, they turned in the road and as a consequence the road became blocked. A large number of people were seen on the far side of the water at Moulsey, and many small boats were pressed into action to convey the anxious spectators across to witness the battle in time. Despite the rumour that Moulsey was going to be the battleground, 'Shepperton' was again given as the signal. The toll keeper of the Walton Bridge saw an opportunity, and quickly put up a board at the end of the lane stating, 'This is the road to the fight', and by this means secured a good haul of coppers, although the route was much out of the way. At Shepperton, a ring had already been formed and Turner had ducked between the ropes, and thrown up his hat as an indication of his willingness to do battle. Scroggins had not appeared, and 2/1 was being offered that there would be no fight. To prevent complete disappointment, the two youths who were to do battle after the main contest were told to strip and commence fighting as a diversion.

At this moment, a cry of 'Scroggins, Scroggins' went up and the sailor appeared in their midst. The two youthful pugilists quickly exited the ring, and a friend approached Scroggins and asked if he intended to fight. 'Yes, and win it,' he confidently replied. Jack Scroggins appeared in far superior condition to Ned Turner as a result of his dedication to training. Tom Owen and Painter served as seconds to Turner, while Paddington Jones and Tom Spring had been retained to assist Scroggins. The colours of the combatants were tied to the stakes of the ring, and at two o'clock the fight began.

The first round was very similar to the previous fight between Ned Turner and Jack Scroggins at Sawbridgeworth, but with greater caution shown on both sides. Scroggins appeared to have adapted his tactics and was reluctant to dash in, and principally concerned himself with getting away. Turner was also on the alert, and the round lengthened to five and a half minutes before they closed, both going down after exchanging a few blows. Scroggins was bleeding as early as the second round after two clean hits from Turner, and both men went down again, with Ned under the sailor. Anxious to punish his adversary, Scroggins resumed his rushing tactics in the following round, and had some success, planting a severe punch under the jaw of Turner. In the rally that followed, Scroggins slipped down, receiving only a light blow in the fall. Turner started coming to the front in the fourth, and succeeded in landing two sharp blows, and barely avoided a return before Scroggins seized him and threw him to the ground.

Ned Turner's advantage in height and reach ensured that while Scroggins landed punches when he had forced his way to close quarters, he was severely punished by heavy hitting at range. Within a few rounds the sailor resumed his usual rushing style, and in this he had some limited success. In the seventh, Scroggy landed a tremendous blow to Turner's face as he was coming in that made Ned's head bob, and followed it with two further punches that sent him into a state of confusion. Scroggins continued to show the advantage in throwing and Turner did not resist him, not wishing to expend his energy by struggling against his stronger adversary. The attacks made by Scroggins had become more desperate by the tenth round, and Turner planted three blows in quick succession on his opponent's face, blood flowing copiously each time, although as usual, the round ended with Ned being thrown down. The 13th was probably the best round that Scroggins had ever fought, and in no previous contests had he ever displayed such skill. He stopped Turner's blows with undeniable skill, and fought his opponent manfully. With both men now beginning to tire, some blows did not land cleanly, and at the end Scroggins was seen to go down.

The savagery of their punches continued, Scroggins occasionally landing good blows, only to be punished in return by Turner, who punched so hard and fast that Scroggins seemed to be confused as to know how to respond. By the 19th round, Turner's hands were covered with the blood of Scroggins, and the brave sailor was sent to the turf with greater frequency at the end of each round. The first signs of Turner's weariness were seen in the 23rd round, when sighing loudly as if out of breath, Ned let his hands drop, and although Scroggins followed him, he missed several opportunities to punish his foe. In the 25th round on coming up to the scratch, Turner's knees trembled violently, which appeared to be a bad omen. The following round saw Scroggins deliver such terrible blows to his kidneys that Ned went down from weakness.

Jack Scroggins appeared to be the stronger man on his legs after an hour and three minutes of hard fighting, although the awkwardness of Turner's stance made it difficult to attack without fear of reprisal. Scroggy continued to come forward, and Turner retreated all round the ring. Ned was not finished just yet, and still had enough strength to send his antagonist to the turf from a severe body blow in the 32nd round. Having regained his wind, the Welshman pummelled the face of Scroggy in the following round until the sailor collapsed from exhaustion. In the next three rounds, poor Scroggins was punched to the turf almost as soon as he stepped up to the scratch, and although his legs appeared quite firm, his head was in such a terrible state that by the 37th round a cry went up of 'Take him away' from all corners of the ring. Brave until the last, Jack Scroggins came out for the 38th round and was sent down by little more than a touch on the part of Ned Turner.

The 39th round proved to be the last,[96] and there was no man at ringside who could have questioned the bravery of Scroggins, who had done everything that might have been expected of him

96 Some later sources record the third fight between Turner and Scroggins as having lasted for 99 rounds. This would appear to have been as a result of the number of rounds having been incorrectly transcribed in *Fistiana*, where 99 rounds are recorded as the duration of the fight instead of 39.

to secure victory. At the start of this final round, the punishment dished out to Scroggins was so severe that he turned away from his adversary in a state of confusion, and fell backwards upon the ropes. Turner, recognising the courage of his stubborn opponent, patted him upon the back. The battle ended with Jack Scroggins unable to come up to the scratch, and Ned Turner immediately approached his corner to shake the sailor's hand before leaving the ring. The battle had lasted an hour and 32 minutes.

The conduct of Jack Scroggins, and the great bravery he displayed in this third fight, silenced the criticisms that had been levelled at him following his previous battle against Turner at Sawbridgeworth, and re-established his reputation as a game and determined pugilist. Though he had been defeated, he had not been disgraced, and was seen to have been forced to yield due to the superior height, reach and skill of Edward Turner. As a result of this final battle against Scroggins, Turner now found himself at the top of the pugilistic tree. Although Turner could not be deemed a showy fighter on his performance in this contest, he had proved that he was cool and collected in the heat of battle, and had revealed his courage at every turn. The only obvious visible damage that was seen as he left the ring was a slight mark upon his ear.

Ned Turner was afterwards presented with the whole of the battle money and returned to London the same evening, appearing at the Castle Tavern in Holborn to celebrate as if nothing of consequence had happened. He had now fought four prize battles, and had been imprisoned for two months after a distressing trial, all within 12 months. Following this second victory over Scroggins, the name of Ned Turner was on the lips of the entire sporting world, having won his popularity as a direct result of the initial contempt with which his abilities had been spoken of by Scroggins and his admirers. The Welshman was modest in victory, although elated by his success, and drank liberally in celebration of his triumph in the company of his friends. Having secured the praise of the Fancy, a dangerous new adversary was soon to appear in the form of one of the most accomplished prize fighters of the period, known to all as 'the Nonpareil'.

Chapter 8

The Nonpareil

Pats who saw *Jack Randall* fight,
That filled the FANCY with delight,
Oh! it was a manly sight,
Such game lads to see,

Back'd by the *Welch*, Ned took his ground,
A better man could ne'er be found,
Showing fine science ev'ry round,
And not a flincher he!

An *Out-and-Outer* is Randall's due,
And Turner's an *Out-and-Outer* too,
Like such Trumps there are but few-
T'wards Victory.

(*Pierce Egan's Book of Sports, and Mirror of Life: Embracing the Turf, the Chase, the Ring and the Stage Interspersed with Original Memoirs of Sporting Men, etc*, London: Thomas Tegg & Son, 1836).

Jack Randall was born on 25 November 1794 at St Giles in London, and his pugilistic abilities were well developed even as a young boy, earning him a small measure of fame after he conquered an opponent named 'Young Snuff' on three separate occasions at the Archery Ground in Long Fields. At the same place, Jack thrashed a man named Leonard, who was a stone heavier than himself, defeating him in three-quarters of an hour when he was just 14 years old.[97] The first recorded battle of Jack Randall, which

97 As recorded in *Boxiana*.

brought him to the attention of the Fancy, had been his battle against the butcher, Jack Payne, who Randall had beaten in just 20 minutes in 1811. Randall's debut in the professional ring had been exceedingly brief: Walton, the 'Twickenham Youth', was defeated in ten minutes for a purse of five guineas at Coombe Wood in 1815, when Jack had been seconded by Paddington Jones and Dick Whale. Abby Belasco and Joe Parish both fell under Randall's fist in 1817, and by the time he defeated Burke of Woolwich in 23 rounds in June 1818, he had remained undefeated after nine battles in the prize ring in just under three years. Jack Randall was the toast of the Fancy, developing into an extraordinary fighter, with a supreme understanding of strategy and ring craft that enabled him to secure victory over opponents far larger and stronger than himself. In attack, he was ferocious and completely without fear of any opponent who dared to stand against him, and had earned himself the title of 'the Nonpareil' from the Fancy.

By 1818, the Fancy were all but unanimous in their opinion that there wasn't a man in England of his weight who Jack Randall would not destroy with ease. Randall began to think that it was time he retired from the ring altogether and settled down as the patron of a public house, feeling that there were no pugilists over which he needed to prove his superiority. The only fighter waiting in the wings who some thought might prove a difficult nut for Randall to crack was Ned Turner, having just risen to the height of his fame following his second victory over Jack Scroggins, and people started to say that if Jack Randall wished to retain his crown as Champion of the Lightweights, he would have to defeat the gallant Welshman. The Nonpareil had been eager to terminate his prize ring career by defeating Ned Turner following Ned's first defeat of Scroggins so that he might enter into his new business as a publican with a final shining victory. Turner was not, however, as eager to engage Randall at this point, hoping to first secure victory for the second time over Scroggy, and lay any lingering doubts as to his superiority over the sailor to rest. As a consequence, Jack Randall let two or three opportunities to secure a good public house slip through his fingers. Less than a week after Ned Turner's second victory over Jack Scroggins, a meeting was announced to be held at the Lion and Goat public house at Grosvenor Square, where the following articles were signed:

> Articles of agreement, October 13, 1818, entered into at Mr Franklin's, the Lion and Goat, Lower Grosvenor Street, Grosvenor Square, between John Randall and Edward Turner, to fight for the sum of £100 a-side on Tuesday, the 1st of December. The above battle to be a fair stand up fight–half minute time, in a twenty four foot ring. The place to be named by Mr. Jackson; but the distance from London not to be less than twenty-five, nor to exceed thirty miles. Randall, on the one side, to choose his own umpire, as to a time keeper, and Turner also to appoint a time keeper, on his part; but to prevent any disputes, Mr Jackson to appoint a third umpire as a referee, whose decision shall be final. The whole of the stakes to be made good on Tuesday, the 10th of November, at Mr. Franklin's, between the hours of seven and nine in the evening; but if either Randall or Turner wish to increase the sum to £200 a-side, this latter sum to be made good on Tuesday, the 24th of November. Mr Jackson to hold the stakes, or any person whom he may appoint. A deposit of £20 a-side was placed in the hands of Mr Franklin; but if the whole of the stakes of £100 a-side are not made good on the 10th of November, the above deposit to be forfeited accordingly.
>
> (Signed) BAXTER
>
> Witness P.E. FRANKLIN

The sporting world was greatly excited by this match; to see Jack Randall fight was in itself a treat, but to see the Nonpareil do battle against the best man that had ever stood up to him ignited unprecedented public interest and lengthy debate. Randall was the favourite, but Turner was by no means looked upon as an easy opponent, and his Welsh supporters were convinced that Turner would win, and were heard to say, 'Cot splutter her nails, hur's sure to win it.' Jack Randall went into training at Hampstead Heath, and took up residence at the Horse and Groom, while Turner also threw himself into strenuous training. Turner attended a grand dinner held at the Chequers Inn at Brentwood in Essex on 24 November , where pheasants, partridges and venison were served in honour of 'the heroes of the ring'. In the course of the evening, mention was made of Ned Turner's previous victories and his pre-eminence amongst the lightweights. Turner gave thanks for the praise that had been placed upon his shoulders, and stated with modesty and candour that 'he would win if he could; but if he lost the match, he trusted that the amateurs would not have to complain that he had not done everything to give them satisfaction'.

As a result of the death of Queen Charlotte, the match between Jack Randall and Ned Turner was postponed until Saturday, 5 December 1818. Randall was confidence personified that he would emerge triumphant, but the faith of his backers waned a little as the day of reckoning drew near. A few days before the fight, the odds stood at 2/1 and 7/4 on Randall, but this fell to guineas to pounds when people saw how strong and confident Ned Turner appeared, and his Welsh supporters wagered large sums on his victory. Reports had also circulated as to whether Randall might be in poor health, and it was rumoured that a doctor had been engaged to apply leeches to his neck to bring down an ugly swelling just three days before the contest. Crawley Downs, situated about halfway between London and Brighton, was appointed as the battle ground. From the break of dawn, coaches, carriages, riders and pedestrians took to the road and poured through Croydon in an unbroken stream towards the venue. The crowds must have numbered at least 20,000 and they gathered round the ring in a state of great excitement as the combatants appeared. Ned Turner was waited upon by Tom Owen and Bill Richmond, while Jack Randall was supported by Tom Oliver and Blake.

Jack Randall, 'the Nonpareil'.

Despite the rumours regarding the health of Jack Randall, it did not look as though there was anything amiss as he entered the ring. Standing 5ft 6in and scaling 10st 6lbs, with a powerful and well-knit frame that hinted at his tremendous punching power, Randall appeared a very ugly customer to tackle. Ned Turner stood an inch taller than the Nonpareil, scaling 10st 4lbs, and was built along slightly lighter lines than his adversary, suggestive of greater activity but possibly of lesser physical strength. This first impression was perhaps deceptive, for Ned Turner's arms had been hardened through his use of 18lb dumbbells, which he was said to have routinely lifted 300 times before his arms began to feel tired.[98]

At one o'clock, Ned Turner and Jack Randall shook hands and the fight began. Neither was eager to engage in combat, and they 'eyed each other with the acute precision of fencing masters' as they dodged, feinted and circled one another for a number of minutes. Turner was the first to strike out, but Randall laughed and got away, and shortly afterwards caught the Welshman on the jaw and the ribs. Rushing to close quarters, the Nonpareil seized his opponent in a vice-like grip and a severe struggle for the throw took place before both men went down. In the second round, sparring was the order of the day, until Randall attacked. Turner, by way of a return, attempted to land a tremendous blow with his left, but the Nonpareil jumped back a full two yards and avoided the punch with ease. With both men having now tested the defences of their opponent, lengthy and cautious sparring resumed to the dismay of the spectators, who called out, 'When shall we get home?' Turner then launched a successful assault through the guard of Randall to cries of, 'Go it, Neddy' as Randall threw two punches at Turner's head, forcing the fight to close range. The finish of the second round was severely contested and marked by a prolonged struggle until both men went down, by which time 20 minutes had elapsed.

Ned Turner's mouth had a tinge of blood about it as the third round began, and his breathing was noticeably quicker, showing the first signs of his distress. The strategy of both men was so shrewd that neither could afford to put a foot wrong, and their caution was marked. Jack Randall had never tangled with such a difficult customer before, and the round took 13 minutes to reach a conclusion, with a few jokers at ringside suggesting to Turner's second, Tom Owen, that he might as well smoke a pipe while he

98 As recorded in *Boxiana*.

was waiting for Turner to enter the fray. After numerous feints, the round ended when both men went down, Randall falling over Turner rather awkwardly on to his neck. In the following round, it became evident that a long fight was likely, as Randall put in two body blows, and Turner landed a left hand on his mouth. The hitting and stopping on both sides was masterful, but at the close the Welshman's nose was bleeding copiously, although Randall's face had also been pinked by Turner's knuckles.

Not to be outdone, Turner landed heavily with his left on Randall's nose in the sixth, and the blood ran down into his mouth, forcing the Nonpareil to spit his blood on to the turf. Caution on the part of both men marked their movements as the fight reached the 50-minute mark. Ned hit out manfully with his left, but Jack stopped the blow with supreme skill. An exchange of blows followed in which Ned punched with both his left and his right, although the blows he landed appeared to be of little consequence. Jack retreated, although the injury to his nose now appeared to be troubling him. Turner was flagging and started to lower his hands, but pulled them up as Randall threatened to strike. The Nonpareil caught Turner napping, and he landed a severe body blow, but the Out-and-Outer was seen to land a sharp punch in return. Changing his mode of attack, Randall now targeted the body, although he found Turner exceedingly difficult to get at, and Randall was forced to use more than his usual degree of caution. Ned started to show his left with greater success, although Jack was equally as quick in stopping his blows, showing great science. In the struggle for the throw, both men went down, with Turner on top. Turner was now bleeding copiously and blood was also running like a tap from Jack Randall's nose. Randall pulled ahead in the rounds that followed, with Turner's distress becoming more marked as the fight wore on. The tenth round was one of exceptional skill and the hitting and stopping on both sides was thought to have been of 'the finest order of the art'. Turner complained at one stage, thinking that Randall had stepped on his foot, and asked, 'Do you call that fair, Jack?' Randall was quick to reply, 'I did not', and in the struggle for the throw that followed, Turner threw Randall over him.

Despite Turner's success at throwing Randall, the Nonpareil seemed to be having the best of it, although the pluck of Turner was so well known that the Welshman still had plenty of backers. Jack skilfully manoeuvred his opponent so that he was looking into the sun, and then landed a telling blow on Ned's left eye that left him winking, although Turner landed a tremendous blow to his rival's stomach in reply. In going down, Ned received a return blow to the stomach that Tom Owen called 'Foul', but he was ignored by the umpires. Although Turner continued to hit his opponent right and left, he seemed to lack the strength to slow the advance of Randall, who laid into Ned with such terrible punches in the 13th round that his blood flowed in 'torrents' before he was knocked down. Despite the punishment he was receiving, Ned showed remarkable coolness as he continued to come up to the scratch. In the 16th round, Turner let his left hand go to Randall's body, but received a heavy return that nearly dislodged his teeth, and his mouth poured blood. The round ended with Turner falling to the turf, his weariness now growing increasingly apparent as each round wore on. Ned still somehow managed to throw the Nonpareil out of the ring in the following round, but was afterwards forced to lean heavily on the ropes, having exhausted himself with the effort.

While Ned Turner fought on with commendable bravery, his blows seemed to have little impact upon Randall, who peppered the Welshman at will in the 19th round until Turner finally went down, by which time they had been fighting for an hour and 35 minutes. In the 21st round, Jack Randall received a hard left on the nose from his opponent, and this blow seemed to trouble him more than any other he had received in the course of the fight. His mouth was now bleeding and it was clear that he was also tiring as a result of his labours.

Even at this late stage of the contest, Ned Turner refused to believe he was facing defeat, and came to the scratch with undiminished confidence at the start of the 24th round, landing a clever right hand to Randall's face. In the struggle that followed, the spectators were amazed to see the strength that the game Welshman was still able to summon, and he threw the Nonpareil with great violence. Two hours had now elapsed. The effort of the throw did as much harm to Turner as to his foe, and his strength now ebbed slowly and surely. Randall had his revenge in the 27th round, and floored his opponent grandly. While looking at Turner as he lay on the turf, Randall stooped down and winked to his friends as if to say he thought he had the measure of his man. Turner was by no means licked just yet, however, and in the next round he managed to land some good hits, and in the struggle, Jack Randall was under Turner in the fall.

Ned Turner continued to keep Randall at range, but the Nonpareil followed him, and a terrible struggle took place in closing. The Welsh pugilist stopped a severe blow that had been launched by Randall, and in return landed a hard punch on his opponent's jaw. Randall nailed Turner mercilessly, and it was now becoming clear that Ned was too weak to stop the blows of his opponent from landing. Turner had been fearfully punished about the head and face, but he continued to fight as coolly as if he had only just commenced the fight. By the 31st round, the spectators were crying, 'Take him away – he's too game.' Two rounds later, Ned's state had become so pitiful that the spectators resumed their cry, not wanting to see such a brave and gallant man punished any further, and began shouting, 'Do not let him fight any more.' Tom Owen would not hear of conceding Turner's defeat, replying, 'Don't say that, gentlemen,' stating in reply that Ned was 'worth 20 beaten men'. Despite the protestations of Tom Owen, Ned went down soon afterwards from a blow to the face and he apparently had no fight left in him.

To the astonishment of all, Turner recovered enough to come up to the scratch at the call of 'Time', and although he was exhausted he was still as game as ever, exhibiting the same cool and collected demeanour that he had shown throughout the battle. After an exchange of blows in which Ned came off second best, a fearful punch to the left side of his head floored him and he was unable to come up to the scratch when called. The conqueror of Jack Scroggins had been defeated for the first time.

After 34 rounds, and two hours, 19 minutes and 30 seconds of determined fighting, Jack Randall had won the hardest-earned victory of his prize-fighting career. Once his fist had been raised in victory, the Nonpareil pushed away the crowd that had gathered around him, and went to clasp the hand of the gallant Welshman in an act of genuine friendship with tears rolling down his cheeks. Ned Turner felt no anger at the loss, and gently patted the back of his conqueror's hand in recognition of the fact that Randall had proved himself the better man. The spectators loudly applauded their efforts and pronounced the two combatants to be the 'best two bits of stuff at their weight in this country'. Throughout the latter rounds, Ned Turner had been repeatedly pressed to give in, but had bravely rejected this advice, believing he still had a chance of turning the tide. His brother-in-law, Mr Baxter, the East Smithfield hat maker, had finally insisted that Ned should fight no more, and had brought an end to the contest.

Ned Turner was immediately carried from the battleground to a nearby farmhouse, and was put to bed to recover from his injuries. Despite the physical pain he felt from the severity of the punishment he had received, complaining of the hardness of the body blows that Randall had rained upon him, Turner felt even greater anguish at the knowledge that he had been defeated for the first time in the prize ring. Jack Randall was in such good health that he returned to London that evening. As a result of his injuries, Turner was forced to stay the night at Crawley.

The downfall of Ned Turner had been witnessed by an estimated 20,000 spectators, who were drawn from every segment of London society. Amongst their number were the poets Thomas Moore and John Keats. Keats had attended the battle ground to take his mind off the death of his brother, Tom, having been encouraged to do so by his friends. John Keats would later record his recollection of the contest in October of 1820:[99]

> ...off we went to Crawley, my friends and I, a more rowdy band of fancy fellows you never saw, all trying a little too much to make me enjoy the occasion, off we went to watch the boxing match between Jack Randall and Ned Turner – a boisterous, tumultuous affair that had all the life, all the brutal savagery that animals might display in the wild, and here we were, the crowd about the ring pressing forward, baying for blood like hounds, and getting it, too, for it went to thirty-four rounds, as I recall, with both men

99 John Keats recorded his recollections of the Jack Randall vs. Ned Turner contest on 29 October 1820, following his confinement under quarantine on the 'Maria Crowther' on 21 October 1820, at the Bay of Naples. Keats had set sail for Italy hoping that the warmer climate might be beneficial to his health, having been seriously ill with tuberculosis.

> beaten down and beaten down, only to rise again. Both were bloody and bruised, trading blows, before Turner was floored by a tremendous series of sharp punches to the head, and down he went, covered in gore, to the cheers and roar of the crowd. Here was life raw and natural, here was blood and spittle and sweat and here were bruises and blows and broken teeth and split knuckles and grunts and groans galore. Here was a fine show of two colossal men, like Cibber's giants come to life, set jaws and clenched fists and heaving lungs and life defiant.

The Fancy were no less appreciative of the intense drama and physicality of the contest than John Keats, and the reputation of Jack Randall was even further enhanced in the sporting world by virtue of having defeated Ned Turner. The glory of Jack Randall's crowing victory would be recorded at length by Pierce Egan in *Boxiana*:

> RANDALL, from the above victory over the cautious, scientific and *game Turner*, was fully considered as having *worked* his way to the *top of the tree*; and it was also asserted by many of the most experienced amateurs connected with the patronage of the Prize Ring, that the late phenomenon, *Dutch Sam*, in the best of his days, must have yielded to the potent arm of the *prime Irish lad*. It is a positive fact, that RANDALL never received instructions from any pugilist whatever: and it is owing to his natural mode of fighting that he has gained all his conquests. It is true, that *Turner* never decidedly took the lead in any one round, but he appeared conspicuous in many of them; and while RANDALL was *fibbing* his *nob*, he, in turn, was endeavouring to knock the wind out of his opponent. This latter essential quality to a boxer, was soon found to be defective in *Turner*. As early as the third round he was piping; which either proved that his condition might have been better, or the tremendous hits of RANDALL floored *condition* as well as *pluck*: but it astonished every one present to see how soon Turner recovered himself upon this spoiling suit, from the advantages of long sparring.

Ned Turner's loss to Jack Randall did not damage the reputation of the Welsh pugilist. Through having fought so valiantly against such a highly skilled performer as Randall, Turner received a great deal of praise amongst the Fancy. Pierce Egan's tribute to the fighting abilities of Ned Turner following his defeat at the hands of the Nonpareil signalled that the Welshman was now considered the second greatest lightweight pugilist of the day:

> *Turner* is an *out-and-outer*... although defeated, he raised himself in the estimation of the Sporting World. He is deficient in nothing else as a pugilist, but in being a *hard hitter*.[100] That is a physical defect, and it cannot be placed to his account as a fault.

Ned also received a great deal of praise from Egan for the manner in which he endured such a phenomenal amount of punishment at the fists of Jack Randall, which was beyond anything that he had encountered in his previous battles:

> It is... singular, that though *Turner* never bled in all his previous fight, in this battle the *claret* flowed from him most profusely. The whole records of pugilism cannot produce anything like the above scientific fight, carried on for such a length of time, with so much consummate skill on both sides, between *Turner* and RANDALL. The latter, it cannot be denied, received more *punishment* than in any of his previous conquests; but he remained strong till the last, and united, like a skilful general, his judgement with his strength. One word more for the brave *Turner*, by way of conclusion: he observed, "*if he lost*, that he trusted the amateurs should not have to complain that he had not given them satisfaction." He most assuredly kept his promise.

100 *Boxiana* includes the following footnote regarding this statement: 'Respecting Turner's being a hard hitter, if RANDALL may be considered as any authority upon this thumping subject, the NONPAREIL has since asserted, that his arms were not free from bruises, and extremely tender, for upwards of three weeks after the contest'.

Public interest in the outcome of the fight in the city of London was immense, and by the evening, hundreds of pedestrians gathered at the turnpikes along the road to the city, waiting for news of whether Randall or Turner had won the day. At sunrise the following morning, the remains of several gigs that had been turned over and abandoned were revealed, as a result of collisions due to the narrowness and the poor quality of the roads. Every roadside inn had been filled to capacity, and with no beds available, hundreds of spectators had trudged wearily homeward through the night.

Jack Randall's followers gathered in their hundreds at his home in Tottenham Court Road, waiting for news of the result. On the arrival of the Nonpareil, the applause he received from his loyal supporters 'almost rent the air'. Every pugilistic pub in the city was crowded and surrounded by sportsmen eager to learn whether the Nonpareil or the Out-and-Outer had triumphed. Newspaper sellers did a roaring trade, and interest in reading the first reports of the fight was 'as great as if some important victory had been achieved on the content, so much anxiety was expressed upon this battle'. Initial reports claimed that Ned had won the contest, and numerous further wagers were made on the accuracy of the information, and the rumour was not dispelled until ten o'clock on the Sunday evening on the arrival of Turner. Many were surprised to find that although the Welshman had evidently been much punished about the face in the course of the battle, 'it was astonishing to see how quickly the appearance of severity had left it'.[101]

With such heavy gambling having taken place on the outcome of the contest throughout all parts of England, Ireland and Wales, the losses were deemed to be 'immense'. That the Fancy recognised that the battle had been one that had been well fought to the best of the ability of both men can be gathered by the fact that despite these heavy losses, no grumbling was heard from the 'amateurs' about the performance of the combatants.

101 As recorded in the *Morning Chronicle*, 7 December 1818.

Chapter 9

The Bristol Boy and the Bruising Baker

Jack Randall and Ned Turner had both expressed a desire to retire from the ring prior to their great battle, regardless of which side claimed victory. Randall had decided that win or lose he would retire from prize fighting and begin a new life as a publican. Turner, having met and lost to the greatest fighter of his weight and having known defeat for the first time, also seemed content that an honourable loss to the Nonpareil was a good point at which to bow out of the prize ring. With both pugilists having become celebrated throughout the land as the greatest fighters of their weight, they changed their minds and decided to continue in their prize ring careers.

That Jack Randall and Ned Turner were thought to be amongst the most prominent pugilists in Britain can be seen by the fact that both prize fighters were called upon to demonstrate their proficiency in sparring before visiting royalty in March of 1819, for the entertainment of Archduke Maximilian Joseph of Austria-Este. The event had been organised by 'Gentleman' John Jackson and was held in Grosvenor Square. Following a set-to between Tom Cribb and Tom Oliver, Ned Turner, who had recently returned from a sparring tour, demonstrated his skills against Bill Eales. The tour had greatly sharpened the skills of the Welsh pugilist, as recalled by Pierce Egan:

> *Turner*, who had recently returned from a sparring tour in fine condition, had a turn with the scientific *Eales*. Notwithstanding the superior tactics of the latter, *Turner* had made such rapid improvement from his late practice

> that he appeared to stand upon equal ground with his opponent; and once or twice, like the acknowledgment of *Laertes* to *Hamlet*, 'palpable hits' were admitted. It was pronounced by all present an admirable display of the art of Self-defence; and thunders of applause crowned their exertions.

Bill Richmond and Jack Randall afterwards demonstrated 'various traits of milling', with the Archduke having been greatly impressed by the method of hitting demonstrated by Jack Randall, and stated that he imagined Randall's blow would prove to be advantageous in combat, by virtue of its velocity. Having witnessed such an impressive display by some of the most celebrated pugilistic stars, the Archduke afterwards retired, liberally praising 'the manliness of the English character'.[102]

With the fame of Edward Turner having now become widespread, another challenger who was eager to topple the Welshman's crown stepped forward. A young boxer from Bristol named Cyrus Davis had begun to receive a great deal of attention amongst the Fancy, and it was thought that he might prove to be an excellent match for Ned Turner.

Cyrus Davis was born at Broadway in the city of Bristol on 27 November 1795. At the age of 14, he had been apprenticed to a butcher and received his first lessons in boxing from George Nicholls, the only man to have conquered Tom Cribb. Cyrus was afterwards introduced to the prize fighting fraternity of London by Tom Belcher, Jem Belcher's brother, and the speed of his fighting when sparring and his precision in hitting drew a great deal of attention from the Fancy. Tom Belcher took his young protégé to see the fight between Tom Oliver and Bill Neat in June of 1818 at Rickmansworth. After the main event there was a purse of 20 guineas to be disposed of, with five guineas to go to the loser. Aby Belasco stated his willingness to fight and Cy Davis stepped into the ring to challenge him.

Cyrus demonstrated such speed and power that he completely demolished Belasco, who refused to continue after just nine rounds, lasting 15 minutes, had been fought. Soon after this, the

102 As stated in *Boxiana*.

'Gay Bristol Boy' returned to his home city but had made such an impression on the Fancy that he was brought back to London to meet Ned Turner in a match organised by Tom Belcher for £100 a-side. Wallingham Common at Surrey, some 17 miles from London, was chosen as the venue, and on the morning of Friday, 18 June 1819, hours of torrential rain finally ceased and preparation was made for the combat to commence. The Welshman threw his hat into the ring and was attended by Jack Randall, who had become a close friend of Turner following their great battle, and Tom Cribb. After some minutes had elapsed, Cy Davis appeared in the company of Tom Belcher and Harry Harmer, and also threw his hat into the ring to signify his desire to meet Turner in battle. At 1.45pm, the men stepped between the ropes, with a blue handkerchief having been tied to the stakes by Randall for Turner, and the colours of Davis, a 'yellow-man', tied over the blue by Tom Belcher.

The youth and freshness of Cy Davis was much in evidence as the men stripped for battle. Although there appeared to have been some doubt regarding the condition of Turner as the date of the battle approached, Ned looked better than had been expected, although the difference between the two fighters was decidedly marked. Davis had a 'fine and elegant form', and was considered to be 'the beau ideal of the ring-goers', while Turner by comparison looked more like a 'weather-beaten Greenwich pensioner'. Ned's constitution had been noticeably undermined by the excesses of drink and the undisciplined life he had pursued following his third battle against Jack Scroggins the previous year. Davis had the advantage of both weight and height, standing some two inches taller than Turner at 5ft 9in, and weighing a little under 11st to Turner's 10st 4lbs. It had been thought by some that Davis would go to work without ceremony, and punish Turner in a style reminiscent of the manner in which he had polished off Aby Belasco.

Instead, as the fight began, Cyrus Davis was seen to show a great deal of caution, perhaps having been wary due to the great fame of the Welshman, and Turner was the first to hit out slightly with his left. After sparring, Cy kept retreating and Ned successfully landed five light hits to Davis's body as he felt out his man. Jack Randall sat on the ropes minutely eyeing the tactics of both combatants, until at length, after an exchange, the right cheek of Davis was reddened, which was accompanied by loud shouting. Ned Turner planted a blow to the body of his foe that sent Cyrus Davis staggering before going down. Astonishment turned to amazement in the second round when Davis went down again after Turner had scarcely landed the first blow to cries of, 'Turner, my boy, you'll win it without a scratch'. Davis appeared to lack any confidence as he stood up for the third, and went down due to a blow so light it was difficult to perceive whether it had landed at all. As a consequence, the seconds of the Bristol Boy were advised by the umpires that he should be more cautious about the manner in which he went down, as if he continued to go down without significant punishment, the battle would be terminated.

Ned continued to use both hands with success, although the youthful strength of Cyrus was apparent as he smiled before launching a terrific right hand that landed on Turner's head, sending Turner to the turf bleeding. Having scored the first knockdown blow and having secured first blood, the supporters of Cyrus were elated, shouting, 'Go along Davis, you can do it if you like. Another such hit, and it will be all right.' To the surprise of his followers, however, Cy failed to follow up his success, and went down again from a slight hit, almost without a blow. In the sixth round, Turner was again the aggressor, and the Bristol Boy retreated, not wishing to stand against him. It was thought that as Davis was little more than a novice in the prize ring, Cyrus might have been panic-struck, and again he went down with the cries of the Bristol men ringing in his ears, angrily shouting, 'Davis, what are you at?' Hearing the reproaches of his townsmen, Davis went to work in earnest in the following round. 'Look, look,' they shouted. 'This chap may win it now, if he will, but go in and fight. He can do something if he likes'. Although it was a good round, Cy was again punched down most severely by Turner, and cries went up around the ring. 'Bravo, Turner,' they shouted, followed by, 'Give him a little one for me', contrasted with a few yells of, 'Well done, Davis' from the supporters of Cyrus. The Bristol Boy seemed afraid to hit out, and despite having had the better of the hitting, his head was by now quite damaged and he was bleeding with more severity than the Welshman.

It was in the tenth round that Cy attempted to turn the tables, and despite his shy style of fighting, Davis lashed out and hit Turner so hard with his right hand that Ned went down as if shot, and he afterwards seemed to be in a state of stupor. 'Go it, Davis,' cried his supporters. 'That's the way to mill, and you'll win.' Ned was all at sea; his eyes appeared dim and listless while he was sitting on the knee of his second, and it seemed certain that if he received another such blow, he would be defeated. Jack Randall shook his head, not knowing what to think of this turn of events, and Turner's backers wore long faces fearing that his defeat was imminent as Davis's supporters started rejoicing.

The celebrations were premature, however, for Cyrus Davis still failed to seize the advantage. In the exchanges that followed he landed some blows, and Ned Turner's face was covered in blood, but Davis appeared shy and turned away from Ned's punches. Some thought that Turner hit Davis when he was down, and a cry of 'Foul, foul!' quickly went up. Turner had now been alerted to the danger of Davis's jaw-breaking right hand, and becoming wary of it, concentrated on stopping it with a great deal of judgement and skill. Davis appeared to have shed the earlier caution that had marked his movements, and received some praise for the way in which he went about his work, one ringside judge exclaiming, 'Davis may win it now.' Despite Davis's dangerous right hand, Turner fought him to a standstill in the 15th round to cries of, 'What's o'clock now?' from his second, Tom Cribb, who jubilantly claimed, 'It's all up, I believe.' Turner stopped most of Davis's blows, but one got through, a dreadful punch that landed over his right eye and almost sent Ned to the turf. The Welshman's blood flowed freely, but undismayed, he took the fight to Davis, who was quick to seek the turf, seemingly to escape further punishment.

In the 20th round, Ned Turner trapped his foe in a corner and Randall called out, 'Ned, do as I do; keep that in your eye, my boy, and you'll soon fetch him out.' Once again, Cy Davis was quick to turn away from Turner's blows and went down once more. The 21st round proved to be one of great confusion, as Tom Belcher stooped down and picked up a piece of paper, which he put in the left hand of Cyrus. Ned believed that Belcher had given Davis a stone to conceal in his hand and refused to fight on. Jack Randall, anxious to do his duty as a second to his friend, rushed in and tore the paper from Belcher, who was showing it and explaining that no unfair practice had been attempted. There was some agitation amongst the spectators, who thought that it had been a bank note and a wager had been proposed, with the deception ensuring that Davis might receive additional time to recover in the delay that followed. After the umpires had been satisfied that nothing unjust had been attempted, a sharp, well-fought round followed before both men went down.

Cy Davis fought better from the 23rd round onwards, but in the 26th he received a body blow that damaged him severely, and in closing, Turner 'slung him round like a cat', and it was clear that the strength of the Bristol butcher was beginning to fade. In the following round, the Welshman landed a dreadful punch behind the ear of Davis, which opened up a large gash like a knife wound, and the blood flowed profusely from the injury as Davis went down in a pitiful state. The eyes of Cyrus began to swell up, and an ugly egg-shaped lump was now rapidly appearing on his forehead. Davis fought on, with sharp hitting being much in evidence, but the possibility of victory seemed to be disappearing minute by minute. Brave Cyrus fell without a blow in the 30th, and Turner further punished him by falling on top of him.

Cy Davis appeared to be finished by the 31st round, having been beaten to a standstill, and could not lift his hands. His eyes were now unfocused, and his strength had deserted him. Turner hit him down without any cruel remarks from the spectators, who now viewed the destruction of the Bristol prize fighter in silence with pity. In the 32nd round, Cy made it up to the scratch, but turned away from Ned's blows once more and fell down. As Cyrus was afterwards unable to rise, the contest finally terminated in victory for the bruised and bloodied Ned Turner after 45 gruelling minutes of combat.

After the contest, it was thought possible that too much praise had been heaped upon the shoulders of Cyrus Davis after his defeat of Aby Belasco, and that there had been too much excitement at the thought that another Bristol pugilist might be joining the lists alongside such luminaries as Jem and Tom Belcher, Hen Pearce, and Tom Cribb. Cy Davis had the advantage of youth, weight, freshness and strength, and it was felt that he ought to have beaten Turner. The supporters of Davis attributed the frequency with which he had gone down to a weakness in the knees brought about by rheumatism, which had affected him a few days before the fight. The appearance of Cy Davis after the contest was said to have been 'terrifying to the beholder'; he had been beaten terribly about the head, with one of his hands, and his arms and shoulders exhibiting 'the most dreadful punishment'. Davis's reluctance to stand up to the punches of Ned Turner was attributed to nervousness at meeting such a well-regarded fighter as Turner so early in his ring career, and some of the Fancy maintained it had been poor judgement for Tom Belcher to have made a match against Turner based on the victory of Cyrus Davis over a lesser pugilist like Aby Belasco.

On this occasion, Ned Turner had fought offensively, rather than defensively, to secure the win. Although he had proved throughout that he was Davis's master in ring craft, and his experience had propelled him to victory, it should perhaps have been evident from the poor condition of his physique on entering the ring that the Welshman's skill could only carry him through so many contests, before his declining physical condition would begin to let him down. Given Turner's well-known drinking habits, it seemed only a matter of time before problems would arise.

According to *Boxiana*, following the defeat of Cyrus Davis by Ned Turner, the sporting world was eager to witness a battle between Turner and Jack Martin. Jack Martin had originally challenged Turner after beating Jack Scroggins on 8 December 1818, just three days after Jack Randall and Ned Turner had fought. The proposed match against Turner was abandoned after a nobleman had rather hastily backed Jack Randall against Jack Martin. As a result of the Nonpareil having consequently secured a victory over Jack Martin, and having therefore conquered both Turner and Martin, it was thought that a fight between Randall's defeated opponents might provide good sport.[103]

There is an interesting back story to the match being made between Ned Turner and Jack Martin, which is worth retelling; although the details were recounted in *Famous Fights Past and Present*

---

103 *Boxiana (Vol. 3)*, records that it was Edward Turner who challenged Jack Martin. This statement can be seen to override the previous statement made about Turner in *Boxiana (Vol. 2)* that 'never, in any instance whatever,...*did* a CHALLENGE FIRST *emanate from his feelings to fight*!'

by Frank J. Bradley over 80 years after the contest took place.[104] Although this newspaper is one of the more graphic sources for information regarding the days of the prize ring, it must be said that along with Fred Henning's *Fights For the Championship: the men and their times*, published by the Licensed Victuallers' Gazette,[105] and consisting of articles mostly taken from it, both publications must be considered with a great deal of caution as accurate sources of information, and not only due to having been written so many years after the days of the early prize fighters. While *Famous Fights* relies extensively upon *Boxiana* to provide the bulk of its accounts of the earlier days of the prize ring, it frequently inserts 'factual' information not recorded by contemporary sources, and often recounts lengthy dialogue that appears to be artistic invention on the part of the author. In some instances, this information is given as having been recounted by retired pugilists in conversation or in correspondence with Frank Bradley. Other details recorded in *Famous Fights* beyond those recorded in the newspapers of the period have to be queried as regards both honesty and accuracy, as in many instances the author does not provide any verifiable sources that would substantiate his claims.[106]

According to Bradley's account, in July 1819, Tom Spring headed a travelling sparring troupe that contained a number of

104 *Famous Fights, Past and Present*, Vol. XI No. 142 – 'The First Great Fight between Ned Turner and Jack Martin'. This newspaper was published between 1901–1904, many years after the death of the prize ring.

105 Fred Henning wrote for the *Licensed Victuallers' Gazette* under the *nom-de-plume* of 'Tourist'.

106 As a publication, *Famous Fights, Past and Present* contains a large number of errors, and has to be viewed with a great deal of caution as a source of information. For example, Vol. III No. 35 contains an article entitled 'The Story of the Fatal Fight between Ned Turner and George Curtis,' which mistakenly confuses George Curtis with his brother Jack. Jack Curtis was the pugilist who died following his contest against Turner, for which Turner was imprisoned at Newgate, and not George. The same article also supplies further details (and quoted speech) regarding Turner's earlier opponent, John Balch (Balche), not recorded in any other sources, including *Boxiana*, as well as also 'inserting' additional details and statements attributed to George (*Jack*) Curtis prior to their contest not recorded elsewhere. Additionally, Fred Henning's *Fights for the Championship* also contains a great deal of 'colourful' accounts that have been greatly embellished by the author.

the leading pugilists, including Tom Shelton, Ned Turner and Jack Martin. Seeing a lucrative opportunity, Tom Spring took his troupe to Brighton to display their sparring skills before an appreciative audience, and reaped a 'golden harvest' from their nightly entertainments. At one of these shows, Ned Turner sparred against Jack Martin, who had been conquered in May of that year by Jack Randall, after 19 rounds and 49 minutes of hard fighting. Martin was 2in taller than Turner, and outweighed the Welshman by a little over a stone.[107] The exhibition would appear to have been well received, and the pugilists were so well matched in terms of their skill with the gloves that Brighton was divided into two factions, those who claimed that the Ned was the superior boxer, and those who were convinced that Jack Martin was the better man.

Night after night, Tom Spring afterwards put the two pugilists together, with the result that the house was continually packed for this 'turn' alone, and as a consequence, Jack Martin and Ned Turner began to view each other as rivals. Tom Spring quickly realised that there was an opportunity to organise a match between the two pugilists and fanned the flames of their rivalry so that on their return to London, a contest with the knuckles could be arranged. Lord Egremont supposedly told Tom Spring that he was willing to put forward ten guineas towards Jack Martin's stake for a match against Turner, so Spring waited for a favourable opportunity to clinch the affair.

Jack Martin had been given the punning cognomen of the 'Master of the Rolls' due to his profession as a baker, and was born on 10 July 1796, near Kennington Church. His first prize ring battle took place eight days after his 20th birthday at Ilford in Essex against Tom Oliver's brother, George. Jack Martin emerged victorious after 21 rounds, and received 20 guineas and a great deal of praise for the blossoming science that he displayed in the course of the contest. He afterwards conquered 'Paddington' Johnson, a pupil of Paddington Jones, at Coventry Farm, the Hale, Middlesex, on 15 September 1818, beating Johnson with ease in just 18 rounds and 30 minutes and left the ring with barely a

107 *Boxiana* records Jack Martin's fighting weight as 'about' 11st 6lbs to Edward Turner's 10st 4lbs.

scratch. With his pugilistic reputation growing, a match was made for Jack Martin to meet Jack Scroggins, who, notwithstanding his defeats at the hands of Ned Turner, was still highly regarded by the Fancy. Although Martin was victorious, it took him 65 rounds and two hours and two minutes to defeat Scroggy, despite the fact the sailor appeared 'stale' and 'used up'. It was thought that it was only the strength of Jack Martin's youth and his constitution that enabled him to win. Jack Scroggins punished the baker most dreadfully, and Martin was ill for several days afterwards. A question mark had afterwards been drawn by the Fancy as to how the 'Master of the Rolls' would perform should he enter the ring against a first-rate scientific boxer. That question had been effectively answered when Jack Martin had been demolished by Jack Randall in 19 rounds, and it was said that Randall 'never won a battle with more comparative ease'. At the end of the fight, Randall only had the slightest of bruises under his left eye and a scratch upon his ear to suggest that he had engaged in a prize fight at all. It now only remained to be seen how Jack Martin might fare against Edward Turner.

Jack Randall had long desired to go into business as a publican, and had only delayed his decision to do so to engage Turner and then Martin in battle prior to his retirement from the ring. Having now beaten both men, it was time for the Nonpareil to settle down into his new role as an innkeeper, so, on Tuesday, 17 August 1819, Jack Randall held a dinner at his new public house, The Hole in the Wall at Chancery Lane, to celebrate in the company of those who had supported him throughout his prize ring career. It was at this dinner that Frank J. Bradley related that Tom Spring saw an opportunity to engineer a contest between Ned Turner and Jack Martin. A newspaper advertised this event as follows:

> TO THE PATRONS OF THE NOBLE ART
>
> A most interesting match will take place on Tuesday, August 17, 1819, at five o'clock in the afternoon, in which The Nonpareil will exhibit in a new character.
>
> The Commander-in-Chief will preside. It will be a game-set-to, and cutting-up will prevail, while the claret will be in full supply. The visitors, if they do not find themselves in Chancery, will be in the lane that leads

to it. The Hole-in-the-Wall will be the *rendezvous* on this occasion, when friendship and harmony will do their best to crown Jack Randall's latest hit.

According to Frank Bradley, it was at this dinner that Randall's friend, General Barton, was called upon to make a speech. In the course of his observations, Barton said that Jack Randall had been well named as 'the Nonpareil' as there was no one who could claim to be his equal in the prize ring. After Barton had finished addressing the company, Randall himself said a few words. The Nonpareil graciously responded that he was wholly undeserving of the title that he had been given, but that he had retired from the prize ring leaving behind an opponent who was every bit as good as he had been, and pointed to Ned Turner. Everyone present knew that Jack Randall had conquered Turner, but the remarks were met with applause as Turner's worth as a pugilist was known to all, regardless of his defeat by Randall.

Tom Spring's voice was then heard above the cheering, saying that he knew a man who was better than Ned Turner. A great excitement rippled through the room, and although Randall immediately demanded to know who Tom Spring thought was a better pugilist than Turner, Spring refused to name the man, and waited for the right moment to arrive. A baronet then

A baronet jumped up and offered to back Ned Turner for twenty to one.

jumped up and said he would back Turner at 20/1. A lord quickly followed him, stating his willingness to bet 2/1 on Turner up to £10,000, and the excitement mounted as everybody present eagerly waited for the announcement of the name of the mystery man. Tom Spring now knew that he would have no difficulty in organising a fight, and proclaimed that his nominee to take down the colours of Ned Turner was Jack Martin, the Master of the Rolls. The announcement brought surprise and disbelief before some members of the company voiced their open scorn at Spring's suggestion that the baker who had been beaten by Scroggins and Randall had any chance against Turner. Spring waited until the excitement died down and calmly said that he was prepared to accept 2/1 on Turner, and would put £5,000 on Martin. This cooled the ardour of many, but several gentlemen took Spring at his word, and a number of bets were quickly placed. Tom Spring's strategy had worked, and with wagers having now been laid on the outcome of the proposed match, many said that it was only proper that a fight should take place.

Ned Turner had long been thought of as the 'Pugilistic Prince of Wales' by his fellow countrymen, and was also held in high esteem by those Welsh sportsmen who maintained an interest in the London Prize Ring. With Turner's reputation and Welsh national pride at stake, the Pugilistic Club member Sir Watkin Williams Wynn, the 5th Baronet of Wynnstay, was the first to throw his support behind the gallant Welshman, announcing, 'I'll stand ten on Turner.' The next voice that was heard was that of Mr Morgan Evans of Glamorgan. 'And I'll stand ten more,' he asserted. The floodgates having now been opened, one Welsh gentleman after another offered £5 or £10, and in one case, £20, until 100 guineas had been raised. Satisfied that the match had been made, Spring placed ten sovereigns in the hand of Captain Barclay as Jack Martin's first deposit to bind the match, and Sir Watkin Williams Wynn did the same on Ned Turner's behalf. It was agreed that the second deposit of £40 should be staked by 30 August at the Castle Tavern in Holborn and the remaining balance should be deposited at Tom Spring's new public house, The Catherine Wheel at Little St James's Street, Pall Mall.

News of the contest was received with great interest by the sporting world, and the outcome of a fight between Ned Turner and Jack Martin was discussed at length with thoughtful criticism. No one doubted the worth of Turner; he had triumphed on two occasions over Scroggins, while Jack Martin had taken two hours to beat the sailor when Scroggy was deemed to have been in 'stale' condition. While both men had fought Jack Randall and lost, it had taken Jack Randall even longer to defeat Turner than it had taken Jack Martin to beat Scroggy. In fact, no one had ever stood up to Jack Randall as long as Turner. Aby Belasco had somehow lasted for 45 minutes – less than half the time that the valiant Welshman had managed – but most of the Nonpareil's opponents had been defeated in less than half an hour. On the date appointed for the final deposit at the Catherine Wheel, debate flew thick and fast as to whom was the better man. Jack Scroggins was present but would not be drawn on his opinion as to who might triumph, saying that, '...he would not give *tup-pence* for choice – he had *tried* both the men – TURNER was the *awkwardest* man alive to *get at*; but *Martin was the hardest hitter.* Two *gamer* lads never entered the ring–and when either of the men said "No!" the other would be very glad of it'.

Jack Randall favoured Ned Turner, pointing out that Martin had taken nearly twice as long as Turner to defeat Scroggins, and even then he had only narrowly saved the day by the 'toss up of a halfpenny'. The Welshmen present seconded Randall's opinion, and refused to believe that their man could be beaten. With the final deposit having been paid, Turner was sent back to Wales to train for the contest, but had hardly been there a week before worrying rumours reached London about Ned's activities. Turner was said to be visiting the houses of his friends, making merry and enjoying their food and hospitality, and drinking liberally in their company and acting as he would if he was celebrating having won a fight rather than in training for one. The second rumour was equally worrying, that Turner had met with a severe accident, having fallen while climbing a hill and fractured his right kneecap. Concerned about their man, Turner's backers engaged Tom Belcher to travel to Newtown to discover whether there was any truth in the rumours. After arriving in Wales, Belcher discovered that while the first story was untrue, there was some truth in the second. Ned Turner had met with a slight accident, but thankfully his kneecap had not been fractured and was only slightly displaced.

On his return to London, Tom Belcher explained the nature of Turner's injury and pushed for a postponement the battle, which had been fixed for the first week of September. After a number of meetings and long discussions, it was finally agreed that the battle between Ned Turner and Jack Martin should be fought at Wallingham Common in Surrey on 26 October 1819.

Chapter 10

The Baker and the Blue Ruin

On the day of the battle, the road to Wallingham Common was all bustle. Despite the concern over Turner's right knee, it was thought that failing any disasters the Welshman must be a certainty to win. At one o'clock, Edward Turner was on the ground and threw his hat into the ring, attended by Jack Randall and Tom Belcher. Jack Martin did the same, having secured the services of Tom Cribb and Tom Spring as his seconds. Turner lost the toss for corners, and ended up having the corner facing into the sun. Without further ado, the fighters stripped for battle, and at first glance both men appeared to be in superb condition. Jack Martin had been trained with exceptional care, and while he appeared large, there was no excessive weight on his frame, although some thought he looked a little more like a foot runner than a pugilist, due to the heavy build of his lower body. Ned Turner was also in fine fettle, and there were only a few worries about the injury he had sustained to his knee. In weight, Martin was the heavier man at 11st 4lbs, while Turner had been trained so finely as to weigh 'considerably' under 11st.

Cautious sparring was the order of the day, with Jack Martin having been seen to retreat, until at length he led off, but his blow was neatly stopped by Ned Turner. There was another pause until Turner tried his right, although Martin avoided the punch. The Welshman, ever watchful for an opportunity, tried for the body and missed, but Jack Martin's counter fell short. Martin seemed to have already tired of holding up his arms, and on dropping them he cast a look towards the ground. Quick as a flash, Ned seized the opportunity, landing a blow to Jack's head. A fast rally followed in which Turner was seen to good advantage, and in short time one of Martin's eyes was damaged and oozing blood. The baker retreated to the corner of the ring, but Turner followed him and sent him to the turf after a spirited exchange. Martin was heard to exclaim, 'Isn't that foul?' after being sent down, but the referee shook his head in reply.

In the second round, Turner landed a severe body blow and repeated it without a return, but on attempting to land it for the third time was stopped by Martin. Ned then landed a smarting blow to the face and got home with a dig to the ribs. Martin, however, gamely stuck to his work, and made some of his blows tell. In the struggle that followed to secure the throw, both men went down. The Master of the Rolls did not attempt to hit first, and foolishly retreated to the corner of the ring. He was pursued by Turner and seemed to lack the skill to be able to extract himself from his perilous situation, and was quickly sent down by a blow from Ned. Showing his fighting spirit, Martin landed a number of blows in the fourth, and was seen to good advantage in the struggle for the throw, when at length both men went down, with Martin on top. The confidence of some of Martin's backers was restored by the baker's good showing in this round and they cried, 'Well done, Martin' in support of their man.

Their hopes received a setback in the fifth round, when it became clear that Jack Martin's strength was beginning to flag, and he received a terrible blow to the nose, which was followed by other damaging punches. Another prolonged struggle for the throw followed in which Turner proved to be the victor, falling heavily on top of Martin. Despite his distress, Martin commenced fighting in earnest in the following round, landing a punch to Turner's head. The Out-and-Outer was unaffected by the blow and he landed a shot to the baker's throat that nearly deprived him of breath, following it up with another telling punch to the body. In getting away from Turner, Martin fell as a result of his increasing weakness. Fighting on the retreat, Jack Martin's strength was now ebbing fast and he continued to be sent down. By the eighth round, his head was 'rolling like a top'. The game baker continued to stagger up to the scratch but by now the tide was already turning firmly in favour of Turner, and Martin went down at every opportunity to avoid further punishment and allow himself recovery time. Turner's punches were starting to make Martin flag and in the throwing he was also proving to be the stronger, slinging the baker around in the 17th and 18th rounds with ease. In the following round, Ned was seen to stop all of Martin's blows without difficulty and all those at ringside were in unanimous agreement that he was winning convincingly. Jack still had the ability to surprise and in the following round he managed to throw Ned heavily, and it was clear that Turner was shaken by the severity of the fall. Martin improved in the rounds that followed and, tired by his exertions, Turner began to look a little weak and was given brandy to fortify his spirit. From the 24th to the 26th round, Martin improved considerably, and there was a moment of concern when upon throwing his opponent, Turner's leg came into contact with the post, and he narrowly avoiding injuring his bad knee.

In the three succeeding rounds, Ned paced himself and put in a telling punch now and then, gradually wearing Jack down, and extended his advantage. Martin rallied in the 31st round and landed some smashing blows, sending Turner to the turf. In spite of this, Ned was the first to lead off on coming to the scratch for the 33rd time and landed a terrific crack under the ear that seemed to separate Martin from his senses, and the bruised baker went down once more, dazed and confused. The 34th round was the deciding round of the fight. After a few blows had been exchanged, Ned Turner threw his right and landed full force on the mark, and then hooked Martin round the neck, holding him in chancery. Ned repeatedly punched his man to the body, and Martin was quickly sent down to cries of, 'Well done, Turner'.

Ned Turner's exceptional skill was witnessed in the following round, and he parried Jack Martin's attacks with the judgement of a master. The round only terminated when his knee began to fail him and he slipped down from a slight hit. Martin now appeared in a state of complete exhaustion, and in trying to get away from Turner in the 37th round he fell without a blow. In the next round, Ned was heard to say, 'Jack, if I am to be beat, stand up and win it like a man.' Martin was by now in such a state of stupor that he was unable to reply, and he went down once more from sheer weakness. The 39th round saw Martin fall again without having received a punch and the baker seemed on the edge of collapse. The umpire found it necessary to say, 'Martin, recollect this is to be a stand up fight', but it seemed unlikely that the battered baker even heard him. The 40th round proved to be the last; Martin tried to put in one last desperate blow, and went down after the slightest of hits. Jack Martin was in terrible shape and had to be assisted to his second's knee, and on 'Time' being called it was clear to all that he had no hope of making it up to the scratch. Tom Cribb was heard to say, 'I believe we may say it's all over', so after one hour and seven minutes of combat, Ned Turner was declared the victor.

Jack Martin had been severely punished and his throat, chest and body all showed the marks of his beating at the hands of Ned Turner. Some of the spectators cast doubt on the notion that Martin was a skilled pugilist, but it would be fairer to say that he had been matched against one of the finest boxers of the day and had been found wanting. Martin had fought valiantly, but in vain, and all his efforts had been stopped by a superior opponent. Turner's skill with his right hand had been evident throughout, and although he had lost the toss for corners, he had manoeuvred Jack Martin so cleverly that the baker was constantly facing into the sun. Ned revealed himself to be unflappable when taking punishment as well, his punches never swaying from their course. It was thought that had Turner's knee been undamaged he would have secured the victory inside 50 minutes. Ned Turner retired from the battleground almost without a scratch on his face, despite the fact that Jack Martin was not an easy man to get at, as he was tall and prone to leaning backwards to avoid punishment when setting-to.

Jack Martin, the 'Master of the Rolls'.

Jack Martin was gracious in defeat, acknowledging his own shortcomings as a pugilist soon afterwards. The bravery of the Master of the Rolls could not be denied, having now tried his arm against both Jack Randall and Ned Turner. Martin had contended with the two greatest lightweights of the day and had been decisively beaten. According to *Boxiana*, Martin's reasoning in having chosen to do so was that *'he would not have been satisfied in his own mind, if he had not fought with Randall and Turner'*. He also afterwards stated, with great candour and honesty, that *'these heroes were too good fighters for him; and he therefore acknowledged, with the utmost sincerity of heart, they were his* CONQUERORS!'

With Jack Randall having retired from the prize ring, Ned Turner now stood alone as the greatest of the lightweights. His nearest rivals, Jack Scroggins and Jack Martin, had both been defeated. It would perhaps have been the moment at which the Welshman should have taken a leaf from Randall's book and chosen to retire from the prize ring. Prior to the fight with Jack Martin, rumour had already spread of Ned Turner's drinking habits, his love of the 'blue ruin', or gin, which he liberally consumed while enjoying the entertainments and night life of London. With no challengers on the horizon, Ned was a popular figure, famous throughout the land, good natured and kind, and found himself with no shortage of drinking companions. Caution was not a word readily associated with Ned Turner. Pierce Egan would say of him in *Boxiana* that, 'A higher courage man does not exist; nor is there a more feeling or generous fellow to be met with in the whole circle of British pugilists than NED TURNER. Taking *care of himself*, he has no idea of; indeed, NED is a perfect creature of the moment. He knows nothing about the value of TIME, (except it is in the Ring, and there, it may be asked, who keeps it better, or any thing like so well, as TURNER?) As a game man, not the slightest dispute exists on that point; and it is only in the space of 24 feet, when in battle, that he may be viewed as a terrific character. In society, he is truly inoffensive; and, as a tradesman he is an excellent workman.'

While Ned Turner apparently continued working as a skin tanner, his nights were spent in the company of his fellow pugilists and rubbing shoulders with the Fancy. Ned was a frequent visitor at the meetings of the sportsmen who comprised the famous Daffy Club, where the gin flowed and the songs followed, and Ned was as keen a drinker of the 'blue ruin' as any. The year after Ned Turner's defeat of Jack Martin, a meeting of the Daffy Club was held at the Bear and Ragged Staff public house in Smithfield, which had recently been taken over by Ned Turner's old opponent, Cyrus Davis, and a one-off meeting of the club at Davis's establishment was organised to support him in his new endeavour. On the evening of the meeting, 9 August 1820, a challenge was issued to Ned Turner from an unexpected quarter. Tom Belcher was accompanied by a well-known member of the Fancy, and both had been drinking heavily throughout the afternoon. Following a number of glasses of gin, Belcher announced his desire to fight any 11st man in England for 500 guineas a-side. This astonished the members of the club, as on most occasions Tom Belcher's conduct was without reproach, and with several of the leading lightweights being present, the President of the Daffy Club, Mr James Soares, asked Tom if he was being 'personal', but his answer was 'No!' The matter having seemingly now been settled, a few more glasses were drunk, and rousing chaunts followed, at which point Tom Belcher stated his willingness to fight Jack Randall or Ned Turner for 500 guineas a-side. Jack Randall was quick to dismiss Belcher's words as having resulted from drunkenness, and did not take offence at his foolishness. Ned Turner appeared at the public house soon afterwards, and after he had been told of Belcher's challenge, Ned stated his willingness to engage him, but said that he would rather 'run a mile, or spend a guinea, than fight Belcher' from the respect that he had for him. 'But if you wish it,' said Ned, 'I am ready'. Five guineas were swiftly put down on both sides and articles of agreement for the proposed match were drafted.

Tom Belcher announced that he would rather fight Jack Randall, and wanted to present the Nonpareil with two guineas to make a match for £500. Win or lose against Turner, he was willing to fight Randall three months afterwards. Jack Randall then consented to fight Belcher in the event that he defeated Turner. After a spirited disagreement with Tom Shelton, Belcher belligerently stated his willingness to fight Shelton there and then, although Shelton politely declined, explaining that he was not in a fit enough condition to fight.

The following Saturday, both Jack Randall and Ned Turner came forward to make the match, but General Barton, Randall's great friend and patron, stepped forward to reason with Tom Belcher. Belcher admitted that it had been the liquor that had been at fault, and offered to pay for the training expenses of Turner, and apologised to Randall. The matter having been put to rest, all parties sat down together for a friendly drink, and laughed at the thought that the Bear and Ragged Staff had been well prepared for another lively meeting of the Daffy Club. Belcher said that he had made the challenge after having been upset that his cousin had been overlooked to perform at a benefit event held at the Fives Court, so the whole notion of a fight between Tom Belcher and Ned Turner quickly went up in a puff of smoke.

Ned Turner's kind and friendly nature would make him a popular figure amongst his fellow pugilists, and it was said by his supporters that his skills were even more apparent on those occasions when Turner had felt compelled to raise his hands outside the confines of the prize ring, as recalled by Pierce Egan in *Boxiana*:

> It is...urged by the friends of TURNER that his boxing requisites have been seen to greater advantage in his accidental *skirmishes* than in those PRIZE FIGHTS which have so much enhanced his *milling* reputation, owning to labouring under those peculiar feelings which he cannot get the better of for some time after his entering the ring with an opponent, merely to obtain a purse.

Turner's skills were such that that despite his sometimes wayward lifestyle, there were few who would wish to fight him, sober or otherwise. West Country Dick had once challenged Turner to a turn-up, and despite Ned having been drunk, he polished off Dick in three rounds. Another impromptu fight would occur a few months after the aborted contest between Tom Belcher and Ned Turner, against Josh Hudson, who had fought a 'swell' by the name of Williams at Moulsey Hurst on 5 December 1820. Despite having been a novice in the prize ring, the swell was thought to have a great deal of skill with the gloves. Josh Hudson had been suffering from a shoulder injury and it was thought that Williams might be able to benefit and triumph over Hudson. This notion was disproved when Hudson, seconded by Ned Turner and Tom Owen, completely destroyed Williams in six brutal and bloody rounds. Hudson celebrated the victory in fine style, drinking liberally for a number of days after the contest. Perhaps a little too emboldened by the manner in which he had defeated Williams, and with his pride having been fortified by drink, Hudson mistakenly believed that he was more than ready to stand up against Ned Turner himself. Pierce Egan relates the incident in *Boxiana* as follows:

> MORE WONDERS. – *A fight for Love between two distinguished heroes of the Prize Ring; perhaps, it might be more correct to say, "for honour."* – JOSH HUDSON, who so recently disposed of the *Swell* in such a *swellish* manner... and who, in consequence, had been making "*too free*" for a few days, when almost as *groggy* as a sailor three sheets in the wind, being in company with *Turner*, *Shelton*, *Randall*, *Martin* and *Purcell*, at the house of a *Swell*, near Lincoln's-Inn Fields, on Thursday evening, December 14, 1820, JOSH *talked* of thrashing the *Welshman*, *Shelton*, &c. at which they only smiled in the most perfect good humour. JOSH, however, would not be denied; fight he would, observing, at the same time, that he could beat both the *Nonpareils*. *Turner* declared over and over again, he had much rather not fight; but Ned was compelled to take a turn. The action immediately commenced. The *science* of *Turner* was fine and effective; and, in two instances, where he might have *punished* JOSH in a severe manner, he *tapped* him on the shoulder, and said, "*Josh, I will not hit you.*" There was no *closing*. JOSH went down heavily several times; and he was also *punished* sharply about the mouth. The *game* of JOSH was excellent; but he had no *chance*; and *Turner* had not a scratch. After fighting about a quarter of an hour, it was observed to the combatants, "they were not fighting for a prize, and it was better to *tie it* up." JOSH was taken away, and shed *tears* on being defeated. He, however, talked about fighting another day. It was the *Daffy* in JOSH that *kicked* up all the row.'

Having beaten Josh Hudson in 15 minutes, Ned Turner was shown to be more than capable of defeating a pugilist of above-average ability, even when under the influence of alcohol. With his reputation having been cemented by his victories over Jack Scroggins, Cyrus Davis and Jack Martin, Turner was the toast of the Fancy. Having no reason to fear that there were any opponents waiting in the wings, Ned continued to enjoy his success and lived life on his own terms. He did not guess that one of his opponents would soon return, emboldened by a string of victories, and with a burning desire to claim the Welshman's crown.

Chapter 11

The Return of the Fallen – Part 1

A new opponent for Ned Turner had been suggested at the end of November in 1820, in quite unusual circumstances.[108] A leading member of the Fancy gave a dinner at his residence in Chancery Lane for a number of prominent pugilists, to discuss possible future matches. Ned Turner, Jack Randall, Jack Martin, Tom Hickman, Phil Sampson, Harry Holt and Jack Scroggins all attended. A proposal had been made for Scroggins, who was suffering with a bad cold, to fight Harry Holt in six weeks' time. Scroggy proved himself to be as pugnacious as ever, responding, 'Why as to that there matter, it is no match between me and Holt, I can lick him like a baby. I never was so ill with a cold in my life; but I will fight him any time you like, even now, bad as I am'. Harry Holt was diplomatic in his response, thanking Scroggins for his candour but stating that he felt the sailor had no chance of beating him. Scroggins was eager to fight, so a contest was made on the spot for 20 guineas with the winner to take the whole of the purse. The room quickly divided, with the supporters of Scroggins moving to one side of the room, and the followers of Harry Holt taking to the other. The floor having been cleared, Ned Turner and Jack Martin stepped into the breach to second Scroggins, and Bob Purcell and Phil Sampson, 'The Birmingham Youth', attended to Harry Holt, while Tom Spring was chosen as the timekeeper. Although Holt demonstrated noticeable science, he was unable to contend with the ferocity of the attack of Scroggins, who followed

108 *Fistiana* records that the fight between Jack Scroggins and Harry Holt occurred in a 'room' at Chancery Lane, 30 November 1820, although states that the fight was for ten guineas, not 20.

his usual rushing strategy of engaging his opponent. In the 33 rounds that followed, Holt was soundly beaten. Scarcely able to make it on to the knee of his second at the end of the final round, Phil Sampson gave in for Harry Holt, saying that he should not fight on. Scroggins was the first to approach Holt at the end of the battle and said, 'Harry, give us your hand; you are a good fellow and here's a guinea for you!'

After the battle had ended, discussion took place as to what future contests might be agreed, and a fight was suggested between Ned Turner and Tom Hickman, the 'Gas-light man' who agreed to fight for 150 guineas to 80. A few eyebrows were raised at the match, as Turner was under 11st, and 'Gas' was above 12st. Despite this, Turner was convinced that he had the measure of Hickman, and Hickman was seen to be equally as confident that he would thrash Turner. Bets were taken and favoured Hickman at 2/1.[109] Once news of the proposed match had reached the ears of the Welshman's supporters, they were quick to try to persuade Turner that he did not have a chance of victory, although Turner was apparently 'too *game* to forfeit'.[110] Despite the well-meaning advice of his friends, Ned wished to continue with the match, and the stakes were increased at a subsequent meeting at Jack Randall's public house. Turner decided to train[111] alongside Tom Oliver and Bob Purcell in Essex.[112] Turner's contest against Tom Hickman was called off soon afterwards due to 'forfeiture' that caused Ned a great deal of anger, as related by Pierce Egan in *Boxiana*:

> TURNER AND HICKMAN – During some conversation one evening early in December, 1820, the friends of the *Gas-Light Man* offered to back him £150 to £80 against *Turner*, when a small deposit on each side was immediately put down. A second meeting took place, when the former deposits were increased; but upon the third meeting, at

---

109 As recorded in the *Public Ledger and Daily Advertiser*, 2 December 1820. This account also states that the Jack Scroggins vs Harry Holt match was for 20 guineas.

110 As recorded in the *Morning Post*, 1 January 1821.

111 As recorded in the *Morning Post*, 8 January 1821.

112 As recorded in the *Morning Post*, 18 January 1821.

> *Randall's*, to the great mortification and even *anger* of *Turner*, a forfeiture was the result. In consequence of *Ned* being engaged at the Royalty Theatre, to exhibit the art of Self-Defence with *Harmer*, he was not present; but he asserts, that he commanded an amateur to make the stakes good for him, and who also promised to attend the meeting. The person alluded to did attend, but when called upon to cover, said, "He had no authority to put any money down; indeed, he had nothing to do with it." It was thus this match went off. The amateurs in general entertained an opinion, that *Turner* in opposition to *Hickman*, would not have had the slightest chance to win; nay, that he must have been smashed all to pieces. However, on Monday evening, Jan. 22, 1821, at *Parish's* benefit, at the Woolpack Tavern, in Cornhill, *Turner* and *Hickman* set-to. The general opinion then expressed by the spectators was, that *Turner* "had decidedly the best of it." But the *Gas-Light Man*, in answer, said "he gammoned it."

Despite Ned Turner's good showing against Hickman at the Woolpack Tavern, it seems likely that his supporters breathed a sigh of relief that he was not to meet the Gas Man with the knuckles. It had been over a year since Turner's last battle in the prize ring against Jack Martin, and outside his appearances sparring at the Fives Court, Turner had rested easy and continued to indulge his love of the 'blue ruin' and the company of his fellow pugilists with little thought to the future. His reckless lifestyle would appear to have been noted by one wily ex-opponent who had been exceedingly busy throughout the time that Ned had been enjoying his place at the top of the tree. Jack Martin had found himself at a loose end following the cancellation of his contest against Bob Purcell, although he was £50 the richer after Purcell's supporters had been forced to forfeit the deposit as a result of Bob having fallen sick. Martin was quick to announce his willingness to engage Ned Turner, for £100 a side, with the money waiting.[113]

113 As recorded in the *Morning Post*, 19 February 1821.

Game as ever, Ned Turner was as willing as always to fight when challenged, and the match was made on the evening of Monday, 5 March 1821 for Turner and Martin to fight for 100 guineas, with the battle to take place on Tuesday, 5 June, the day before the Epsom races.[114] Despite the previous reluctance of Turner's supporters for their champion to engage the Gas Man, the match against Martin was widely viewed as a 'gift' of 100 guineas to the Welshman, whose followers keenly recalled how cleverly he had beaten Martin in an hour and seven minutes in 1819, when Turner had fought with an injured knee. They believed that Ned was sure to triumph and bets were quickly wagered in his hand being raised in victory in under an hour. Odds of 6/4 had been laid on Ned's triumph, and despite the confidence of the Turnerites, there were a few who thought that Ned should view the match with greater caution, believing that Martin would 'prove a much more *troublesome* customer to Turner than heretofore'.[115]

Those who confidently predicted a win for Turner would have been best advised to look with greater scrutiny at the string of victories the baker had notched up since his defeat by Ned. In December of 1819, less than two months after having fought Turner, Jack Martin had defeated Josh Hudson in nine minutes, dislocating Hudson's left shoulder in the second round with a 'tremendous hit'. Sadly, the Fancy were not satisfied that Martin had proved himself, feeling that the shortness of the contest had given limited opportunity to measure Martin's skill against Hudson, and most were of the opinion that if Hudson had not been injured, he would have thrashed Martin. In March of 1820, the Master of the Rolls had engaged Jack Strong, known as 'Iron-hitting Cabbage'. Cabbage had gained a great deal of notoriety following his

Thomas Hickman, 'The Gas-Man'.

114 As recorded in *The Globe*, 7 March 1821.

115 As recorded in the *Salisbury and Winchester Journal*, 9 April 9 1821.

previous victories and was considered to be the champion of the Bristol lightweights. Against Jack Martin, however, Cabbage was found to be wanting. Despite having been extremely weak and sick through rheumatism, and being scarcely able to walk in the week prior to the fight, Martin triumphed after 76 rounds in a battle lasting two hours.[116] Cabbage was dreadfully punished and was left unconscious for a quarter of an hour at the end of the battle, with blood pouring from his right ear. The Bristol pugilist was in a bad way for a number of hours afterwards and for a time it was feared that he might not recover at all.[117] Although the abilities of Cabbage were thought in hindsight to have been much inflated, being a rushing fighter of similar quality to Scroggins, albeit of lesser quality, Jack Martin's standing was greatly improved by the ferocity of his performance given his poor health at the time of the fight.

Ned Turner should perhaps have been taking more careful note of the manner in which Jack Martin was steadily improving his record in the prize ring, particularly as Turner had served as one of Phil Sampson's seconds in his fight against Martin in July of 1820. It is possible that Ned was unimpressed with the manner in which Martin secured victory over the 'Birmingham Youth' in 29 rounds. In a rough and ready fight, characterised by more 'pulling and hauling' than hitting on Jack Martin's part, the baker had at one stage pulled Sampson to the turf by his thighs to shouts of 'Foul', but the cries of the spectators had been ignored by the referee. Although the contest ended in a win for Martin, his poor performance brought murmurs of criticism amongst the spectators, and had cast further doubts on his standing as a scientific boxer.

Despite the naysayers, Jack Martin had also conquered David Hudson, Josh Hudson's brother, in October of 1820, although it was thought a certainty that Hudson would emerge victorious. Hudson was decisively beaten in 18 rounds, lasting 39 minutes and ten seconds, and was severely damaged by Martin's heavy blows,

116 As recorded in *The Globe*, 29 March 1820. Most of the newspaper accounts of this fight record the contest as having been 76 rounds, which lasted two hours. *Fistiana* curiously records this fight as having lasted 75 rounds over 72 minutes.

117 As recorded in *Boxiana*.

which were as hard as 'a horse's kick'. Martin had such an easy time of it that it was said he could have afterwards beaten another David Hudson in the same ring. The success of Jack Martin led the sporting world to conclude that his merits as a boxer had been held 'much too cheap', and by conquering Hudson, considered one of the best lightweights of the day, the baker finally succeeded in raising his profile sufficiently to be considered amongst those men of the first rank. Having toiled continuously to improve his pugilistic record in the year and a half since he had been defeated by Ned Turner, the Master of the Rolls relocated to train at Hertfordshire for the rematch against Turner, and was reportedly in fine form the week before the contest.[118] The day of reckoning against his Welsh rival was drawing ever nearer.

A fairly select number of the Fancy took to the road on the day of the battle and headed from London to Crawley Hurst, a little over 30 miles away. The distance and the fact that the date of the fight had fallen so close to Epsom races meant that a sizeable number stayed away. Additionally, as it was thought that Ned Turner was almost certain to win, the match failed to attract a great deal of speculation, many contenting themselves with the knowledge that they would hear of Turner's victory later. The power of the morning sun was so strong that those horses that had been used for the journey suffered terribly, and were forced to a standstill at every mile along the road. Some didn't even manage to make it to Crawley, and fell by the side of the road exhausted, where they lay, doomed to being sent to the knacker's yard.[119]

The bad omens continued. Ned Turner was the first to appear on the battleground and tried to throw his hat into the ring, but the wind blew it away, forcing him to pick it up and throw it in for a second time. Turner must have felt some alarm – a hat falling outside the ring had always been viewed as a sign that a pugilist's efforts would be doomed to failure.[120] Tom Belcher and Jack Randall accompanied Turner as his seconds. A few minutes afterwards Jack Martin appeared on the scene, accompanied by

---

118 As recorded in the *Cheltenham Chronicle*, 31 May 1821.

119 As recorded in the *Morning Chronicle*, 6 June 1821.

120 As recorded in the *Cumberland Pacquet, and Ware's Whitehaven Advertiser*, 11 June 1821.

Tom Spring and an amateur from Norwich, all of whom were wearing white top hats and looking exceedingly 'swellish'. The colours were quickly tied to the stakes, dark blue for Turner and a lighter blue for Martin, and the men stripped for battle. At the call of time, both men approached the scratch and the fight began without delay.

Jack Martin was the first to launch an attack with his right hand, Ned Turner skilfully avoided it, but the baker continued to throw punches and push forwards so quickly that Ned nearly lost his balance and a fast exchange of blows occurred. So determined was Jack Martin's attack that Ned Turner was heard to cry out, 'Hollo! Hollo! Go it my lad!' in surprise. Martin then launched a heavy blow that landed on Turner's throat, although Turner got in one of his own with his left on Martin's eye, nearly closing it. Undeterred, the baker landed a heavy body shot and followed it up with another to the face. Turner quickly went about his work, and sharp punches passed between them until at length both combatants went down.

In the second round, Ned Turner hit Jack Martin's guard down and afterwards landed a telling punch to the head with his left hand before getting away, although in the close at the ropes, he was sent down. It was now evident that the baker was determined to fight and both men pursued each other in turn all over the ring. Grasping Turner in the close, Martin punished him until he either slipped or went down from a slight blow. The battle was now beginning to turn in Jack's favour as he landed further blows in the fourth round just as Ned was nearly falling down. Ned Turner's knees were trembling, and it was clear that despite initial appearances, he was not in good condition. Seizing the advantage, Jack Martin bored into close range and got Ned down again. In the rounds that followed, although Turner was landing punches, they did not appear as strong as in his previous battles, although he somehow managed to score first blood. Every blow from Turner was matched by Martin, and from the 12th round onwards, Martin landed several hurtful punches to the kidneys of Turner. He followed these with a number of 'facers' to the head. By now, the Master of the Rolls was clearly having the best of it, but the supporters of the Out-and-Outer could not perceive it, so confident were they of Turner's skill.

In the 16th, Jack Martin landed three blows to the face without return and although Ned Turner attempted to rally, he was sent down after another severe clout. 'I'll have Martin to win for five hundred guineas,' said Tom Spring, gratified by his man's performance. Martin again proved to be the better man in the following round; blood was now streaming from Turner's nose and he was sent down awkwardly once more. Martin had the best of it, taking all the rounds that followed, and by the 30th it was evident that Ned could no longer stop the body shots of his opponent and was weakening under each onslaught. The referee announced that the fight had now passed the one-hour mark. Martin's confidence was growing with every round, and he nonchalantly replied, 'I can fight for six hours.'

The odds were rapidly changing to reflect Jack Martin's dominance and now stood at 2/1 in his favour. Ned Turner continued to go down, once seemingly without a blow, and an appeal was made to the umpires. 'You are mistaken,' one replied, adding, 'I should not like to have had it.' By the 41st round, it was obvious that Ned could not fight against the tide much longer, and after an exchange of punches he went down after having been pursued all over the ring. In the 43rd round, it seemed as though Ned was finding his second wind, landing a hard left hand on Jack Martin's forehead that made the blood flow profusely. 'It's all right now,' cried a few of the spectators. 'Give him the Bermondsey screw, Ned.' Although Martin had the worst of this round, Turner went down again. The 46th round was marked by dispute. Turner hit Martin hard in the head before getting away, and after a brief exchange Martin followed Turner, who dropped, causing the baker to remark that 'Ned went down without a blow,' and he complained to the umpires. 'Fair, fair' and 'Foul, foul' resounded from all around the ring. In a fit of passion, the Master of the Rolls complained that 'he was not used well' and tried to leave the ring. One of Martin's legs was already between the ropes before he was seized by Tom Spring, who refused to let him leave, saving him from forfeiting the battle. At this point, Mr Jackson stepped in and said that neither the combatants nor their seconds had any right to interfere, and that the only people who could do so were the umpires appointed to observe the contest, with final appeals being made to the referee.

Jack Martin appeared very angry as he came up in the following round, but his temper soon cooled and a good round was the result. Turner was again sent down at its termination to loud shouts from the baker's supporters, who jubilantly cried, 'It's all right again, and Jack's alive.' Their elation did not appear to reach the ears of Turner, who seemed to think he was winning the battle as he sat on his second's knee, and he smiled with confidence at his supporters, although he was again sent down in the next three rounds. In the 51st round, although Turner started proceedings with a sharp 'facer', following an exchange, Ned went down again, and Jack Martin complained that he had done so without having been hit. Mr Jackson was again forced to intercede, saying, 'I shall decide fairly, depend upon it, he not only received a hit, but his foot caught in a hole,' and pointed to the depression in the ground that had caught Turner's foot. The next three rounds were well

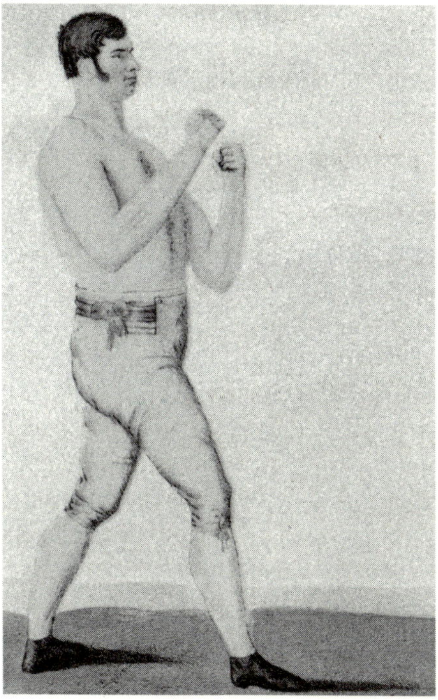

An engraving of Ned Turner published by Samuel William Fores (1827), entitled 'Edwd. Turner', which is captioned 'A Welchman about 27 Years of Age, stands 5 feet 7 Inches high, he weighs about 10 stone 5 pounds'. Note Turner's unorthodox stance with right foot forward.

fought, although Martin made another appeal to the umpires, and Jackson was forced to step forward again and say that if there was anything amiss the umpires would notice.

Jack Martin landed a severe 'facer' in the 55th round following an exchange, and there was a short pause in proceedings, and the baker was heard to exclaim, 'You are a game man, Ned, but you must lose it.' Shortly afterwards, Turner was sent down once more. It now appeared as though one of Turner's hands had gone, and Martin's right hand was also in very poor condition. Weakening by the second, Turner was again sent down in the following round and now appeared 'terribly distressed'. The 58th was another punishing round for Turner, and he tumbled to the turf following a severe blow to the body and another 'sharp one' to the head. The next round saw Jack Martin do as he pleased with Ned Turner; he grasped Ned around the neck with one arm and 'fibbed' away with his free hand, punching him repeatedly until Turner finally went down. Martin then fell on him with his knee, landing nearly at Turner's throat, prompting Tom Belcher to cry, 'What do you call that? Is it foul?'

The 60th round proved to be the last, and Jack Martin terminated the round by falling with all his weight upon Ned Turner. The brave Welshman was picked up and placed on his second's knee, as Martin nervously looked first at his opponent and then at the umpires, waiting for the call of 'Time'. When the call finally came, it went unheeded by Turner. After being given the victory, Jack Martin gave a jump of joy and he ran out of the ring towards his carriage. Ned Turner's injuries were then attended to and he was gently led from the ring, having battled against Martin for 88 minutes.[121] The reason for Ned's defeat was clear to all, with a number of newspaper reports on the contest remarking that, 'Sooner or later the *Daffy* will find them all out, and fighting men will be *floored* by it'.[122] Ned Turner's constitution had suffered because of his heavy drinking, and he lacked the punishing power that had previously won him such fame. Jack Martin received a great deal of credit for his noticeable improvement in science, and

121 As recorded in *Fistiana*.

122 As recorded in the *Cumberland Pacquet, and Ware's Whitehaven Advertiser*, 11 June 1821.

was thought to have demonstrated a great deal of cleverness in the manner in which he had defeated Ned Turner, although drew some criticism for having taken an hour and 28 minutes to do so. Ned Turner's abilities were thought to be on the wane; keen eyes had noted the fact at one point he had received 14 body blows without stopping one. A collection was afterwards made for the fallen hero, to which a number of his supporters contributed, despite many having lost considerable sums as a result of Turner's defeat.

None of the spectators were as angry at Jack Martin's victory over Ned Turner as the Welshman's second, and one-time rival, Jack Randall. After Turner had been taken from the ring, the Nonpareil threw his hat in the air and announced his willingness to fight Jack Martin in three months time for £300 a-side. 'I'll bet 5/1,' said a spectator, 'no one dares to make it'.

The day after the battle, Ned Turner and Jack Martin met on the return journey home at Riddlesdown, and after shaking hands they drank to each other's health in a friendly manner. Ned Turner's friends refused to concede that he had been decisively beaten, maintaining that as Ned had beaten the baker, and Martin had then defeated Turner, 'the test of it is yet to be decided' and were prepared to put down £100 on a third match against Jack Martin, when Turner was fit enough to engage him.[123] The Master of the Rolls was not without options, as his old opponent Josh Hudson was waiting in the wings for a second shot, and Cyrus Davis had also been put forward as a potential challenger for £100 a-side. It remained to be seen whether Martin might be so bold as to take up the challenge of Jack Randall, the celebrated Nonpareil – who seethed at the thought that Jack Martin had uncrowned his close friend, Ned Turner.

123 As recorded in *Saunders's News-Letter*, 12 June 1821.

Chapter 12

The Return of the Fallen – Part 2

The defeat of Ned Turner at the hands of Jack Martin was the first loss that Turner had known since his defeat by Jack Randall back in December of 1818. The two and a half years that followed had seen the Welshman's pugilistic skill and ability raise his name to the forefront of the sporting world. Turner had been negligent in his training, with his love of gin having been largely responsible for his defeat, and was admitted by Turner the month after the fight. Ned had been called upon to second a man named Marshall against a fighter named Coultham, in a disappointing contest that came off at Fordwich, near Canterbury, in July of 1821, alongside his old rival, Jack Scroggins. Despite having two such celebrated pugilistic heroes in his corner, Marshall was decisively beaten in ten rounds and 18 minutes. After having been asked for his opinion on his loss to Jack Martin, Turner freely admitted that his 'having made too free with the daffy was the cause of Martin's beating him'.[124]

Ned Turner was engaged in August to appear at a benefit event held at the Tennis Court for the black veteran pugilist, Bill Richmond. Following a number of exhibitions by some of the leading boxers, Richmond and Turner wound up the evening with a 'good set-to' to the delight of the spectators.[125] Soon after this event, stakes of £300 a-side were laid by the backers of Jack Randall and Jack Martin at the Hole in the Wall, Chancery Lane, to make a match between the two men. The Nonpareil was the favourite and odds of 70/40 were offered on his victory, but there

---

124 As recorded in the *Kentish Weekly Post* or *Canterbury Journal*, 13 July 1821.

125 As recorded in *Saunders's News-Letter*, 4 August 1821.

were no takers.[126] Randall's furious challenge to Martin following the defeat of Ned Turner had not been immediately accepted by the baker's supporters, having been wary of laying such a large sum on Martin beating an opponent of such tremendous ability as Jack Randall. It was only after some time had elapsed that Martin's backers summoned up enough courage to put their money behind their man, with certain key factors having bolstered their confidence. Firstly, Jack Randall had retired from the ring some two years previously, and it was thought that he had lived a somewhat 'soft' life as a publican. Along with Turner, Randall had become known for a fondness for gin, which was thought likely to have undermined his constitution in his time outside the ring. Secondly, the Nonpareil had also only just recovered from a serious illness, it having been thought by an eminent physician in late April that he was unlikely to recover at all.[127]

The fight between Jack Martin and Jack Randall took place at Crawley Downs in Sussex on 16 September 1821. Despite the rumours of Randall's decline, on stripping for battle it was clear that Randall was every inch the man he once was, and was a picture of physical perfection. Randall seemed to have complete mastery over Martin right from the start, and after a few minutes of cautious exchanges, a severe right hand from Randall to Martin's stomach made the baker bite his lips. Jack Randall's mind quickly turned to 'fibbing' his opponent, a tactic at which the Nonpareil was unequalled. Seizing Martin around the neck with the right arm, Randall punched him with great rapidity with his left. Randall then changed arms, grabbing him with the left as he continued to strike at the head and neck with his right. His hands landed so fast that one eyewitness compared the sight to the 'motion of a mill wheel in full speed'. Landing repeated blows on the jugular vein ensured that Martin's eyes soon rolled upwards, and the hapless baker began foaming at the mouth. Beaten to near unconsciousness, a cry of 'It's all up' soon followed. The Master of the Rolls was carried out of the ring after just one round lasting eight and a half minutes.[128] Jack Martin was quickly put to bed and

126 As recorded in the *Cheltenham Chronicle*, 30 August 1821.

127 As recorded in the *Dublin Evening Post*, 13 September 1821.

128 As recorded in *Fistiana*.

it took him the best part of half an hour to recognise his second, Tom Spring, and in a state of confusion asked where he was, and whether he had lost the fight. There had perhaps never been a prize fight decided so quickly or so decisively, the excellence of Randall's skill being undeniable. The Nonpareil had avenged Ned Turner's defeat by Jack Martin in the grandest style imaginable.

Jack Martin did not take this second hammering by Jack Randall at all well and believed that his failure to seize victory was an 'accident'. Eager to repair his lost pride, the baker issued a challenge for a third contest against Randall, despite Randall having declared that this second fight against Martin was to be his last, having only decided to come out of retirement to engage Martin as a result of Martin's victory over Turner. Jack Randall's refusal to fight angered Martin a great deal, so the month after the contest, on Monday, 15 October 1821, a gang of Martin's followers, led by Tom Spring, descended on the Hole in the Wall to offer Randall £300 to £600 a-side to induce him to fight Martin for a third time. Randall refused to be swayed, stating that he had 'quilted' the baker twice, and was satisfied that he had proven his superiority. In the argument between Tom Spring and Jack Randall that followed, Spring was sufficiently enraged to call Randall a cur, and with Randall unable to stomach being insulted in this fashion in his own establishment, a tear-up swiftly followed. Ned Turner sailed in to defend Randall, and in the confusion that followed the Welshman accidentally hit Randall instead of Tom Spring. At the end of the scuffle, Tom Spring was well punished for his impertinence, and Randall told Spring that he was an honest fighter, who had won all his battles, and that he had never been beaten by a '*thing*' – alluding to Tom Spring's defeat by Ned Painter, about which Spring was said to be particularly sensitive.[129] Although the dispute between Randall and Martin wore on for an exceedingly long time afterwards, resulting in many bitter words being exchanged between the two men, the Nonpareil was true to his word and never entered the prize ring again after having avenged Ned Turner's defeat.

The following month, Ned Turner and Jack Randall appeared at the Tennis Court for a benefit event held for Turner, which was

129 As recorded in the *Sheffield Independent*, 20 October 1821.

'The Interior of the Fives Court, with Randall and Turner Sparring' engraved by Charles Turner, (originally created in 1818).

well attended. A number of spirited exhibitions were witnessed, although the sparring between Turner and Randall was 'far foremost in science' and deemed to be 'altogether perfection'. Jack Rasher, the Welsh butcher from Whitechapel market, was also present, and being exceedingly drunk, made a nuisance of himself. Rasher 'mounted the stage in a beastly state', forcing Jack Scroggins and Phil Sampson to punish 'Ironface' by spilling a little of his 'claret', by 'clarifying' his head.[130]

It might be imagined that Ned Turner was not in the best of spirits; his best days now appeared to be rapidly slipping into the past, although he remained a popular figure amongst his fellow pugilists by virtue of his friendly nature and the courage that he had displayed in all his contests within the prize ring. On 10 April 1822, Turner found himself besieged by multiple female assailants following an invite to Tom Belcher's house for an evening of revelry with his fellow prize fighters. Jack Scroggins had been in attendance and slid off to the kitchen in pursuit of a kiss from Tom Belcher's cook after having had his passions inflamed by too much gin. The cook proved reluctant to give in to Scroggy's charms and took up a posture of defence, which

130 As recorded in *Saunders's News-Letter*, 9 November 1821.

excited the drunken sailor even more. After scratching the face of Scroggins while defending herself, the cook quickly took to her heels in search of the lady of the house to inform her of his roguish behaviour. After a confrontation with Scroggins, Tom Belcher was summoned, and remonstrated with him at some length, but to no avail as the sailor was as unrepentant and as insolent as ever. Following an energetic row, it was decided that the matter could only be settled with the fists, and Ned Turner was engaged to oversee the battle. In the fight that followed, Scroggins tried his usual rushing tactics, although he was well thrashed by the superior fighting style of Tom Belcher. Drunkenly pursuing the same battle plan, Scroggins's rushes were halted each time by Belcher's fists, which 'transmogrified' Scroggy's face, leaving it a 'frightful spectacle' and the blood that poured from his face stained the wooden floors. At length, Scroggins finally gave in having taken a tremendous beating, but feeling that he had at least proved his manhood.[131] At the end of the fight, the cook, leading a 'party of petticoats', broke into the ring and for some unknown reason in the confusion that followed, the gang of women pitched into Ned Turner 'without mercy' before the fight was broken up.[132]

Ned was apparently also engaged in teaching boxing at this time; in May he had seconded Joe Nash, the Kingston baker, alongside Josh Hudson, and assisted him in his 35-round victory over T. Emmit.[133] Following this battle, a 'Birmingham youth', who was a pupil of Turner's, entered the ring and beat an unnamed 'countryman'.[134] It seems likely that Turner may well have needed the money that he earned from tuition, and his friends had by this stage started calling him 'Poor Ould Ned' despite his having only just reached the age of 30. Another benefit event was held for Turner on 15 July 1822, with the intention of setting Turner up in the world once more. Harry Holt and Turner himself were the

131 The *Morning Advertiser*, 25 April 1822, states that the fight was of six rounds duration and lasted for 20 minutes. *Fistiana* records that the fight between Scroggins and Belcher was five rounds and lasted for 29 minutes.

132 As recorded in the *Morning Advertiser*, 25 April 1822, and in *Bell's Life in London and Sporting Chronicle*, 28 April 1822.

133 *Fistiana* records the name 'T. Emmett' and not Emmit, as reported in the *Morning Advertiser*, 8 May 1822.

134 As recorded in the *Morning Advertiser*, 8 May 1822.

main attractions, and Tom Hickman, the Gasman, and Tom Spring also demonstrated their skills with the gloves. At the end of the evening, Ned mounted the stage and thanked the spectators for their support, and stated that he was willing to fight Jack Martin for the third time for £100 a-side. Martin was quick to take up the challenge, although he still smarted at his defeat by Randall, and addressed the crowd as follows: 'Gentlemen, first and foremost, I will fight Randall in one, two or three months, for £300; but if Randall does not accept this challenge, I will accommodate Turner for £100, whenever he pleases'[135]. Nothing would come of the challenge, possibly because Turner's health was still in the balance, and many thought that his continued heavy drinking would ensure that Ned would not enter the prize ring again.

It was soon after this benefit event that James 'Jemmy' Soares, the President of the Daffy Club, took the only step he thought might help save Ned Turner. Soares induced some friends of Cyrus Davis to rally around their man and challenge Turner, believing that if a matter of honour forced Turner into training, the Welshman might turn away from his reckless lifestyle and a combination of fresh air and healthy living might save him from further decline. Cy had been mortified by his defeat at the hands of Turner and was often heard to say that he would never feel satisfied until he had had the chance of a second fight against Ned, and was quick to agree to the proposal. Ned Turner took up the gauntlet with more readiness than he had ever demonstrated before, having been keen to dispel the remarks that had been made about his noticeable decline following his defeat by Jack Martin. Jemmy Soares was so overjoyed by the success of his scheme that he backed Turner in the battle against Cy Davis. The articles of agreement to fight were signed in November of 1822 at the Castle Tavern, Holborn. The news of the match created something of a minor sensation as Turner's agreement to fight was 'contrary to all expectations,' with most of the Fancy believing that '*dissipation* had told him out'. A dramatic turnaround in the Welshman's attitude had already been seen since the challenge had been made, and it was reported that 'Turner... has materially improved in health; and he confidently asserts that the effects of a few weeks training will

135 As recorded in the *Morning Post*, 17 July 1822.

not only renovate his frame, but he shall be in first-rate condition by the appointed time'.[136] On Wednesday, 13 November 1822, the following articles were signed:

> Castle Tavern, Holborn, Wednesday, Nov. 13, 1822.
>
> Edward Turner agrees to fight Cyrus Davis for 100*l.* aside, on the third Tuesday in February, 1823. To be a fair stand-up fight, in a 24 feet ring. Half-minute time. Mr Jackson to name the place; and also the whole of the stakes to be placed in his hands. Two Umpires to be appointed on the ground; one by Turner, and the other by Davis. The Referee to be named by Mr Jackson, if present; otherwise, the Umpires to appoint the Referee. Ten pounds aside are now deposited in the hands of Mr. Belcher; a further deposit of 40*l.* aside to be made good at Mr Harmer's, the Plough in Smithfield, on Tuesday, the 10th of December, between the hours of eight and ten o'clock in the evening; and the whole of the stakes completed at Mr Cyrus Davies's, the Salutation, in Newgate-market, on Tuesday, Feb. 4, 1823, between the same hours; or the deposits to be forfeited.
>
> (Signed) EDWARD TURNER.
>
> Witness, P.E. CYRUS DAVIS.

Cyrus allowed Ned as much time as needed to prepare for the match, probably due to the desire to minimise any possible suggestion that Turner was not in a fit enough state to do battle. After signing the agreement to fight and laying a £10 deposit to bind the match, they shook hands, 'more after the manner of inseparable friends than old opponents'.

Due to Ned Turner's well-publicised health problems, Davis was the favourite in the betting, at 5/4, which was perhaps unsurprising given the contrast in the manner in which they had lived their lives since their first battle. Cyrus was by far the heavier man, weighing over a stone more than Turner, and Ned was heard to observe that 'had he challenged any person 10lb under his weight, instead of a stone and better, he thinks he would

136 As recorded in the *Bristol Mirror*, 16 November 1822.

have been considered by amateurs a "cur"'.[137] Despite Turner's poor health and his opponent's superior weight, Ned enjoyed significant support amongst the Fancy, and it was reported that he did 'not want for backers'.[138] At the suggestion of Jemmy Soares, Ned elected to return to Newtown in Wales in the company of his brother-in-law, Mr Baxter, where it was hoped he might be able to repair the ravages that dissipation had brought to his once splendid constitution, and it was thought that he would benefit from training in the fresh air of his native land. The decision for Ned to undergo his training in Wales was undoubtedly a wise one, as when the Welshman returned to London, he could hardly be recognised as the emaciated creature who had travelled to Newtown early in the year. Ned Turner looked something like the pugilist who had famously defeated Scroggins and Martin, and who had come so close to wrestling the championship from Jack Randall himself.

On the day of the contest, Tuesday, 18 February , the inclement weather dissuaded a large number of casual followers of the ring to travel the 25 miles from London to Harpenden Common, near St Alban's, which had been named as the venue. At one o'clock, Cy Davis appeared on the ground, accompanied by Bill Richmond and Harry Harmer, and he immediately threw his hat into the ring as an indication of his willingness to fight. Ned Turner followed close at his heels, arm-in-arm with his backer, Jemmy Soares, and was followed by his seconds, Tom Cribb and Josh Hudson. Cyrus seemed undaunted by the task ahead of him, and went to shake hands with Turner, smiling all the while. The colours were then tied to the stakes by Tom Cribb and Bill Richmond, blue for the Welshman, and yellow for Davis. As the men stripped for battle and awaited the call to come up to the scratch, it allowed the spectators the first opportunity to criticise their appearance. Turner looked better than anyone could have expected a man to look who had previously appeared to have been near death's door. On closer scrutiny, however, it could be seen that while Ned had been well 'patched up', he was not quite the Ned Turner of old. He barely scaled 10st, some 7lbs less than when he had met Randall.

137 As recorded in *Saunders's News-Letter*, 7 November 1822.

138 As recorded in the *Morning Post*, 11 November 1822.

There was a marked falling off in his physique, and his skin now exhibited a peculiar yellowish hue.

Cy Davis was in beautiful condition, and his physique bore testimony to the careful preparation of his trainer, Bill Richmond, and he was deemed a 'perfect picture of a man in fine health'. His skin was 'transparent, ruddy, and healthful', he was four years younger than 'Poor Ould Ned', and was 2in taller, as well as enjoying the advantage of a full stone in weight. With these points in his favour, the odds of 5/4 in his favour appeared justified. The fight began with great caution on both sides; Davis kept his head well back with both hands extended, and his fists were so close together that they were nearly crossing. Cyrus evidently didn't like the look of Ned, and seemed to be keenly aware of the difficulty of getting at the 'Ould' one. At length, it was Turner who let fly with a left to the body, which landed without force, followed by more dodging. A right hand from Cy was carefully stopped by Turner, who landed another punch to the body. After Turner had stopped another attempted right hand from Davis, they struggled at the ropes to secure the throw, and both combatants went down, with Cyrus under. The first round occupied six minutes, and the supporters of Turner seemed satisfied with their man's performance, shouting that it 'was all right, the Ould one behaves well'.

Ned was the first to attempt an assault in the second round, shooting a well-meant left-handed blow at Davis's body. The sense of danger was playing on the minds of both men, and they seemed reticent to engage each other. Cyrus was eager to bring his favourite right-hand punch into play, and after a series of exchanges he sent Turner down, to the excitement of his supporters. The third round saw Davis come out 'piping' a little for breath as the Welshman continued to target the body. A number of exchanges took place, but the blows appeared light on both sides. At the end of the round, the slippery state of the turf meant that Turner went down from a slight hit. In the next round, Cyrus came up smiling and full of confidence, determined to land his telling right-hand blow, but Turner, demonstrating considerable skill, stopped him once more. In the struggle that followed, both went down. Whether it was bias on the part of Turner's followers or not, his supporters maintained that he was not having the worst of it; in fact there was no severity of punishment on either side. In closing, Turner had the best of the fibbing that followed, and he succeeded in securing first blood, although Davis managed to throw Turner at the end of the round. The sixth round saw Davis try to bring his left hand into play, although it only helped him to hold off his opponent. Some spirited fighting took place in this round, with Cyrus landing heavily on Turner in the fall.

Ned Turner was again seen to advantage in the next round, although had he not shown such exceptional judgement in stopping Davies's dangerous right hand, the contest would have soon drawn to a close. In the fibbing that followed, the Welshman had the advantage, and managed to secure the fall. Turner's supporters were clearly overjoyed at what they seemed to believe was a reversal in his fortunes, and started loudly shouting, 'Turner for ever!' The eighth round of the contest was the most exciting so far, and Ned threw his left hand hard into Davis's face, drawing the 'claret' from his nose and mouth. For an instant, Cyrus looked a little shaky on his pins, and received another hard body blow, but recovered well enough to launch a tremendous right hand, which sent Turner to the turf. 'It's all over,' shouted Cyrus's supporters. 'You have won it, Davis!' Turner's supporters began to fear the worst as their man came out at the start of the ninth, and it was clear that the terrible blow from the previous round had taken its toll. Although he came up to the scratch obviously weak and bleeding, Turner's courage was never in doubt. Cy Davis eagerly went to work, but to his credit, Ned returned fire and matched him hit for hit until he finally fell to the ground exhausted. The anxiety of his supporters was matched by his seconds and Jack Randall, Harry Holt and Dick Curtis rallied round Turner as he sat on his second's knee, advising the 'Ould One' on his strategy.

Encouraged by the support of his fellow pugilists, Ned came up to the scratch determined to do his best to secure the victory and he seemed to have no thought that he might lose the battle. Despite his confidence, it was clear that Turner was no longer the force he had once been, and the effects of his reckless lifestyle could no longer be concealed. Before long, Ned received a telling blow that sent him down again, to shouts of support from Davis's friends. Cy continued his assault in the following round, and landed a severe blow with his right hand to the body of Turner.

Ned stood up manfully and threw some skilful blows, until growing exhaustion forced a pause on both sides. Cyrus began sparring for wind, although he was smiling all the while. Turner was now bleeding from a severe blow to his left ear, and in trying to pursue his foe, he went down from either a slip or from a slight blow. With every round that passed Ned was fading, and although he was as game as ever, the truth was clear: his stamina was failing him, and his well was now all but dry. Jack Randall heaved a sigh at ringside, and exclaimed with great sorrow, 'I am afraid it is all over.'

Grimly, Turner fought on, and to the surprise of all, the 12th round showed him to excellent advantage. In spite of his distress, Turner's stops to Davis's blows were so skilfully executed that they drew forth applause from all corners of the ring. Not to be outdone, Cyrus continued to score with his punches, and his blows fell harder than Ned's. Turner fought on in vain, but at the close of the round he fell once more, overcome with fatigue. Although Ned continued to fight valiantly, there was no comparison in the strength of their punches. Cyrus's blows were far harder and although Ned matched him for milling, it was clear that his strength was rapidly flagging. The combatants followed each other all over the ring, exchanging punches until both men were puffing for wind. A struggle took place at the ropes and as both men fell, Turner was under. Their efforts were applauded by all. 'Well done, both,' was heard from all quarters.

Cyrus opened up the 14th round with a punch to the body with his right hand, but it was seen to fall rather low, 'Come,' said Josh Hudson, 'fight fair, recollect you are to hit above the waistband.' This was a good round but at the end Turner was again sent down exhausted. A group of anxious pugilists collected in Turner's corner and advised Ned on a strategy to try to secure the victory. Sadly, their advice assisted Turner little as in the next round, Davis had all the best of the hitting, and threw Turner, falling so heavily upon him that the shout quickly went up, 'He cannot come again'. Ned was so shaken by this throw that he was placed upon the knee of his second with great difficulty. It appeared as though the battle was now won.

Tom Belcher saw Ned Turner's distress so clearly in the following round that he was heard to suggest to Cyrus, 'Why not use both of your hands?' Josh Hudson was quick to take exception

Cyrus Davis jumps over the ropes after his defeat of Ned Turner.

to Belcher's remarks, saying that he had no business interfering in the fight and his decision to offer advice was unfair. 'It was not my intention to have said a single word,' replied Belcher, 'if I had not seen so many fighting men breaking in the ring, and, like Trueman's cocks,[139] all on one side. I have not one farthing on the battle; all I want is fair play.' Cy Davis took Belcher's suggestion and utilised both his fists, with Turner gamely opposing him until he was finally sent down. In the 17th round, Turner still met his man punch for punch, until at last, and quite exhausted, he was hit down. On coming up to the scratch, Cy went immediately to work with his right hand, and landed to Turner's body, sending him down in the twinkling of an eye. It was at this point that Jemmy Soares realised that Turner no longer stood any chance of victory and stepped forward, saying that 'he should not fight any more'. The fight thus ended in 18 rounds and 35 minutes. Cyrus at once approached Turner and shook hands with his fallen adversary, although Ned was by now too stupefied to realise that he had been beaten. Having overturned his defeat at the hands of Ned Turner, Cyrus Davis gave a jump for joy and made a victory cry before jumping over the ropes and leaving the battleground.

It appeared that Ned Turner had no one to blame but himself, having been in no condition to fight, and he afterwards freely

139 Trueman's Cocks – 'those persons who act truly by each other, in evil or in good'. *Sportsman's Slang: A New Dictionary of Terms Used in the Affairs of the Turf, etc.* by Jon Bee, (London: W. Lewis 1825).

admitted that he could not have fought another round, attributing the loss to fatigue and exhaustion. It was clear that Turner was a shadow of the fighter he had once been, although the brave and manly conduct of Cyrus Davis also drew favourable comment. Davis had fought from the seventh round onwards in considerable pain after his right hand had met with an injury, and it was very swollen afterwards. Unfortunately for Cyrus Davis, the victory was a pretty dear triumph, and it soon became apparent that the injury to his right hand was much worse than was first thought. The forefinger of his right hand had come into contact with Ned Turner's teeth, and was in a very poor state. The injury baffled the most skilful surgeons for some time, before it was finally decided that the finger must be amputated. With a useless right hand, Cyrus Davis was forced to announce his pugilistic retirement. The 'Gay Bristol Boy' was consequently never seen in the prize ring ever again, and he returned to his previous life as a publican.

Chapter 13

Enter the Phenomenon

Despite Ned Turner's efforts to repair his damaged constitution, it was clear that things were taking a downward turn in the career of the gallant Welshman. Owing to the absence of the guiding influence of 'Gentleman' John Jackson at the fight, the Fancy could not be compelled to offer up so much as a shilling to reward the efforts of 'Ould' Ned Turner. A benefit event held for Turner at the Fives Court on Thursday, 20 February 1823, was 'respectably attended', however. Tom Belcher and Harry Harmer, Bill Richmond and Tom Shelton, and a number of lesser lights demonstrated their skills on the stage. The best bout of the event was that between Dick Curtis and Jack Teasdale, which drew 'peals of applause' from an appreciative crowd. Jack Martin, Tom Spring, Jack Scroggins and Tom Cribb were all present, as was Cyrus Davis, who had sold a large number of tickets for the event to assist Ned in his time of need. After mounting the stage, Turner thanked the audience for their support, and expressed sadness at having lost his battle against Cyrus, admitting that 'although he had done his best to prove the conqueror', he had 'since found out that he had not time enough to restore an old constitution'. Furthermore, Turner stated that he hoped that the 'liberality of the amateurs towards him would never be erased from his heart', and the candid honesty of his words brought great applause from all corners of the Fives Court.[140]

Ned Turner had appeared the night before at Jack Randall's establishment, the Hole in the Wall, and was reportedly 'rather dejected on account of his defeat'. Ned had lamented that he had

140 As recorded in *Bell's Life in London and Sporting Chronicle*, 23 February 1823.

'found out, too late, that intemperance has been his only enemy'.[141] Somewhat predictably, in his depression at his loss to Davis, Ned Turner hit the 'blue ruin' once more and sought to drown his sorrows, with some sources claiming that Ned soon afterwards became a fixture at George Belshaw's establishments, the Gordon Hotel and the Britannia Tavern at the corner of James Street in Covent Garden. At Belshaw's a number of fighting men could be found, although mostly pugilists of the second rank. They were employed by the 'swells' as paid bouncers to accompany them on their evening adventures when venturing into the rougher areas of the city, and it might be imagined that Ned Turner found a useful way to prop up his income by joining the ranks of these lower-level pugilistic security guards. Despite his desire to win back his laurels in the prize ring, Turner's defeat by Cy Davis, and the manner in which his strength had broken down in the course of their battle, was uppermost in the minds of the sporting world, so he failed to secure any future contests, with the general opinion being that to back Ned would be to throw good money after bad. In April, an attempt had been made to match Ned against a pugilist known as 'Young' Weston (George), but brought little interest, and nothing came of it.[142] Another contest was reported as having been made against an unnamed Scotsman to take place within 20 miles of Manchester for 50 sovereigns on 6 October, but also faltered.[143]

In August, it had been announced that Ned Turner could be backed for £100 against Bishop Sharpe,[144] although attempts to bind this match also appear to have failed, as it was reported in October that 'some little surprise has been expressed among the amateurs, that a match has not been made between Bishop Sharp and Ned Turner, more especially as the late boxer is under the weight of Sharp'.[145] Soon afterwards, Dick Defoe, 'the Westminster champion', was stated to have been about to be matched to fight Ned Turner for £100 a-side. Ned's backers were perhaps reticent

141 As recorded in the *Morning Post,* 21 February 1823.

142 As recorded in the *Morning Post,* 21 April 1823.

143 As recorded in the *Hull Packet,* 1 September 1823.

144 As recorded in *Saunders's News-Letter,* 21 August 1823.

145 As recorded in the *Dublin Correspondent*, 11 October 1823.

to commit to the match, given that *Bell's Life* reported that, 'The match, in point of weight and science, is thought to be equal, both being about eleven stone; though some fears are entertained that Ned may have affected his stamina by copious libations of... Evans' blue ruin'.[146]

With interest flagging in Ned Turner's prize fighting career, there were no other potential opponents in 1823, and it wasn't until the following year that a brave new challenger stepped forward, eager to win further acclaim in the prize ring by defeating Turner. Ned had appeared at the Fives Court for the benefit event arranged to honour Bill Richmond in January of 1824, and was seen to make a 'very fine and a brave set to' against Gipsy Cooper.[147] There was little to excite the interest of the Fancy in the way of prize fights at this time; Tom Spring was 'inactive', Tom Belcher was behind the bar of the Castle Tavern and Tom Shelton was 'seldom heard of'. The *Morning Chronicle* was quick to summarise this disappointing state of affairs in early February, telling its readers that, 'Randall declares himself satisfied with the past. Martin has retired. Scroggins is used up. Turner is worn out. Harry Holt and Inglis are tongue and pen-sparring. Langan and Reynolds are both eager without the chance of a customer. Josh Hudson is as warm as ever in the cause, but his east-end friends think him too fat for combat.' With this fairly gloomy outlook, it was unsurprising that the *Chronicle* came to the conclusion that 'all confidence is at an end, and pugilism may be fairly considered on the decline'.[148]

It had apparently gone largely unnoticed by the sporting world that Ned Turner had been matched against Peace Inglis just a few days previously to fight for £50 a-side in six weeks time. Inglis had been engaged in a bitter war of words to try to get Harry Holt to fight him for £100 a-side, but with the possibility of a contest against the famous Welshman, the proposed fight against Holt went off. Despite concerns that Turner was 'worn out', Ned still had enough supporters willing to put their faith in him and he was

146 As recorded in *Bell's Life in London and Sporting Chronicle*, 26 October 1823.

147 As recorded in the *Morning Post*, 14 January 1824.

148 As recorded in the *Morning Chronicle*, 7 February 1824.

viewed as the 'favourite' for victory.[149] On Tuesday, 24 February 1824, Peace Inglis made an appearance at the Castle Tavern, wanting to make good on his stake of £50 to bind the match against Turner. Despite a limited amount of publicity announcing the contest, there was a large turn-out of the Fancy. Inglis was left waiting some time for Turner to appear, and expressed his doubts as to whether Ned would make good on the agreement to fight. It wasn't until after 10pm, and after 'Time' had been called on the matter, that Turner arrived in the company of Jack Randall. In short time, the signed articles were produced, and read as follows: 'The men to fight in a 24 foot roped ring – half-minute time – an umpire to be chosen by each – and a referee to be named by Mr Jackson. The fight on the 20th April, between twelve and two o'clock, and the whole stakes to be made good on the 6th April at Randall's'.

After some good-natured chaffing between Turner and Inglis, the £50 a-side was made good and deposited in the hands of the treasurer. The match having now been made, the two combatants made the toast 'May the best man win' before draining a glass of blackstrap.[150] Ned's supporters were quick to offer odds of 6/4, but there were no takers.[151] It was thought that the match might well be 'one of the best fights that has been for some years' as there was 'no lack either of courage or science' on either side.[152] Before going into training, another lucrative benefit event was organised for Ned Turner at the Fives Court, and the appearance of a host of pugilistic heroes ensured that the occasion was a success. Turner wound up proceedings with a set-to with Jack Randall, and the 'elegancies of science' between the Out-and-Outer and the Nonpareil were applauded by all, with Ned taking a bow at the end of the performance.[153]

Soon after this event, Ned Turner left London in the company of his brother-in-law, Mr Baxter, and fellow Welshman, Paddington Jones, and headed for Wales. Turner had elected

149 As recorded in the *Morning Advertiser*, 7 February 1824.

150 *Blackstrap* – an alcoholic drink made from rum and molasses.

151 As recorded in the *Public Ledger and Daily Advertiser*, 26 February 1824.

152 As recorded in the *Morning Advertiser*, 26 February 1824.

153 As recorded in the *Morning Post*, 27 February 1824.

to travel to Newtown in Montgomeryshire once more, hoping that training under the care of his uncle, Llewellyn Turner, might help restore strength and hardiness to his weakened frame. There would appear to have been a strategy on the part of Ned Turner in having engaged Paddington Jones to assist with his preparations, as 'Ould' Paddington had served as Peace Inglis's second in two of the three prize fights that had won Inglis the cognomen of 'the Phenomenon' among the Fancy. This impressive title had replaced his previous nickname of 'the Mattress Maker', which had been given to him by his friends, as the young pugilist was employed as a feather-bed maker outside his prize fighting career.

Peace Inglis had made his debut appearance in the ring less than a year and a half previously, on 22 October 1822,[154] when he fought a young waterman named Hamilton, considered one of the most promising students of Josh Hudson, and was seconded by Paddington Jones. To the disgust of Josh Hudson, his protégé was polished off by Inglis in 40 minutes and 28 rounds.[155] His next opponent was Bill Davis, better known as 'Deaf Davis', a man of some reputation, and they met at Harpenden Common near St Alban's on 18 February 1823, immediately after the second fight between Ned Turner and Cy Davis. It proved to be an extraordinary fight. Deaf Davis initially took the lead and punished Inglis so severely that it was feared that he might be killed within the first few rounds. Against all odds, Inglis rallied and hit Davis down shortly afterwards, and subsequently beat him to pieces. Deaf Davis was thrashed senseless in the eighth round in just eight minutes, amid scenes of excitement rarely witnessed before. It is perhaps to be wondered whether Peace Inglis, having witnessed the fight between Ned Turner and Cy Davis, might well have concluded even at this early stage of his pugilistic career that he might well be the man to take Turner's scalp. Inglis possibly formed the same conclusion that *Bell's Life* had drawn, the newspaper having commented on the Inglis vs.

---

154 There is some discrepancy in the date of this contest; *Fistiana* records the battle as having occurred on 23 October 1822, while *Pugilistica* records it as having taken place on 22 October 1822.

155 *Fistiana* records the duration as being 48 minutes and 28 rounds. *Pugilistica* records the contest as having taken 42 minutes.

Davis battle that, 'Davis, like Turner, is too stale for a young opponent'.[156]

The supporters of Peace Inglis tried to match him against Dick Curtis, but after reflecting on the matter, they were not so keen on making the match against such a battle-tested and well-regarded opponent. Instead, a match was made against Dick's brother, George Curtis. They fought at Moulsey Hurst on 12 August 1823, and Paddington Jones served as Inglis's second once more. It was the first time George Curtis had appeared within the prize ring, but his skill with the gloves was so well known that it was thought that the sporting world might witness the rise of a second 'Pet of the Fancy'. Their hopes were disappointed, however, and the young Phenomenon proved to be too strong for Curtis. His superior condition allowed him to outlast his foe, and he revealed himself to be a hard hitter with both hands, beating Curtis in 15 rounds and 55 minutes.

This was Peace Inglis's last appearance in the prize ring before the match against Ned Turner was agreed. Although he had only fought in the prize ring on three separate occasions prior to the contest in hand, he had proved himself to be a courageous fighter. The bravery of Inglis had been in evidence shortly before the match against Turner was made, when the house in Whitechapel in which Inglis resided had caught light. Inglis had been asleep and the house was almost completely consumed by flames before he woke up. With no thought for his personal safety, Peace crossed a single charred and flaming rafter, and rescued one of his sisters from her room, carrying her back across the treacherous beam to safety. Peace returned to the flaming inferno, and crossed the fragile bridge for a second time to reach his other sister, and also saved her life. The brave pugilist was afterwards thought to be exceedingly lucky to have received no injury other than having his hair scorched.[157]

Peace Inglis elected to train at Carshalton in Surrey, and was placed under the care of the veteran Isaac Bitton, conqueror of Paddington Jones. Turner undoubtedly had the harder job, and although favourable reports were sent to London from time to

---

156 As recorded in *Bell's Life in London and Sporting Chronicle*, 23 February 1823.

157 As recorded in the *Sussex Advertiser*, 8 March 1824.

Peace Inglis saves his sister from the roaring flames.

time of his progress in Wales, all was not well with 'Ould' Ned. A few weeks prior to the fight, Turner was struck down by a severe attack of inflammatory fever, which was thought to have been 'chiefly brought on by the intemperance in which he had so freely indulged'. His constitution was so shattered as to leave him enfeebled, and those doctors who examined him tried to dissuade him from continuing with the fight. As the stakes had already been laid on the contest, Turner felt that he had to continue with the match rather than forfeit the money already put down.[158]

158 As recorded in the *North Wales Gazette*, 25 November 1824.

The fight was fixed for Tuesday, 20 April 1824. It had initially been thought that Moulsey Hurst would be the battleground, although with the 'Beaks' having been angered by the decision to hold a prize fight on Easter Monday, it was decided that the village of Colnbrook was a better meeting place. The close proximity of the River Colne, dividing Middlesex and Buckinghamshire, was an additional bonus for the Fancy as they could easily hop from one county to the other and thus avoid the law of both. The nomination was kept secret until the day before the contest and was only made known to a select few to ensure that the village was not swarmed by less-desirable characters. Ned Turner arrived at Colnbrook on the Sunday before the battle, accompanied by his backers and friends. How aware they were of Turner's breakdown due to inflammatory fever in Wales can only be guessed, but there must have been some anxiety amongst his supporters. Ned had repeatedly pressed for one more opportunity to prove himself, following his defeats to Jack Martin and Cy Davis. It had been hoped that if he won the battle against the Phenomenon, Turner's share of the battle money might enable him to retire from the prize ring with his reputation intact, and solvent enough to pursue some other occupation. As always, the reckless manner in which Turner had lived his life stood uppermost in the minds of many, with *Bell's Life* commenting that in 'late years... his frequent defeats seem to have rendered him careless of his health, and with a view probably to drown care, his application to the daffy bottle has been so frequent, as almost entirely to undermine his constitution'[159].

A select gathering of the Fancy woke early on the Tuesday morning and took to the road towards Hounslow. There were all manner of vehicles on the move, but there was a scarcity of the riff-raff that would ordinarily be found on the journey to a fight. Rumour abounded as to the state of the combatants. Inglis was said to be in excellent condition, having been trained to a hair by Isaac Bitton, and he was being backed at 6/4 to win. Of Turner, reports were less than favourable, with it being whispered that, 'some of the best judges had kindly squeezed his *mawley*, and reported that it was hot and feverish, and he was far from that state which betokened good condition'.

---

159 As recorded in *Bell's Life in London and Sporting Chronicle,* 25 April 1823.

A field a little beyond the village of Colnbrook on the left-hand side of the road was chosen as the best spot to pitch the ring. Everything was now ready for the fight. Shortly before 1pm, the men appeared on the ground, and Turner was the first on the scene, accompanied by Josh Hudson and Paddington Jones. The initial impression of Ned was good, and his appearance was warmly received by all. A short delay occurred as Turner waited for the appearance of Inglis, Josh Hudson roaring out, 'Come, you Inglis! Where are you? Don't you like it? We are ready'. The Phenomenon immediately appeared, accompanied by his seconds, Maurice Delay and Dan M'Kenzie. Turner was the first to enter the ring, appearing both cool and collected. Inglis followed, throwing up his hat with bravado and confidence. At ringside, Jack Martin and Turner's faithful friend, Jack Randall, cheered the appearance of Turner, observing that, 'things must be come to a pretty pass indeed if such a man were floored by a *bag of feathers*'. Ned's dark blue colours were tied to the stakes, followed by the light blue of Inglis, and the stage was set for the fight.

Despite the confidence of Jack Randall and Jack Martin, on stripping for the battle it was clear that Peace Inglis was in far superior condition to Ned Turner. The Welshman was a 'shadow of himself' and although his face showed 'all the calculating firmness and caution of a good old general, it was clear that he foresaw he had a hard day's work cut out for him'. Youth and freshness was on Inglis's side, and he had every motivation to fight to the bitter end, having been so eager to engage Turner in battle that he and his brother had pooled their resources and had staked £52 of the battle money, with £48 being made up by subscription.

As the two men stepped up to the scratch, Ned Turner's eyes brightened as if a flash of his former victories in the ring revived his vigour. The moment of reckoning having now arrived, Inglis appeared nervous and both men settled into sparring for the first opening. Inglis carefully went about his work, and his muscular superiority was much in evidence, although Turner, undeterred, brought his right hand into play. Turner stopped a few of the Phenomenon's blows before throwing a hard left hand that forcibly landed on his throat, to a thunderclap of applause. Another left hand landed on Inglis's stomach that drew forth a discordant squeak from the mattress maker before Inglis was sent to the turf with a bump. The first round thus having ended with a 'floorer' for Turner, the ring resounded with cheers for the 'ould one'. As Inglis came out for the second round, the marks on his throat were visible to all, and again Turner showed to good advantage, 'nobbing' Inglis on the 'canister' repeatedly with his left hand. Josh Hudson was delighted and bellowed 'the day is our own'. A few more nasty punches to the mouth saw Turner gain first blood from Inglis's 'ivory case', and a few more saw the Welshman 'draw the cork' from the mattress maker's nose. 'First blood! My eye, what a hobble you have got into, my covey', exclaimed Josh Hudson with delight.

Peace Inglis was in no way daunted and held his ground; he received a facer for his trouble but succeeded in returning on Turner's body. Turner 'nobbed' his foe again, which drew further approval from the excitable Hudson, who wondered with admiration, 'Talk of Old Ones, is there anything like the good Old Ones?' Jack Randall was similarly impressed with Turner's performance, offering 50/20 on his friend. Inglis tried to push into close range but Turner was wise to his plans and caught him under his arm, in readiness for 'fibbing'. Inglis wrestled for the fall until at length both went down, with Turner under.

Ned Turner landed some telling left-hand punches in the third, although Inglis was now wary of being fibbed at close quarters, and commenced sparring. His wariness was justified; in the close Turner swung around and attempted to grab Inglis again, but he was unsuccessful and fell. Ned's superior fighting skills were much in evidence and Inglis took a great number of punches, which he attempted to return in kind. The Phenomenon sparred for an opening but got a hard punch on the 'nozzle' for his pains and Turner repeated his visits to Inglis's 'nob' several times with both right and left, although he did not receive a scratch in return. It was a long and arduous round and in the close Turner went down, visibly weakened from his exertions.

From the fifth round to the tenth, it was all Turner, and he continued to stop Inglis's blows, while landing with his left. Inglis succeeded in giving Turner a 'clink on the gob' in the fifth, which made him spill a little claret, but Turner quickly returned the favour, and in the rally that followed it was clear that Turner was proving superior to his foe. At the close of the fifth, a body blow sent Turner down, although he appeared to go down more through tiredness than actual punishment. In the seventh, Turner continued to punish the head of Inglis and sent his blood splashing after landing a blow under the chin. Inglis fought on, his youthful strength coming to his aid, although Turner was all alive and stopped a number of heavy blows. In the rally that followed it was hit for hit, but Turner's punches told more tales and the nose of the Phenomenon was streaming blood by the end of the tenth round.

'Come, Scroggin's ruin,' exclaimed Hudson as the 11th round began. 'We are at home, we have won it'. Although Ned Turner's weakness was now evidently growing, he fought bravely on, landing on his opponent with the greatest of ease, and his 'mawleys' were seen to travel 'steady and heavy to their destination'. He had everything his own way, although at the end he went down through tiredness once more. The manner of Turner's assault astonished the spectators in the following round, and he hit Inglis as and when he pleased with a one-two that fell with the 'rapidity of lightning', leaving visible marks of his handywork. Inglis weathered the storm and following a sharp exchange of blows, Turner went down. 'Bravo! Well done both sides!' cried the Fancy. It was now thought that the Welshman must win, if his stamina held up. 'Such another round and it's your own,' cried Josh Hudson. Taking the hint, Turner gathered all his energy and went to work, exhibiting 'the skill of a master'. Hitting Inglis right and left, Ned appeared to be getting the better of his man, stopping all his opponents blows, but in the close he went down once more, exhausted by his exertions. By now Ned was breathing heavily, but despite his growing weariness he still managed to hold Inglis off, but had any of the Phenomenon's blows reached their destination, it was felt that a change would be witnessed in the course of the fight. Turner continued plugging away with his one-two, but Inglis rushed in after landing a punch to the body, and Turner fell weak without a follow-up blow.

Ned's astonishing game was still in evidence in the 15th round as he threw off the shackles of age and contrived to take the lead once more, nobbing his antagonist with astonishing energy, right and left. 'If Ned does not tire,' said an old ring-goer, 'he must win the battle; but he has too much work to perform'.

Inglis could not keep Turner's hands out of his face but he was as strong as ever and at the close of the round he bored in, and Ned went down again. In the 16th round, Ned Turner's superiority was still in evidence, and while Inglis occasionally planted a blow, they were not of sufficient strength to reduce the activity of Turner. At the close, Ned succeeded in fibbing and then throwing his man, accompanied by a great cheer from all corners of the ring. Josh Hudson was still as vocal as ever in his support of Turner, announcing, 'A fine old cock, this Ned is,' as the Welshman came out for the 17th. 'This is the weather for the old cocks to tip it them.' Ned was told to go in and finish but this was no easy task as although Inglis had been punished, he was still fresh. Turner stopped all the heavy blows directed at him in beautiful style. The fight reached the 38-minute mark and Turner, to the surprise of all, though tired, was still fighting manfully, although at the close he went down again. In the following round, Peace Inglis fought at close range and hit Turner right and left in the face before throwing him in the close.

Seeing that his man was flagging, it fell to Josh Hudson's talent as a second to encourage and support Ned Turner, and before the 19th round he gave Ned a few sips from his brandy bottle to invigorate him. It seemed to do the trick and an excellent rally followed in which Turner had all the best of the fighting, although he was once again thrown by Inglis, whose youthful strength appeared undimmed. Ned came up as game as ever in the 20th and after having collected his strength, he hit Peace a tremendous blow on the mouth and floored him to deafening applause from the spectators. The exertions of Turner were now beginning to tire him, and although he continued to land punches on Inglis with some success, the feather-bed maker was undaunted, and at the close Ned chose to go down after a slight 'facer' to avoid receiving further punishment. The Phenomenon now showed signs of Turner's handiwork and his left eye was nearly entirely closed. Turner continued to punish him at length, and had he not missed with one particularly hard, well-aimed blow, it seemed likely that Ned might well have finished Inglis. Turner's strength was waning fast, and although as game as ever, he 'staggered to his work like a *lushy* one'.

Peace Inglis's supporters thought he should have won long beforehand and it was something of a surprise to them that Ned Turner had stood before their man so long. Although Turner continued to go down at the close of the rounds, he was seen to throw the harder punches. In the 25th round, Ned again showed that he was not to be underestimated and attacked Inglis with a vengeance, hitting right and left, landing four successive blows, with one 'jobber' on the 'muzzle' bringing forth a 'purple stream' from the nose of Inglis. After a few more swigs of brandy to strengthen Ned's resolve, the 26th round proved to be a tremendous one. Although Inglis had been hit to pieces, he fought like a bull-dog. After a heavy rally, Ned closed and threw Inglis to the turf. The reaction at ringside was jubilant. 'What a round! Here's a fight! Why, it is worth going to see if it had been five hundred miles from London!' they cried.

The Phenomenon continued to bore in to close range. Although Turner now appeared groggy, he could not be touched at stand-up fighting and continued to hit away when Inglis attacked. The condition of the mattress maker was extremely bad by the 30th round, and Turner continued to punch him about his head until at length Peace slipped down to the turf through weakness. Wise to Peace's tactic of boring in, Ned retreated in the 31st round, continuing to punish him as Inglis advanced, before a struggle occurred at the ropes, in which Inglis fell over. As he was falling, with his knee on the ground, Turner accidentally hit him on the neck to cries of 'Foul!' from Inglis's supporters. It was not an intentional foul on the part of Turner and the umpires pronounced that it had not been meant unfairly. Ned's face appeared little the worse for wear, although the superior strength of Peace was beginning to take its toll. The Welshman was hit heavily and took more punishment in the 33rd round than he had in any of the preceding ones. From the 35th round until the 38th, Ned continued to land almost at will on Peace Inglis and had it not been for the courage and stamina of the Phenomenon, it seemed likely that Inglis would have been beaten long before this period of the battle. Grimly, Peace Inglis battled on, pursuing the notion that 'Ould Ned' could not last. At the close of the 38th round, Inglis fell heavily on to the ropes and into Turner.

The Fancy were astonished to see Turner successfully fend off Inglis's attacks and take the lead in such a superior manner against such a young and strong opponent. Each time Inglis bored in, Turner would launch an uppercut and every time it landed, the 'claret flowed in profusion'. The sun was now beating down on the ring and between rounds Ned appeared languid as he sat on the knee of his second, and it was only when fighting that he appeared to be fully alive. Despite his obvious fatigue, he continued to land on Inglis's face and head with the greatest of ease, and the Phenomenon was almost hit to a standstill in the 42nd round.

'Go in, Inglis,' cried his friends. 'You can't lose if you do.'

Taking their advice, Inglis forced the battle to close range, fighting furiously until Turner went down.

Ned was not defeated yet, however, and the 44th round nearly decided the battle in his favour. It was hit for hit until Turner punched his foe to a standstill. Refusing to give Inglis a chance, he planted another blow on the head and it was only the great courage of the mattress maker that saw him weather the storm, fighting like a lion until the Out-and-Outer finally went down. 'Bravo Inglis!' cried the Phenomenon's supporters. 'Your fellow is not to be met with every day in the week.'

Peace Inglis continued to rush in but was punished each time by Turner. Ned doggedly fought on but his strength could no longer keep pace with his skill, and in the 46th round he again went down through his exhaustion, to the dismay of his friends. 'Take the good Old One away. If he wins, he cannot raise himself higher in the estimation of the Fancy,' they shouted, adding, 'The chance is against him.' Their fears proved to be correct, and the 47th round was Turner's last. It was well fought and both men were visibly distressed, although the youth of Peace Inglis came to his aid. Despite his injuries, he could almost be thought of as 'fresh' compared to his game opponent. Ned Turner made one last expiring effort, before Inglis, gathering all his strength, landed one last tremendous punch, which sent Turner down. While Turner was sitting on the knee of his second, a number of concerned onlookers said he should not fight any more. Harry Holt could not watch any longer and jumped into the ring, throwing his hat in the air and declaring, 'Permit me, gentlemen, to give in for Turner.' Ned was so weak that he was unable to protest, and although he would not say he had had enough, his silence voiced his weary consent. The battle had lasted an hour and 18 minutes. In his excitement, Peace Inglis immediately scrambled out of the ring to receive the congratulations of his uncle and brother-in-law, and

'Fifty pounds to twenty on Turner', cried Jack Randall.

the Phenomenon then returned to the ring to shake the hand of his fallen opponent.

Ned Turner had fought bravely and it was afterwards remarked that 'never did age, science, and experience so admirably resist youth, strength and sound bottom'.[160] Ned had proved to be the superior fighter until after the 30th round, when his strength had started to fail him, although his skills had dazzled as brightly as ever and even in the face of defeat. Although the pugilistic ability of Peace Inglis was applauded, it was clear that he would not have stood a chance against the Ned Turner of yesteryear, who had defeated Scroggins and Martin and who had stood before Jack Randall for over two hours. Although he had lost, Ned had only received a trifling degree of punishment, whereas Peace Inglis was bruised, beaten and bleeding long before the end of the contest. The manliness, courage and strength that had been demonstrated by the Phenomenon ensured that his performance was afterwards applauded by the sporting world, although it was with sadness that it had to be admitted that, 'Ned was not licked; he was tired, worn out, and Nature refused to second his efforts'.[161]

---

160 As recorded in *Bell's Life in London and Sporting Chronicle,* 25 April 1824.

161 As recorded in *Pugilistica.*

Chapter 14

The Pugilistic Prince of Wales

Ned Turner found the defeat to Peace Inglis impossibly galling by virtue of the fact that Inglis, despite his impressive title of 'The Phenomenon', was a comparative novice in the prize ring. Following a benefit event that was held for Turner at the Cock and Cross in Redcross Street, East Smithfield, on 6 May 1824[162], Turner challenged Inglis to a rematch for £100. Peace Inglis appeared ready to do battle against Ned again if his supporters could be persuaded to back him, having been reportedly unwilling to risk his own money on a second match against Turner.[163] Although Ned was keen to fight Inglis and prove that he was the better man, his supporters were in favour of his retirement from the ring, having known that his 'convivial habits' were 'against his pugilistic exertions'.[164] A deposit was made for a match soon afterwards, but it seems that Turner's friends forfeited on the deposit and elected to make a new match for October, so that their man might have a longer training period and more time to repair his damaged health.[165] As it happened, Ned was allowed a little more time than they had hoped and an agreement was made in August for the fight to come off in November.[166]

Once again, the President of the Daffy Club, James Soares, had come to Ned Turner's aid, and announced that he was willing to assist in raising the battle money on Ned's behalf. Ned was also

---

162 As recorded in the *Morning Advertiser*, 5 May 1824.

163 As recorded in the *Morning Chronicle*, 6 May 1824.

164 As recorded in the *Morning Advertiser*, 5 July 1824.

165 As recorded in the *Morning Chronicle*, 21 July 1824.

166 As recorded in *Bell's Life in London and Sporting Chronicle*, 15 August 1824.

lucky enough to secure a new and liberal patron in a young Welsh squire, Mr Llewellyn Lloyd. Lloyd was a native of Montgomeryshire and a grandnephew of the veteran Welsh sportsman and one-time backer of Daniel Mendoza, Sir Thomas Apreece. With the pride of Wales at stake, Llewellyn Lloyd stated his willingness to stand for half of Turner's battle money, as well as paying his training expenses. As it had always been found that the bracing Welsh air was the best restorative for Ned's health, it was decided that he should undergo his training at Newtown in Montgomeryshire once more. Old Paddington Jones was engaged to assist Ned in his preparations and travelled to Wales in the company of the broken-down hero, along with his faithful brother-in-law, Mr Baxter, and his new patron, Llewellyn Lloyd.

The news that Ned Turner was to fight Peace Inglis for the second time was received with a great deal of interest by the Welsh supporters of Turner. For this reason, the *North Wales Gazette* begrudgingly published a report on the match, duplicating the following report 'from a London paper', stating its 'regret that the *fancy* in some of our readers, demands such statements':

> Ned Turner is the pugilistic Prince of Wales – the champion of the West Britons. When he was beaten by Randall in his best day, there was great wailing and sorrow among his people; but when he was vanquished by Inglis, last spring, the whole principality was in despair. The sides of Penmaen Mawr grew black with mortification, while its head lost itself in cloud clad in eternal snows, in mourning, after the Chinese fashion – The vale of Langollen became a vale of tears – every brook swelled to a torrent of indignation, and from Cernioge to Tredegar, all was lamentation, and woe! To be beaten by Randall was painful enough – but to be demolished by a bed-maker, as Inglis was – by a pugilistic chamberlain – by a ticker of feathers, was beyond Welch endurance! Taffy was thunderstruck – Cambria was in consternation, and were it not for one Mr. Llewellyn ap Jenkins ap Lloyd, who plucked up courage to put down money for another try for the honour of his country, no one can tell what might have been the consequence on so sensitive a people.

> Like Dr. Morgan, in Rodrick Random, he exclaimed, "we will put valour in his pelly and strength in his limbs, and peradventure we shall behold what we shall see." A new match was made, and Turner was taken in hand-nursed with goat's whey, and fed upon strong ale, to repair all the havoc which late hours and gin punch had made in his constitution. Few men have been in a worse way than honest Ned; he had not only to repair a shattered frame, but to stifle an attachment for ardent spirits to which he was almost a victim – but be it said to his credit, that out of gratitude to his backer, he carefully abstained from the excess, and underwent the severities of training without relaxation, until he improved his stamina, and rallied the energies of his nature, as far as early hours, hard work, and regular living could go, to recruit a man of four and thirty, with a constitution of another score.[167]

Ned Turner's arrival in Newtown was met with concern on the part of his Welsh supporters, who were less than reassured by the poor state of his health. With such an important contest on the cards, the opinions of the local medical advisors who had been consulted following Turner's breakdown due to an attack of inflammatory fever prior to his first contest against Peace Inglis were sought. They decided that the best course of action was for Ned to relocate to Llandrindod Wells, where he was committed to 'a course of the Llandrindod waters'. It was hoped that the 'salubrious effects' of the 'celebrated springs' might assist as a restorative to Turner's physical health that would enable him to enter the ring 'in such condition as to render victory certain'.[168]

Ned Turner remained in Wales until October, returning to London to complete his training under the watchful eye of the veteran pugilist, Tom Owen, at Walton-on-Thames, while Peace Inglis decided to undergo his training at Carshalton. The condition of Inglis was exceptional even before having entered into training and his strength was furthered by his subsequent exertions. It must be said that Peace was not a particularly popular

---

167 As recorded in the *North Wales Gazette*, 18 November 1824.

168 As recorded in the *North Wales Gazette*, 18 November 1824.

Ned Turner returns to London from Newtown, Wales, with his health restored.

pugilist amongst the followers of the ring. He was 'simple in his habits, demure in his manners' and did not drink, and was never heard to have indulged in any excess. In point of fact, the Phenomenon drew a sharp contrast in every respect to Turner. Even his friends might be heard to agree that 'a little spice of the Devil would qualify him better for the Ring'.[169] The sober and abstemious habits of Peace Inglis brought little patronage from the Fancy, and he experienced some difficulty in gaining support before finding a sporting gentleman willing to lay down stakes on his behalf. It was said that Inglis laid as much as £60 of his own money to cover his share, with the rest being made up mostly by his brother and father, and a few friends. By the end of his training period, it was reported that the Phenomenon was not only 5lbs heavier than when he had last engaged Turner, but that in terms of strength and pugilistic 'science', he had greatly improved.

It was perhaps more with the sympathy for an old favourite that the sporting men of London gathered to wish good luck to Ned Turner on his return to the metropolis a few days prior to the fight. It could not be imagined that 'Poor Old Ned' had much chance of beating his young, strong opponent. A sudden and quite unexpected change took place after Turner presented himself

169 As recorded in the *North Wales Gazette*, 18 November 1824.

before the Fancy on his return from Wales. Ned was greeted by his doubters with astonishment; the sickliness that had marked his appearance prior to his departure had been 'completely removed'. The Welsh pugilist was a changed man in every respect, appearing strong, active and hearty, with a 'healthful glow on his cheek' that had bloomed in his absence. Ned Turner was also nearly three-quarters of a stone heavier, and he had abandoned his hard drinking habits in his desire to defeat Inglis. Any notion as to the likelihood of the Phenomenon's youth ensuring his victory was set aside, and the old admirers of Ned Turner rallied round him with renewed faith to such a degree that a few days prior to the fight, he was being freely backed at 5/4.

The day of the contest was fixed for 9 November 1824, which was thought to be a wise decision as it fell on the same date as the Lord Mayor's pageant. This procession, which followed the Mayor from Guildhall to Westminster and back again, was undoubtedly a greater draw to the ruffians, thieves, pickpockets and blackguards who were frequently found plying their trades amongst the crowds surrounding the ring of a prize fight. Finding such lucrative opportunities on their doorstep on the streets of London ensured few of these rogues felt any necessity to travel 20 miles in search of plunder, so on the day of the fight it was only the admirers of pugilism who elected to journey to Colnbrook, where the fight was to take place at the same location where the first Turner vs Inglis contest had been fought. A large number of Ned's old patrons decided to make the journey from London, pleased at the prospect that Turner might retrieve his fame, and make an exit from the prize ring in a manner that would do credit to his dazzling early career inside the ropes.

The stakes and ropes had been pitched by the Commissary of the Pugilistic Club, Bill Gibbons, with assistance from his Deputy Commissary, Joe Fishwick. On the field of battle, a host of catering tents had sprung up, seeking to take advantage of the sense of occasion. Amongst their number was Jack Scroggins, who had seen an opportunity to make some money and adorned his cart with a notice advertising his stocks of bread and beef to feed those who had trotted and tramped so many miles to witness the fight. As the hour of battle grew ever nearer, and as greater numbers of horses and carriages appeared on the scene, it became apparent that the prospect of seeing Turner in action one last time had drawn forth a greater assembly of gentlemen than had been seen at a prize fight for many years. The 'Nobles of the land, gallant cavaliers and fanciers of the real sort' who travelled to see the fight were said to have included such prominent ring patrons as Lord Fife, Lord Yarmouth, Lord Longford, Lord Gwydyr (a strong supporter of Turner), Lord Petersham, Lord Henry Seymour and a few noblemen of lesser fame. The most surprising spectator to be seen on the battleground was Sir Thomas Ap Rhys (Apreece), now past his 80th year. Ap Rhys had been induced to attend the contest by his grandnephew, Llewellyn Lloyd, who had wanted the old baronet to see Ned Turner uphold the honour of Wales in what was likely to be his last performance in the prize ring.

At one o'clock, Ned Turner was driven to the ground by an 'aristocratic' carriage drawn by four horses, having waited for the hour of battle at a nearby inn. His appearance was greeted with loud cheers, and after stepping down from his carriage Turner was surrounded by admirers wishing to shake his hand. Advancing to the ring, Ned threw in his hat with conviction and was attended by his seconds, Harry Holt and Tom Shelton. Shortly afterwards, Peace Inglis arrived at the battleground, accompanied by Jem Ward and Ned O'Neal (the Streatham Youth), looking as though he was in the pink of health and greeted by a crowd of well-wishers. Stepping up to the ring he threw his hat but due to the force of the throw, and a sudden gust of wind, it was carried beyond the ring before falling to the turf. It was undoubtedly something that caused the supporters of Peace Inglis a degree of concern – for a hat to fall outside of the ring was long perceived by the Fancy as an ill omen. All being now in readiness for the fight, the spectators were driven back and Ned Turner and Peace Inglis stripped ready for battle.

It was obvious that Ned showed considerable improvement in the contours of his frame, and looked like a new man, being a far cry from the emaciated and wasted figure he had cut on previous occasions. 'Old Ned' took up his position at the scratch in his familiar and awkward stance with his right leg foremost, like Bishop Sharpe and Bendigo, a position that made him exceedingly difficult to get at, as all his opponents, and particularly Scroggins, had found to their cost. Peace Inglis also prepared for battle and it was clear that he was in the best possible condition for the contest.

The two combatants drew a stark contrast. Turner showed the calm, determined manner in which he approached every battle between the ropes. Inglis appeared fresh and youthful by comparison, and his face revealed a determination to take danger by the horns and boldly stand up to his experienced foe, in the hope of seizing victory once more.

A hushed silence fell around the ring as 'Time' was called. Ned Turner was the first to advance, with his eye steadily fixed on his youthful rival. Peace Inglis seemed to shrink a little as he retreated but the Welshman followed him and covered him with scientific precision. As Turner advanced, Inglis stepped back, almost to the corner of the ring. After some dodging, Inglis threw a few blows at Turner's head, which did not bother his opponent, and broke free of the corner. Turner stopped and tried to catch Inglis with an uppercut, but Inglis managed to avoid it. Ned's supporters were elated, shouting, 'Well done, Turner, that's the way to finish him.' Ned continued to follow Inglis as the Phenomenon broke ground before him, landing his right hand on the head of Inglis, which staggered the mattress maker. 'Beautiful!' exclaimed Turner's backers. In his eagerness, Ned launched himself at his opponent but in doing so he laid himself open to a heavy right-hander that landed between his eyes and made them water. The strength of this blow alarmed Turner's backers, and for a moment the face of Jack Randall took on a serious aspect, revealing his anxiety for the safety of his friend. Luckily, Ned was quick to recover and he went in again, launching another uppercut, which, had it got home, would have greatly shortened the battle. The Phenomenon was very quick on his legs and narrowly dodged the blow. For all his activity, Inglis found it impossible to break through his opponent's guard. At length, Ned Turner planted a slashing hit, knocking Inglis down on one knee. Cries of joy, hands clapping and roars of celebration were heard all round the ring from Turner's supporters as the first round ended.

Ned was determined not to give another chance away and every time it seemed as if his concentration had begun to wane, Harry Holt was heard to roar out, 'Look out, he's coming with his right hand.' Ned Turner meant to win this time and would not allow himself to be worn down until he was no longer physically strong enough to beat his foe. Inglis trusted in bobbing and ducking and while he launched some heavy-handed blows, Turner stopped them and the Phenomenon received plenty back in return for his efforts. Ned fought on with a measure of the spirit of the Turner of old and struck out with the severity and precision that had carried him to victory in all his great fights. Towards the close of the round, Ned landed a blow of such fearsome force on the nose of Inglis that the blood spurted out in a jet, leaving the feather-bed maker dazed and confused. A cry immediately went up, 'Bravo, Turner; the ould one is a little bit stronger than he was last time.' In the scuffle that followed, Inglis was seen to land a few shots and a couple of drops of blood appeared on Turner's face before both combatants went down.

The third round proved to be a short one; Ned had proved himself to be the hero of the first stage of the fight, but there were still concerns regarding his strength and stamina. Turner's friends looked grave. 'If he can but last, it's as safe as the bank,' they murmured. The nose of Inglis was looking a little worse for wear as he retreated to the corner of the ring once more, pursued by Turner, who appeared determined that the Phenomenon should not escape. Inglis was again forced to fight his way out, driving Ned before him by threatening him with a 'facer'. Warming to his game, he tried to creep in to land a body blow on Turner, but was stopped. Inglis was lucky to escape without a return but in the close he succeeded in boring Turner down at the ropes. The fourth saw Peace retreating with marked caution as Turner advanced, until the Welshman planted two heavy hits in succession with right and left to the feather-bed maker's head. Inglis, as strong as ever, was undismayed by the blows and threw some punches of his own, but in the close for the throw Ned was triumphant in sending the Phenomenon to the turf once more. Turner again pushed for the advantage in the following round and in closing received a blow to the face, which was followed by a sly punch to the body from Inglis. The odds on Turner increased considerably as the round ended, when Ned caught his foe with an uppercut that dropped Inglis to the turf accompanied by a cheer from his supporters. 'It's all your own,' they cried.

Turner's confidence was growing round by round and he again went in to fight, and although Inglis broke away he caught a staggering blow that sent him twirling round in a state of confusion. Inglis managed to regain his balance, and boldly closed on Turner, hitting him severely to the throat in the rally that followed. In the wrestling at the end of the round, Inglis was thrown once more. Spurred on by his successes, Ned opened the seventh with a right to the temple, but his distance was off. Inglis fought back gamely, and threw a number of skilful counter-punches, but they lacked the power to make any serious impression on his antagonist. The Welshman was now beginning to tire of his exertions and was blowing increasingly hard as the round wore on. The feather-bed maker pushed to close range, and good stops were seen on both sides, but Peace paid the price, receiving a blow to the mouth for his efforts, and returning in kind to Turner's chest. He attempted to repeat the feat, but was stopped each time, until at last he caught Ned under his guard and beneath his waistband with his right hand. Feeling the blow, Turner pointed to where it had landed, saying that it had been a foul blow, accompanied by cries of 'Fair' and 'Foul' from all sides, although the umpires took no notice. Long sparring followed, with both combatants appearing grateful for a pause in the proceedings. Turner attempted to throw a slashing hit at the head of Inglis, but the Phenomenon was as cautious as ever, and bobbed to avoid the blow. Immediately afterwards, Inglis rushed to close range, pushing Turner back towards the ropes, although he could not land any significant punches as Ned was shrewdly covering himself with great judgement. At length, Peace closed and grappled Ned in an effort to secure the cross-buttock throw, although the Out-and-Outer slipped from his grasp, and in retreating fell to the turf, finally bringing a long and exhausting round to a close.

The eighth round saw cautious sparring on both sides, with neither combatant wanting to risk leaving an opening or throw a chance away. Finally, Inglis rushed into close range but in the struggle that followed, the veteran had the advantage and both men went down, with Inglis under. At the start of the ninth, Ned again proved to have the measure of the mattress maker, landing on the side of the head of Inglis with his right, and drew the Phenomenon's counter, which twice landed on Turner's chest. Squaring up for a tremendous body blow, Inglis's efforts were seen to be in vain as Turner stopped the blow with ease. The superiority of Ned was witnessed soon after when he caught Peace around the neck, and getting his man into chancery, punished him at length, locking his head underneath one arm while 'fibbing' away with the other, and afterwards continued to hit and get away from his youthful opponent. The Phenomenon valiantly fought on but it was Turner who came to the front once more, landing twice on the nose and making his opponent's blood flow copiously. Harry Holt was as alert as ever, warning Ned of the advance of Inglis. Although Turner was now breathing heavily from his exertions, he profited greatly from his second's advice until at length he dropped Inglis with a right hand to the head. Jubilant cries of 'It's all over' were heard amongst the supporters of Turner and 6/1 was now being offered on his victory.

Despite the bloody and battered appearance of Peace Inglis, he again came up at the call of time. The Phenomenon's supporters still clung to the slimmest of hopes that his physical strength might overcome Ned's science and strategy. A terrific blow came from Turner's right, which Inglis was lucky to duck. Turner's supporters cried 'Steady, Ned', fearing that victory might still slip through their man's fingers. Inglis rushed to close range, and attempted to rally, but was met with a punch flush on his nose, which brought instant grogginess. Despite the severity of the blow, Inglis would not fall until a punch that was 'almost severe enough to have knocked a stone out of a wall' finally floored him. By now, cries of 'Take him away, he's a brave fellow' were starting to be heard around the ring.

It was now becoming evident that Peace Inglis could not win. He staggered about like a drunken man, his courage was unshaken, but he had little strength left. Showing his bravery to the last, Inglis hit out boldly but his punches were stopped. Ned moved into close range to finish his handiwork and caught Inglis with an uppercut. As Inglis started to go down, Turner was in a position whereby he might have thrown a finisher, but refused to take any advantage and walked away with his hands held up, and brave Peace Inglis fell down, nearly 'choked with blood'.

It was obvious that Peace Inglis no longer stood a chance in the 12th round, which ended in an instant. Inglis came up to the scratch and was immediately floored with a 'dreadful facer'. Again the spectators cried out, 'Take the brave fellow away.' As 'Time' was called for the 13th, the Phenomenon's seconds tried in vain

The Fancy congratulates Ned Turner on his triumph over Peace Inglis, 'the Phenomenon'.

to rouse him from his stupor. They were forced into shaking Peace Inglis into consciousness and roaring, 'Ned's coming' in his ear, and when they did, Inglis opened his eyes wildly and frantically prepared to fight, as if responding on instinct alone. Inglis rushed out to meet Turner once more, but it was only to be hit down again. Somehow, Peace managed to come out for the 14th but having now been hit ragged, he was again punched to the turf. A hat was thrown in the air, which was taken as the signal for Ned Turner's victory, but it was ignored and Peace staggered up to the scratch for what proved to be the 15th and final round.

Peace Inglis was by now barely conscious and had suffered a tremendous amount of punishment, and rolled and reeled about the ring as Turner viewed him with compassion, refusing to attack. Finally, the brave Phenomenon lurched forward and fell upon his face in a stupor without having received a single blow. After 46 minutes and 15 rounds of hard fighting, Ned Turner had finally triumphed over the brave Peace Inglis to tumultuous applause from his ecstatic supporters.

Chapter 15

Alas, Poor Ned

Alas, poor Ned! –
He's floor'd-he's dead;
His fighting days are ended.
The *Champion* DEATH
Has stopp'd his breath;
His *bellows* can't be *mended.*

('Elegiac Stanzas on the Death of Ned Turner', by Frosty-Faced Fogo, Poet Laureate of the Ring, *Bell's Life in London and Sporting Chronicle*, 30 April 30 1826)

The victory of Ned Turner over Peace Inglis was celebrated enthusiastically by all of the Welshman's supporters who had believed that despite his physical decline, Turner's undoubted ability as a scientific pugilist would enable him to defeat his youthful opponent. *Bell's Life* would afterwards pay ample tribute to the bravery of both pugilists, commenting:

> Turner, by this victory, has regained his lost credit, and has proved that, although a stale man, he is one of the best generals of the age. For scientific excellence, and determined game, he has scarce a superior. His victory also affords another illustration of the advantages of good training. Such was the admirable manner in which he covered his person, that few blows of any consequence reached him, and he may be said to have won almost without a scratch. Of Inglis, it is impossible to speak but in terms of warm eulogium; from the first round it was clear he was opposed to his superior, and indeed he seemed so

> to feel himself from his system of retreat; nevertheless he did not shrink from the attack, but went in at all hazards to do his best. In the last few rounds he proved that he had no personal fear; and it was evident that it was nature, and not his heart, which at last cried "enough". Had Turner been in condition when he fought him on the former occasion, he never could have had a chance, nor would he have been exposed to the mortification of having his hard earned laurels torn from his brow. A fairer or a better fight was never witnessed, and we are glad to add, that good order prevailed throughout. A few such days will restore the character of the Ring.[170]

Some sources record that after the initial excitement of Ned Turner's victory had subsided, the Welshman went to Inglis's corner, where Peace lay in a half-dazed state with his head supported by Jem Ward's knee. Shaking the hand of Inglis, Ned is said to have pressed two £5 notes into the Phenomenon's hand in acknowledgement of his courage. Peace Inglis was then 'bled' by a surgeon at the battleground, prior to having been taken to his quarters at the King's Arms in Colnbrook and being put to bed. Ned Turner felt that that his own injuries did not warrant immediate medical attention, and elected to stay to watch a second fight that was arranged for a subscription purse, and £5 was collected from a 'Noble Lord' for a contest to be fought between Ned Brown (the Sprig of Myrtle) and Harry Scott of Windsor. Despite a great height and weight advantage in favour of Scott, Brown proved to be the victor, Scott having fallen senseless at the start of the 20th round. He was carried from the field and died shortly afterwards.

Following this tragic contest, Ned Turner returned to his quarters at the George Inn. The most severe injury that he had received in his fight against Peace Inglis was a fracture of a metacarpal bone in his left hand, which nearly protruded through the skin. Ned thought it likely that the injury had occurred around the middle of the fight, when in stopping one of Inglis's powerful right hand blows, he had received a punch to the knuckle of his

170 As recorded in *Bell's Life in London and Sporting Chronicle*, 14 November 1824.

middle finger. With the exception of this injury, he had sustained no major damage and was without a scratch. Turner was also quick to correct his supporters, who remarked that Inglis's blows must have been light, saying, 'Don't tell me that, I felt them, and know that they were extremely heavy.'[171]

Ned Turner was evidently largely unhurt, having attended Aby Belasco's benefit event at the Fives Court the day after the fight with Inglis. The swelling to his nose, which had at first been greatly puffed up, had gone down and he wore his arm in a sling. As sportsmanlike as ever, Ned was keen to pay tribute to the tremendous power of Inglis's right hand. The Welshman stated that had he not constantly parried the Phenomenon's blows, he feared that over time the strength of Inglis may well have turned the tide against him. The doctor that attended to Inglis was of the opinion that Peace was not as strong as he had been in the previous fight, having been beaten in less time and with much less personal injury. The additional 5lbs of weight that Inglis had been carrying was afterwards deemed more of a hindrance than a benefit, as although it had increased his bulk it had diminished his activity.[172]

The victory over Peace Inglis brought almost inexpressible joy to Ned Turner, and a dinner was held by his supporters and friends at the establishment of the veteran sportsman Bill Moss, at the Crown, in the Borough, on Monday, 15 November 1824. Most of the past opponents of Turner attended, in order to pay tribute to the Welshman. Jack Scroggins, Jack Randall, Jack Martin, Cyrus Davis, Josh Hudson and Peace Inglis all raised their glasses and drank to the health of Ned Turner. Ned appeared to be overcome with emotion at the display of fondness from those he had opposed in the ring, and the admiration of those who had supported him. The Out-and-Outer wound up his brief speech by saying that 'it was very likely that he should not fight any more; but if he did alter his mind, he would always behave like a man'.

It was with this final burst of glory that the pugilistic career of the great Welshman Ned Turner ended, and his scientific fighting skills would never be witnessed between the ropes and stakes again. Peace Inglis felt the defeat at Turner's hands keenly, and

---

171 As recorded in the *Morning Post*, 11 November 1824.

172 As recorded in *Bell's Life in London and Sporting Chronicle*, 14 November 1824.

was quick to try to secure a third fight. A month after his battle against Turner, the following letter penned by the Phenomenon was published in the *Weekly Dispatch*:

> "TO EDWARD TURNER
>
> "SIR, –
>
> "My friends have agreed to give me another trial; I therefore challenge you to fight me for £100 a-side, within two months from the date hereof, and am ready to make a deposit within a fortnight. If this challenge be not accepted, I propose to retire from the ring altogether.
>
> "I remain yours, etc.
>
> "PEACE INGLIS.
>
> "December 10, 1824."

Ned Turner had already left London and travelled to Newtown in Wales, where he was celebrating his victory over Inglis in the company of those friends who had supported him so loyally throughout his pugilistic career. Turner sent the following reply, in answer to the challenge of the Phenomenon:

> "TO PEACE INGLIS.
>
> "SIR, -
>
> "I have seen your challenge in the papers, and in reply beg to state that the only terms that will induce me to meet you, or anyone else, in the ring, and which, considering the battle I have fought, will not, I trust, be thought out of the way. £200 a-side is the least I meant to fight for. And when you talk of two months you must have forgotten the state of my left hand; but if the last Tuesday in April will answer your purpose, and your friends are willing to agree to the sum I propose, I will be most happy to accommodate you. I should be very sorry to think my refusal the cause of your leaving the Ring, in which I wish you success; but I must take care to leave off fighting before fighting leaves me.
>
> "I am yours, etc.
>
> "EDWARD TURNER.
>
> "Newtown, Montgomeryshire, North Wales,
>
> "December 15, 1824"

Nothing came of this correspondence, and neither man ever entered the ring again. It seems as though Peace Inglis made good on his promise to retire from prize fighting and returned to his previous occupation as a mattress maker. Ned Turner remained a popular figure in pugilistic circles, by virtue of his exemplary fistic record, and St David's Day, 1 March 1825, was chosen for another benefit event in his honour at the Fives Court in London. The Court was crowded with fellow Welshmen, wishing to pay tribute to the great pugilist, and the 'Knights of the Leek' were reportedly highly amused by the sparring that took place. There were a number of performances by lesser pugilistic stars before Jonathan Bissell, better known as 'Young Gas' (named due to his striking resemblance in appearance and fighting style to 'The Gas Man', Tom Hickman), demonstrated his skills against a Welshman named Jones. Bissell reportedly took the 'most disrespectful liberties' with the head of Jones, before concerned spectators convinced Jones to retire.[173] Better-known pugilists Jem Ward, Tom Shelton, Tom Gaynor and George Cooper all demonstrated their skills afterwards, with the set-to between Ward and Shelton having been deemed one of the better exhibitions of the day. Ned Turner and Peace Inglis mounted the stage for the final bout, although it was obvious that Ned was no longer the pugilistic force he had once been and that the 'spirit was willing, but the flesh was weak'. It was apparent that the fighting days of Ned Turner had now passed, and the *Morning Advertiser* strongly suggested that,

> Ned must fight no more, but console himself with the recollection of his achievements in his early days.

Ned Turner's health, which had been the cause of so much concern in the final years of his prize fighting career, was in steady decline and just two months later a sympathetic notice in *Bell's Life* would draw attention to the precarious state of the Welshman's constitution. Fearing that a meeting with the grim reaper was on the cards, it commented,

---

173 As recorded in the *Morning Advertiser*, 2 March 1825 and *Bell's Life in London and Sporting Chronicle*, 6 March 1825.

> We are sorry to state that Ned Turner is very unwell; he must take care of himself, or he will be booked for the darkey.[174]

Despite having been quite ill by this stage, Ned Turner would appear to have retained an interest in the prize ring, particularly when one of the combatants was a fellow Welshman. Robert Smout, a 'Welchman' from 'Taffy's Land', was backed by Ned in a fight for five sovereigns a-side against a Scotsman named William Shields, which took place on 16 May 1825, at Peckham fields. The match was deemed 'as gallant a battle as had been witnessed for some time', and both men 'went to work fearlessly, and smashed each other in the most finished style'. Smout initially took the lead, justifying Turner's confidence in him, but Shields fought back, and although he was severely punished the Scotsman succeeded in securing victory over the Welshman in the 12th round.[175] It is clear that Ned Turner's health declined steadily in the months that followed, and by 1826 his breathing became laboured and he was also reportedly lame.[176]. Another benefit was arranged for Turner at the Fives Court on 28 March 1826, but due to the fact that Tom Brown had pre-booked the Court, the event was postponed. Ned remained in poor health and it was hoped that his 'past services ought not to be forgotten by the friends of the Ring' and that the venue would be filled to its capacity.[177] Turner managed to attend a dinner given for Josh Hudson on 31 March, by which time he was very ill indeed. At the benefit event arranged for Phil Sampson at the Fives Court on Monday, 3 April 1826, Tom Spring

---

174 As recorded in *Bell's Life in London and Sporting Chronicle,* 1 May 1825.

175 As recorded in *Bell's Life in London and Sporting Chronicle,* 22 May 1825.

176 *Pugilistica* records that Turner 'became lame' and was 'labouring under the effects of an asthma'. By 'an asthma' we can deduce that Turner was suffering from shortness of breath by this time, and not that he was asthmatic. Asthma was not refined as a medical term until the late 19th century. Prior to this time, the term asthma, taken from the Greek meaning 'short of breath', was applied to any patient experiencing breathlessness. Despite Ned Turner having been recorded by some modern sources as an 'asthmatic', there is no evidence that he suffered from asthma prior to the decline in his health before his death.

177 As recorded in *Bell's Life in London and Sporting Chronicle,* 5 March 1826.

Jack Scroggins speaks of his sadness after hearing of the death of Ned Turner.

mounted the stage and made an appeal on behalf of Turner, telling the concerned spectators that Turner's health was in steep decline, and he was now quickly sinking into the grave.

The date of the gallant Welshman's farewell benefit was announced for Tuesday, 18 April, and it was hoped that the event might attract the patronage of those who had admired the ailing pugilist. A number of tickets were sold on the spot, due to the sympathy that had been elicited amongst the crowd by the tragic news.[178] Surprisingly, Turner managed to attend Sampson's benefit, and looked extremely ill, and his brother-in-law, Mr Baxter, prophetically stated that the brave pugilist would be unlikely to reap any reward from any funds collected in his honour. After the benefit, Ned Turner returned to Baxter's house and took to his bed. It would prove to be the last public appearance of the pugilistic Prince of Wales.[179] *Bell's Life*, having been made aware of the perilous condition of the Out-and-Outer, issued the following plea to its readers on Turner's behalf,

> NED TURNER – We trust the Fancy will not forget the 18th instant, when poor old Ned Turner, who is extremely ill, will take his benefit at the Tennis Court. His lamp is nearly extinguished; but we hope it may be made to live a little longer still by the kind aid of the 'oil of human kindness.[180]

On the day of this final benefit, the Royal Tennis Court in Great Windmill Street, Haymarket, was filled to suffocation, and there was a full bill of sparring featuring such well-known pugilists as Harry Jones 'the Sailor Boy', Jack Randall and Harry Holt, Alec Reid 'the Chelsea Snob', Jem Ward, Jem Burns, Dick Curtis and Harry Harmer.

The conqueror of old Paddington Jones, Isaac Bitton, also put in an appearance, introducing the Jewish pugilist, Elias Spree – who at nearly 70 years of age was one of the oldest pugilists still living. Few of those present were made aware that the great Ned Turner, second only to Jack Randall in the days of his glory, had passed away in his bed at the home of his brother-in-law, Mr Baxter, at eight o'clock the previous evening on Monday, April 17, 1826, at East Smithfield.[181] Given the slow decline of Turner and his well-publicised drinking habits, his end had long been

178 As recorded in *Bell's Life in London and Sporting Chronicle*, 9 April 1826.

179 As recorded in *Bell's Life in London and Sporting Chronicle*, 23 April 1826.

180 As recorded in *Bell's Life in London and Sporting Chronicle*, 9 April 1826.

181 *Bell's Life in London and Sporting Chronicle*, 23 April 1826, records eight o'clock in the evening on Monday, 17 April 1826 as Turner's time of death. *Pugilistica* records his time of death as two minutes to five in the afternoon.

predicted, and the cause of his death was afterwards recorded as having been due to a 'decay of nature".[182]

After the sparring had ended, Jack Randall and Jack Scroggins mounted the stage together, and after both had taken their bows, Randall stepped forward. Tears were already appearing in his eyes as he remembered his great friend and one time opponent, and said,

> Gentlemen, I am requested by the friends of poor Turner, to come forward and express their thanks in his behalf for the kind and liberal manner in which you have this day manifested an interest in his fate. Gentlemen, Ned and I have been opponents in the ring, but we have always been friends in private, and no man feels more for his situation than I do. That we shall be able to see him here at any future time, I think, is more than doubtful; but let us hope we may all see him hereafter.

Jack Randall's brief speech to his fallen friend was received with loud applause, and it was clear that the Nonpareil was greatly affected by the response from the crowd, and he was unable to repeat his speech when called to do so from the far side of the Court. Jack Scroggins, ordinarily a rough sort of man, followed him and said a few words that touched those present more deeply than any eloquent and well-crafted speech could have done:

> 'Gem'men,' said Scroggins, 'Ned was always a gentlemanly sort of a man – he is now going or gone to his long home, and I hope God will forgive him as well as everybody else. Let us all live while we can, and when we can't live no longer, well I supposes we must die; and I don't see why a fighting man shouldn't see eternity as well as anybody else.'

182 The *North Wales Chronicle* of 26 July 1890, reproduced an obituary for Turner, 'Death of a Welsh Pugilist', under the title 'Leaves from our Early Issues, (from April 13 to May 25, 1826)', in which it is stated that 'so small was one of his kidneys that the physicians were surprised he lived so long'. This might account for the inability of Turner's body to cope with his liberal consumption of alcohol for which he was well known, and possibly hastened his physical decline.

Ned Turner was taken to his final resting place in Aldgate Cemetery on Sunday, 23 April 1826, from the house of Mr Baxter. The funeral procession was of the most respectable description. The hearse bearing the body of Turner was followed by two mourning coaches, which contained Ned's father, Mr Baxter, and a large number of celebrated pugilists wishing to pay their respects to the great Welshman, including Jack Randall, Jack Scroggins, Tom Owen, Tom Cribb, Josh Hudson, Harry Holt, Harry Harmer and the famous scribe of the prize ring, Pierce Egan.

A report on the funeral reads as follows and pays ample testimony to the scientific fighting skills of Ned Turner, and his valiant and honourable conduct, both in and out of the ring, as well as the respect that he had earned amongst his fellow pugilists. There can be no doubt that the Fancy had seen the death of the greatest fighting Welshman of the age:

> From an early hour in the morning, the house of Mr Baxter was surrounded by numbers of persons anxious to pay respect to the remains of a man who once stood so high amongst the admirers of the art of self-defence. The church and churchyard also were crowded. We noticed many of the *corps pugilstique*. Scroggins, for the feeling and respect he paid to the deceased, deserves the highest praise. Forgetting all former differences; nay, more following the side of the hearse, and dropping a tear over the grave of the man who had proved his conqueror, speak a volume in his favour as a generous-minded English boxer. Every person present appeared sorry for the loss of Turner. In all his battles he behaved like an honest, honourable man; in fact, throughout his life he was never known to have committed a dishonourable action – his conduct was always upon the square. His last moments were marked by resignation and Christian-like behaviour; and he expired without a sigh in the arms of his cousin, Mr Baxter.[183] Turner was in the thirty-fourth year of his age.

183 Although recorded as Ned Turner's 'cousin' in this extract, Mr Baxter the hat maker of East Smithfield is recorded as Turner's uncle, and also his brother-in-law by other sources. In the course of this book, Baxter is referred to as Turner's brother-in-law, as stated in Ned Turner's obituary published in *Bell's Life in London and Sporting Chronicle*, 23 April 1826.

The reporter adds:

> Turner was a most difficult boxer to be got at; standing with his right leg first, he proved at all times a truly awkward and dangerous customer. In a set-to with the gloves with Tom Spring, at a benefit in the city of Norwich, previous to the fight between Painter and Oliver, the science of Ned Turner was so much admired, and his blows were so effective, as to produce thunders of applause. In point of true courage, Turner was never excelled in or out of the ring. He was a most modest, unassuming fellow, and, notwithstanding his intercourse with various grades of society, he was a 'bashful' man. In company he was cheerful and good natured, always anxious to serve his brethren in the prize ring, and throughout the sporting world he was as much respected for his civility as his high courage.[184]

184 As recorded in *Pugilistica*.

Chapter 16

Ironface, the Hardy Mountaineer

Jack Rasher had a reputation as a fighter prior to entering the prize ring. The Welshman was well known as the 'tremendous butcher' of Whitechapel Market, as a result of the numerous impromptu 'turn-ups' this 'knight of the cleaver' had fought in the neighbourhood. Rasher stood about 5ft 6in tall and weighed in at about 12st, his frame was said to be 'exceedingly hardy and well put together', [185] and he was noted as having been 'a native of Wales, possessing great strength'.[186]

Jack Rasher was perhaps not the most skilled boxer but having been blessed with prodigious strength, he was thought to be 'a terror to most of the *cutting-up* tribe in the... market'. Rasher's fame spread before him and as a result virtually no one had the courage to enter the prize ring against him. Jack Rasher's backer had a great deal of confidence in the butcher's powers and elected to support him in an off-hand match for ten guineas to eight against the highly regarded Josh Hudson. The contest took place at Plaistow, in Essex, on Tuesday, 11 January 1820. Hudson was seconded by Tom Owen and his brother, David, while Rasher had Daniel Mendoza and Cyrus Davis in his corner. The first round proved to be tremendously contested but after this Hudson had it all his own way. Josh Hudson's skills were much admired and he feinted well with the left hand in order to bring his right into

---

185 As recorded in *Boxiana*.

186 *Sporting Magazine: Or, Monthly Calendar of the Transactions of the Turf, the Chase and Every Other Diversion Interesting to the Man of Pleasure, Enterprize, and Spirit*, Volume 6, (London: Rogerson & Tuxford, 1820).

play. Before the end, Jack Rasher was covered with blood and while his 'gameness astonished every person present', it could be seen that he was too slow in his movements. Although he was floored and rendered senseless in the last round, on having been brought round, Rasher wanted to renew the fight. As a result, 'in this battle he was not only taught that *strength* alone would not insure conquest, but soon defeated without a shadow of a chance; he, however, satisfied all the spectators, that he was an *out-and-out* GAME man.'[187] The fight thus terminated in victory for Josh Hudson in 15 rounds, after 29½ minutes.

Josh Hudson, the 'John Bull Fighter'.

Despite the defeat to Hudson, Jack Rasher entered his next engagement shortly afterwards against one Adams, a fellow butcher, with considerable and, as it turned out, justifiable, confidence. The match was fought on a common near Billericay, in Essex, on Tuesday, 4 April 1820, for £15, straight after a contest between Josh Hudson and Benniworth, the Essex Foulness Island Champion, in which Hudson proved to be the conqueror. Against Adams, Rasher 'had so much the superiority' that he took the lead and kept it in fine style; and won the battle in short time, scarcely giving his opponent 'anything like a *chance*'.[188] Rasher was seconded in this battle by Tom Oliver and Bill Gibbons, while Bob Purcell and Jack Scroggins attended upon Adams. The battle was a particularly hard one and 16 rounds were fought in just 12 minutes.[189]

It was as a consequence of this victory that Jack Rasher was matched without hesitation for £20 a-side against Charles

---

187 As recorded in *Boxiana*.

188 As recorded in *Boxiana*.

189 As recorded in *Fistiana*.

Giblet (Gyblett/Gibletts).[190] The battle took place at Epsom Downs on Tuesday, 16 May 1820, after the contest between Tom Spring and Bob Burns, in which Spring emerged triumphant after 18 rounds. Rasher was seconded by his conqueror, Josh Hudson, and Harry Harmer, while Giblet was supported by Jack Randall and Tom Shelton. As it was the first appearance of both Rasher and Giblet in the Prize Ring, a spectator asked Jack Scroggins the name of Rasher. Scroggins, noting the hardy appearance of Jack Rasher, replied 'Ironface', and thus christened the Welsh butcher with his well-deserved cognomen.[191]

At the start of the fight, the formidable appearance of Jack Rasher was much in evidence, his 'frame and *mug*... seemed as hard as the mountains from which he dates his early days, in Wales.' Giblet was also seen to be in 'equally *tip-top*' condition and a keen battle was anticipated. The first round met all expectations and after some cautious manoeuvring, both men engaged in a determined and ferocious rally at the ropes, until at length, both went down to a great applause and cries of 'Did you ever see such a first round?' At the start of the second, both men were bleeding from their faces on coming up to the scratch. A sharp rally ended when Jack Rasher was hit down onto one knee, although he merely laughed and jumped up to resume the contest until both pugilists went down.

As the rounds rolled on, Jack Rasher showed astonishing fight and he resumed each attack with fury, and with little regard for his safety. Charles Giblet showed much greater caution, and was seen to get away from his man most cleverly. It was in the fourth that Rasher showed his powerful left hand, landing twice with such venom that Giblet's right eye was damaged. Regardless of the injury to Giblet, it was Jack Rasher that was sent down over and over. Rasher gamely rose each time and went about punishing his man, banging his left into Giblet's face, and damaging his eye.

With his superior skill in avoiding punishment, Giblet was the stronger man by the 13th round and blood was now running down

---

190 The name of Charles 'Giblet' is given as Charles Grantham in *Boxiana*.

191 *Sporting Magazine: Or, Monthly Calendar of the Transactions of the Turf, the Chase and Every Other Diversion Interesting to the Man of Pleasure, Enterprize, and Spirit*, Volume 6, (London: Rogerson & Tuxford, 1820).

Rasher's face in streams. The butcher showed startling resilience in the light of the treatment he was receiving and answered a tremendous blow to the body with one to the face in return. At the end of the round, the spectators were exhilarated by their display, shouting, 'Well done, upon both sides – the Welshman is game indeed.'

By the 18th round, Giblet was stopping blows with dexterity and yet his right eye had now 'swelled up as big as a halfpenny ball'. It was in the 21st round that '*Taffy*, on setting-to put in so severe a blow on Giblet's puffed eye, that it was cut open, and the claret ran down from it'. The struggle continued but it was Giblet who more often than not was sending his opponent to the turf. In the rounds that followed, exhaustion seemed to take hold of Ironface and although in the exchanges he continued to land solid blows, it was Giblet who began pulling ahead and by the 26th round he was landing at will, fighting Rasher all over the ring. Rasher seemed unbothered by the severity of his punishment, and he came out for the 27th round laughing as if he had not been fighting at all, although by now his head was so beaten and bloody that it 'was like a rainbow, all manner of colours'. He seemed to entertain no thought that he might be defeated and the 'gameness' he displayed was 'equal to any thing ever exhibited', although it was perhaps telling that Rasher slipped down from weakness at the end of the round. The 28th round was one of terrific punishment and the combatants took no heed of tactics and slogged each other until they both stood still. Receiving two staggering blows, Ironface was sent to the ropes. He refused to go down and returned to the centre of the ring, laughing once more, although by now he was nearly defenceless due to exhaustion.

As the round multiplied, it looked as though Jack Rasher must drop, and yet he fought on, regardless of his injuries. The 31st round saw terrible exchanges, with Giblet pursuing him to the ropes, where he held Rasher almost off the ground with one hand and punched him mercilessly with the other. Giblet quickly made a 'slaughter-house' of Rasher's face and unceremoniously dropped the Welshman in exhaustion as the round closed. Rasher continued to take a tremendous beating. 'He'll not come any more' the spectators cried, and yet Ironface continued to step forward, receiving a near jaw-breaking punch in the 34th

The Public Ledger,

AND DAILY ADVERTISER.

Boxing.

Gyblett and Rasher fought for more than an hour and a half for a purse, and unmercifully milled each other. In the early part of the battle one of Gyblett's peepers was darkened, and Rasher's left ear was nearly hit from his head. Each round was manfully contested, and Gyblett won it.

The Jack Rasher vs. Charles 'Gyblett' (Giblet) prize fight, as reported in the Public Ledger and Daily Advertiser, *May 17, 1820.*

round. His ear showed horrific damage by the 36th round and was 'terrible to view – it was nearly cut off, and swelled as big as a two-penny loaf'.

By the 38th round, entreaties were being made to Jack Rasher to give up the contest but he refused to entertain the notion and the fight continued, with it being 'astonishing, notwithstanding the *nobbing* Rasher had received, to witness the strength he still retained' as the butcher fought on. Giblet was by now outfighting the game Welshman at every turn and Rasher continued to show signs of the tremendous punishment he was taking. Astonishingly, he remained in good humour and by the 45th round 'the *ear* and *mug* of Rasher was damaged so severely, that it was terrific to view them; but he kept laughing, and exchanging hits, till he went down'.

Charles Giblet continued to pepper his man with punches, often managing to get away without a return, and Jack Rasher continued to fall with frequency at the end of each round. By the 52nd round, no one could quite believe the punishment that Rasher was absorbing, an amateur of distinction exclaiming, 'Did you ever see such a game fellow? He ought not to be suffered to fight any longer.' It was useless to try to get the Welsh butcher to give in and he continued to show fight each time until he was sent down. The contest could have ended in the 56th round. Giblet tried to bring the fight to a close and landed a smashing blow to

Rasher's injured ear. He continued to punch Rasher at will on the ropes until he fell onto his knees and then dropped on to his face. A shout was heard, 'It's all up, take him away' – but still Ironface fought on. Coming up for the next round, the Welshman left his second's knee, spat on his fists and commenced his attack, but he was again battered into submission by Giblet, and sent down once more. The 58th round was the finisher, Jack Rasher having finally been induced to give in by his second. Charles Giblet celebrated in unusual style and jumped over the ropes, which stood about 4ft high, and ran from the ring in exultation. The gruelling battle had taken an hour and 23 minutes before Jack Rasher's fortitude was finally broken.

It wasn't until the following year that Ironface would do battle in the prize ring again. The Welshman was matched against another butcher by the name of Spencer.[192] The contest was scheduled for Crawley Hurst for £30 on 5 June 1821, immediately after the second fight between Ned Turner and Jack Martin, which ended in victory for Martin after 60 hard-fought rounds. In this fight, as in his battle with Giblet, Rasher was 'dreadfully punished' but would eventually triumph over his stubborn antagonist.

'A most desperate slaughtering fight took place between two of the *cutting-up tribe*, Rasher and Spencer, for 30*l.* a-side, occupying seventy rounds, and one hour and a quarter. It was won by Rasher, who was seconded by Randall and Smith; and Spencer, by Jones and Purcell. Both of the men were dreadfully punished; and Spencer shewed the most science, but the hardy *Mountaineer* would not be *stalled off*, although at one time he was told to go and look for his *nob*, from the severe blows he had received upon it.'[193]

Spencer, having not apparently been sufficiently convinced of Ironface's pugilistic superiority, elected to fight Jack Rasher a second time for £50, and the fight was contested at Crawley Downs on 11 September 1821. It was an even lengthier battle in which an astonishing amount of punishment was dealt on both sides, and

192 The first name of Spencer is given as 'Joe' by Fred Henning in *Fights for the Championship, The Men and Their Times* (London: Licensed Victualler's Gazette, 1902).

193 *Sporting Magazine: Or, Monthly Calendar of the Transactions of the Turf, the Chase and Every Other Diversion Interesting to the Man of Pleasure, Enterprize, and Spirit,* Volume 8, (London: Rogerson & Tuxford, 1821).

lasted one hour and 48 minutes before Rasher was proclaimed the victor once more. Jack Rasher had fought three incredibly hard battles in less than a year and a half. The fight against Spencer proved to be his last, and the ferocious Welsh butcher never fought in the prize ring again.

In speaking of 'gameness' and courage, Pierce Egan would name a number of boxers who had exhibited these qualities in the course of their battles, but would state that 'RASHER is entitled to a high place among them'. In closing on the brief, bloody, and brutal career of Jack Rasher, Egan would write in *Boxiana* that,

> He is not a good fighter, and he does not calculate open points; but depends more upon his *bottom* than the advantages of *science*, for obtaining *victory*. In his fight with *Josh Hudson*, he was very angry on being taken out of the ring, and wished to resume the contest; and previous to his battle with *Giblet*, he declared to his second, that if he was taken away, without he said "*No*;" he would have satisfaction for it at another period. Instead of the term *Iron Face*, *Iron Frame* and disposition might be more applicable to RASHER; and he will always prove to be a *troublesome* customer.

Chapter 17

The Welsh Savage

A Welsh pugilist would take to the stage of the Fives Court, situated at Little St Martin's Street, Leicester Fields, London in January of 1823 at a benefit event celebrating the fighting career of Jack Scroggins.[194] Edward (Ned) Savage was unknown to the majority of the spectators who had gathered to pay their respects to 'Scroggy', and it would appear to have been Ned's first appearance before the leading lights of the London Prize Ring.

It seems likely that Ned Savage may have gained something of a minor reputation in 'turn-ups' before this time, and had chosen to appear at the Fives Court in order to further his pugilistic reputation. The Fives Court, while originally a place to play the game of fives, which was a form of handball, or hand tennis, became better known in the years that followed as a place where the skills of some of the greatest pugilists of the period might be witnessed in sparring matches, exhibitions, and benefits, all of which were held with the gloves. Presided over by 'Gentleman' John Jackson, the matches drew a great deal of interest from many noblemen and people of high rank, who paid as much as a guinea a ticket to view proceedings from an elevated position seated in a gallery set in the high walls overlooking the court. Up to 1,000 people could be accommodated at the Court, and when full the takings at the door might draw as much as £200. From 1802 to 1820, the Fives Court served as the principal location where leading pugilists demonstrated their abilities in exhibitions and in benefit events.

194 The Jack Scroggins benefit took place on 14 January 1823, as recorded in *Bell's Life in London and Sporting Chronicle*, 19 January 1823.

The Royal Tennis Court, in Great Windmill Street, Haymarket had opened its doors to sparring exhibitions in 1820, with a benefit event taking place for Bill Richmond on 20 February of that year. The decision to feature sparring at the Tennis Court led to a strong rivalry between the two venues, which only came to an end six years later when the Fives Court was demolished in 1826.[195] The Fives Court played a vital role in promoting pugilism as a legitimate form of entertainment, providing a location where respectable gentlemen who would not dream of appearing at a prize fight could witness the prominent fighters of the day in sparring matches. It also served to educate spectators in the finer aspects of the 'science' of boxing, and introduced new fighters such as Ned Savage to the Fancy, raising their public profile and enabling them to find financial backers.

Ned Savage was a London-based cabriolet driver and had been matched to appear on the stage at the Fives Court against a 'west countryman' carpenter named Gainer. The match would appear to have been well received, having been a 'rare manly bout'. Savage was hit and thrown in the opening round, with the combatants having drawn admiration for their 'gameness', although the contest was marked by a degree of awkwardness due to their relative inexperience. The third round saw Savage land a heavy punch that sent Gainer reeling, although he showed a great deal of pluck in defence and the match was thought to be a good but 'ruffianing bout' that lasted nearly 15 minutes. Following the contest, the feeling amongst the spectators was that both Savage and Gainer would benefit from 'much practise before they could enter the ring'.

Ned Savage was so keen to make his prize fighting debut that he appeared in the London Prize Ring just a month later on 19 February 1823, against a man named Cope. The fight took place at Copenhagen Fields for £5 a-side. It would bear similarity to the match that Savage had fought against Gainer, and was deemed to have been 'a real ruffianing battle'. The inexperience of both men was obvious from the first round; both combatants were too

195 The last benefit held for a pugilist at the Fives Court was for Peter Warren on 30 August 1825. The Fives Court was demolished in 1826 for the site to be redeveloped.

eager to set-to and both went down in the struggle. Cope landed heavily in the second, smashing Savage's eye, which soon puffed up, and the cabriolet driver was floored shortly afterwards. Ned came back with a vengeance in the third, throwing Cope to the turf to take the round. Cope successfully targeted Ned Savage's swollen eye in the fourth, striking him with such force that he split the Welshman's eye, making blood pour down his face as if the swelling had been lanced, the force of the blow sending him to earth.

The fight continued in this give-and-take manner until the 12th round, when an unusual event occurred. Both men landed heavy punches simultaneously and fell on their faces. The battleground had by this time been reduced to mud, and a great deal of merriment followed when the fighters came up to the scratch, their faces having been completely covered by black mud. The fight continued for 22 rounds as the fortunes of both pugilists swung first one way then the other, although ultimately Savage triumphed by knocking Cope out of time, and the Welshman was declared the victor.[196]

Ned Savage's head would appear to have swelled more than a little following this battle, and made him view his limited pugilistic skills through rose-tinted spectacles. Savage would quickly discover that while roughhouse mauling might well secure him victory over the flotsam and jetsam of the prize ring, it helped little when facing a pugilist of merit. A 'turn-up' took place between Ned Savage and the celebrated Dick Curtis, the 'Pet of the Fancy', early in August of 1824, when both men had watched two glass blowers demonstrating their sparring skills at Battersea Fields. Dick had courteously offered some friendly advice to one of them, to which Ned seemingly took offence before attacking Dick without warning. Not to be underestimated, although much the smaller man, Dick dished out a sound beating to Ned, who was sent off in short time nursing a bloodied nose, having had both his pride and his face bruised by Curtis's knuckles.[197]

196 The *Morning Advertiser*, 20 February 1923, states that the fight went 22 rounds, although *Fistiana* records this fight as having lasted 14 rounds.

197 As recorded in *Bell's Life in London and Sporting Chronicle*, 15 August 1824.

Ned was back in the ring the following month, when he engaged an opponent by the name of Tom Schofield for ten sovereigns and a stake at Hampstead Fields on 1 September 1824, which was attended by thousands of spectators.[198] Despite the scorching heat of the day, a total of 49 rounds would be fought. After a cautious start, Schofield was floored by a blow on the side of the head in the third round, and from the ninth onwards Savage began to outfight his opponent, landing repeatedly with his left hand. As the fight progressed, Schofield grew increasingly weary, and Ned Savage's superior endurance won him the victory in 52 minutes.

It doesn't appear as though Savage fought any other contests worthy of note until the following year, when he elected to do battle against a fellow cabriolet driver named Locke (Lock) after the conclusion of Ascot races on 4 June 1825, for £25 a-side. The match was of little interest to the crowds at the racecourse, with both men having been deemed of 'third-rate consideration'. An initial attempt to set up the ring before the betting booth was met with reluctance, so the ring was formed in front of the Royal Stand, although the aristocracy who had watched the races had long since departed. The lack of enthusiasm for the battle can be gauged by the fact that although there were a number of collectors on the ground, a mere £4 was raised before the men were brought to the scratch.

Lock's appearance did not inspire a great deal of confidence; he was 'long and thin' and although he was 'possessed of some science and bottom', he was thought to be somewhat wild and lacking in steadiness. On paper, Savage looked the more capable of the two, being 'a middle-sized, well-set fellow, a hard hitter, active, and ready at his business'. The odds favoured Savage with 6/4 having been offered on his victory. Gypsy Cooper and West Country Dick stood as Lock's seconds, and Ben Burns and Tom Gaynor took the corner of Ned Savage.

Ned Savage launched into battle at the start of the fight, making play with his right before catching Lock heavily on the ribs with his left, and they began exchanging blows with gusto. Savage was quick to take the offensive, forcing his man to the ropes and

198 As recorded in *The Morning Advertiser*, 2 September 1824. Although this contest is also mentioned briefly in *Bell's Life,* it is omitted from the fight record of Ned Savage in *Fistiana*.

throwing Lock across them. They continued to fight until Savage fell over with Lock falling upon him. The second round showed the inexperience of both fighters; Lock attacked with a good body blow, but he left himself open and was nailed to the head by Savage, and the round ended with both men down once more.

The third saw Lock come up to the scratch with confidence, although his body was already showing marks from the ropes and the stinging knuckles of Savage. Many of his blows to Savage's head were stopped and he received a 'chattering crack' on the mouth for his pains, which cut his lips and drew first blood. Lock was unceremoniously thrown on to the ropes once more, and fell over them on to his shoulders. The betting now reflected Lock's wearied state, with 2/1 now being offered on Savage. In the next round Lock landed a slight blow to Ned Savage's eye, but received a heavy punch to the stomach in return. In the scrambling rally that followed, the Welsh cab driver was seen to have some success while Lock grimly fought on without judgement. Once again, Lock went down at the ropes. Ned Savage continued his attack in the following rounds, bloodying Lock's nose, and while he tried to finish his man, Lock continued to fight courageously, although was again thrown in the sixth, with Savage falling heavily upon him.

The seventh round proved to be the last. Ned Savage now found his attacks scoring with greater frequency. Lock was thrown upon the ropes and as he fell, Savage launched a heavy blow, striking his opponent on the mouth. A cry of 'Foul' immediately sprang up amongst those gathered round the ring, with the umpires voicing agreement. As a consequence of the foul blow, Lock declined to resume the fight despite having been loudly called upon to do so by Ned Savage. The decision therefore went to Lock, who had seemed to be on his way to a crushing defeat at the hands of Savage prior to the foul. Ned Savage's conduct reflected badly upon him and it was thought that in future, 'Master Savage' should 'feel the advantage of commanding his temper'. Despite the disappointment, the exposure of having fought at Ascot seemingly did the Welshman's reputation some good, as an honourable baronet afterwards offered to match Savage against Gypsy Cooper for £25, although nothing would come of it. Ned preferred the prospect of a contest against Bishop Sharpe and tried to secure a match for £50, but his challenge went unheard.

BELL'S

LIFE IN LONDON,

AND SPORTING CHRONICLE;

DICK CURTIS AND SAVAGE.

These men had a *turn-up* in Battersea-fields, on Monday. Two glass-blowers were shewing off their milling qualities in a *friendly* way, when Dick gave a little advice to one of them to whose success Savage was hostile. Savage in consequence made a *Savage* attack on Dick, but Dick soon reduced him to a state of civilization, and sent him off with his *nose in a sling*.

The first 'turn-up' between Ned Savage and Dick Curtis, as reported in Bell's Life in London and Sporting Chronicle, *15 August 1824.*

A few months later, Ned locked horns with Dick Curtis for a second time at the Castle Holborn public house, run by Tom Belcher, and a favourite watering hole of the leading figures of the London Prize Ring. Savage was perhaps foolish to neglect to mind his manners on the evening of Wednesday, 3 August 1825, when his harsh criticism of a fellow cabriolet driver drinking in the company of Dick Curtis would lead to a hasty 'turn-up' in which Ned Savage was well thrashed. The entertaining account of their unscheduled fight from *Bell's Life* is worth reprinting in full:

> On Wednesday evening last, the Pet was enjoying a sober glass of negus and a friendly gossip, at the house of an old friend in Holborn, when Ned Savage made his appearance, and joined the group. Ned was not exactly in the best temper in the world, and having made a hasty, if not an offensive observation to a *Knight of the Whip*, who was in Dick's company, the latter remonstrated with him on his want of *politeness*. "Touch my honour, touch my life;" cried Ned, "if you say any more, I'll give you a slap in the chops!" "If you do," said Dick, very quietly,

Dick Curtis, the celebrated 'Pet of the Fancy'.

"you shall have another." No sooner said than done – and bang went Ned's *fives* against Dick's *canister*, and a most unseemly hit it was, for Dick's eye sparkled as if flint and steel had come in contact; but he was as good as his word, and with the rapidity of lightning, he caught Ned such a cutter on the side of the nob as laid the flesh open to the bone, and then breaking away he met him coming in with his left, in such a way as to show he was not to be daunted, even by a man two stone heavier than himself.

The room was electrified and the spirit and valour of Dick was loudly applauded. There was an immediate cry for an open field of action, and in a very few minutes the decks were cleared of all superfluous furniture, the door was barred and free elbow-room afforded to the combatants. Both doffed their upper *togs*, and to it they went. Ned, who is a game fellow, went to work in downright earnest, thinking he could soon finish his *tiny* opponent; but he reckoned without his host. Dick said "he had been too long in the woods to be frightened by an *owl*". He drew back, and as Ned bored in he met him with his left, and then with his right, smack in the *mazzard*; on which Ned closed for the fall, but there again he was out, and got a heavy throw. Thirteen other rounds were fought in which Dick showed a decided superiority in judgement and science, nobbing, fibbing and throwing his man as he liked; but receiving a few clumsy thumps in return.

At last Ned got a little *foggy* in his *glimmers*, and fought wild-in one round catching a spectator an ugly smack, which was intended for Dick. Dick laughed, and had him at all points, watching his opportunities, and hitting him under and over as seemed most agreeable to his own style of punishment. Ned became confused, but he was too much of a man to say "enough" with such an antagonist. He had round after round, and punch after punch, till his head was a perfect *spectacle*. At last, the bystanders were fearful that if Dick pursued his *carving* system, the *Coroner* would have a *job*; and to prevent all discredit to the house, the Host interfered and prevented further warfare. Dick wished to *finish* his man, as he had been the first aggressor;

> but all were satisfied with what he had already done, and gave him the highest praise for the manliness which he had displayed. Dick was allowed to be entitled to the *laurel*, and it was universally agreed that Savage had been properly treated. There is an old saying "Civil words cost little," and Savage will in future feel the value of preserving his temper. Dick was hit heavy with Ned's right on the side of the head, and was much bruised on the elbows and hips from rummaging about. His hands, too, were considerably swelled. As for Ned, his nurse gave his *cab* a holiday, for his *phisog* won't be fit for genteel company for at least a week.[199]

News spread rather fast of the beating that Dick Curtis had dealt to Ned Savage, so much so in fact that Ned gained more fame, or possibly notoriety, from this encounter than any of his previous appearances in the prize ring. The host of the Castle Holborn, Tom Belcher, long remembered their memorable battle and would often recall the scrap between Curtis and Savage in the years that followed, concluding, 'It wouldn't be lucky for some of us if Dick was 12 stone. There wouldn't be much chaff about who would be champion then"[200]

---

199 This account is taken from *Bell's Life in London and Sporting Chronicle*, 7 August 1825. *Pugilistica* also records this event prominently in its chapter on Dick Curtis. The account in *Pugilistica* differs slightly and alleges that Ned Savage insulted Curtis by remarking that he wished he might be able to get down to Curtis's weight to give him a beating, and afterwards landed a punch on Curtis as he was leaving the Castle Tavern, Holborn, which started the fight. *Pugilistica* records the duration of the fight as being over 16 minutes, but incorrectly records the event as having occurred on 5 August 1824, perhaps confusing this second turn-up with Curtis with their first meeting at Battersea Fields the previous year, although it makes no reference to this first 'turn-up' at all. The second incident at the Castle Tavern definitely occurred in 1825, having been recorded in the 'Chronology of the Ring for 1825' in *Bell's Life* the following year. In addition to Ned Savage and his brother William, *Pugilistica* also mentions another brother of Ned Savage named Cab (or Jack) Savage, who is also stated to have been a boxer, albeit one of lesser renown, who fought with far less frequency than Ned and Bill Savage. A rare mention of Cab can be found in *Bell's Life* on 17 September 1826, in which he was challenged by a cab driver named Wilson to fight for £25 a-side, and who wished to meet at the Castle Tavern in Holborn to make a match.

200 As recorded in *Pugilistica*.

Ned Savage's next battle was against James (Jem) Kirkman, a hackney-coach driver, at Shearmere in Bedfordshire for £25 a-side on 18 October 1825, having been scheduled to take place after an aborted battle between Jonathan Bissell (Young Gas) and Reuben Martin, and following a contest in which the celebrated Young Dutch Sam decisively beat his opponent, Harry Jones the 'Sailor Boy', in 18 rounds.

After the fight between Young Dutch Sam and Jones had concluded, Ned Savage and Jem Kirkman stripped for battle and entered the ring. Savage had the advantage in height and reach, although Kirkman appeared to be in 'very fine condition' and despite his smaller stature, he was deemed to be 'well set', and appeared 'better calculated to go well through a hard day's work' than Savage. Kirkman had much less experience than Savage but had proved the power of his punch to his supporters, having broken the jaws of two previous opponents. Despite his quarrel with Ned Savage, Dick Curtis didn't hold a grudge and appeared as Savage's second alongside Tom Gaynor. Bandy Tom, the fighting brickmaker, and a friend appeared in the same capacity for Jem Kirkman.

At the start of the contest the odds favoured the Welshman, but the battle proved to be exceedingly disappointing, 'all science' having been 'set at nought'. Hammering without judgement was the order of the day, each round ending in severe falls, between scrambling and hugging on the ropes. The rough-and-ready nature of the fight was echoed by the conduct of the spectators, who broke into the ring, causing scenes of chaos. The combatants showed 'uncommon game' and it wasn't until the 58th round after a fight of an hour and ten minutes of hard, scrappy fighting that Kirkman was declared the winner. Both men showed signs of complete exhaustion, caused in part by the slippery state of the ground, which was reduced to mud. Ned Savage was evidently unsatisfied with the result, attributing the loss to an awkward fall on his shoulder, and immediately made a public challenge to Jem Kirkman to fight a second time for a similar stake.[201] Kirkman was perhaps a little more reticent, stating his willingness to fight either Ned Savage or his brother Bill, but refusing to do so unless the

201 As recorded in *Bell's Life in London and Sporting Chronicle,* 23 October 1825.

stakes were raised to £100. While Savage somehow found backers willing to cover the stakes, and appeared at the Castle Holborn the following week to make the match, Kirkman was a no-show[202].

At the start of the year in January, 1826 Ned Savage's skill in wrestling was to be put to the test against a Shropshire wrestler named George Pigg, with £10 a-side having been laid on a collar-and-elbow match. The victor would have to secure the best of two out of three falls, and was to be decided following a dog fight for £20 a-side at the Sluice House the following month.[203] On the day appointed for the battle, Pigg did not show so the meeting was abandoned.[204] According to *Fistiana*, Ned Savage's next battle in the prize ring was against an opponent named 'Avis', who was beaten by Ned in seven rounds and 15 minutes at a place named Wedgebury's Pitt on 9 March 1826.[205]

The Welsh cab driver pursued the possibility of a rematch against Jem Kirkman, and finally persuaded the coach driver to meet him, but there were doubts as to whether Savage would be able to defeat him. In June, Ned had appeared at the Tennis Court in order to spar against an opponent named Johnson, on the occasion of a benefit event organised for Peter Crawley, at which Savage's sparring style drew criticism. Ned worked his arms as if 'stirring a porridge pot' having relied heavily on his antiquated over-handed left-hand chop, and showed bad sportsmanship by tripping his opponent to secure the advantage. It was thought in consequence that Savage 'must look to his training' if he meant to beat Jem Kirkman,[206] although most believed he would secure the victory.[207]

On a hot and sunny afternoon in July[208] at Norman's Land near St Albans, in Hertfordshire, Ned Savage met Kirkman for the

202 As recorded in *Bell's Life in London and Sporting Chronicle*, 30 October 1825.

203 As recorded in *Bell's Life in London and Sporting Chronicle*, 29 January 1826.

204 As recorded in *Bell's Life in London and Sporting Chronicle*, 12 February 1826.

205 This fight between Ned Savage and Avis does not appear to be recorded by any sources other than *Fistiana*. It seems possible that 'Wedgebury's Pitt' was located at the town of Wedgebury in Staffordshire.

206 As recorded in *Bell's Life in London and Sporting Chronicle*, 18 June 1826.

207 As recorded in *Bell's Life in London and Sporting Chronicle*, 9 July 1826.

208 The second fight between Ned Savage and Jem Kirkman took place on 11 July 1826.

second time for £25 a-side. While both men's reputations amongst the followers of the prize ring remained of little consequence, they enjoyed a loyal following amongst their fellow cab and coach drivers, being viewed 'as champions of the rival classes to which they belong'. The proposed scene of the battle, Bernard's Common, had been abandoned following police interference after the news of the impending fight had reached the ears of the local Mayor. The 40 or so cab and coach drivers present were forced to travel onwards to Norman's Land, where after a lengthy delay the men entered the ring at 2.30pm. On this occasion, Ned Savage had secured the services of Tom Gaynor and 'Young Gas', while Jem Kirkman was seconded by Harry Holt and Reuben Marten. There were roughly 200 spectators present, although many had been drawn from surrounding farms, indicating that the contest was not of particularly great interest to the Fancy at large.

The fight began in a tedious fashion, neither man showing a great deal of interest in engaging the other in battle. Savage was the first to step up, and although he hit out with both right and left, his blows were of little consequence and he touched rather than thumped his man. Ned continually tried to bring his right into action, although as usual, his judgement and distance were at fault, and he failed to land any telling blow until the tenth round, when he finally scored first blood. The rounds ended with falls that went first one way then the other, Kirkman being thrown with a little more frequency than Savage. The impatience of the spectators was obvious by the 13th, and a general cry went up that a 'Jew boy would lick them both'. Hugging, scrambling and throwing featured heavily in the rounds that followed. In the 31st round, the frustration of Kirkman's second, Harry Holt, was witnessed when after a heavy fall in which Ned Savage afterwards fell upon his opponent, Savage was roughly shoved by Holt on rising.

Cries of 'Foul' naturally sprung up amongst the cab drivers at ringside, although these were ignored by the umpires. A violent struggle against the ropes in the 39th round was also halted by the interference of Holt, who pulled his man away. The umpires disagreed on whether his actions were 'Fair' or 'Foul', but the referee decided that both parties had acted unfairly and ordered the combatants to fight on.

As the battle wore on, Ned Savage made a number of attempts to strike out, but his efforts invariably concluded in struggles and falls. Harry Holt softened the severity of Kirkman's falls on a couple of occasions, having been too close to his man, and was knocked underneath the hackney-coach driver. A few voices of dissent were heard amongst Savage's supporters, who voiced their reluctance to pay up in the event that Kirkman won, although no appeals were made to the umpire to intervene.

From the 42nd round onwards, the same tiresome style of fighting continued. The weariness of the spectators at ringside was voiced by fellow pugilist Josh Hudson, who was heard to say that, 'Lady Barrymore would have licked the two with ease'. The last major blow to be landed by either man was that planted by Jem Kirkman in the 66th round on Ned Savage's left eye, which swelled immediately. For 101 rounds and two and a half hours they fought. In the last ten rounds, Savage had the best of the throwing and fell heavily on his opponent time and again. At the end of the fight, Jem Kirkman had to be lifted up upon the knee of his second and at the call of 'Time' was unable to make his way to the scratch. The victory was then awarded to Ned Savage. Kirkman was placed in a carriage in a senseless state and driven off. Savage was in good enough health to mount his gig without assistance and drove off satisfied that he had reversed his previous defeat at the hands of the coach driver.

There was a general feeling of fatigue amongst the spectators who had witnessed the drawn-out battle, and the lack of scientific hitting had been a great disappointment to all. The contest was consequently looked upon as more of a 'trial of wrestling than of boxing' and it was said that there were 'many nine stone, and some eight stone men in the ring, who would have licked them both in half an hour'. Despite the match having been viewed as one of the 'most tedious and least interesting ever witnessed by the lovers of the fistic art', both pugilists received some praise for their courage and physical strength. Given the heat of the day and the hardness of the ground, it was thought that few men would have been able to endure the number of falls that they had sustained over the course of the fight.

A match against an opponent by the name of Wilson was afterwards proposed for Ned Savage in September, and while

Savage was eager to make a match, Wilson did not show at the appointed time, so the proposed contest was abandoned.[209] The following month, another fight was floated against a fighter named Lansward, and although the patrons of the Castle Tavern witnessed a great deal of bravado or 'chaffing' on the part of the two men, they failed to make an agreement to fight.[210]

Despite having been defeated by Ned Savage, Jem Kirkman believed that he was the better fighter and continued to boast that he was willing to meet Savage 'at any time'. Ned quickly issued a challenge via the pages of *Bell's Life*, but Kirkman afterwards fell silent.[211] The following month, the Welshman set his sights considerably higher, challenging the gifted pupil of Dick Curtis, Young Dutch Sam, to meet him for £50 a-side.[212] The following week, Ned Savage was at the Castle Tavern, hoping that Sam would make an appearance and agree to fight, but was disappointed.[213]

It wasn't until January of 1827 that Ned Savage would secure another engagement in the prize ring, against an opponent named James (Jem) Wallace, with Savage wagering £25 to Wallace's £20.[214] The event was Wallace's debut in the prize ring and many thought that he might defeat Savage, based on the ability he had shown in his demonstrations in sparring at the Fives Court. Wallace had stationed himself for training at the Bell public house in Hendon, while Ned Savage had trained at Child's Hall, in Hampstead. The Bell also served as the meeting point for the spectators and a large crowd of the Fancy descended on the public house on the morning of 6 March 1827, and began drinking 'like fishes, and paid like Lords'. After satisfying their thirst, a large number of pedestrians, chariots, wagons and gigs took off across Hampstead Heath towards the battleground. Their movements did not go unnoticed by the keen eye of Mr Hoare, a banker and local magistrate, who viewed the motley multitude from his house

209 As recorded in *Bell's Life in London and Sporting Chronicle*, 24 September 1826.

210 As recorded in *Bell's Life in London and Sporting Chronicle*, 29 October 1826.

211 As recorded in *Bell's Life in London and Sporting Chronicle*, 19 November 1826.

212 As recorded in *Bell's Life in London and Sporting Chronicle*, 3 December 1826.

213 As recorded in *Bell's Life in London and Sporting Chronicle*, 10 December 1826.

214 The articles for the fight were published in *Bell's Life in London and Sporting Chronicle* on 14 January 1827.

overlooking the Heath. Mr Hoare was quick to give chase, eager to foil any attempts to bring off a prize fight within his jurisdiction.

The fight had been fixed to come off at a place named Duck Lane, which turned out to be appropriately named, heavy rain having turned it into a 'complete swamp' and made finding a suitable spot for the pitching of the ropes and stakes difficult. The sudden appearance of Mr Hoare made it impossible, having announced on his arrival, 'Gentlemen, I am a magistrate and I will not suffer a breach of the peace in this country.' Fortunately, one of the Fancy came forward and announced that he had a farm within distance, through which the River Brent ran, dividing the counties of Middlesex and Hertfordshire. By pitching the ring in neighbouring Hertfordshire, it was thought that further interference might be avoided. A rendezvous was made for the Swan with Two Necks public house, and so those whose spirits had not been dampened by the endless rain tramped on towards Whetstone on the Barnet road.

Further instructions were not long in coming and the Fancy pushed onwards, unbothered by a tremendous storm that threw torrents of rain and hail down around their ears. Some failed to reach the venue, as the River Brent, swelled by the continual rain, presented an ever-growing barrier. A few decided to try to jump the river and lost their footholds in the mud, plunging into the grey waters, to the great amusement of their companions. It was not until a hasty bridge of planks had been cobbled together that a safe passage across could be made. In spite of these difficulties, a large crowd found themselves on the far bank of the river, where the ring was quickly pitched within 30 yards of the county boundary. Having finally reached the land of promise, the scale of suffering was marked. Some were only wet to their knees and were amused to watch those who had plunged into the water stripping off and wringing out their muddy clothes while shivering in the rain. In a short time, all were ankle-deep in mud once more, and Ned Savage and Jem Wallace made ready for battle. Wallace was accompanied by Jack Randall and Ben Burns. Ned Savage was looked after by Peter Crawley and Tom Gaynor. At 2.45pm, the men toed the scratch and began to exchange blows.

Sadly, it was not to be the best of performances, being deemed 'bad on both sides', and neither man had enough skill to draw the fight to a close. At the start, Ned attacked in his routinely clumsy fashion. Wallace was seen to hit straight with more frequency but he was incapable of making much headway in attack. The hesitant manner of Jem Wallace in fighting on the retreat and the tenacity of Ned Savage in his attempts to land heavy blows suggested that the wild and ill-directed blows of Savage might pay off in the long run. The valour of the combatants was without doubt, with no flinching seen on either side. Ned's superior weight ensured that he got the better of Wallace in the throwing, and by falling on his opponent, he exhausted Wallace a great deal. Wallace's right hand flashed out with good intentions but he failed to make a dent in the efforts of the glutinous Welshman. As the rounds climbed into double figures, both pugilists wore the effects of the fight on their faces, having been 'dreadfully disfigured' almost to a 'state of stupefaction'. Their decline was accompanied by a tremendous battle of the elements, with wind, rain and hail now pelting down around them.

The ring was broken into and a melee between a dozen rival supporters broke out. Before long, the scene was one of both chaos and confusion. The slush was now ankle-deep as the men fell in turn and were then taken to the scratch to fight again. Many of the spectators became so fatigued by the spectacle that they abandoned the turf in search of shelter. Ned Savage and Jem Wallace fought to a near standstill, the fight taking two hours and 27 minutes, with 127 rounds being fought before exhaustion brought the contest to a close in favour of Ned Savage. He would pay a heavy price for the victory. Both men were taken to the Swan Inn and put to bed with medical assistance being required. Ned Savage required particularly close attention and was so severely damaged on the left side of the head and forehead that it was feared that his injuries might result in the loss of his life. It was some time before his condition became stable. The 'Welsh Savage' had proved that while he may have lacked the skill and strategy of a top-ranking pugilist, it seemed unlikely that his courage and 'gameness' could ever be doubted.

Chapter 18

The Coach Driver and the Conjuror

Soon after the fight between Ned Savage and Jem Wallace, Wallace voiced his desire for a rematch. Ned Savage accepted the challenge and stated his willingness to put between £50 and £100 on the outcome, and also wished to stake £50 on the success of his brother, Bill, in a fight against David Hudson.[215] While Ned was unsuccessful in securing a contest for his brother, Jem Wallace was eager for revenge, so articles were signed for a second Savage vs Wallace fight on Wednesday 29 March, at the Castle Tavern in Holborn, with the match to come off at the end of May for £50 a-side at Epsom Downs.[216]

The battleground that was finally settled upon for their second fight was Banstead Downs in Surrey, near the same spot where Daniel Mendoza had fought and lost his last fight against Tom Owen seven years previously, at the age of 55. The fight was prudently relocated from Epsom to Banstead Downs due to the interference of the authorities, and was fixed for £50 a-side to come off less than three months after their first fight, on 29 May 1827. Ned Savage decided to train at Child's Hill, in Hampstead, once more, while Jem Wallace was stationed at Harry Lancaster's establishment, the Bell in Hendon. On this occasion, both men were seen to be in the pink of condition on the day appointed for the fight. Ned was the heavier man, weighing in at 12st to Jem's 10st 6lbs. The advantages of weight on Ned Savage's side were

215 As recorded in *Bell's Life in London and Sporting Chronicle*, 25 March 1827.

216 The fight articles for this second contest were published in *Bell's Life in London and Sporting Chronicle* on 1 April 1827.

BELL'S LIFE IN LONDON,

AND SPORTING CHRONICLE.

SAVAGE AND JEM WALLACE.

Edward Savage agrees to fight James Wallace for 50*l.* aside. A fair stand-up fight, in a twenty-four foot roped ring. Half minute time. The battle to take place on Tuesday, the 29th of May. Four pounds are now deposited in the hands of P. E. The second deposit of eight pounds aside to be made good at Mr. Spratt's, the Hole in the Wall, Fleet-street, on Tuesday, April 3. The third deposit, at Mr. Holt's, Cross-lane, Long Acre, ten pounds aside, on Tuesday, April 17. The fourth deposit of ten pounds aside at Mr. Gibson's, Hole in the Wall, Gate-street, Lincoln's Inn Fields, on Tuesday, the 1st of May. The fifth deposit of ten pounds aside at Mr. Belcher's, Castle Tavern, Holborn, on Tuesday, May 8; and the sixth and last deposit of ten pounds aside, also to be made good at Mr. Belcher's, Castle Tavern, Holborn, on Tuesday, the 15th of May. The above deposits to be made good between the hours of eight and ten o'clock on the above evenings, or the money down to be forfeited. Two umpires to be chosen; and also a referee on the ground. The fight to take place within thirty miles of London.

Ned Savage vs. Jem Wallace fight agreement, published in Bell's Life in London and Sporting Chronicle, *1 April 1827.*

thought to be counterbalanced by the superior fistic science of Jem Wallace, so betting was even. For the rematch, Ned secured the services of his brother, Bill Savage, as a second, along with Ned O'Neal, while Wallace was supported by Tom Oliver and Young Gas.

In spite of his commitment to training, Ned Savage had failed to hone his primitive skills and strategy to any appreciative degree in the interim. After coming up to the scratch he began flourishing his left and circling it in readiness for his favourite 'old-style' over-handed chop. By contrast Wallace's stance was steady, with a solid defensive posture and his hands held up. Each attempt to land his chop brought Savage a straight blow to the nose and in his impatience Savage continually rushed his man, receiving jab after jab for his pains. Savage's thoughts soon turned to throwing, and in this he was seen to have greater success than in landing his chopping blows. Ned paid dearly for his recklessness, having been smashed by a severe blow to the nose as early as the fifth round, which made him bleed profusely, causing a cry from Wallace's supporters of, 'It's all over.' They had not, however, reckoned on the endurance of the Welshman, who would take another tremendous blow to the nose, 'drawing more claret' in the following round. As the rounds wore on, Savage became ever more reckless in his wild attacks, although his persistence resulted in some success. By and large, however, his continued efforts to land his 'chopper' were stopped and countered by Wallace's careful use of straight punches, Wallace showing a great deal of judgement in fighting on the retreat. Savage appeared as game and as merry as ever, even coming up to the scratch laughing in the rounds that followed, seemingly unbothered by the punishment he was receiving.

By the 17th round, Jem Wallace's hands were puffy and trembling, and were fast failing him from the sustained punishment that he was dealing out to Savage. Ned fought on, without judgement and seemingly without strategy, landing a tremendous blow in the 22nd round. The scrambling nature of the battle continued, with nail marks appearing on Wallace's neck as Savage's recklessness in the falls became more apparent. They fought for one hour and 24 minutes, totalling 61 rounds, although the interest of the spectators had waned long before this time. Savage's courage and endurance was in evidence right to the last, although finally, when 'quite groggy, stupefied, and almost blind, his friends gave in for him', conceding their man's defeat, although on hearing the news, Ned still wanted to toe the scratch and fight on. Had Wallace possessed greater punching power, it seemed likely that the fight would have ended much sooner, Savage's performance had been more than lacklustre, and it was reported that Ned's blows were '... of that wild description which had no certain direction, and nothing but his powers of endurance and strength could have kept him so long on his legs'.

In conclusion, *Bell's Life* would conclude that Ned was 'decidedly a bad fighter', and had 'only his game to recommend him'. At the termination of the battle, Ned Savage said that the blow to the nose in the sixth round had caused him the most damage, and that he had swallowed a great deal of blood. Ned had also fractured all the small bones of his left hand as a result of his reliance on his old style left-handed chop, so his arm was placed in a sling.

The defeat did not sit easily with Ned, and he would quickly issue a challenge through the pages of *Bell's Life* to Wallace on 3 June stating the willingness of his brother, Bill, to fight in his place until such time as the bones in his left hand had healed:

> TO THE EDITOR OF BELL'S LIFE IN LONDON.
> SIR – You will oblige me by informing Wallace, with whom I fought for the second time on Tuesday last, that I am not satisfied, and that I am anxious for another trial. We have now won a battle a piece, and I think he can have no objection, in fairness, to fight the odd one, so that our friends may judge which is really the best man. I shall be at Mr. Belcher's, the Castle Tavern, on Tuesday evening, to sign articles to fight in three months, for 50*l.* or 100*l.*; or, if Wallace wishes not to remain idle so long, my brother William will fight him at his own time for the like sum, and he can take me after.
>
> EDWARD SAVAGE.

Prior to a benefit event arranged for Ned Savage at the Three Compasses public houses in Holborn on 22 June, he again made his desire to secure a third and deciding match against either Jem Wallace, or his old rival, Jem Kirkman for 100 sovereigns, to finally prove his fistic superiority.[217] The challenges were ignored, and neither Wallace nor Kirkman bothered to show up at the event, leaving Ned to brood on the matter. Determined to force Wallace into fighting him again, Ned was propping up the bar at the Castle Tavern the following month, after having again issued a statement of his willingness to meet Wallace.[218] With bad feeling at an all-time high, an irritable Jem Kirkman appeared in the Castle Tavern the following Monday, having been considerably annoyed by the continual 'chaffing' of Ned Savage. While the coach driver professed that he had no desire to seek his fame with the knuckles, Kirkman felt honour-bound to meet Savage, announcing that he 'could not suffer himself to be attacked upon all occasions with impunity' by his Welsh cab-driving rival. Kirkman proposed

217 As recorded *in Bell's Life in London and Sporting Chronicle,* 17 June 1827.

218 As recorded in *Bell's Life in London and Sporting Chronicle,* 8 July 1827.

fighting his truculent antagonist for £10 of his own money and a purse. The battle money was quickly covered by Ned Savage, so the match was made for the following month.[219]

The fractured bones of Ned Savage's left hand had apparently healed enough in the time that had elapsed for him to fight Kirkman on 28 August 1827, at Colney Heath. Wounded pride and honour had forced the contest, and while the grudge match may have drawn interest from their fellow cab and hackney coach drivers, the Fancy were disinterested in the result. *Bell's Life* wearily reported that 'the merit of the men, if they possess any, are well-known to our readers' and that their reputations as fighters were of 'a very questionable description' and that 'their pretensions to the pugilistic art are extremely slender'.

The fight might not have come off at all as a few weeks prior to the contest, Jem Kirkman had a narrow escape when travelling to Smithfield races on an old 'Dragoon horse', which was to be auctioned. While Kirkman was riding the beast, a friend had jumped on to the horse's back. Startled, the steed had raced off at full gallop in a state of alarm, and threw Jem on to the spikes of some iron railings at Euston Square. Fortunately, Kirkman escaped all injury, with the spikes having only penetrated his clothes, leaving him in need of a trip to his tailor, and not a doctor.[220] Despite having secured a match against Kirkman, the loss to Jem Wallace still rankled Ned Savage, and just a couple of weeks before his match against Kirkman he attended a benefit event held in honour of his brother, Bill, at the Rising Sun public house in Windmill Street, hoping to make a match with Wallace,[221] for £50 or a hundred pounds a-side, for three months time.[222]

As regards the match with Jem Kirkman, Ned was confident of securing the victory over his rival, boasting that he was prepared to back himself to the tune of £100. Jem Kirkman, undergoing his training at the Castle Inn at Highgate, was greatly angered by the statement, and replied that if Savage or his supporters wished

219 As recorded in *Bell's Life in London and Sporting Chronicle*, 15 July 1827.

220 As recorded in *Bell's Life in London and Sporting Chronicle*, 12 August 1827.

221 As recorded in *Bell's Life in London and Sporting Chronicle*, 12 August 1827.

222 As recorded in *Bell's Life in London and Sporting Chronicle*, 5 August 1827.

to make an appearance at his training quarters, he would be more than happy to cover their money.[223]

On the day of the fight, while both men looked in reasonable health, their fighting condition could be said to be anything but good. When Jem Kirkman pulled off his shirt, his physique was exceedingly disappointing, being 'as fat as Bacchus', and he was quite as flabby and rotund as the Roman God of fertility and wine. This decline in condition was ascribed to Kirkman's recently found love, a washerwoman who doted on Jem to the degree that he had been fed 'fowls for breakfast, rabbits for dinner, fish with his tea, and God knows what with his supper'. Having led a life of considerable ease and gluttony for some time, the coach driver appeared in poor condition to fight Ned for the third time. On this occasion, Savage had engaged the services of Jem Burns and Ike Dodd as seconds, while Kirkman was supported by Tom Mason and Jem Landsdowne. A short delay to the start of the fight took place due to the length of the nails in Ned Savage's fighting shoes, and a hammer was quickly procured and used to shorten them.

In keeping with Ned Savage's contests on previous occasions, the battle would prove to be a tedious testament to his unquestionable powers of endurance, lasting some two hours and two minutes, and 93 rounds in total, with the fight swinging first one way and then the other. Both would show the marks of the punches that they had received, which was 'pretty much upon a par; each had the *bark* of his *conck* scraped, and his *claret* tapped, while diver's bumps proved that their *knuckular* visitations to each other's nobs were not without effect'. Savage's face was terribly swollen and one ear was 'fearfully smashed'. Typically, Ned had the advantage in throwing, although he received a great deal of criticism for his habit of falling on his man with his knees when down, for which angry exclamations of 'Foul' were quick in coming from Jem Kirkman's supporters.

The falls sustained by Kirkman brought him to a near standstill by the 55th round, although he showed remarkable powers of recovery and delivered heavy blows to his antagonist in the following rounds, which left Savage looking 'foggy' although still strong on his legs. The fight continued in this manner until the 93rd round,

223 As recorded in *Bell's Life in London and Sporting Chronicle*, 19 August 1827.

when Kirkman, with his strength now failing, was thrown heavily. Savage stood near him for a moment and then dropped on to Kirkman with both knees. Instantaneously, Kirkman's supporters shouted 'Foul' and appealed to the umpires, who disagreed.

The referee was asked for his judgement, but he was unable to say whether Savage had fallen on Kirkman with his knees intentionally or not. In the disagreement that followed, Jem Kirkman's followers were adamant that Ned Savage had breached the rules, and after a lengthy dispute it was agreed to draw the stakes, thus rendering all the bets void.

While it was thought that Kirkman's failing strength meant that he was unlikely to win, Savage's conduct was looked upon with great distaste, *Bell's Life* stating that 'Savage... from the repetition of his foul practises, scarcely deserved success; and it is to be hoped that this may operate as a lesson to him to be more cautious in his future fights'.

Once again, Ned Savage's deficiencies in the finer points of the art had been much in evidence, and had he known how to take advantage of Jem Kirkman's distress and shown more caution in the placement of his blows, the fight would likely have ended in his favour in a fraction of the time taken. Kirkman was carried from the battleground in poor shape, although his heart was stirred by the sight of his besotted washerwoman, who brought a pigeon pie to console her man before he was conveyed to her home and was put to bed.

Sadly, this contest would cement the reputation of Ned Savage as a dirty fighter, and it was some time before he would enter the ring again, after having fallen out of favour with the Fancy. Ned was quick to issue a statement of his willingness to fight Kirkman again, having been prepared to lay down either £50 to £40 or £25 to £20 on a fourth prize fight.[224] In his eagerness to secure a fight against Kirkman, a subsequent challenge to Ned Savage from Ned Harwood to fight for £25 was ignored.[225]

Ned Savage continued to try to engage Kirkman in a match and was reportedly prepared to stake £30 to £25 in order to make the fight. While Kirkman's supporters seemed willing to commit

224 As recorded in *Bell's Life in London and Sporting Chronicle,* 2 September 1827.

225 As recorded in *Bell's Life in London and Sporting Chronicle,* 2 September 1827.

to putting an initial £10 deposit on the contest in November,[226] it was Savage's supporters that seemed unable to come up with the remainder of the stake money the following month.[227] Further attempts to settle the match would appear to have faltered, and were subsequently shelved until the new year[228].

In January of 1828, a new challenger stepped up to the mark, when a novice by the name of Harry Wood, better known as 'Spring the Conjuror',[229] made his desire to fight Ned known, so a match was hastily agreed at the Norfolk Arms on Friday, 11 January.[230] Spring had elected to try his luck in the London Prize Ring after having enjoyed some minor success in the Liverpool Ring. On his arrival in London, Spring had been seeking a match for some time in vain, and had utilised his skills as a magician to entertain the Fancy at the various sporting public houses to improve his public profile while seeking an opponent to do battle against in the London Prize Ring. The Conjuror had also sparred at the Fives Court and at benefit events, where his appearances had been met with a great deal of merriment due to the fact he possessed a physique unlikely to assist him in his desire to become a professional pugilist:

> Like the Living Skeleton, his bones seemed to be altogether unencumbered with flesh; and from the extraordinary pliancy of his joints, he looks rather like a puppet worked by wires, than anything human.

The battle between Spring the Conjuror and Ned Savage was fixed to come off on Tuesday, 15 January at Banstead Downs for £5 a-side, following a contest between Ned Savage's brother, Bill, and Paddy Flynn, the St Giles Irishman. With just three days

226 As recorded in *Bell's Life in London and Sporting Chronicle,* 25 November 1827.

227 As recorded in *Bell's Life in London and Sporting Chronicle,* 9 December 1827.

228 As recorded in *Bell's Life in London and Sporting Chronicle,* 16 December 1827.

229 Harry Wood fought under the name 'Spring the Conjuror' while trying to establish himself in the London Prize Ring. Spring is recorded as Harry Wood in *Fistiana* in the fight entry for Ned Savage on 15 January 1828. Spring would later fight in the Liverpool Ring with some success under his real name.

230 As recorded in *Bell's Life in London and Sporting Chronicle,* 13 January 1828.

between the match being made and the day of the battle, Spring's supporters had an impossible job to get their man into optimum physical condition in such a short period of time. Jem Hood of the Norfolk Arms was charged with doing what he could, and fed the Conjuror platefuls of beef steaks to try and strengthen his constitution as much as possible in the few days prior to the fight. Outwardly, the Conjuror remained unchanged on the day of the contest, and when he stripped for battle a yokel was heard to remark that he looked as though he had come from a neighbouring churchyard rather than having been a creature of flesh and blood. Contrary to all expectations, the merriment of the crowd soon turned to admiration when Spring was seen to exhibit a degree of talent and bravery that no one could have imagined.

By comparison, Ned Savage was a picture of athleticism, weighing upwards of 12st, and drew sharp contrast to the long, stringy figure of Spring, whose weight was under 10st. The Conjuror was ill-prepared for the fight and had been forced to borrow a pair of breeches from the Chelsea Snob, which did not come to within 2in of his knees. His ludicrous appearance drew forth roars of laughter when his skeletal body toed the scratch in fighting pose. Ned Savage laughed along with them, but he was not laughing for long. In the second round, Spring landed a smashing blow to the left cheek of Savage that left him with a gaping wound. Unsurprisingly, Ned's thoughts quickly turned to throwing and in the following round he hurled the Conjuror with brutal force, Spring making a despairing squeak as Savage fell on him.

As Ned continued to bore in, Spring jumped away like a grasshopper, trying to evade the Welshman's swinging blows, and receiving some criticism for occasionally falling without a blow. With each fall, it seemed likely that the Conjuror was going to be severely hurt, falling like the 'downfall of a house of cards' with 'every limb seeming to tumble in different directions', but he somehow managed to renew the battle with undiminished vigour each time. Astonishingly, Spring was seen to hit out right and left with 'uncommon severity' as the rounds mounted, and in time both of Savage's ears had swelled to four times their normal size, his right eye had been closed and his forehead had been cut. Many of the spectators began to feel that despite his inexperience, Spring was proving to be the better man.

The fight reached a turning point in the 117th round, when Ned Savage, resorting to the tactics that had made him notorious, fell heavily on the exhausted Conjuror with his knee as he lay on the ropes, by which time Spring was nearly insensible. While there were complaints of foul conduct, Savage's actions were looked upon as being in the spirit of 'give and take', so the objections of Spring's supporters were ignored. The Conjuror would bravely come up to the scratch for three more rounds, by which time he was almost unconscious and his seconds finally gave in for him. The contest was then awarded to Ned Savage, whose face had been dreadfully disfigured by the Conjuror's knuckles after 120 rounds had been fought over the course of an hour and 43 minutes.

The stakes were handed over to Ned at Jack Randall's establishment, the Hole in the Wall at Chancery Lane, the following evening. Ned's backers apparently felt so sorry for Spring's wounded pride that they presented him with a sovereign to cheer his spirits. Curiously, Spring was apparently eager to meet Savage a second time, with Ned replying that he was willing to meet the Conjuror for £50 a-side, although nothing came of it.[231] Ned's spirits must have been at a low ebb; although he had beaten Spring, the underhanded manner in which he had secured victory against the novice had further undermined his poor reputation in the London Prize Ring.

231 As recorded in *Bell's Life in London and Sporting Chronicle,* 27 January 1828.

Chapter 19

A Shamed Savage

Ned Savage finally arranged to meet Jem Kirkman for the fourth time at Epsom Downs on 20 May 1828, for a mere £5 a-side and a purse. The contest was viewed with absolute disinterest; the collection gathered from the spectators brought forth just £4 and the scrambling fight that followed proved as big a disappointment as it was expected to be. Ned Savage fought more wildly than ever before and Kirkman outshone the Welshman, throwing him heavily several times. On this occasion, Savage's legendary endurance failed him, and after 25 minutes he was forced to give in, being unable to come up to the scratch at the call of time.

With interest flagging in Ned Savage's pugilistic career, Ned was again resorting to 'chaffing' and goading potential opponents in order to make matches and stir public interest. A butcher by the name of Peter Sweeney decided he was the man to shut Ned's big mouth once and for all. To this end, Sweeney sent a letter to *Bell's Life*, which was published on 24 August 1828, stating his willingness to fight:

> TO THE EDITOR OF BELL'S LIFE IN LONDON.
> SIR – Ned Savage having more than once bounced in an extraordinary way respecting his intention to fight me, when I had not a friend present, I have now only to say that if "he means what he says," and does not, as usual, merely intend to chaff, I can be matched against him for 50*l.* a-side; and if he will meet me on Wednesday evening next, at Frank Redmond's, Lomond's Pond, I shall be prepared to stake ten pounds, and sign articles. If he does

> not come, I shall take it for granted that his Welsh blood has got cool, and his Welch friends still cooler. Yours, &c.
>
> PETER SWEENEY.

Ned Savage was as eager to irritate Sweeney as ever, stating that he was prepared to make the match for £25 a-side rather than £50, as his friends had gone shooting in the country and he could not raise the full sum. Savage dismissively observed that this sum should be more than enough to please Sweeney, as he had never fought for a purse exceeding a paltry £2. A great deal of chaffing followed, with Sweeney angrily agreeing to fight for £30 a-side.[232]

After a few further complications, the match was finally made for £25 a-side, although the drama was ongoing. Three deposits were made by both men in the weeks that followed, with the date for the final deposit having been fixed for Wednesday, 17 September, before 10pm at the City of London public house in Berwick Street. At seven minutes past ten, Peter Sweeney threw his money down on the table, although there was no sign of a friend of Ned Savage, who had been engaged to put down the final deposit on Ned's behalf. The friend appeared a mere seven minutes later, although by this time Sweeney had already claimed forfeit and left the premises, stating that Savage would have to make a fresh match for larger stakes, and signified his intention to pocket the £20 that had already been staked by the Welshman.[233] The resulting disagreement dragged on for some time, and meetings were scheduled by the Fair Play Club, the body set up to regulate the prize ring, to settle the dispute. Peter Sweeney finally agreed to the match continuing for £30 a-side, after it was pointed out to him that he was also late in making his final deposit. The butcher won the toss for the choice of venue and picked Norwood in Surrey, near his training quarters at the Jolly Sailor, as the location for the battle on 14 October.[234] It was a foolish choice of battleground, being one of the more heavily populated parts of the county of Surrey, and falling under the jurisdiction of two magistrates. The organisers received word that Mr Cato, one of the

232 As recorded in *Bell's Life in London and Sporting Chronicle,* 31 August 1828.

233 As recorded in *Bell's Life in London and Sporting Chronicle,* 21 September 1828.

234 As recorded in *Bell's Life in London and Sporting Chronicle,* 28 September 1828.

FISTIANA;

OR,

THE ORACLE OF THE RING:

Savage, Ned, b Cope, 5*l* a side, 14r, Copenhagen Fields, Feb 19, 1823.
— b Avis, a purse, 7r, 15m, Wedgebury's Pitt, March 9, 1826.
— bn by Locke.
— bn by Dick Curtis.
— bn by Kirkman twice.
— b Kirkman, 25*l* a side, 101r, 2h 30m, Noman's Land, July 11, 1826.
— b Wallace, 25*l* a side, 127r, 2h 27m, Whetstone, March 6, 1827.
— bn by Wallace.
— dr with Kirkman (foul blow and wrangle), Aug 28, 1827.
— b Harry Wood, 5*l*, 120r, Banstead Downs, Jan 15, 1828.
— bn by T. Sweeney.
— fought Peter Sweeney, 30*l* a side, 16r, beaks interfered, Norwood, Oct 14, 1828.
— paid ft to Sweeney, Oct 29, 1828.
— bn by Peter Sweeney.
— bn by Gow.

The fight record of Ned Savage, published in Fistiana; or, the Oracle of the Ring *(1867).*

more troublesome magistrates with a reputation for breaking up prize fights in the past, was currently in France, so it was deemed safe for the fight to go ahead.

On the morning of the fight, a field was selected on the south side of the Croydon Canal, and the ring was hastily assembled. At one o'clock, Savage and Sweeney entered the ring; Ned Savage was attended to by Harry Holt and Ned Neal, while Peter Sweeney was accompanied by Alec Reid and Frank Redmond. Savage's blue colours, sporting a 'bird's eye' design, were tied in his corner, while Sweeney tied a yellow handkerchief around his corner stake. After having stripped for battle, Sweeney appeared to be in superior condition to Savage, who complained of swelling in the glands of his neck as the result of a cold. Sweeney was confident of success and shook five sovereigns in his fist at Savage, offering to lay them on his victory. The bet went uncovered as Ned Savage's backers had already emptied their pockets and laid sizeable bets on the Welshman's victory.

At the start of the contest, both men were eager to fight, although Ned Savage, seeking to land his over-handed chop, was seen to hit wildly and clumsily. Peter Sweeney showed superior judgement, landing on Savage's ribs, and had some success in visiting his opponent's face during the in-fighting that followed. It wasn't until the fourth round that Ned's fierce attacks benefitted him, Sweeney bled from his nose and Savage afterwards caught the butcher a smack on his left eye. By the seventh, Peter Sweeney was pulling ahead, and dropped Ned Savage with a heavy swinging punch to the jaw, after which Savage was picked up by his attendants. When time was called, the Welsh cab driver made it up to the scratch, but his legs were seen to be 'quite abroad'. In the 13th round, the punishment meted out by Sweeney was beginning to show, and Savage was bleeding from his ear. As the rounds mounted, however, Ned succeeded in landing heavy body blows and continued to rush in, to the cheers of his admirers. It was in the 16th, as the fight went first one way and then the other, that matters were brought to an abrupt end by the interference of a posse of police officers, to the great disappointment of both men, who had been equally confident of victory.

It was decided that the battle should be resumed at the Old Oak Common, in Middlesex, so the spectators travelled to the new scene of battle in advance of the combatants, and set up a ring. Savage and Sweeney did not appear, the police having threatened to follow them to the location where the ring had been pitched and take them into custody if they attempted to resume the battle. Appearing at the Castle Tavern in Holborn that night, neither Savage nor Sweeney were greatly the worse for wear as a result of their brief struggle. Savage was puffy round the face and ear, although still fresh and capable. Sweeney, by comparison, only showed the slightest hint of a black eye. Ned Savage's backers felt satisfied that had the battle continued, Ned's superiority in throwing, supported by his 'everlasting' endurance, would have seen him emerge victorious. Peter Sweeney's supporters were equally confident of their man, having believed that the butcher's superior science and skill at in-fighting would have paved his way to success.

Before they were able to settle the matter, Ned Savage and Peter Sweeney were forced to attend court to explain their actions along with their seconds and bottle holders. Their defence was handled by Harry Holt, who sent a letter to the magistrate, Mr Chambers, to apologise for the offence, stating that the organisers had made a regrettable mistake by pitching the ring within the Surrey boundary, having believed that it had been pitched within the county of Kent. Holt assured Chambers that if he treated the matter with leniency, the men would never fight within the Surrey county boundary again. Gratified with their pledge, Mr Chambers took their entreaties to the Magistrates in Sessions, and on his return stated that the offenders must go before the court and enter their personal recognisances not to reoffend. After having been bound over to keep the peace, the men were allowed to leave court. The decision as to whether Ned Savage or Peter Sweeney was the better man lay unresolved for the time being, although Sweeney was quick to vow his intention to chop Ned to 'sausage meat', a sentiment echoed by his Welsh rival.[235]

There were further problems before a contest could be arranged. After both men had posted a £5 deposit for a rematch, there were scenes of some drama at the Duke of Wirtemberg in Hatfield Street, Blackfriars, on 9 December 1828, where the two fighters were meant to put down a further £10 a-side before 10pm. Once again, Ned Savage's backers disappointed him and, as the clock struck ten, there was still no sign of them, so a forfeit was declared. Overcome with emotion, Ned burst into tears, lamenting that his friends had failed him again and he wailed that he wished to fight Peter Sweeney above all things, turning three shillings out of his pockets and begging the butcher to accept them as a token of his desire to fight. Sweeney was unmoved and,

---

235 As recorded in *Bell's Life in London and Sporting Chronicle,* 26 October 1828.

in his desperation, Ned offered to sell his clothes in order to make the sum up to £5. In the midst of this unfolding drama, one of Ned's backers arrived and threw ten sovereigns on the table, having run all the way from Islington to meet the deadline, but it was too late.[236]

In the argument that followed, a new opponent stepped up. Peter Sweeney's brother, Terence Sweeney, offered to fight Ned for £5 a-side within the month. Although Peter Sweeney's refusal to fight was a great disappointment to Ned, he was determined to make a match and elected to take what he could get. Terence Sweeney was both taller and heavier than his brother and while he was a novice in the prize ring, he had been taking lessons in the boxing school of Alec Reid, the Chelsea Snob. It was only after Ned agreed to fight Terence that Peter Sweeney was persuaded to make a new match against Ned for £50 a-side the following March. The money that had already been given to the stakeholder, Tom Spring, remained on the table as part of the new battle money. In a surprising turn of events, Ned would now be facing both Sweeney brothers in the ring.[237]

The contest against Terence Sweeney came off at Epping Forest on 23 December 1828, near the Old May Pole. Ned Savage seemed to believe that the match was unlikely to extend his limited skills, observing that 'it would be a little pleasant pastime previous to his entering upon the festivities of Christmas'. With Terence having been a novice in the prize ring, and Ned's reputation at an all-time low, there were few spectators beyond a small party consisting of the friends of both fighters. As a ring had been unavailable for use, a few rough poles and ropes were fashioned into a makeshift ring by Jack Carter and Alec Reid. On this occasion, Ned Savage was attended by Jack Carter and Bob Castles, while Terence Sweeney was seconded by his brother, Peter, and Alec Reid, who appeared in support of his pupil. At the start of the fight, Ned Savage was quick to take the lead, nearly closing Sweeney's eye with his right and cutting his opponent's cheek. Terence, for his part, proved that he was not to be taken lightly, and hit out with great severity with both hands, peppering Ned's face dreadfully. Ned Savage's

236 As recorded in *Bell's Life in London and Sporting Chronicle*, 14 December 1828.

237 As recorded in *Bell's Life in London and Sporting Chronicle*, 14 December 1828.

endurance seemingly failed him and his lack of training was clear to see. After 26 rounds lasting 33 minutes, Ned's seconds saw that there was no chance for him to seize victory over his opponent and gave in for their man. Little the worse for wear, Terence Sweeney was afterwards conveyed home, although Ned Savage's injuries were so severe that he had to be put to bed to recover from his beating. Ned's reputation was at an all-time low amongst his own supporters and he had been at Tom Spring's public house the night before the fight, drinking from every glass that had been offered to him.

None of Ned's regular band of supporters had accompanied him to the battleground, and he had been forced to request the assistance of Carter and Castles as seconds without notice. They were completely unprepared for the task, and did not even have a sponge in their possession, so in a short time Ned Savage's face had been covered in gore. The horrific appearance of Ned had merely spurred Terence Sweeney on to greater efforts. *Bell's Life* commented that, 'We have heard of *Savages* in distant climes, who were wont to daub their *phizzes* with various colours, in the hope of terrifying their enemies in battle – whether our Welsh *Savage* had this object in view when he presented his *nob* to Sweeney, in all its unmitigated horrors of the sanguinary drippings from his wounds, we know not; but certainly, if such were his motive, it was ill-founded, for Sweeney, so far from taking alarm, only derived fresh energies from the display, and "leathered away" rather to increase rather than to lessen the horrors of the spectacle presented to him.'

Having emerged victorious in his first prize ring battle, Terence Sweeney was seen to do ample credit to the training of his tutor, Alec Reid, and it was thought with a little more instruction, Sweeney might well prove to be a troublesome customer in the future. The long-awaited fight that came off a few months later against Peter Sweeney also did little to improve Ned Savage's increasingly poor reputation amongst the Fancy. Colney Heath had been named as the venue for the fight as it was thought that the somewhat wild and desolate spot might prove to be a place unlikely to attract the same kind of interest from the authorities that had brought their previous meeting to an abrupt and premature end. Ned Savage was no stranger to the inside of a public house and the battleground was compromised by the Welshman's thirst for alcohol the night before the fight, on 2 March. Savage had pitched up at The Cock public house on the borders of the Heath and had drunkenly bragged to all and sundry of the impending fight the following day. The news quickly reached a neighbouring magistrate, who promptly stopped the contest being fought in the county of Hertfordshire. For this reason, Tom Spring, the stakeholder, was forced to name Shearmere, in Bedfordshire, as an alternative battleground, so Ned Savage and Peter Sweeney, and the ever-decreasing members of the Fancy who were drawn by the prospect of a 'Savage battle', numbering less than a hundred, set out at full trot in their carriages and gigs on 3 March 1829. On this occasion, Ned Savage wore a leek on his hat to honour his home country of Wales and his followers put yellow neckerchiefs, or the 'yellow man', round their necks to indicate their support. Sweeney's partisans donned blue-and-white spotted neckerchiefs to signify their faith in their man.

Shortly after three o'clock, the men stepped up to the scratch, Ned Savage attended by Harry Holt and Tom Gaynor, and Peter Sweeney being accompanied by Savage's old rival, Dick Curtis, and Alec Reid. On stripping, both men were in excellent condition, Ned Savage weighing 12st to Sweeney's 10st 12lbs. In addition to the advantage of weight, Ned was of superior height and reach to the butcher, whose short arms cast doubts amongst the spectators that he was cut out to be a pugilist of consequence in the London Prize Ring. Regardless of these concerns, the betting was still 6/4 in Peter Sweeney's favour at the start of the contest. As the fight began, it became obvious that Ned Savage had attempted to address some of the deficiencies of his fighting style, holding his hands in better position, instead of relying on the twirling motion of his right hand to try to distract from his use of the old-style over-handed chop with his left, which he had previously favoured. Peter Sweeney struck out with his right, landing on Savage's head, but received a blow in return on the mouth. The butcher proved his gameness as the fight continued and Sweeney rushed in and planted his right to the body and followed it up with a left to the ear. A final right hand brought Savage to the turf. Ned, not to be outdone, promptly landed a blow to Sweeney's ear, which drew first blood. Despite the improvement in the Welshman's style, his blows were not effectively executed and in the rounds that followed, he was jabbed repeatedly by Sweeney, who visibly damaged Savage's nose and closed his right eye. The cab driver's ears also started to show the effects of heavy punishment and quickly swelled to an extraordinary size as the fight unfolded. Ned Savage continually hit out and yet he frequently missed his opponent until at last he landed a nasty punch with his left under Peter Sweeney's right eye, leaving a gaping wound. The flow of blood was stopped by the application of a patch of beaver taken from the hat of a spectator.

By the middle of the battle, Peter Sweeney was beginning to look more than a little ragged, his hands had puffed up and in the vast majority of the rounds, the butcher was either floored or went down. Ned Savage, showing his usual eagerness to attack, was thrown heavily on his head several times as a consequence of his reckless assaults. The odds swung first one way then the other. With Sweeney's hands now failing rapidly, the butcher was forced to rely on shoving rather than punching and in this sloppy manner he succeeded in sending Savage down once more. It was in the 94th round that Ned was finally thrown on his head with such force as to be rendered unconscious, and Sweeney was declared the victor after one hour and 55 minutes. Peter Sweeney was exhausted but an initial inspection of his wounds merely showed the cut on his cheek and the 'utter demolition' of his hands. On the arrival of his carriage at the Bull public house in Harpenden, however, it was found that Sweeney was so weak that he was incapable of walking from his carriage. Ned Savage was reportedly 'dreadfully punished' and was taken to the Cross Keys public house in the same village, where he was forced to remain that night.

After the defeat, Ned Savage's few remaining staunch supporters were quick to speak up in defence of their man, pointing out the great improvement in his style of fighting and the bottomless courage that had marked his appearances in the ring on previous occasions. Despite their dogged support, the correspondent for *Bell's Life* who reported on the contest, would find little merit in the efforts of either man, commenting, 'Viewing the qualifications of both impartially, we should recommend them, in future, to abandon the ring, and seek reputation in some more peaceable walks in life.'

The battle money was handed over to Peter Sweeney at the Castle Tavern the following Friday, with Ned Savage having been bitterly disappointed with the result. Ned was quick to claim the defeat was an accident and stated that his loyal followers were willing to find the money to back him in one more contest. Peter Sweeney exhibited much greater marks of the punishment than were previously thought, with his right eye having been completely closed and his left eye also showing signs of extensive injury. The butcher's hands and wrists were greatly swollen and he also complained of having been stiff and sore all over, so declined Ned Savage's invitation to fight again.

It had perhaps been a valiant effort on the part of Ned Savage to reverse his diminishing fortunes in the prize ring, and he received some credit for his attempts to address the obvious flaws in his style of fighting. He had also resisted the temptation to fall on his opponent with his knees to secure victory, as he had in the past. Sadly, Ned's next fixture in the prize ring would sever the last threads on which his declining reputation hung once and for all.

A new opponent, John Davis, known as 'the Manchester Black', had been selected by Tom Spring as a likely candidate to lower Ned Savage's colours for £25 a-side. With backers for the Welshman now being thin on the ground, Savage had induced an Irish traveller, whose judgement was clouded by alcohol, to put down the initial £5 deposit on his behalf. The remainder of the money was meant to be found by Savage himself, although he failed to find the outstanding £20. In an attempt to save his £5, the Irishman was induced to find a further £15, after being convinced by Ned Savage that he would win with ease. On 9 June 1829, Ned Savage was transported to the battleground, Harpenden Common, in Hertfordshire, in a post-chaise, with no indication that he had any thoughts other than to meet the Manchester Black in battle. It was only after the ring had been pitched that rumour spread that Ned Savage did not intend to fight. His Irish patron was aghast. 'Not fight?' exclaimed his astonished backer. 'What do you mane [mean]? 'It isn't in arnest you are?' Ned, smirking to himself, replied, 'Indeed hur is, hur was climbing up a tree to get a starling's nest, and hur fell down and hurt hur loins, and so hur can't fight at all.' The Irishman looked at Ned in a state of shock, and then at John Davis, who had already entered the ring in readiness for the battle. 'Can't you go into the ring and get a licking, whether or no,' he said to Savage, 'so that I may have something for my money?' Ned was unmoved and refused to fight, so John Davis promptly claimed the stakes and the match was abandoned.

The spectators were naturally incredulous and many doubted the story of the starling's nest, which was viewed as an excuse invented by Ned on the spur of the moment, being fearful of receiving a thrashing at the hands of Davis. The patience of the Fancy and Ned's fellow pugilists was now at an end, and the following night he was turned out of the Castle Tavern public house for the last time amidst the hisses and groans of the patrons, and was told in no uncertain terms that he would never enter the pub again. As far as *Bell's Life* was concerned, Ned Savage's reputation was now beyond repair, scathingly commenting, 'so much for the game Welchman and such the gratitude which such fellows exhibit towards those who may be inclined to do them a service'. The anger of the Fancy at Ned's conduct would be made apparent in the reporter's irritable remarks that he hoped that 'the next time Savage is elevated beyond the level of his mother earth, either to seek a bird's nest, or for any other adventurous purpose, he will be apt to injure some part of his person more immediately connected with his wind than his loins.'

The condemnation of Ned Savage's fellow pugilists was not slow in coming and at a subsequent meeting of the Fair Play Club, a resolution was passed excluding Ned Savage from using the official ropes and stakes of the Fair Play Club ever again. It was also recommended that he should, in future, 'be deprived of the countenance of every friend to the Prize Ring, as a person utterly unworthy of confidence', as a result of his refusal to fight John Davis, 'without assigning any rational cause'.[238]

Ned Savage's final contest would come off on 22 December 1829, against an untested opponent named Jack Gow, for a mere £12 to £10 a-side at Norman's Land, in Hertfordshire, after the toss for the battleground had been won by Gow. With the Fancy having turned their back on Ned Savage, only 50 spectators could

---

238 As recorded in *Bell's Life in London and Sporting Chronicle*, 14 June 1829.

be bothered to show up to witness the contest. Ned reverted to his previous scrambling style and although he drew first blood, it was clear that he did not have a chance as the fight continued, having been outfought on all fronts by the novice, Gow. By this stage of his career, even Ned's astonishing physical endurance was now failing him and he was soundly beaten in 23 rounds and 23 minutes. There was no betting on the fight and even the 'small fry' had proved unwilling to put down a few coins on the outcome. A final black mark would be put against Ned Savage's disappointing end to his nine-year career in the Prize Ring, with it having been reported that 'Savage, it appears, offered to sell the fight, but he was not worth purchasing'.

So ended the less-than-illustrious career of the Welsh cab driver, Ned Savage, whose attempts to raise himself above the common herd of the lesser lights of the London Prize Ring had been doomed to failure. While he had never shown the skill and promise of those names destined to become synonymous with pugilistic greatness, in his time Ned had at least been applauded for his merits as a 'game Welchman', and drawn favourable comment from the Fancy through his courage and his ability to endure phenomenal amounts of punishment. Sadly, his continued reliance on underhanded tactics devastated his reputation and resulted in his supporters choosing to abandon him. Ned's refusal to meet John Davis, the Manchester Black, in battle, followed by his decision to resort to offering to fix his final contest, meant that he would end his days as a professional pugilist in disgrace. The 'Welsh Savage' disappeared into the shadows and never darkened the London Prize Ring ever again.

Chapter 20

A Savage Brother

The first instance in which Bill Savage, Ned Savage's brother, had come to the attention of the Fancy had been one that had caused something of a minor sensation, after Bill had tangled with Alec Reid, the 'Chelsea Snob', in rather unusual circumstances. Bill Savage would fight a 'turn-up' with Reid following a fight between Harry Jones, the 'Sailor Boy', and Ned Stockman at Epping Forest on 21 September 1824, in which Stockman proved to be the victor. At the conclusion of the battle, the spectators assembled at the King's Arms, in Stratford, on the way home for some refreshment, and the notion of a turn-up was floated, which was promptly taken up by Alec Reid, who was half-drunk and agreed to meet Bill Savage for £5. The terms having been agreed, the men adjourned to a field behind the King's Arms, where Harry Holt and Jem Burns stepped up as seconds for the Chelsea Snob, with Bill Savage being looked after by his brother Ned and George Weston.

With Reid labouring under the liberal quantities of alcohol he had consumed, the first four rounds showed him as second best, with Savage 'proving himself in every way worthy of his name'. It was only thanks to the efforts of Harry Holt in tending to his man with cold water that Reid was induced to snap out of his drunken state with enough clarity to defend himself with his usual judgement. Reid was afterwards well on his way to overpowering Savage, when the Welshman's supporters, seeing the change in his fortunes, hastily decided to take up arms in defence of their man and began raining sticks down upon the head of the Chelsea Snob. Those spectators who tried to defend the interests of fair play had their skulls cracked by sticks, and in the scenes that followed,

Reid's followers agreed to halve the purse, fearing for the safety of Alec Reid. Reid himself suffered only a few scratches to the face in the attack and was well on his way to winning the fight when the supporters of Bill Savage had turned on him.[239]

The turn-up with the Chelsea Snob ensured that Bill Savage's name was quickly known to all, even though he had not contended against any opponent within the prize ring, and it would be some time before he would make his debut in the London Prize Ring. Bill Savage was, like his brother Ned, a wrestler of some skill and he elected to engage William Moyles, the brother in-law of prominent pugilist Ben Burns in a wrestling contest held at the Sluice House on the banks of the New River on 13 October 1824. The conditions of the contest were that the first man to secure three back falls against his opponent was to be declared the winner, with £10 a-side having initially been staked on the outcome, which was later raised to £50. Bill was a cab driver, like his brother Ned, and had laid some groundwork for his career as a professional pugilist by appearing at the Fives Court prior to the encounter with Moyles. Although the men were well matched as regards their size, William Moyles had been picked as the favourite.

At the start of the match, there was little advantage on either side until Bill drove his antagonist against a table, and afterwards threw Moyles, gaining the first fall. Moyles secured the second fall in the following round, throwing Savage cleverly, making the score one-all. The battle continued with Bill Savage being seen to get the advantage with greater frequency over Moyle, who appeared somewhat winded. In the seventh round, Moyles again

Alec Reid, the 'Chelsea Snob'.

239 This account is taken from *Bell's Life in London and Sporting Chronicle,* 26 September 1824. *Pugilistica* reports this event exceedingly briefly in its chapter on Alec Reid, making no reference to the interference on the part of the spectators, and states that the contest was halted due to the fact that darkness was falling, and the money afterwards divided, after 37 minutes.

successfully threw Savage and the umpires declared that the score was 2/1 in Moyles's favour. In the ninth round Moyles pressed Savage hard for the final fall and Bill forgot for a moment that he was wrestling and not boxing, and took a pugilistic attitude. Moyles took advantage of his error and grabbed hold of Bill, and threw him, although it was afterwards deemed to be a no-fall by the umpires. The 11th round would see a prolonged struggle end with Bill being thrown again, although the umpires decreed that the fall had been a foul. After a lengthy 25-minute dispute, William Moyles was deemed to have taken the second fall. Bill Savage was thrown for the third time in the 17th round and was finally defeated by his skilful opponent. One spectator who believed he could do far better than Bill was his own brother, Ned Savage, who thought that he could have beaten Moyles. As a consequence, Bill and Ned had a brief wrestling contest straight afterwards, in which Ned proved to be an inferior wrestler than Bill and was thrown twice in just a few minutes by his brother.

Bill Savage's entry into the ranks of the professional pugilists of the London Prize Ring would be brought to an abrupt halt in April of 1826, when he was hauled before the court in Middlesex in scandalous circumstances. Described as a 'notorious pugilist', Bill Savage faced the judgement of the court for having tried to sexually assault his young stepdaughter, Mary Ann Chapman. On a Sunday morning in February, Bill Savage's wife had left their home in Princes Street in Bedford Row to visit Uxbridge, and was unable to travel home the same night. Arriving home late that evening and finding his wife absent, Bill told his stepdaughter that she would be sleeping with him that night. Being scared of Bill's temper, and having witnessed Bill throwing knives at her mother following heated arguments on previous occasions, his step-daughter agreed to his demands. After having been awoken and assaulted by Bill in the middle of the night, Mary Ann cried out, 'Pray, father, let me go! Do, father, let me go!' Her cries were heard by a female lodger, Mrs Webb, in the next room, who banged on the partition wall and called out to Bill, saying that he should be ashamed of himself, and implored Mary Ann to come to her room. Bill refused to let his stepdaughter go and locked the door, barring Mary Ann's escape, callously answering that the matter was of no concern to Mrs Webb, and was unmoved by her threat that she would go tell the nightwatchman. Hearing someone at the door soon afterwards, Bill looked out of the window, and saw that it was his wife, and told his terrified stepdaughter to return to her own bed, before opening the door.

The following morning, Bill attempted to conceal his crime after escorting the girl to her workplace, where she was employed as a lace-maker, and implored her not to tell her mother what had taken place the night before. Learning of the assault on her daughter the same day, Bill's long-suffering wife lost no time in bringing the matter to the attention of the authorities. Mary Ann Chapman tearfully recounted the attack before the court, and her testimony was afterwards corroborated by Mrs Webb, who had stayed up until dawn on the night of the incident, fearful that Bill might renew his assault on the innocent girl. The judgement of the court was quick in coming, and Bill Savage was found guilty of assault, and he was sentenced to imprisonment for 12 months and given hard labour for his sins.[240]

Bill Savage would fight his first match in the London Prize Ring a month after having finished serving his sentence, although given his status as a 'notorious pugilist' at the trial, it seems likely that he might well have indulged in a number of skirmishes of minor importance before this time. Bill made relatively quick work of his opponent, which would appear to have been for the sake of 'honour' and not a purse, against a stonemason named Griffiths, beating him in 23 rounds and 45 minutes, which is intriguingly recorded as having come off near the 'Penitentiary' on 7 May 1827.[241]

The following month saw Bill trying to make a match against either Ike Dodd or one 'Hurley', but neither man appeared on the date of the proposed meet to discuss the contest at the Three Compasses in Holborn. Bill would also be disappointed in his attempts to make a match against 'Jennings', likely to have been one John (or Pat) Jennings, with Savage having placed £1 as his first deposit on a fight to come off on 18 September, with £25

240 As recorded in the *Morning Chronicle,* 10 April 1826.

241 This contest is recorded in *Fistiana* under the fight record of Bill Savage. Bill had reportedly been trying to secure a match against Robert Clegg for £50 about 11 days prior to the match, as reported in *Bell's Life in London and Sporting Chronicle* on 6 May 1827.

a-side to be deposited at the Castle Tavern in Holborn, on the first day of August. Unfortunately, Bill failed to raise the cash required for the second deposit the following week and was forced to forfeit. In an attempt to raise money and interest in the fight, Bill hastily organised a benefit event for himself at Ben Burn's establishment, the Rising Sun public house in Windmill Street, having wanted to stake £10 in the hope of landing a match for £50 a-side against Jennings, but was again disappointed in his ambitions.

Undeterred, Bill Savage's next prize fight of consequence would come off on 28 August 1827, against John Brunston, also known as 'Brimstone Jack' or 'Jack of Finchley', for a purse of 40 shillings. The battleground was at Colney Heath and took place straight after the third battle between his brother Ned and his long-standing rival, Jem Kirkman. Brimstone Jack had earned his nickname after disposing of all the brickmakers, tradesmen and labourers to be found in the neighbourhood of Finchley. The fight was preceded by some drama, with Brimstone Jack's wife having followed him to the field of battle and attempted to persuade him not to undertake the fight. Despite her repeated coaxing and scolding, Jack would not be persuaded to give up the match, although it might have been wise if he had. Jack gave a slashing and game performance, but the straight hitting, wrestling abilities and superior experience of Bill Savage would mean that the Finchley man was ultimately outclassed. According to the *Weekly Dispatch*, Jack gave up the contest after 20 rounds and declared himself satisfied that Savage was the better man and pocketed ten shillings as a reward for his valour.[242] *Bell's Life* recorded that the fight lasted just 14 rounds and its account was a little less colourful than that of the *Dispatch*, which had claimed that Brunston's wife was the main cause of his defeat, having insisted on staying within the ropes and apparently 'more than once made free use of her mauleys for the correcting of those who dared to speak a word against her husband', while simultaneously berating her unfortunate spouse for his fighting abilities. At the end of the contest, Jack's wife reportedly led her conquered husband from the ring and promised to give him 'a rare time of it when she got him home'.

---

242 This fight was also recorded as having lasted 20 rounds in *Fistiana*.

The next opponent firmly fixed in Bill Savage's sights was Harry Jones, the 'Sailor Boy' who had previously made his willingness to fight Savage known, in the event his preferred opponents, Barney Aaron or Ned Stockman, were not prepared to meet him.[243]

At a benefit event for Tom Gaynor held at the Tennis Court, Bill mounted the stage and announced his willingness to fight Harry Jones for £25 a-side. Jones made no hesitation in joining Bill on stage, staking a sovereign on the meeting, with two more to be put down to bind the match that evening at the Castle Tavern. At the public house that evening, Harry Jones's backers failed to put in an appearance and the money already put down was forfeit.

For some unknown reason, after offering to post the £25 to secure the fight and the whole of the money was produced, the supporters of Jones promptly backed out of making any agreement, so nothing was done.[244]

Attempts to make an agreement to fight faltered in the weeks that followed, with Harry Jones having been a no-show at Hood's, the fighting tailor's establishment on the Strand, when Bill Savage appeared with his backer to meet Jones.[245] The Sailor Boy would again forfeit a couple of weeks later, having apparently been more tempted to make a match against Dan M'Kenzie.[246] With the proposed match against Jones having stalled, Bill Savage would state his willingness to meet Paddy Flynn, in the event that Harry Jones would not come to terms.[247]

Bill Savage and Harry Jones finally agreed to fight on the evening of 18 December, although after having finally made a match, Harry Jones was sufficiently angered by Bill's conduct at the meeting to write a letter to the editor of *Bell's Life*, highlighting the underhand behaviour of both Bill and his brother, Ned:[248]

---

243 As recorded in *Bell's Life in London and Sporting Chronicle*, 11 November 1827.

244 As recorded in *Bell's Life in London and Sporting Chronicle*, 25 November 1827.

245 As recorded in *Bell's Life in London and Sporting Chronicle*, 2 December 1827.

246 As recorded in *Bell's Life in London and Sporting Chronicle*, 16 December 1827.

247 As recorded in *Bell's Life in London and Sporting Chronicle*, 16 December 1827.

248 As recorded in *Bell's Life in London and Sporting Chronicle*, 23 December 1827.

TO THE EDITOR OF BELL'S LIFE IN LONDON.

SIR – The cowardly conduct of Bill Savage, on Tuesday, compels me to lay the same before the public, for them to judge whether such men ought to be admitted into the Ring. After I had won the toss to name the place of fighting, he declined making the match, and afterwards told my backer (who will come forward at any time) that he and his brother Ned would both pitch into me together. Now I have only to say, I will fight the pair of them in a fortnight for 25*l*. each. If they decline this, I am open to fight any man of my weight for 25*l*. I should like to give Dan M'Kenzie a chance.

HARRY JONES, Sailor Boy.

By this time, Bill Savage had already entered into negotiations with Paddy Flynn, so for the time being, his rivalry with Harry Jones was put to one side. Bill sent an answer to the Sailor Boy's letter, which was published in the newspaper the following week:[249]

TO THE EDITOR OF BELL'S LIFE IN LONDON.

SIR – In answer to Harry Jones's *chaff* in your last, I have only to say, I would have had great pleasure in giving him the preference to Paddy Flynn; but my friends thought Paddy an easier customer, and gave him the turn. I will, however, make a match with Harry, win or lose with Flynn, for fifty or a hundred pounds.

Yours, &c. WILLIAM SAVAGE.

On Tuesday, 15 January 1828, Bill Savage and Paddy Flynn appeared at the appointed battleground at Banstead Downs. While both men had support amongst their friends and followers, neither could be said to have enjoyed a sound reputation amongst the Fancy. In Bill's case, it was said that both 'Bill Savage and his brother Ned are both well known in the sporting houses, and perhaps, more *jaw work* has taken place in their attempts to make matches, than has been observed with any other men in the Ring'. Despite his limited pugilistic record, some people thought

249 As recorded in *Bell's Life in London and Sporting Chronicle*, 30 December 1827.

Bill was a superior fighter to his brother, given Ned's reliance on underhanded techniques and his rather old-fashioned left-handed 'chop', and Bill's supporters were confident of his victory against Flynn. Paddy Flynn, known as a 'St Giles Irishman', had never before fought in the London Prize Ring, but had won some praise for the manner in which he had distinguished himself in contests against other amateurs at the Old Oak Common. As a consequence of his great strength, athletic frame and his notable ability in throwing an opponent, the odds favoured Flynn at 6/4 and it was thought that his superior weight of 12st 6lbs would be too much for the 11st Welshman to overcome.

After having arrived at the battleground, the superiority of Paddy Flynn's physique was obvious to all. On this occasion, Bill Savage retained the services of Harry Holt and Josh Hudson as seconds, while Alec Reid and Savage's rival, Harry Jones, had been engaged by Paddy Flynn. As the fight began, it was Flynn who attacked from the outset and, after some exchanges, the Irishman took the upper hand in the throwing that followed until the 84th round, when Bill Savage was heavily cross-buttocked and Flynn fell upon him. At one point in the fight, the contest was temporarily drawn to a halt by a bulldog owned by a member of the Fancy, which broke into the ring and seized Flynn and then Savage by the drawers while the men were struggling with each other on the ropes. After the dog had been retrieved, the fight was able to continue. Heavily spurred on by the encouragement of his second, Harry Jones, Paddy Flynn punished Savage at will in the rounds that followed. Seeing that their man no longer stood a chance of victory, Bill Savage's seconds gave in for him after 91 rounds and one hour and 35 minutes of hard fighting. At the end of the fight, both of Bill's eyes and ears were dreadfully puffed up and he was conveyed to his carriage and taken away. Despite a few marks upon his left eye and nose, Flynn was not nearly as badly punished and elected to stay on the battleground to watch the following fight between Bill's brother, Ned, and Spring the Conjuror.

Bill Savage's performance was viewed with a great deal of disappointment and it was thought that apart from fighting badly, he had been overmatched, having 'nothing decisive in his style of fighting', and had exhibited the same deficiencies of his brother, Ned, in not being a 'finishing hitter'. Paddy Flynn owed his victory to his ability in throwing; Bill Savage had been thrown in almost every round, even though Flynn had showed a reluctance to seize the advantage by falling on the Welshman with his full weight. It was to be a disappointing demonstration of skill on the part of both Savage brothers, as Ned had resorted to falling on 'Spring the Conjuror' with his knees to secure victory in the match that followed. Undeterred by the defeat to Flynn, Bill Savage announced himself as willing to engage Harry Jones in a contest for £25 or £50 a short time later.[250] With the Sailor Boy having finally agreed to fight, deposits to bind the match were made throughout February to meet towards the end of March for £25 a-side.

On the day of the battle, 25 March 1828, the Fancy met at the New Inn public house in Staines, run by a Mr Shirley, who had also overseen the training of Harry Jones in preparation for the fight. Harry Jones was in excellent condition as a result of his exertions, weighing 10st, and was supremely confident of victory. Although Bill Savage was a full stone heavier, and enjoyed an advantage in reach, it was thought that the comparative youth and vigour of the Sailor Boy made him the favourite. Dick Curtis and Young Dutch Sam arrived at the New Inn, having been retained to second Harry Jones, although a rumour had spread that Dick Curtis had expressed a doubt that Jones would emerge victorious. With doubts being cast upon Curtis's impartiality, Harry Jones's backer declined his services. Feeling his honour had been undermined, Dick Curtis at once decided to throw his assistance behind Bill Savage, joining Alec Reid as Bill Savage's second. Ned Stockman then elected to join Young Dutch Sam in seconding Harry Jones, in place of Curtis.

The party made their way to a meadow close to the town of Chertsey, where a select band of spectators watched with interest as the men entered the ring. Harry Jones was the first to throw his hat in the air as a mark of his willingness to do battle, although a gust of wind blew it out of the ring, which some thought to be a bad omen for his success in the battle to come. Bill Savage then dropped his hat within the ropes and it remained exactly where it lay, and Dick Curtis, perhaps fearing the Fancy might take it as

250 As recorded in *Bell's Life in London and Sporting Chronicle*, 27 January 1828.

a further indication that his impartiality had been undermined, exclaimed, 'Blow it! I wish it had gone out', and kicked it out of the ring and across the field.

After a cautious start, Harry Jones was the first to attack and landed hard blows on Bill Savage's mouth, and while Bill showed a great deal of caution and judgement in stopping punches, he was often thrown violently in the close by his opponent. While Jones targeted the head of Savage, Bill showed a determination to punish the Sailor Boy's body and had a great deal of success, although by the fourth round it was Bill who was bleeding as he came up to the scratch. More claret was spilled by the end of the round, when a smashing left hand from Jones caused further damage. Both men fought for all they were worth in the following rounds, Bill Savage continually hitting at the ribs of his antagonist, while Jones continued to punish his opponent with heavy shots to the head. As the rounds mounted, it was clear that while Bill remained as game as ever, his chance of securing victory was becoming more slender as the fight progressed. The strength of Harry Jones remained undimmed and he began to punch Savage at will until the 29th round. After one hour and two minutes of fighting, Savage was forced back on to the ropes and was hit until he went down, almost insensible. At this point, it was thought that the fight was over, but to the surprise of all, Bill Savage recovered sufficiently to again come to the scratch at the call of time.

It looked as though a turning point had been reached in the 37th round, when Jones had become sickened by the repeated punishment to his body and Savage was told to seize the advantage. Bill Savage's hopes disappeared in an instant as Harry Jones vomited his stomach contents and resumed battle, going on to floor Bill with a great deal of cleverness. It was in the 53rd round that Bill's brother, Ned, started shedding tears at the deplorable state of his brother and threw his hat into the ring as a token of Bill's defeat. Bill refused to acknowledge that he was beaten and fought on for another three rounds, but received such heavy blows that he was unable to continue, having been left completely blind after one hour and 35 minutes of hard fighting. Caution at the beginning of the match had undermined Bill's chances of success, the Welshman having tried to fight the Sailor Boy at distance, although he had refused to admit defeat and it was said that it

Bill Savage tried to fight on, despite being almost completely blinded by the 'Sailor Boy'.

was 'impossible for a human being to have shown more game than Savage'. The 'dreadful state' of Bill Savage as he was led from the ring was strongly contrasted with the condition of Harry Jones, who did not shed a drop of blood during the fight and looked to all intents and purposes unmarked, although he admitted to his backers that he had been severely battered about the body by the strength of Savage's hitting in the closes.

There is an interesting back-story to the fight between Bill Savage and Harry Jones, which is related by Frank J Bradley in *Famous Fights Past and Present*, although not recorded in any of the newspaper reports of the contest. Following the Sailor Boy's early battles against Ned Stockman and his questionable defeat of Young Dutch Sam, a question mark had been drawn over his honesty, with it being suspected by many that Harry Jones had only made a point of winning when it had been worth his while to do so. Prior to the fight against Bill Savage, a rumour had circulated that Jones had been approached to throw the fight. Frank Bradley claims that these reports were well founded and that Harry Jones was forced to seek out the counsel of his backers after he had been offered £50 to lose the fight to Savage. His backers suggested that Jones should pocket the money and deceive the miscreants into thinking that he intended on losing to Savage until entering the ring and then defeat the Welshman. The Sailor Boy afterwards pretended to go along with the fixers and attempted to get them to hand over the money prior to the contest, but they refused to trust in the pugilist's word, so the negotiations fell through. Having been disappointed in their initial efforts to fix the fight, the band of rogues decided to try another tactic to ensure the victory of Bill Savage.

As the backers of Harry Jones had been alerted to the possibility of foul play, they made sure to bring their own water bottles and brandy from London, concerned that someone might try to drug the Sailor Boy. Their fears proved to be well founded and in the 22nd round the water bottle of Harry Jones was skilfully swapped for a doctored bottle by one of the scoundrels. Luckily, the principal backer of Jones noticed the substitution and alerted Jones's second, Young Dutch Sam, to their deceitful plan. When the bottle was poured out, it revealed a 'thick, puddled mess' which was thought likely to be a 'poisonous narcotic drug' that would paralyse Harry Jones, winning the villains the stakes and the bets. The supporters of Jones were furious that someone had tried to tamper with their man, and the bottle was put to one side so that the contents could be analysed after the fight. Unfortunately, in the excitement of the later rounds, Dick Curtis accidentally broke the bottle, so the truth of its contents was never established.[251]

The fight between Harry Jones and Bill Savage would be the last big fight in which Bill Savage would appear in the London Prize Ring, and although he would occasionally second other pugilists, and appeared at the Fives Court, there would be no further contests of note. In May, a potential opponent named 'Sabes' came forward, offering £30 to £25 to try to secure a match,

251 As recorded in *Famous Fights Past and Present*, Volume X, No. 126. This account has to be viewed with extreme caution (as with many accounts within *Famous Fights* that are unverified and unsupported by comparison with other sources, including newspaper reports). *Famous Fights* was published over 70 years after the contest in question and many of the articles contained within it appear to be exceedingly 'colourful' when compared to contemporary newspaper reports, with many additional details having seemingly been inserted by Frank J Bradley that are not recorded elsewhere.

although nothing would come of it.[252] Bill Savage's last recorded fight took place on the evening of 23 September 1828, against 'Pick, the Bristol Youth' at Battle bridge, as a consequence of a dispute that had started in a public house. Bill's gameness was as much in evidence as ever, although both men were reportedly out of condition and after a hard battle lasting an hour and three quarters for a mere £3 a-side, Pick was declared the winner.[253] While Bill Savage hoped to reverse the decision in a rematch, staking a sovereign to try to induce Pick to meet him, Pick forfeited, despite Savage's desire to make a fresh contest for £25 a-side.[254]

With no challengers or paydays on the horizon, Bill Savage would appear to have gone back to his day job as a London cab driver. He was summoned to Bow Street court in August the following year to answer charges of dangerous driving by a hackney-coach driver. The coach driver alleged that Bill Savage had been driving his horse at a gallop in the opposite direction, when one of Bill's wheel shafts had apparently come loose and pierced the breast of his horse, penetrating its heart and instantly killing his steed. Witnesses to the affair were quick to defend Bill Savage's innocence, stating that the coachman had been racing against another, trying to impress a 'girl of the town' that was seated beside each of them, so the charges against Bill Savage were dismissed.[255]

Despite having never won a prize fight of consequence after his victory against Brimstone Jack, Bill had been viewed as a talented wrestler and perhaps a boxer of greater technical ability than his brother, Ned. Sadly, with the departure of Bill Savage from the ring, and the disgrace of his brother, the careers of the 'Welsh Savages' were quickly forgotten in the chronicles of the prize ring, beyond the footnotes recording their ill-conceived

252 As recorded in *Bell's Life in London and Sporting Chronicle,* 11 May 1828.

253 As recorded in *Bell's Life in London and Sporting Chronicle,* 28 September 1828.

254 As recorded in *Bell's Life in London and Sporting Chronicle,* 12 October 1828.

255 As recorded in *Bell's Life in London and Sporting Chronicle,* 6 September 1829.

turn-ups against Dick Curtis and Alec Reid.[256] The next Welsh pugilist of prominence would do a great deal more to restore the reputation of Welsh prize fighters on home ground. William Charles of Newport would appear to be the first Welshman to have been widely supported by his countrymen as having been the 'Welch Champion' in the long years that had passed since Ellis Pannwr had first raised his clenched fist.

256 Although Ned Savage fought a great deal more battles than his brother, Bill Savage, because Ned Savage's record is comprised of fights against opponents of limited ability, he is consequently only recorded in passing as a result of his turn-up with Dick Curtis in *Pugilistica*. Bill Savage was perhaps remembered more fondly by the followers of the ring, due to his more honourable conduct within the London Prize Ring, but also as a consequence of his fight against Harry Jones, the Sailor Boy, in which he was seen to fight courageously. Bill Savage's fight against Harry Jones is recorded in full in *Pugilistica* in the chapter dealing with Harry Jones.

Chapter 21

Songs of Blood and Glory

Behold the ring! How strange the groupe appears
Of dirty blackguards, commoners, and peers.

(*The Age of Frivolity: a Poem Addressed to the Fashionable, the Busy and the Religious World, Third Edition, Revised and Enlarged, by the Reverend Thomas Beck, published by Maxwell & Wilson, 1809*)

The Reverend Thomas Beck, in the third and enlarged edition of his lengthy poem condemning the obsessions of the 'Age of Frivolity' at the start of the 19th century, reserved some of his most scathing verses for the growing sport of pugilism and the collective followers of the prize ring known as the Fancy. The reverend's disgust at the spectacle of two men battling with bare fists for the entertainment of the crowd and for the financial benefit and personal fame of the combatants was undoubtedly shared by many others. Beck had a particular loathing for those influential patrons of the ring who had assisted pugilism in developing into an activity that was starting to enjoy a vast public following:

Say, man of wealth! Say what applause is due
For scenes like these, when patroniz'd by you?

It was perhaps only in prize fighting circles that the victories of pugilistic heroes could be celebrated at length in verse and in song, with a great many verses having been composed by the talented Pierce Egan. The first volume of *Boxiana* was published in 1812, followed by the second in 1818, and the third in 1821. What separated Egan's history of the prize ring from other works of the period, such as William Oxberry's *Pancratia* (1812), was the author's obvious enthusiasm for the prize ring and his unforgettable (and often imitated) style. Egan was afterwards named 'the Great Lexicographer of the Fancy' as he did not merely record the language of the followers of the ring; in many instances he created it. The 1822 edition of Francis Grose's Classical *Dictionary of the Vulgar Tongue*, which had been edited by Pierce Egan, would include many terms that had been coined by Egan himself.

The second volume of *Boxiana* contains a lengthy section that records those lyrics that Egan composed in commemoration of some of the more famous pugilists of the period, which were set to the music of popular songs. The section entitled 'Chaunts for the Fancy' is subtitled 'As Sung at the Convivial Meetings held at Belcher's, the Castle Tavern, Holborn', which served as one of the headquarters of the London Prize Ring, and where Egan had been a welcome member of the party on many occasions. When Tom Belcher was landlord, the Tavern would become the leading sporting house in London, and played host to the famous 'Daffy Club', whose founder and permanent president was James 'Jemmy' Soares. The club took the 'Daffy' part of its name from a slang term for gin, and was a somewhat informal gathering; there were no specified times for meeting, and no fines for non-attendance. The club motto was, 'To do what is right!' and its members gathered in a long room that had its walls adorned by portraits of the prominent pugilists and sportsmen of the day. At the meetings of the Daffy Club, the inner circle of the prize-fighting fraternity would meet, and its members enjoyed many dinners and presentations where peers and lords of the realm mixed freely with the pugilists, backers and leading members of the Fancy. Fights were organised, deposits on future fixtures made and, following important contests, toasts with wine, sherry and, of course, 'blue ruin' or gin were made to courageous winners and disappointed losers alike.

Tom Belcher, brother of Jem Belcher, and the host of the Castle Tavern, Holborn.

The Castle Tavern in Holborn, London, taken from Pierce Egan's Book of Sports, and Mirror of Life *by Pierce Egan, (London: T. Tegg, 1836).*

In these surroundings, far removed from muddy battlefields, and the accompanying con men, blackguards, scoundrels and pickpockets that were inevitably drawn to a prize fight, the virtues of pugilism and pugilists was enthusiastically sung, and in time many songs would become familiar to the sporting world beyond the confines of the Castle Tavern. Regulars at the Daffy Club included such intriguing characters as Adey the Greek, Lucky Bob and 'Di the table-lifter', who was so strong that he could bend iron bars but was known to have had no stomach for a fight.

A dinner had been given at the Chequers Inn at Brentwood, Essex, by the supporters of Ned Turner prior to his battle with Jack Randall on 24 November 1818. Following the extravagant meal of 'hares, pheasants, partridges and venison, served up in the highest style of culinary perfection', the company was entertained by songs sung by Mr Webber of the Royalty Theatre accompanied by a Mr Higman, as well as the celebrated theatrical performer, Mr Herring. A song attributed to the pugilist Tom Owen, 'Rum Old Mog', was sung, and then followed by one of Pierce Egan's own compositions, sung to the tune of 'The Land of Sweet Erin', and entitled 'The Lads of the Fancy'. Egan's lyrics focus on the sense of brotherhood shared by the supporters of the prize ring who gathered at the Castle Tavern due to their mutual interest in pugilism. It is clear from the lyrics of the first verse of the song that the author of *Boxiana* revels in the company of these fellow supporters of the prize ring almost as much as in the spectacle of witnessing a prize fight itself:

You Lads of the Fancy, who wish to impart
The tokens of friendship and soundness of heart,
To BELCHER's repair, at the *Castle* so strong,
Where he'll *serve* you all well, and you'll hear a good song.
The company cheerful, and SPORTING'S the go –
Though *milling's* the theme, you'll not meet with a foe;
But each in good humour, enjoying his pipe,
With tales of the FANCY – and knowledge of life!

CHORUS

Then let us be merry,
While drinking our sherry,
For friendship and harmony can't last too long –
Be still our endeavour,
That nothing shall sever
The LADS OF THE FANCY at the *Castle* so strong!

Pierce Egan was an enthusiastic admirer of Ned Turner, and amongst the numerous songs recorded in *Boxiana* Vol. 2 that specifically celebrate the pugilistic achievements of such men as Jack Randall, Dutch Sam and Jack Carter, is a song entitled 'The Three Fights Between Scroggins and Turner', which was sung to the tune of 'Paddy Carey':

THE THREE FIGHTS
BETWEEN SCROGGINS AND TURNER
AT
HAYES, SAWBRIDGEWORTH, and SHEPPERTON
By P.EGAN.
TUNE – "Paddy Carey"

'TWAS at Hayes, TURNER saw the ring,
So primely made for *milling* glory,
Of heroes too he's heard 'em sing,
Boxers that wish'd to live in story!
Of FIGG so bold, and BROUGHTON'S fame,

Those millers of a century back;
Till modern days rais'd SCROGGY'S name,
When TURNER came and got the *crack*.

He stripp'd so gay, – And mill'd away,
Till ring got broke, – Then all a joke;
Prime delusion, – Glorious confusion;
Such a row was ne'er before seen!
Among the *slang* faces, – At the donkey races,
From Tothill-fields to the Epping hunt,
All anxious to *draw* their blunt.

CHORUS

Now chanting with glee, – I should like to see,
This milling boy, – THE FANCY'S toy,
Who's got the charm, – With his long arm,
Victory to gain, – Without any strain;
Nimble footed, black eye's, whisker'd cheek,
Milling Neddy Turner,
O Prime Neddy,
Get away Neddy,
Prime, hit away, *milling* Turner.

At *Sawbridgeworth* NED took the lead,
So full of spunk, light and airy,
With confidence he show'd WELSH breed,
He hit and sprung about like a fairy!
While SCROGGY puzzled, lost his rote,
His temper gone and smashing play,
NED made a hit upon his throat,
So sharply that he won the day.

Old and young, – Were struck dumb,
To see retreat, – And SCROG'S defeat,
The "three to one," – Completely done,
Such long *mugs*, – And precious shrugs!
Among the keen faces, – At Newmarket races,
From GULLEY'S odds on that boxing pet,
On TURNER'S name they wouldn't bet.

CHORUS

At Shepperton again they met,
But TURNER'S now the FANCY man;
SCROGGINS so teas'd, and on the fret:
Anxious to win, – changing his plan;
But NED awake, he *spoilt* in style,
The *boring* traits of brave SCROGGY;
His length of arm was like a foil,
Repeated hits made JACK *groggy*!

Poor SCROGGY done, – Beat like fun,
He fought with *pluck*, – But out of luck;
Yet still his name – Deserves good fame.
A better "little one" ne'er was seen,
Among the hard faces,- – At Newmarket races,
From Belcher's time to prime TOM CRIBB,
Those precious ones to *mill* and *fib*.

CHORUS

Now chanting with glee...&c.

As the most prominent pugilist to have been connected with Wales up to this time, it is perhaps unsurprising that Ned Turner should have been singled out for such praise amongst the Welsh pugilists of the period. Turner's victories against Jack Scroggins were still fresh in the minds of the followers of the ring, and there were no pugilists of the time that were as closely linked to Wales as Ned Turner.[257]

Many of the songs and verses penned by Egan give voice to the notion of the pugilist fighting for the national pride of his countrymen. The confidence with which Turner met Scroggins in their second contest at Sawbridgeworth is directly attributed to Turner having been of Welsh 'breed'. Egan had previously drawn attention to the role that he believed Ned Turner's Welsh roots

257 In spite of having been born in Wales, Tom 'Paddington' Jones, the most famous Welsh pugilist prior to Turner's time, was more closely associated with Paddington in London than Wales.

played in having laid the foundations for his pugilistic courage in the second volume of *Boxiana*, commenting, 'TURNER is descended from that warlike race of people, denominated ANCIENT BRITONS; and he seems to have imbibed those true notions of valour, which so eminently distinguish that loyal and brave description of men.'

In the third volume of *Boxiana*, Egan would offer a further selection of 'Chaunts for the Fancy', with the first offering being a song entitled 'Song Made on the Prize Ring in 1819', which was intended to be sung to the tune of 'Scots wa hae wi' Wallace bled'. A few selected verses from this song on the fight between Jack Randall and Ned Turner were afterwards selected and reprinted in *Pierce Egan's Book of Sports, and Mirror of Life*.[258] Jack Randall is portrayed as the celebrated champion of the Irish people, and the '*Pats* who saw *Jack Randall* fight... filled the FANCY with delight'.

Turner is seen to be equally deserving of his fame, and Egan records the Welsh pugilist as having been fully supported in his endeavours in the prize ring by his countrymen, as a result of the high regard in which his pugilistic skills had been held, due to his superior 'science' and courage:

> Back'd by the *Welch*, Ned took his ground,
> A better man could ne'er be found,
> Showing fine science ev'ry round,
> And not a flincher he!

The chosen representative of the English prize ring selected by Pierce Egan in the song is John Shaw, who had defeated Edward Painter in 1815 and had afterwards been selected as a worthy opponent to contend for championship honours against Tom Cribb.

Unfortunately, Shaw was soon afterwards sent to fight at Waterloo, having been a Corporal in the 2nd Lifeguards. Corporal Shaw single-handedly killed nine Frenchmen in

258 *Pierce Egan's Book of Sports, and Mirror of Life: Embracing the Turf, the Chase, the Ring and the Stage Interspersed with Original Memoirs of Sporting Men, etc*, (London: Thomas Tegg and Son, 1836). These verses are recorded at the beginning of Chapter 8, *The Nonpareil*.

battle before his sword broke, and after having given his life in combat, Shaw's name became synonymous with heroism in battle[259]

The third volume of *Boxiana* contains 'chaunts' and songs mostly penned by writers other than Pierce Egan, and contains a further song celebrating the fight between Ned Turner and Jack Randall, entitled 'The Fight at Crawley between The Nonpareil and The Out-and-Outer'. This song was written by the pugilist, Bob Gregson, who at one point had been named the 'poet laureate' of the prize ring.[260] A second unattributed piece is included, which was written by Thomas Moore, entitled 'Lines on the Fight Between Randall and Turner' and is recorded as having been taken from a 'Literary Journal'.[261] In this poem, Ned Turner is associated with the Welsh national symbol of the leek, and despite his defeat at the hands of Randall, the reputation of Turner himself is seen to be undamaged and upheld:

> Oh, the leek that beam'd gaily on *Turner's* clear brow,
> Glitters still in the wind both purely and bright;
> Though the fast springing buds are close clipp'd round it now,
> Yet the leek is but robbed of the glare of its light.

The week after Ned Turner's death had been announced in *Bell's Life* in 1826, Jack 'Frosty-faced' Fogo contributed a lengthy poem entitled 'Elegiac Stanzas on the Death of Ned Turner'. By this time, Frosty-faced Fogo, an ex-tailor who had received his unusual nickname as a result of his pockmarked face, had replaced Bob

---

259 Some later comparison was made between the manner in which John Shaw was killed and the death of the Welsh late-19th century pugilist Dai St John of Resolven, known as 'The Welsh Giant', who perished in the Boer War at the Battle of Belmont after dispatching multiple assailants with his bayonet in close combat prior to having been shot in the temple.

260 See Appendix 1 for the full text of this song, which is recorded as having been 'sung at the Daffy Club, held at the Castle Tavern, Holborn by TOM OWEN, with the MOST *spirited* applause.' (Footnote to the song in *Boxiana*)

261 'Lines on the Fight between Randall and Turner' was taken from *Jack Randall's Diary of Proceedings at the House of Call for Genius*, by Thomas Moore, and is recorded in full in Appendix 2.

Gregson as the 'poet laureate' of the prize ring. Fogo became a popular figure in the sporting world, and was in great demand to compose and chaunt his poetry in the drinking dens of the Fancy. His poem on the death of Ned Turner pays ample credit to the high esteem in which Turner had been held throughout his prize fighting career, and credits his Welsh heritage, stating that he had been the 'boast of Wales'.[262]

In the years that followed, it became common practice for the characteristics and victories of prominent pugilists to be recorded in both song and poetic verse. In addition to the 'colours' of fighters that were often offered for sale following their victories in the prize ring, song-sheets with outlines of their careers and memorable battles would also be sold before, during and after their contests, earning the vendors a few pennies for each copy sold. Intriguingly, there remains an example of one poem composed in Wales to celebrate the victory of a native pugilist, a fighter recorded only under his nickname of 'Young Bloody'.

The undated prize fight poem 'Young Bloody' was copied from a manuscript that was owned by Mr John Davies, who was the parish clerk of Montgomery from 1891, and published by a historical society, the Powys-Land Club, in its journal in 1938.[263] In the course of the poem, one 'Squire Harrison' is mentioned who was thought likely to be Major Robert J Harrison (born approx. 1780). Major Harrison was the father of the Reverend R J Harrison, the Vicar of Forden, and the grandfather of Major R J Harrison, the first Mayor of Montgomery. John Davies would recall that Squire Harrison supposedly wagered his carriage and horses on the outcome of the fight. It seems plausible on the face value of the poem that it may have been composed after the start of the 19th century, when prize fighting in Montgomeryshire had increased in popularity following the widespread fame of Ned Turner. Additionally, the poem shows

---

262 'Elegiac Stanzas on the Death of Ned Turner' by Jack 'Frosty-faced' Fogo, was published in *Bell's Life in London and Sporting Chronicle* on 30 April 1826, and is reprinted in full for the first time in Appendix 3.

263 'Young Bloody, A Prize-Fight Poem' was published in *Historical & Archaeological Collections Relating to Montgomeryshire and its Borders, Vol. XLV., Issued by the Powys-Land Club* (Welshpool: David Rowlands Ltd.,1938). For the full text of this poem, see Appendix 4.

a familiarity with Egan's pugilistic terminology, including such terms as 'knowledge-box' (head) and the more familiar 'claret', meaning blood.[264] It seems possible that the composer of the poem may have been inspired by the songs published in *Boxiana* celebrating Turner himself.

The poem recalls the visit of an English pugilist named 'Bristol Jack', who appeared at Ludlow Castle in Shropshire, close to the Welsh border, to fight a 'Montgomery lad, Not twenty years of age'. The contest had been fixed to result in the victory of Bristol Jack, with the Montgomeryshire opponent having received a bribe from a Newtown clothier to throw the fight. The ruse having been discovered, Squire Harrison was quick to raise his objections, saying, 'I'll be bound for all your gold, if bribery there is ta'en.'

It is at this point that 'Young Bloody' speaks up, and it is clear that in doing so he becomes the representative of Welsh national honour, defending the reputation of his countrymen against the English pugilist. Bristol was a city of pugilistic renown, having been the birthplace of many fighters who had achieved fame and glory in the London Prize Ring. In later years, the relatively close proximity of the city to the Welsh border ensured that a strong rivalry developed between the Bristol pugilists and their Welsh counterparts.[265] With Young Bloody having been forced to challenge Bristol Jack to defend the reputation of his countrymen, the Welsh pugilist revealed himself willing to die before sacrificing his personal honour and that of Wales:

> Then up spoke young Bloody,
> Saying it never shall be told

264 Appendix 5 – *Pugilistic Terminology*, contains many terms coined by Pierce Egan, taken from Francis Grose's *Classical Dictionary of the Vulgar Tongue*, Revised by Pierce Egan, (London: Sherwood, Neely and Jones, 1823), and *Sportsman's Slang: A New Dictionary of Terms Used in the Affairs of the Turf, the Ring, the Chase and the Cock-pit*, etc., by Jon Bee, (London: W. Lewis, 1825) with some additions by the author.

265 One of the best examples of the Bristol–Welsh pugilistic rivalry can be seen in the background to the fight between Jem Bailey of Bristol, and William Charles, the 'Welsh Champion' of Newport. Prior to this time, Bill Thomas the Chepstow butcher had sent a public challenge to the 'best man' in Bristol, which was accepted by George Nicolls, who 'won it off-hand'. (*Boxiana*).

That I would sell my country
For silver or for gold.
So make sure of your betts, me men,
To flinch I'll ne'er be seen,
Before your money shall be lost,
I'll die upon the green.

Having been impressed with the strength of Young Bloody's speech, a 'butcher lad' was the first to decide to put his faith in the 'Welch boy', and put down 20 guineas on his victory. The response from Bristol Jack is swift, with his initial deception in arranging a fixed contest having been exposed; his 'honour' demands that he meets the wager. Bristol Jack cannot conceal his anger at this challenge to his fistic superiority, and he threatens the butcher's boy with a beating after he has met Young Bloody:

The champion pulled out twenty more,
And this to him replied,
Before I leave this country
I'll tan thy greecy hide.

With the match having been made, the fight begins at one o'clock in the afternoon, and it can be seen that the contest is one that has assumed great local importance, with thousands having crowded on to Ludlow Castle Green to witness the battle.

It is worth noting that the author has already impressed upon the reader that the spectacle of the prize fight is one that appeals to men drawn from all sections of society, with the commoners rubbing shoulders with those from the upper echelons, such as the well-heeled clothier from Newtown, as well as Squire Harrison himself.

Young Bloody threw himself into battle at the start of the fight, and with his first blow split the nose of Bristol Jack. He continued to punish his antagonist in the third round, making him 'reel about', and in the seventh round landed a severe blow on the ear, which almost 'took it from his head'.

With Young Bloody repeatedly targeting the head of Bristol Jack, resulting in streams of blood running down his face, Jack's courage failed him, and he was reduced to a figure of pity. After refusing to fight on, Bristol Jack was forced to throw himself on the mercy of the crowd:

> Poor Jack began to cry
> My head it is so mangled,
> My body is so sore,
> I must give in, kind gentlemen,
> I cannot fight no more.

The victory of Young Bloody is met with great satisfaction on the part of the author, who hopes Bloody might be relied upon in the future to defend the honour of his countrymen, and pays tribute to the hero who has successfully defended the reputation of 'Montgomery boys' by having vanquished the 'foreign invader':

> So now the battle it is o'er,
> And Bloody as won the day.
> And now let him fight when he will
> I hope he alway may.
> The element did roar like thunder
> With the echo of their noise
> Hosaw! Hosaw! was all their cry,
> Hosaw! Montgomery boys!

While there appears to be no information recorded regarding the fighting career of the gallant 'Young Bloody' beyond this song, a couple of intriguing references can be found to another Montgomery pugilist known as 'Bloody' recorded in the London Press. The *Whitehall Evening-Post* of 11–14 December 1784 reported that a 'few days ago a most terrible battle was fought at Ludlow, consisting of 35 rounds, between one Bloody, a butcher of Montgomery, and another noted bruiser'. The battle was for £25, and Bloody proved to be the victor, while his opponent was said to have afterwards died of his injuries.[266] Six years later, the same Bloody was mistakenly described as the 'noted Shropshire

266 This fight was also reported in the *London Chronicle*, 16–18 December 1784, and in the *St. James' Chronicle* of the same date, and with similar information, although Bloody's name is not given and he is merely recorded as having been a 'Butcher of Montgomery'.

bruiser' when he was matched against William Warr (Ward) for 100 guineas a-side.[267] The contest was 'expected to be a battle of much game and science', but there appears to be no further written reports to confirm whether the fight actually took place. Nevertheless, as Warr was considered to have been one of the best men around at that time, Bloody must have been thought a very capable fighter for there to have been an attempt made to bring them together.

It must be wondered whether 'Bloody', the butcher of Montgomery, and 'Young Bloody' of the prize fight poem are actually the same man, given the similarity in names and the link to Montgomery. Assuming that John Davies, the parish clerk of Montgomery, is correct in his statement that Squire Harrison wagered his carriage and horses on the outcome of the fight between Young Bloody and Bristol Jack, Harrison would not have been in a position to do so in 1784, when 'Bloody' the butcher of Montgomery had presumably already developed enough of a reputation to meet a 'noted' opponent in battle. At the time when Bloody was later matched against Bill Ward in 1790, Squire Harrison (born approx. 1780) would have been approximately ten years of age. It would seem to be a possibility that 'Young Bloody' may well have earned his cognomen as a result of having been the son of Bloody the Montgomery butcher, or that his fighting ability drew favourable comparison with the earlier fighter and that he was named 'Young' Bloody in tribute to him.

Regardless of the connection between the two men, it is worth underlining the fact that Bloody the Montgomery butcher was meeting 'noted' opponents in 1784 within Wales and that this information was deemed of sufficient interest as to be reported by London-based newspapers.[268] It is also significant that by 1790, Bloody was thought to have been so well regarded as to be considered a difficult opponent for Bill Warr. The logical conclusion to draw is that by this time prize fighting in Wales had developed to the point where local champions such as Bloody

---

267 As recorded in the *Gazetteer, and New Daily Advertiser*, 3 December 1790.

268 The contest between Bloody the Montgomery butcher and his unnamed opponent in December of 1784 at Ludlow would appear to be the earliest reference currently traced regarding an organised prize fight fought within Wales to date.

had emerged from a pool of lesser pugilists and were celebrated by the general public, and their pugilistic abilities were well known to a larger cross-section of Welsh society. Although there appears to be no further information recorded on the second-rate pugilists who were active within Wales around this period, at the time that Bloody was being matched against Warr, Ellis Pannwr had already been 'looked upon' as the Champion of Wales for a number of years, having fought 'seven pitched battles' against unnamed opponents prior to his meeting with Roderick Lewis. It seems plausible to conclude that, by 1791, Ellis Pannwr's challenger, Roderick Lewis, was just one of the more well-known Welsh pugilists to have developed enough skill to raise himself above the common herd, and that there would have been a significant number of Welsh knuckle fighters of mixed ability competing at a lower level within Wales before this time.

At a later time, when the reputations of native Welsh prize fighters were more widely known, verses penned to recognise their accomplishments and deeds would become more commonplace. Songs and poems would become an easy way to share news of the outcome of important contests with the general public, and aided in relating the previous victories of a fighter, serving to publicise the credentials of a local 'Champion'. By recording this information in verse and song, names of prominent pugilists would be remembered by those members of the public who were either ignorant of their careers, or were perhaps unable to read of their battles in such newspapers as *Bell's Life*. In the case of 'Young Bloody', the tale of his great battle against Bristol Jack being recorded in verse ensured that while the name of this valiant Welsh pugilist has now been forgotten, his courage and bravery have not.

Chapter 22
The Game Welchmen

The 1820s saw an increase in the number of prize-fighting Welshmen. This upturn in the number of Welsh pugilists might well be ascribed in part to the widespread fame of Ned Turner. Following the defeat of such stars as Jack Scroggins and Jack Martin, Turner was considered to be amongst the cream of the lightweights, and second only to Jack Randall. Turner was more closely associated with Wales than any other prize fighter up to his time, despite having been born in the borough of Southwark in London. Having fought his way to glory in the London Prize Ring, Turner's contests received far more newspaper coverage than any of his Welsh contemporaries.

Only a handful of minor contests in Wales would be reported in brief by the Welsh newspapers in the first years of the 19th century, with most newspaper editors having frowned upon prize fighting as a socially acceptable sport. References to the activities of the more familiar champions of the London Prize Ring are a little more prevalent, with the fledgling Welsh newspapers, perhaps begrudgingly, recognising that such matters made for good copy and were of interest to a significant proportion of their readership. That there was a taste for pugilism and a desire for information on the prize ring had been seen in 1819, when Tom Cribb, Tom Spring and Bill Eales had demonstrated their 'milling talents' at 'Swansea, Neath, and other places' in September.[269]

The prize ring in Wales was by this time starting to adopt roughly the same organisational structure that characterised the London Prize Ring, with numerous sympathetic public houses

269 As recorded in *The Cambrian*, 18 September 1819.

being used by the Welsh pugilists as places where contests could be discussed, organised and planned. As these fights began to assume a more professional nature, they attracted larger stakes, increased gambling and, inevitably, larger crowds. One such early prize fight between two Welshmen named Jones and Penk drew considerable interest from the Welsh Fancy and took place on 25 November 1822. Both combatants appear to have been well known for their pugilistic skills; Jones was a Flintshire man of 'scientific celebrity', while Penk hailed from Denbighshire and was deemed to be 'of no less skill in the art, and of proof bottom'. The 'two pugnacious champions of the lightweights' had been in training for some time, and had engaged the services of 'first-rate professors' to assist them in their endeavours. The fight was for 'love', and there was no purse for the victor, the 'laurels of honour' being the only reward, and took place near Worthenbury in Flintshire. The outcome of the contest was of sufficient interest to draw 'many professors in the science' to the battleground alongside a 'large concourse of spectators'. According to the *Sporting Magazine*, 'most of the beds at the public inns in the vicinity were engaged long before the day of meeting!!'.

Jones was the first to arrive on the scene, at about 7am, in the company of his second. Penk arrived a few minutes later and projected a confident air. The fight commenced soon afterwards, with both men showing 'great muscular powers' in the early rounds. It was in the tenth round that Jones received a 'severe contusion' to his left arm that determined the course of the contest. Although both men 'shewed much game', after 'severe fighting' in which both men 'displayed great science', Jones fell from a slip and was afterwards unable to come up to the scratch, so Penk of Denbighshire seized the victory to the cheers of his supporters.[270]

Despite the reluctance of the Welsh newspapers to report on prize fighting, an impending contest between a Monmouthshire quarryman named Bob Parry 'of local pugilistic fame' and Powell, a blacksmith hailing from Broad Oak in Herefordshire, attracted a great deal of local public interest, and was reported in *The Cambrian*

270 As recorded in the *Sporting Magazine: Or, Monthly Calendar of the Transactions of the Turf, the Chase and Every Other Diversion Interesting to the Man of Pleasure, Enterprize, and Spirit,* Volume 11, (London: Rogerson & Tuxford, 1823).

newspaper in July of 1824.[271] On 17 July , the White Swan Inn at Monmouth had been the venue for the second deposit of £30 a-side, with a final deposit to be made at the same place at the end of the month to seal the match. News of the fight created 'great interest in the neighbourhood' and resulted in excitable scenes in the public house itself, with 'even betting to a considerable amount' having been made over the course of the evening.

The battle came off at Harewood's End in Herefordshire on 2 August 1824, and was witnessed by an estimated 4–5,000 spectators, and amongst those present was Tom Spring, who had been visiting his native county. While the contest drew sufficient interest as to be reported in a number of newspapers,[272] the most detailed report appeared in *The Cambrian* itself,[273] which for the first time reported on a prize fight in detail, and its round-by-round coverage far exceeded the account of the contest published in the pages of *Bell's Life* the previous week.[274] The report published in *The Cambrian* also demonstrated a familiarity with the language that had been used in accounts of prize fights since the publication of *Boxiana,* paying homage to the many imaginative terms coined by Pierce Egan. A punch to the mouth therefore lands on the 'tusk-box', while a blow to the eye is recorded as a 'clink' to the 'ogle' or 'peeper'. The head of an opponent is often referred to as having been his 'cannister'. In some instances, a fighter who had knocked out the teeth of his opponent might be recorded as having successfully 'cabbaged' the 'ivories' of his rival.

On the morning of the fight, a continuous stream of people headed towards the battleground from first light, and the spectators excitedly discussed the physical condition of the two combatants. Powell the blacksmith was said to have been in excellent condition, and had been strongly backed by the Hereford men, although many maintained that the Welshman, Bob Parry, was in far superior condition than he had appeared on previous occasions. After midday, the combatants appeared on the ground.

271 As recorded in *The Cambrian*, 24 July 1824, and also reported in the *Hereford Journal*, 21 July 1824.

272 Reports were also published in the *Hereford Journal*, 4 August 1824, the *Morning Advertiser*, 17 August 1824, and the *Morning Chronicle*, 17 August 1824.

273 As recorded in *The Cambrian*, 14 August 1824.

274 As recorded in *Bell's Life in London and Sporting Chronicle,* 8 August, 1824.

Bob Parry was the first to enter the ring, and his appearance drew concern from his Welsh supporters as he did not seem to have 'the undaunted look of anticipated conquest' that many had hoped to see. Powell followed, and threw up his hat 'with great spirit and confidence' to the sounds of cheering from the supporters of both men. After having stripped for battle, Powell's 'size and his looks' appeared in his favour, although the blacksmith had a disadvantage in reach, being inferior to 'great Bob in length of arm'. Despite the favourable reports as to Bob Parry's condition, the quarryman was thought to be a 'shadow of his former self' and although his face spoke of his determination and bravery, it was clear that a difficult fight was ahead of him. Parry was seconded by Ben Worgan and one 'York', while Richard Preece and Mathew Jubb served as the seconds of Powell. Powell was the favourite and was heavily backed right up to the moment that the men toed the scratch.

After initial sparring, Powell's confidence showed as he struck out with all of his muscular power, throwing his left at the throat of the Welshman and following it up with another, but receiving a return from Parry to the head. The second round proved to be a long and busy one, with the blacksmith showing noticeable 'science', landing repeated blows to Parry's head and drawing first blood from above the quarryman's eye. Undaunted, Parry launched an assault of his own that made Powell cautious, and in the close fighting that followed it was Powell who went down. The blacksmith continued to attack and in the fourth round landed a blow on Parry's 'tusk-box' to the cheers of his supporters, although Parry threw Powell with severity at the end of the round. Bob Parry came out with great determination in the following round and managed to draw blood from the blacksmith's nose. The rally that followed was brought to an abrupt end when Parry landed a smashing blow to Powell's face that sent him to the turf. Powell was seen to better effect in the rounds that followed and landed a number of damaging blows, but a turning point was reached in the tenth round when on coming up to the scratch he appeared quite weak from loss of blood.

Despite his tiredness, Powell threw slashing and heavy blows with right and left, but slowly Parry was closing the gap, having sent the blacksmith down from a blow to the stomach in the 12th round. Powell proved that he was as game as ever and even

BELL'S

LIFE IN LONDON,

AND SPORTING CHRONICLE;

BOXING.—Monday last a Grand Mill took place at Harewood's End, Herefordshire, for 60*l*., between two noted provincial Pugilists of the names of PARRY and POWELL. Even betting.—The contest lasted one hour and 40 minutes, during which 103 rounds were fought, and in which more game than science was displayed. Parry, who had a decided advantage in size and weight, was declared the victor, and Powell was very severely punished. The fight excited great interest, upwards of 4,000 persons being present, including Spring, who is on a visit to his friends at Hereford.

A brief report of the contest between Powell the Herefordshire blacksmith and Bob Parry the Monmouthshire quarryman, at Harewood's End, Herefordshire, taken from Bell's Life in London and Sporting Chronicle, *8 August 1824.*

as the Welshman put in some 'tremendous blows' in the 15th, Powell stopped a great number before Parry finally went down. Powell would go down again and again in the next three rounds, gradually becoming weaker due to loss of blood. The blacksmith fought on and succeeded in landing a tremendous punch to Parry's nose in the 25th round that sent blood gushing from it in a stream. In the rounds that followed, blood poured from a wound that had opened up above Powell's eye, but he managed to have the best of it and his 'superior science' gave him the advantage.

From the 43rd round until the 60th, things swung in favour of the Welshman, although Powell launched an assault that nearly closed Parry's eye. The strength of Powell, which had initially been to his advantage, was now being overshadowed by Bob Parry's superior reach, and by the 100th round, the blacksmith received a blow that almost closed both of his eyes. In the final three rounds of the fight, Powell valiantly tried to launch an attack but he had become so weak from blood loss that his backers refused to allow him to come up to the scratch again. At this point Bob Parry, the Monmouthshire quarryman, was declared the winner after 103 rounds and one hour and 47 minutes of fighting.[275]

275 Duration of fight as recorded in *The Cambrian*, 14 August 1824.

The strength of the Herefordshire blacksmith had ebbed gradually from the 23rd round onwards as a result of his increasing loss of blood and, although his strength and science had been superior to that of his antagonist, he was defeated. Bob Parry had been severely punished by the muscular arm of the blacksmith and his victory been very dearly bought.

It is clear that the desire of Welshmen to indulge in prize fighting within Wales was well established by this time, and with greater interest in the prize ring came an increased opportunity for the professional pugilist to make money. Tom Spring certainly thought so, having presumably financially benefitted to such a degree from his pugilistic exhibitions in Wales in 1819 that he elected to demonstrate his boxing skills in the company of John Langan the year after he had been a spectator at the Powell vs Parry contest. Spring and Langan arrived at Brecon in April of 1825, having travelled to the town via the Abergavenny mail coach. The 'Champions of England and Ireland' then gave a 'grand display of pugilistic Science in a crowded room at the Sun-inn' and afterwards sparred again at the Town Hall, 'before a numerous company' two nights later.[276]

John Langan was undoubtedly a popular draw, having briefly visited Wales the previous year following his second defeat at the hands of Tom Spring in June of 1824. The Irish champion had arrived at Bristol early in July intending to sail to Dublin to visit his sick father, but as his ship was not ready to sail he set off by steam-boat for Tenby in order to meet the steam-packet *Ivanhoe*, which was bound for Ireland. *Pugilistica* would afterwards record that,

> In his journey through Pembroke and Milford, he met with a very kind reception from the Welsh people. Langan was put up at the Nelson's Hotel, in Milford. Crowds of people surrounded the house during his stay and the sailors, who were wind-bound, came on shore, along with the crews of two revenue cutters, just to get a peep at the Irish milling cove. The inhabitants of Tenby wished him to spar for a benefit and some gentlemen amateurs offered him their assistance, but Langan refused to accept their kind offer, on account of his

276 As recorded in *The Cambrian*, 30 April 1825.

> father's illness. He sailed in the Ivanhoe steam-packet for Waterford, on the 14th.[277]

The conqueror of John Langan, Tom Spring, would appear to have been an English pugilist who was perhaps better known and more popular in Wales than many of his contemporaries in the London Prize Ring, possibly due to the fact that Spring hailed from neighbouring Herefordshire, on the Welsh border. Spring's popularity amongst the Welsh at Brecon was so pronounced that some had tried to claim the English champion as one of their countrymen, with the *Morning Advertiser* recording in 1824 that,

> The Welchmen of Breconshire claim Spring, whose real name is Wynter, as their countryman. His grandfather's great grandfather, they say, was the best wrestler of his day, and a celebrated genealogist is now making out his pedigree.[278]

Spring's Welsh roots had been claimed by the Breconshire Fancy and recorded in *The Cambrian* newspaper a few weeks previously, which had remarked that,

> We understand that *Spring*, the Champion of England, is a Welshman: his real name is Wynter, and his family are of *Kerigkadarn* in Breconshire.[279]

It had been due to Tom Spring that a prize fight between the Yorkshireman, Matt Robinson,[280] and Jonathan Bissell, 'Young Gas',[281] came off at Monmouth Cap,[282] Monmouthshire, in January of 1827. The contest had initially been arranged to be fought in

277 John Langan's departure from Milford, Wales for Waterford, Ireland, is also recorded in *The Cambrian*, 17 July 1824.

278 As recorded in the *Morning Advertiser*, 5 July 1824.

279 As recorded in *The Cambrian*, 19 June 1824.

280 Robinson's name is given as 'Mat' in *Fistiana*.

281 Jonathan Bissell was given the nickname of 'Young Gas' due to his similarity in appearance and fighting style to the 'Gas Man', Thomas Hickman. The combatant in this fight was Bissell and not Hickman, as stated by some modern sources, as Hickman had died five years previously.

282 The area known as Monmouth Cap was named after the woollen headgear that became fashionable in the 15th and 16th centuries, which was associated with the town of Monmouth.

the vicinity of Hereford, with Bissell having been persuaded to venture so far from London by Tom Spring's promise that £100 would be collected from the townsmen to be divided between the two combatants. Spring was eager that the fight would come off on his native turf, hoping that he might benefit by virtue of increased trade at the Booth Hall Inn, of which he was host.

The fight had been delayed for a fortnight due to the death of the Duke of York, so Jonathan Bissell, in the company of Dick Curtis, was forced to take up training quarters within four miles of Hereford and continued preparing for the postponed contest. Matt Robinson, who was being looked after by Tom Spring, also trained in the locality. As the day of the fight drew closer, news of the contest was being excitedly discussed around Hereford and inevitably reached the ears of one of the local 'beaks who think fighting a deadly sin'. A warrant was soon afterwards issued for Jonathan Bissell and Dick Curtis. On 19 January, as Bissell and Curtis had been taking a walk, they were bundled into a post-chaise by a local constable. Curtis was lucky enough to see the warrant that had been issued and noted that neither his own name, nor that of Bissell, had been entered correctly. Deciding that there was a flaw in the indictment, Curtis opened the chaise door and fled. He was quickly followed by Young Gas, who also took to his heels.

It was quickly decided that to prevent the recapture of the combatants, it was prudent to change the venue of the proposed fight, and the decision as to the new battleground was made in private and kept a secret until the morning of the contest itself. The day before the battle, the backers of Young Gas cornered Tom Spring, demanding the £100 that they had been promised for travelling to Hereford. Spring said that he had only collected about £20 and that those who had promised to contribute the money felt absolved from their promise by virtue of the fact that the fight had been prevented from taking place in the vicinity of the town.

This news was not well received by the backers of Bissell, who maintained that the nomination of the battleground had been made by Spring, and that the promise of the £100 had been made subject to the risk, and without any reservation whatsoever. A great deal of angry debate followed, with the friends of Young Gas arguing that he should receive compensation for the expenses he had incurred in travelling and training. In the end, despite Tom Spring's reluctance to accept responsibility for the matter, Bissell received £25 for his pains.

On 23 January 1827, Jack 'Frosty-Faced' Fogo, the Acting Commissary, set off at the head of a wagon train, followed by Tom Oliver, Bob Baldwin and others, and travelled across the Welsh border into Monmouthshire, stopping in the vicinity of the village of Llangua, on the River Monnow, marking the boundary between Herefordshire and Monmouthshire. The battleground chosen for the contest was a large field near the well-known inn, the Monmouth Cap.

Some indication of the growing popularity of pugilism in the region can be ascertained by the large crowd who gathered to witness the contest. Despite it having been a cold morning, pedestrians from every nearby town and the surrounding countryside ventured forth to the battleground and the spectators quickly grew to an estimated crowd of 4,000, who stood patiently waiting for the start of the contest between the outer ring composed of 32 wagons drawn in a circle and the inner ring. The Yorkshireman, Matt Robinson, was the first to appear, in the company of Tom Spring and Harry Holt. Jonathan Bissell, 'Young Gas', was not far behind, and had Dick Curtis and 'Uncle Ben' as his seconds. A crimson and white handkerchief was tied to the stake in Robinson's corner, and a 'Belcher' tied in the corner for Gas. After stripping for battle, it was seen that both men were in the prime of health. Gas, although shorter in the reach, was the favourite, his stamina and endurance making him the favourite at 6/4.

After a tentative start, Gas fought confidently and managed to secure first blood as early as the second round, but in the third Robinson proved he was not to be underestimated and caught Bissell with a tremendous smack with his right over his opponent's left eye. Robinson was quick to try to secure the advantage and in following up managed to hit Bissell off his legs. It was the turning point of the fight and although Gas fought doggedly on, he was repeatedly 'jobbed' by Robinson. Gas fought as wildly as ever when under pressure, drawing an obvious contrast with Robinson's 'fine judgement'. As the fight progressed, Gas made increasingly desperate lunges and was further punished by the science of Robinson. By the 13th round, the supporters of Robinson were already celebrating an impending win, but Gas fought on as vigorously as ever. He continually rushed to close quarters and attempted to hit right and left, but was again sent to the turf. Robinson seemed astonished that Bissell was still standing by the 18th round and by this point he was exhausted from his efforts. Dick Curtis was quick to perceive the sudden change in Robinson's fortunes and urged Gas to go in and finish.

Gas was quick to heed the call to arms and rushed to close range. Following a dreadful struggle, Robinson was thrown and Gas afterwards fell heavily upon him, with his elbow on Robinson's throat. Despite being peppered with blows by Robinson in the following rounds, Gas came out with 'alertness scarcely credible' in the 21st round to make one last desperate effort, and finally succeeded in hitting Matt Robinson down at the ropes.

By the 23rd, it was clear that the contest was drawing to a close. Robinson was a great deal distressed and Gas, encouraged by the condition of his antagonist, went in vowing to fight until he dropped. Robinson, for his part, did everything a man could do but failed to defend against Bissell's strenuous assault. In the final struggle for the fall, both men went down heavily. The 25th round proved to be the last. Matt Robinson came up to the scratch groggily and Dick Curtis called out to Young Gas to finish him. Bissell rushed to close quarters once more and another desperate struggle took place that ended with both going down – Robinson was underneath and Gas lay heavily on top of him.

When Tom Spring picked up Matt Robinson, he was nearly senseless and unable to stand, so Young Gas was declared the victor after 35 minutes of combat. Having vanquished his opponent, Gas left the ring without any obvious signs of weakness and it appeared as though he could have fought half an hour longer if necessary, although he seemed a little bewildered. Gas was afterwards taken back to Hereford. He had suffered a great deal of punishment throughout the fight, his eyes were partially closed, his forehead was cut and his face was greatly disfigured. Robinson was thought to have been beaten 'rather by exhaustion than punishment' and was carried off to the Monmouth Cap Inn and put to bed.

Following the main event, *Bell's Life* reported that there was a second fight between Bill Smith ('who fought the Bristol Pieman') and a friend of the pugilist Ned Stockman for a purse of £10. Stockman's friend won in ten rounds. Both contests were witnessed by a very well-behaved crowd, who appeared to greatly appreciate the efforts of the combatants.[283]

That Monmouthshire was fast becoming a popular location for prize fights, due to its close proximity to the English border, is shown by the vast numbers of spectators who turned out for another well-contested battle held on 15 December of the same year, when 'Worcestershire Ben' and a 'St Millan's Trump' fought for 100 sovereigns near Quarry Mawe, in the Sirhowy Valley. The 'immense' crowd witnessed a 'fine display of game and science, in which 30 rounds were fought in one hour and 15 minutes', with Worcestershire Ben proving to be the victor.[284]

Despite the emergence of locally renowned pugilistic heroes such as the Monmouthshire quarryman, Bob Parry, with substantial betting taking place on the outcome of important Welsh prize fights, and pugilism having been supported by accommodating public houses, the Welsh prize ring would not have its rules of conduct enforced by anything resembling a governing body. There was no Daffy Club or Pugilistic Club to ensure the fairness of matches and being so remote from the formalities of the London Prize Ring, those who sought to organise matches in Wales did so without concerning themselves with matching men of similar levels of skill, or of similar weight.

Possibly the greatest example of a vast disparity in weight between two early Welsh pugilists can be seen in the fight between Thomas Edwards and James Benbow, which came off at Llangollen in September of 1827.[285] James Benbow, better known as 'Admiral'

---

283 *Bell's Life in London and Sporting Chronicle,* 28 January 1827, maintains that the second fight was between Bill Smith and an unnamed friend of Ned Stockman for £10, with Smith having been defeated. *Fistiana* (1846) records Ben Smith (Hereford) as the winner and fought Bill Painter for £5 under the entry for Ben Smith.

284 As recorded in *Bell's Life in London and Sporting Chronicle,* 23 December 1827.

285 As recorded in *Bell's Life in London and Sporting Chronicle,* 30 September 1827.

Benbow, decided to engage a tailor named Thomas Edwards in battle, despite having weighed just 9st to the tailor's 17st. Benbow was the first to arrive at the battleground in the company of John Mylord, his second.

Benbow had not been there for long when Edwards appeared, accompanied by his second, Mr Baker. The tailor cut an unlikely pugilistic figure and his bulk drew a great deal of amusement from the spectators. At the start of the first round, Benbow threw himself into a solid fighting stance with his left foot foremost, while Edwards put his right foot forward in the manner of Ned Turner. No time was spent in sparring and the 'Admiral' threw shots with his left and right, although the tailor stopped his blows and at length landed a right hand on Benbow's face, dropping him in 'grand style' to the shouts and cheers of the supporters of Edwards. The second round saw both men rush to a close, and they continued to hammer away at each other with gusto. At length, Benbow received a punch on the nose that drew first blood and after a violent struggle both went down, with the imposing bulk of Edwards being underneath the plucky Admiral.

Admiral Benbow continued to slash away left and right in the third, but proved to be a poor judge of distance. Edwards stopped his blows with his left, and threw his right hand, closing Benbow's left eye. In an astonishing end to the round, the Admiral rushed in and threw the 17-stone bulk of the tailor at the close. The fourth round proved to be the last and drew forth a thunder of applause from the spectators. Both men hit with vigour; there was 'no flinching, no scrambling, but all fair stand-up milling'. At length, Benbow rushed into close range, and 'floored his man in grand style', breaking the tailor's arm in the process. The fight was then declared to have been won by Admiral Benbow, to the great disappointment of the supporters of Thomas Edwards.

General interest in the prize ring had increased considerably from the early 1820s onwards, after the founding of the influential sporting paper, *Bell's Life in London & Sporting Chronicle*, by Robert Bell in March of 1822, incorporating William Macdonald's newspaper, *Life in London*, which had been published in January of that year. *Bell's Life* reported briefly on politics but focused mostly on crime reporting and sporting affairs, and quickly became the leading sporting newspaper of the time. The reputation of the newspaper would be built on its coverage of prize fighting, although it also reported in great depth on horse racing and pedestrianism.

Vincent Dowling stood at the helm of *Bell's Life* as its editor and principal contributor for 30 years, and was one of the most ardent supporters of the prize ring. He was both generous and honest, and in a sport that frequently found itself under the spotlight for unfair practice and fixed contests, Dowling proved to be incorruptible and was one of the fiercest critics of those pugilists, rogues and ruffians who brought the ring into disrepute. Dowling frequently served as a referee in some of the most important prize fights of the London Prize Ring and his unbending judgment in this capacity earned him a great deal of respect amongst the pugilists and the Fancy alike. As the editor of *Bell's Life*, Dowling had a great deal of power, as prize fighters who succumbed to the temptation of fixing fights were subject to Vincent Dowling's terrible retribution.

As *Bell's Life* developed a reputation for accurate reporting on prize fighting, it also became its main defender and chief judge in pugilistic matters, and in many instances Dowling would serve as both jury and executioner. Retribution was swift; any pugilists who had fallen foul of the influential editor would receive savage criticism from his pen of any untoward conduct. They would afterwards find themselves unable to advertise their benefits within the paper, and their challenges to other fighters went unpublished in *Bell's Life*. The professional pugilist who came under such a ban found that he was effectively excommunicated from prize fighting circles, and was practically deprived of his livelihood as a result. It was chiefly due to the vigorous influence exercised by *Bell's Life* that the more unseemly aspects of the prize ring were kept in check. As the author of *Fistiana*, first published in 1840, Vincent Dowling also recorded the ring records of the principal pugilists of the ring, and also further cemented public knowledge of the reputations and accomplishments of all the major prize fighters (and many minor ones) to have featured in the prize ring since the days of James Figg and Jack Broughton.

His son, Frank Dowling, would take the helm of *Bell's Life* following his father's retirement and was as defensive of the prize ring's interests as his father. Frank served as both umpire and referee in important contests in the London Prize Ring, and many agreements to fight were made at his parlour at No. 5 Norfolk Street. Criticism of those pugilists who he deemed to have been unsporting in their behaviour was not without its dangers. Frank Dowling is said to have organised his parlour so that his fire irons were at close hand, so that he was able to use them to defend himself from behind his desk in the event of attack from any enraged pugilists who had fallen foul of his pen.

As *Bell's Life* flourished, and brought news of prize fighting matters to readers far removed from the London Prize Ring, it also increased interest in pugilism in the regions. Recognising this interest, *Bell's Life* also reported on local prize fights in a section of its pugilistic coverage entitled 'Provincial Milling', which records a few interesting details regarding some forgotten fighting Welshmen. In July of 1823, a 'Welchman' by the name of Jack Lewis was reported as having fought a clerk by the name of Green in a 'turn-up' at Copenhagen Fields for £10 a-side. Their 'sharp battle' ended in the 18th round in favour of Lewis after Green had injured one of his fingers.[286] The following year, a corpulent Welsh sailor named Griffiths was less fortunate, having been beaten by an equally portly smuggler named Rogers at Mongeham, near Deal. The amusement afforded by their contest seems to have provided enough interest to have been included in the pages of *Bell's Life*, as their 'respective rotundities' were deemed to be 'better calculated for feasting than fighting'. Griffiths appeared to have had a 'week's allowance of junk under his belt', while Rogers seemed to have 'placed a keg of contraband spirits in his locker'. After a few rounds scuffling, followed by 'hitting, grunting and rolling in the mud', Rogers finally 'capsized' the Welshman.[287]

Bell's Life would also record a few short entries regarding Welsh pugilists on the fringes of the prize fighting world, of which there are sadly few records. One of these men would be 'Taffy' Pritchard, who had challenged fellow pugilist 'Purl-nose Jem' of Bath to eat 6lbs of raw liver in less time than the gluttonous Welshman could eat 7lbs of liver fried in tallow, in November of 1826. 'Thick-headed Bob' stood in as referee, Moses Gould supported Purl-nose Jem as his umpire, while 'Bumper' Jones served as Taffy's man. Sadly, Taffy

286 As recorded in *Bell's Life in London & Sporting Chronicle*, 20 July 1823.

287 As recorded in *Bell's Life in London & Sporting Chronicle*, 4 January 1824.

Pritchard was beaten in 'fine style' as Purl-nose Jem had five minutes to spare after clearing his plate.[288] After the initial celebrations, Purl-nose Jem regretted having ever taken part and afterwards challenged Mr Tucker of the Pig and Whistle in Avon-Street at Bath to fight him for £20 a-side, due to the relentless 'chaffing' that had taken place at Jem's home town following the 'Liver Match'.[289]

Another provincial Welshman by the name of Tom Williams, commonly known as the 'Game Welchman', was unlucky in his attempts to topple the experienced pugilist Isaac Hadley at Northerton, near Dudley in 1829. Hadley had already proved victorious in 12 previous battles and had elected to engage the Game Welchman for £5 a-side on 6 November 1829[290]. Twenty eight rounds were fought with 'manly firmness and unshrinking courage'. Hadley had been growing increasingly weak when he rallied and launched a 'clink under the listener', which managed to 'tumble' over Williams 'as stupid as a cat under the influence of prussic acid'. After having been brought around, the Game Welchman was carried off and put to bed. The fight was witnessed by between 3,000 and 4,000 colliers and smelters, who were as black as 'Suspension Monday'. It was a raucous crowd, who demonstrated their enthusiasm 'by a slap at each other's concks, thereby fully identifying themselves with the scene, and affording a pleasing accompaniment to the fistic games'.[291]

Perhaps one of the most intriguing lesser pugilists of the period recorded as having been a 'Welchman' in *Fistiana* is Jack Jones, who frequently contended within the Liverpool Prize Ring in the mid 1820s.[292] In August of 1825,[293] Jack Jones engaged Bill

---

288 As recorded in *Bell's Life in London & Sporting Chronicle*, 19 November 1826.

289 As recorded in *Bell's Life in London & Sporting Chronicle*, 26 November 1826.

290 The date of this contest is recorded in *Fistiana.*

291 As recorded in *Bell's Life in London & Sporting Chronicle,* 8 November 1829.

292 Jack Jones is recorded as having been a 'Welchman' in the 1845, 1846 and 1867 editions of *Fistiana.*

293 There is some confusion regarding the date of this contest. *Bell's Life in London and Sporting Chronicle*, 21 August 1825, gives the date of 'Monday week', which is Monday, 8 August 1825. *Fistiana* (1841) gives the date of 1 August 1825 under the record for Bill Fisher, although there is no entry for Jack Jones at all. In *Fistiana* (1845), the date of 9 August 1825 is given under Fisher's record. *Bell's Life Ring Chronology* for 1825, published in *Bell's Life in London and Sporting Chronicle*, 1 January 1826, records the date as 3 August 1825.

Fisher, also of Liverpool, in a battle held between Woodside Ferry and the village of Bedstone in Cheshire for £25 a-side.[294] An estimated 4,000 spectators witnessed the fight. Jack Jones was the heavier man, weighing 10st to Bill Fisher's 9st 10lbs. The fight lasted 134 rounds before Bill Fisher was declared the winner, having been severely punished by Jones. *Bell's Life*, remarking on the uncommonly long number rounds fought before the contest terminated, took it as 'sufficient evidence that there was something wanting on either the one side or the other' and published extracts taken from a Liverpool sporting newspaper in order to expose the rather unsportsmanlike behaviour of Jack Jones, duplicating the report of the final round:

> Round 134. The crises now unexpectedly arrived and the battle terminated in a way that was not anticipated. On coming to the scratch, sparring for a short period; Jones made a rush, and Fisher retreated from the ropes; but Jones, stooping down his head, as if from a sudden impulse, ran between Fisher's legs and seizing him by the lower part of the thighs, he lifted him a considerable height and threw him with great force upon the ground. 'Foul! Foul!' exclaimed a thousand voices at once; the ring was instantly broken and Fisher was declared the victor.

It would appear that the large number of rounds fought was principally due to Jack Jones having continually 'sought the grass', by having thrown himself down on the turf at the slightest touch, in one instance without receiving a blow. Pointing out that Jones's dubious strategy would be unlikely to be tolerated within the London Prize Ring, *Bell's Life* concluded,

> Perhaps a more cowardly fighter never entered the Prize-ring than Jones, and by his *finesse* he absolutely forfeited his right to win at least three or four times during the fight. If Fisher had justice done him, his friends should have claimed the battle at the close of the 19th round,

294 The contest between Jack Jones and Bill Fisher is recorded as having been for £20 a-side in *Fistiana*.

> when Jones fell without a blow; the battle was then fairly won, and he ought not to have been again brought to the scratch. And yet Jones was suffered to play the same game over again several times, and no notice was taken of it beyond the astounding shouts, and groans, and hisses, from the surrounding spectators. This could not have happened in the London Ring. Had Fisher hit upon the plan of falling on him, he would soon have put an end to his tumbling system, for he would have given him the *gasps*; and as for a fair, manly, stand-up fight, Jones had no notion of it. We hope the event of this battle will teach him to play fair in future, as he may rest assured, it is far more honourable to lose than to win by dishonourable and base means.

The next recorded fight of Jack Jones against Patsy Tunney took place in Cheshire in 1825 for £10 a-side, and ensured that Jack Jones entered the pugilistic history books. The number of rounds fought against Tunney even put the 134 rounds that Jones had fought against Fisher in the shade. The men fought for four hours and 30 minutes comprising 276 rounds before Jack Jones was proclaimed the victor.[295] *Guinness World Records* recognises this fight between Jones and Tunney as being the world record for the greatest number of rounds ever fought in a boxing match. However, it might be guessed that given the previous performance of Jack Jones against Bill Fisher, this seems unlikely to have been the ferocious slugfest that might initially be imagined. Patsy Tunney was apparently not dissuaded from meeting Jack Jones for a second time in 1825 for the same stakes, and was again defeated by Jones after two hours of combat. After having recorded another victory over Tom Knowles in June of 1827, Jack Jones lost to Bill Fisher for a second time in a 70-round fight held at Bootle Marsh in Liverpool, in September of the same year.

Jack Jones revealed that his sportsmanship was as lacking as ever in a fight that came off on 15 January 1828, following an aborted

295 There is some discrepancy in the duration of this fight. *Fistiana* (1846) records the fight as having taken 210 mins (3hrs 30mins) while *Fistiana* (1867) records the duration as having been 4hrs 30mins.

FISTIANA;

OR,

THE ORACLE OF THE RING.

Jones, Jack (Welchman), wt. 10st.
bn. by Fisher Bill, Aug. 1825.
— bn. by Fisher, Bill.
— b. Patsey Tunny, 10*l*. a side, 276r. (most ever fought), 210m. Cheshire.
— Tunny a second time, 10*l*. a side, 120m. Cheshire, both in 1825.
— fought Rogers (of Warrington), 5r. Rogers cut as did his friends with the purse. Southay Common, Jan. 15, 1828. [FISHER.)
— dr. with Fisher, Bill.—(*See*
— b. Tom Knowles, June 9, 1827.
— bn. by Bob Hampson (street fight), Feb. 21, 1831.
— bn. by Jack Adams.
— b. Goodwin (street fight), 1832; (fatal to Goodwin,) Jones sentenced to six weeks' imprisonment.

The fight record of Jack Jones, published in Fistiana; or, the Oracle of the Ring *(1846).*

contest between Bill Fisher and Ned Stockman at Graston-heath, approximately 21 miles from Manchester. Following a dispute about Fisher's weight, Stockman left the battleground and a small purse was collected to ensure that the day was not entirely wasted. Jack Jones stepped forward and challenged Sam Pixton, a Manchester butcher, but Pixton was not present. At length, a 'yokel' was found for Jones, and the yokel apparently fought quite well until Jones finished him off in the fifth round with a kick to the head. Jack Jones would meet Fisher for a third time in November of the same year in a fight for £25 a-side, managing to finally draw against his rival after a fight of 58 rounds lasting 77 minutes.

Jack Jones afterwards lost a street fight to Bob Hampson in 1831, and two years later the notoriety of Jones was earning him column inches even outside of the sporting papers. Jack Jones met an acquaintance named John Goodwin at Ward's public house in Liverpool on 13 February 1832, where after a quarrel Jones and Goodwin agreed to fight, both being known as 'two noted second-rate pugilists'. The battle, which took place in Hood Street, at the corner of Queen Square, resulted in Goodwin having been 'left on the ground almost without life' after 50 minutes of fighting. Goodwin died two days later and Jack Jones was taken into custody. In the trial that followed, a jury found Jack Jones guilty of causing the death of John Goodwin, and the judge sentenced the pugilist to six weeks' imprisonment with hard labour.[296]

The last recorded fight of Jack Jones took place on 31 October 1833, against Jack Adams of London, at Primrose Field at Bootle, Liverpool, for £10 a-side. On this occasion, Jones lost to Adams in 75 minutes.[297] After this time, Jack Jones, who had fought (or probably sought the turf) in more rounds in a single prize fight in the history of the ring, apparently retired from prize fighting altogether and nothing was heard of him again.

296 As recorded in the *Liverpool Mercury*, 17 February 1832, and 16 March 1832. The fatal match was also recorded in the *Monmouthshire Merlin*, 3 March 1832, and the *Cambridge Chronicle and Journal*, 9 March 1832.

297 As recorded in the *Chester Chronicle*, 1 November 1833.

Chapter 23

Rise of the Champions

Fights between Welsh tradesmen in the provinces rather than professional pugilists frequently make up those brief accounts of pugilistic Welshmen found within the pages of *Bell's Life*. One such contest between a tailor named John Mahers and a Welsh groom by the name of Charles Williams took place at Stratfield Saye in Hampshire in 1825.[298] The battle was witnessed by a 'respectable muster of the Fancy' and was fought with all the ceremony of an organised prize fight.Williams had honoured himself with the title of 'the Welsh Champion' by virtue of having been 'a *Taffy* by birth'. In the fight that followed, Charles Williams was as active as a 'buck-goat' and gave a fair account of himself, having demonstrated 'excellent science' before having two of his teeth knocked out by Mahers in the latter part of the fight. In the last four rounds, although Williams was seen to be as 'bold as a lion', he had the worst of it and gave in after 15 rounds. The spectators were satisfied that he had done his best and concluded that Williams was 'as brave a fellow as ever left the Principality of Wales'.

At this time, a number of pugilists began to emerge who showed a keenness to identify themselves as Welshmen, usually by adding the title of 'Welsh Champion' in the event that they had any pretensions as to their skill at prize fighting, whether proven in battle or not. There is another more intriguing reference to a 'Welsh Champion' found amongst the pages of *Bell's Life* in December of 1825, who must have been thought a pugilist of some merit by virtue of the fact that he was being viewed as a potential opponent by the hardy veteran Jack Scroggins. On 11

298 As recorded in *Bell's Life in London & Sporting Chronicle,* 18 December 1825.

December 1825, *Bell's Life* contained a notice drawing attention to a benefit event arranged for Scroggins to be held at the Tennis Court on the following Tuesday. Scroggy was apparently eager to end his long retirement from the ring and was anxious 'to have another *shy* before he departs for "Kingdom come," and is ready to fight the Welsh champion, of Battle-bridge, for 25 or 50; and "no mistake"'.[299] It seems likely that this unnamed Welsh pugilist was John Lewis, a blacksmith, who was 'well known in Battle-bridge' by the cognomen of the 'Welch Champion'[300].

Another lesser pugilist who appears to have been well known as a 'Welsh Champion' was John Thomas of Merthyr, who appeared at the Tennis Court on 19 October 1825, in the company of a number of leading pugilists at a benefit event held for the veteran Tom Shelton. Jem Ward, Tom Oliver and Jack Scroggins all demonstrated their sparring skills at the event. On this occasion, John Thomas, styled as the 'Welch Champion', met an unnamed 'Sawney' or Scottish 'Champion'. It was reported in *Bell's Life* as follows:

> 'THE SCOTCH AND WELCH CHAMPIONS – These worthies mounted the stage to vindicate the pugilistic fame of their respective countries. *Sawney* had exhibited on former occasions. But *Taffy* made his first bow, and merely got up to see what he could do. He is a fine young man, and, with instruction, would puzzle some of the vulgar. Neither of them troubled themselves about stopping, but hit away with vigour. The round hitting of the Scotchman was, however, well met by the straight muzzlers of the Welchman; and in the end, Sawney wished himself away. Taffy retired as proud of one of his native buck goats; and will, no doubt, astonish his friends by the details of his exploits[301].'

The defeat of the 'Scotch Champion' by John Thomas would lead to a rivalry that would drag on for the next two years, following further

299 As recorded in *Bell's Life in London & Sporting Chronicle,* 11 December 1825.

300 As recorded in the *Public Ledger and Daily Advertiser,* 6 October 1828. John Lewis was named in the 'Police' section of the newspaper. Lewis was charged with theft at Hatton-Garden after having deceived a neighbour and laid claim to one of their cockerels as his own.

301 As recorded in *Bell's Life in London & Sporting Chronicle,* 23 October 1825.

meetings at the Fives Court in London, and 'other places' with the gloves as well as with the knuckles. Thomas's confidence was apparently so bolstered by a rematch against the Scotch Champion the following year that Vincent Dowling received a letter from the backers of Thomas a few months later stating their willingness to match him against 'any man in England of his own weight':

> TO THE EDITOR OF BELL'S LIFE IN LONDON.
> Mr. EDITOR – You made handsome mention of the "Welsh Champion" in his set-to at the Tennis Court with the "Scotch Champion," some months ago – this is to inform you that the friends of John Thomas, the Welsh Champion, will back him to fight any man in England of his own weight, 12st. 7lb. for 50*l.* or 100*l.*
> Your's, &c. J.W.
> London, December 6, 1826.
> N.B. Direct to the Bell Inn, Merthyr Tydfil, Glamorganshire.[302]

One reader of *Bell's Life* who was less than impressed with the open challenge was the 'Scotch Champion', who was quick to pen a response to the letter, which was published the following week:

> TO THE EDITOR OF BELL'S LIFE IN LONDON.
> SIR, – The Scotch Champion presents his polite compliments to Mr. Taffy Thomas, and would feel pleased to draw a little of his hot Welch blood on the earliest occasion. The Scotch Champion was in bad condition when he set-to with Mr. Ap Shenkin Thomas, or he would not have had to boast or vaunt about what he did that day with the *gloves*. Taffy will not talk so lightly about the *knuckles*. The Scotch Champion means to visit Glamorganshire in a short time, and will be happy to make a deposit of 20*l.* at the Bell, Merthyr, on the evening of the 22d instant.
> Howard's Cafe House, Dec. 14, 1826.[303]

302 As recorded in *Bell's Life in London & Sporting Chronicle,* 10 December 1826.
303 As recorded in *Bell's Life in London & Sporting Chronicle,* 17 December 1826.

BELL'S
LIFE IN LONDON,
AND SPORTING CHRONICLE;

CHALLENGE TO JEM BURNS.—A letter has arrived in town from Alex. Cropley, of Haverfordwest, South Wales, challenging Jem Burns, for 50*l*. or 100*l*. Cropley says he is a novice, weighing 11st. 10lb.; and will fight Jem any where within 60 miles of London. He will be in town in six weeks, to make the match.

A challenge sent from Alex Cropley of Haverfordwest, South Wales, to Jem Burns, published in Bell's Life in London and Sporting Chronicle, *14 May 1826.*

Despite the apparent willingness of the Scotch Champion to visit Merthyr and lay his money down to make a match against Thomas, he did not appear at the Bell Inn to put down his deposit on the night in question. Suitably annoyed by the Scotsman's boasting, the 'Welsh Champion' drafted a letter and posted it to the offices of *Bell's Life*, pouring scorn on the idle boasting of his Scottish rival:

> TO THE EDITOR OF BELL'S LIFE IN LONDON.
> SIR – I beg to apologise for intruding again on your kindness and to inform the Sporting World, that the "Scotch Champion," who promised in your Paper of the 17th. instant to visit Merthyr-Tydfil and make a deposit of 20*l*. has not done so, nor do I suppose he will. However Sawney may sneer at Taffy, you, Mr. Editor, are aware that there are some good ones in our parts. I shall still hope the "Scotch Champion" will redeem his promise; and should he be punctual to his appointment, I shall meet his chaffing, by pleasing my backer and punishing Sawney's presumption. I remain, Sir, your humble servant,
> JOHN THOMAS, Welsh Champion.
> Bell Inn, Merthyr-Tydfil, Dec. 27, 1826.[304]

304 As recorded in *Bell's Life in London & Sporting Chronicle*, 31 December 1826.

This was not the end of the matter, as the 'Scotch Champion' afterwards travelled to John Thomas's home town of Merthyr and spoke disparagingly of his ability as a pugilist compared to his own. Incensed by the Scotsman's braggadocio, Thomas sent another letter to the offices of *Bell's Life*, outlining the reasons why he had retired from prize fighting, while issuing an exception in the case of the Scotsman in the event that he proved willing to fight:

> TO THE EDITOR OF BELL'S LIFE IN LONDON.
> SIR – I am, at last, become a Benedict, and likely to be comfortably settled in life, and I have promised my wife, and her friends, not to fight any more. But, in consequence of the Scottish Champion (Sawney) having been lately in this place, vauntingly talking of his prowess, and his superiority over me, I will keep myself open to fight him within three months of this time, for one hundred sovereigns a-side. When he was here, he did not come near me; which, as a man, he ought to have done, probably from the recollection of the straight *muzzlers* he has received from me, at our various turns-up at the Fives Court and other places, with the gloves and naked fists, within the last two years. I mean fighting, and nothing else. Indeed, I challenged him, in your Paper, not five months ago, but could not get him to come to the scratch. I, and my friends, will be at the Castle Tavern, on the 19th April, to do every thing needful. By inserting the above in your valuable Paper, you will oblige, Sir,
>
> Your humble servant, JOHN THOMAS,
> Bell Inn, Merthyr-Tidvil, March 19. Welsh
> Champion.[305]

The above letter would appear to be the last published account of the ongoing rivalry between John Thomas and the Scotch Champion. While it appears doubtful that Thomas had any real claim to have been 'Welsh Champion' outside his circle of local backers in Merthyr, the fact that Thomas had laid claim to such

305 As recorded in *Bell's Life in London & Sporting Chronicle,* 25 March 1827.

a title would underline that pugilism had developed to the point where multiple 'Champions' of a regional variety had emerged and were familiar to the Welsh public. Certainly, there appears to have been other self-styled 'Champions', a few of whom received some support from their fellow Welshmen, who looked to them to defend their national pride. In 1826, Phillip Lewis, alias 'Portobello', who claimed to be 'the Glamorganshire Champion', sent word to *Bell's Life* for the second time to announce his desire to meet Big Brown (Tom Brown of Bridgnorth), Phil Sampson (The Birmingham Youth) or 'any other man in England' to fight for the considerable sum of £500. In this desire, the 'Glamorganshire Champion' appears to have had a degree of local support, as it was stated that 'the Welchmen are not a little surprised their former challenge was not noticed, and say, that if their card is treated with silence, they will come to the conclusion that the London Ring thinks more of taking benefits than coming to the *scratch*'.[306]

W. Hoddell (also Hoddel) awarded himself the far grander title of 'Welch Champion' following his drawn battle with R. Humphreys at Fiddler's Green in Radnorshire, about eight miles from Newtown in Montgomeryshire on 30 July 1828. The battleground for the fight had been carefully selected to avoid interference from the authorities. By selecting a location near to the boundaries of Montgomery, Salop and Radnor, in the event that the fight was disturbed in one county, it was thought that by quickly relocating to another, the contest might be able to continue unhindered.

The fight had been of sufficient interest as to be announced in *Bell's Life*,[307] and both men were well known in the locality, with 'the well-known tactics of the combatants' having earned them some measure of fame as a result of their 'various spirited "mills" in the past' and both pugilists had been in training for a long time prior to the contest. It was thought that the fight would draw a large number of spectators as there had been 'numerous bets' made upon the outcome. On the day of the battle at 35 minutes past two, the men entered the ring. Humphreys was the

306 As recorded in *Bell's Life in London & Sporting Chronicle*, 4 June 1827.

307 As recorded in *Bell's Life in London & Sporting Chronicle*, 27 July 1828.

first to throw up his hat, and was attended by Winterflood, the 'Bath Champion', and one Jack Williams. Hoddell had secured the services of a man named Tom Morris and a well-known Montgomeryshire artist named Jack Evans as his seconds. The colours for both men were promptly tied to the stakes, yellow and scarlet for Hoddell, and orange and blue for Humphreys, and the combatants stripped for battle. Hoddell weighed 13st to Humphreys's 12st 6lb, although Humphreys looked much thinner than his opponent.

The fight lasted for one hour and 47 minutes, during which time 'sixty-one rounds were contested with a game and perseverance scarcely ever exceeded'. Hoddell had been winning when the fight stopped after a heated disagreement following a suspected foul blow. The seconds and the backers then agreed to call the contest a draw with Hoddell and Humphreys having been given £10 each. The possibility of a rematch was afterwards discussed for £70 a-side.[308]

Following this match, W. Hoddell was quick to decide that having been on his way to winning his battle against R. Humphreys prior to it having been called as a drawn battle, he was fully entitled to call himself the 'Champion of Wales'. With Hoddell having consistently challenged one Pat M'Donnald, the 'Irish Gasman' from Newtown, in order to prove his superiority, Pat M'Donnald penned a letter to *Bell's Life*, disputing Hoddell's claim to the title and stating his willingness to do battle with the supposed 'Welsh Champion':

> TO THE EDITOR OF BELL'S LIFE IN LONDON.
> SIR – Having received repeated challenges from Hoddell (who stiles himself the Champion of Wales), who last contended with Humphreys, I beg leave to inform him, that I am ready to meet him on his own terms, for a purse of 20*l*., which is ready at the Crown Inn; or I am prepared to post the pony, to make a match for 50*l*. or 100*l*. a-side, to come off in one month, six weeks, or any time convenient to himself. If Hoddell don't like the match, Humphreys will be accepted. I shall be at Shrewsbury Races, on Tuesday

308 As recorded in *Bell's Life in London & Sporting Chronicle*, 10 August 1828.

the 16th. inst., when either of them may be accommodated for the 20*l.* purse, by
Yours, &c.

PAT M'DONNALD, the Irish Gasman.
Newtown, Montgomeryshire, 8th September, 1828.[309]

Sadly, there appears to be no published record of whether the Irish Gasman ever succeeded in deflating the pugilistic pretensions of Hoddell, although it is clear that Hoddell's decision to call himself the 'Champion of Wales' was met with irritation by other Welsh prize fighters, who refused to accept the credibility of his claim. One of these was William Cole, who felt it necessary to write to the editor of *Bell's Life* to pour cold water on Hoddell's title, challenging him to prove his mettle in battle:

CHALLENGE TO HODDEL,
THE WELCH CHAMPION
TO THE EDITOR OF BELL'S LIFE IN LONDON.

SIR – Having seen in your Sporting Chronicle, that Hoddel, who contended with Humphreys, had assumed the title of Champion of Wales, I, being a Welchman myself, conceive he has no pretensions to the title, and am willing to contend with him in a twenty-four feet roped-ring, in a fair stand-up fight, half-minute time, for from five to twenty-five sovs. a-side, or any sum, on any day not exceeding a month from the day the match is made. A deposit shall be made, if the challenge is accepted, at the Chandos Arms Inn, Knighton, Radnorshire, on Thursday, the 23 instant, when a friend of mine will attend, between the hours of two and four in the afternoon, on my behalf, and arrange and enter into articles, as shall be then agreed upon.

Yours, &c. WILLIAM COLE.
Oxford Arms Inn, Presteign, Radnorshire, Oct. 6, 1828.[310]

309 As recorded in *Bell's Life in London & Sporting Chronicle*, 14 September 1828.
310 As recorded in *Bell's Life in London & Sporting Chronicle*, 12 October 1828.

With prize fighting having been quite widespread throughout Wales by the late 1820s, locally defined 'Champions' increased in number, and the outcome of their battles were apparently well known by the public despite the fact that there was little coverage of their deeds in the Welsh press. In the same year that W. Hoddell was laying claim to having been the 'Champion of Wales', a pugilist known by the title of the 'Tram-road Champion' defended his title against a fellow Welsh prize fighter by the name of Williams, another 'acknowledged "good one" amongst his countrymen' at Talgarth. The fight lasted 104 rounds over a period of one hour and 45 minutes. It ended with both pugilists having been so exhausted that they were left unable to come up to the scratch at the call of time, and as a consequence, neither man could claim the victory. Public interest in a rematch ensured that they were matched again, and 'considerable sums' were laid on the result, public opinion being that Williams might well succeed in toppling the Tram-road Champion.[311]

Aside from the various pugilists claiming to be 'Welsh Champions', there were other Welshmen of lesser reputation who were also following the careers of the prominent pugilists of the London Prize Ring through the pages of *Bell's Life*. A few of these men felt sufficiently confident in their fighting abilities to issue challenges of their own. That these challenges were issued from places so far apart in Wales would also confirm that pugilism was of widespread interest to the Welsh sporting public. In May of 1826, Alex Cropley of Haverfordwest posted a letter to the editor of *Bell's Life*, stating his willingness to fight Jem Burns, despite having never fought in the London Prize Ring. Cropley was willing to fight Jem Burns 'any where within 60 miles of London' for £50 or £100, and was apparently so eager to meet Burns that he had decided to travel to London in six weeks' time to make the match.[312] M. Richards, a native of 'Welchpool, North Wales', drafted his own letter to *Bell's Life* on 7 September 1829, from Chester. Richards was also a novice, having never fought in the London Prize Ring before, but had also decided to challenge a pugilist with a well-established reputation in the form of Ned

311 As recorded in *The Cambrian*, 26 April 1828.

312 As recorded in *Bell's Life in London & Sporting Chronicle*, 14 May 1826.

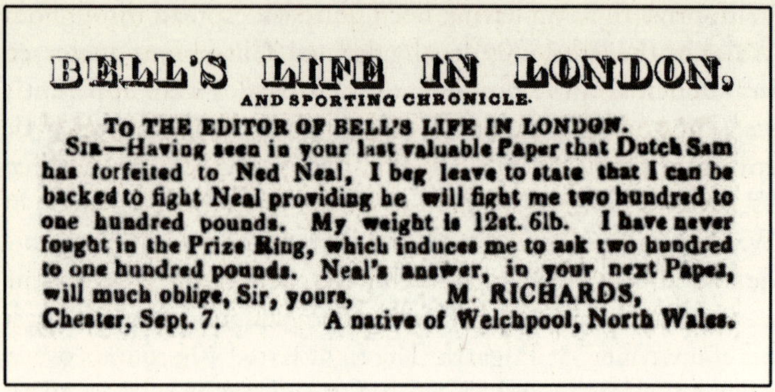

BELL'S LIFE IN LONDON,
AND SPORTING CHRONICLE.

TO THE EDITOR OF BELL'S LIFE IN LONDON.

SIR—Having seen in your last valuable Paper that Dutch Sam has forfeited to Ned Neal, I beg leave to state that I can be backed to fight Neal providing he will fight me two hundred to one hundred pounds. My weight is 12st. 6lb. I have never fought in the Prize Ring, which induces me to ask two hundred to one hundred pounds. Neal's answer, in your next Paper, will much oblige, Sir, yours, M. RICHARDS,
Chester, Sept. 7. A native of Welchpool, North Wales.

A challenge sent from M. Richards of 'Welchpool', North Wales, to Ned Neal, published in Bell's Life in London and Sporting Chronicle, *13 September 1829.*

Neal. Richards was apparently eager to engage Neal after reading that Dutch Sam had forfeited to him, asking if Neal would fight him for £200 to £100, and hoped that Neal would reply in the next edition of the newspaper.[313]

A 'journeyman painter' from Corn Street in Newport, Monmouthshire, named Richard Lewis was bold enough to issue an open challenge through the pages of *Bell's Life* in 1829, writing of his willingness to 'fight any man in England at his weight, 10st. 9 lb., for any sum from 50*l.* to 500*l.*' (£50 to £500). It would seem that Lewis may have had some degree of financial backing as a pugilist, claiming that his money was 'always ready at the Noah's Ark Inn, Newport'.[314] Another confident open challenge from a pugilistic Welshman appeared in *Bell's Life* on 13 September 1829, which was attributed to Henry Edwards, 'The Little Miller' of the Three Salmons, near Monmouth. Edwards was apparently willing to fight 'any of my weight, 10 stone 9 lbs, in the counties of Gloucester, Hereford or Monmouth' for anywhere between £10 to £50, and was reportedly also 'happy to accommodate' either Alec Reid, the Chelsea Snob, or Harry Jones, the Sailor Boy, breezily commenting that he would 'not be particular to a pound or two in weight'.[315]

313 As recorded in *Bell's Life in London & Sporting Chronicle,* 13 September 1829.

314 As recorded in *Bell's Life in London & Sporting Chronicle,* 27 September 1829.

315 As recorded in *Bell's Life in London & Sporting Chronicle,* 13 September 1829.

There was no reader more surprised by this boldly worded challenge than Henry Edwards himself, who was forced to pen a hasty letter to *Bell's Life* to put the record straight, and which was published the following week, stating,

> Henry Edwards, of the Three Salmons, near Monmouth, denies that he ever expressed a desire to fight Harry Jones, Alec Reid, or any other man. His name has been unwarrantably used by some fool in his neighbourhood.[316]

With an increase in prize fighting activity in Wales as the 1820s progressed, the likelihood of a prize fight resulting in serious injury or even the death of a pugilist was greatly increased. Charles Hall was imprisoned for two months following a trial at the Flintshire Assizes in 1825 for the manslaughter of Thomas Oxford, following a pugilistic contest that had arisen as a result of a personal quarrel.[317] In 1829, the disapproval of the magistrates of Montgomeryshire was shown when their vigilance forced a battle for £20 between two pugilists named Price and Humphreys, (possibly the same R. Humphreys to have fought Hoddell), to relocate to Llanbadarn Fynydd in neighbouring Radnorshire on 11 September. Eighty-five rounds were fought in front of an estimated 2,000 spectators before Humphreys was carried unconscious to a nearby inn and died as a result of his injuries. Humphreys left behind a wife and four small children, who were left entirely dependent on the charity of the parish. In its report on the contest, *The Cambrian* would comment with obvious disapproval that the fight was 'the second pitched battle which has been fought near the same spot within the last 12 months, both of which were got up in Montgomeryshire, but through the laudable interposition of the Magistracy of that county they were not suffered to take place therein'.[318]

Despite the apparent distaste with which *The Cambrian* newspaper would reluctantly report on matters relating to the

316 As recorded in *Bell's Life in London & Sporting Chronicle*, 27 September 1829.

317 As recorded in *The Cambrian*, 9 April 1825.

318 As recorded in *The Cambrian*, 26 September 1829, and in the *Carmarthen Journal and South Wales Weekly Advertiser*, 25 September 1829.

Welsh prize ring, the editor of the newspaper seemed to privately accept that pugilism was unlikely to fall out of favour with the general public in the near future. Certainly, by this stage vast numbers of Welsh spectators were prepared to travel great distances in order to watch local pugilistic heroes do battle, and were willing to bet significant sums on the outcome. That *The Cambrian* had decided it was fighting a losing battle on the behalf of public morality by 1830 might be ascertained by its decision to reprint a challenge issued by a Welsh pugilist named Luke Purcell to a rival, Evan James, which was copied directly from the pages of *Bell's Life*:

> Luke Purcell will fight Evan James, one shilling to a sixpence, or £200 to £100, either at Brecon or Swansea; and hopes, if James is not a cur, he will come forward. He will fight either of his friends at the same rate, and prove who is the best man – *Bell's Life*.[319]

---

319 As recorded in *The Cambrian*, 6 February 1830, reprinted from *Bell's Life in London & Sporting Chronicle*, 31 January 1830.

Chapter 24

The Welch Champion

'Charles is considered another Glendower, and is recognised as the Welch Champion.'
(*Bell's Life in London and Sporting Chronicle*, 3 February 1828)

William Charles of Newport was exceedingly annoyed by the arrival of three pugilists from Bristol at his home town in October of 1827. Jem Bailey, accompanied by one Sam Hazel and John Keate (or Keates), the 'Bristol Youth', had posted up bills around Newport on their arrival, announcing their intention to thrash any men of their weight, regardless of whether they were English or Welsh. The townspeople were incensed by the challenge, and a message was quickly sent to William Charles at nearby Pontypool, to return home to do battle with Jem Bailey. Up to this point, William Charles had only ever fought locally, although he had earned something of a reputation as the local champion, having had 'several turns-up in his own neighbourhood, and always beat his man'.[320] The contest against Bailey was made for 8 October 1827, for ten sovereigns a-side and a purse. Jem Bailey had enjoyed a reputation at his hometown, after defeating 'Redman', at Durham Downs, near Bristol back in 1822. Bailey had subsequently improved his pugilistic reputation in a hard-fought contest against the prominent Bristol pugilist 'Jack Cabbage', in which Bailey was beaten, and a defeat over an opponent named Abbenott at Chertsey in 1824.

Despite his reputation as 'a man of sound bottom', it was felt by the supporters of William Charles that unless Bailey could

320 As recorded in *Bell's Life in London and Sporting Chronicle*, 14 October 1827.

hit Charles out of time within the first few rounds, he had little chance of victory as William Charles was known as a 'complete glutton' for punishment.[321]

Jem Bailey would appear to have been a formidable opponent for the Welshman, being 3in taller than Charles at 5ft 10in tall and of muscular build. A large crowd of thousands of Welsh and Bristol spectators crowded round the 24ft roped ring set up in a field near Newport waiting with baited breath for the entrance of the combatants on the afternoon of the fight. Jem Bailey was assisted by W. Danks, Sam Hazel and John Keate, while a man named Jenkins was to be found in the corner of William Charles. At one o'clock the fight commenced, and was reported by *Bell's Life* on 14 October 1827, as follows:

THE FIGHT

Round 1. Charles kept his *mawleys* well up, waiting for the attack. Bailey worked for an opening and at last hit out with his left, catching Charles slightly *on the nob*; when Charles let fly, and Bailey napped it on the *listener*. They then got to close fighting. To it they went pell-mell: stop, give and take on the face and neck was the go on both sides, until Bailey was compelled to give way, and down he went, after three minutes hard hammering. This was a tremendous round, and on which, we think, depended the result. Bailey now, for the first time began to discover his mistake. No untrained or untaught youth ever contested a more severe round with a scientific pugilist better than Charles did here: we really thought this round would have ended the battle.

Round 2. Charles looked at his man for a moment, and then went to work. Bailey more cautious, as if dreading a repetition of the first course. Charles put in a *nobber* with his left hand. Bailey seized him with his right by the back part of the neck, and began jobbing, but found he had "caught a Tartar;" and after a few exchanges, went down, amid the shouts of thousands.

Round 3. Bailey eyed his man seriously, as if bent upon mischief, and put in a blow upon his left *ogle*; but missed to put the shutter up. Charles returned on the *scent-box*, fetching *claret* pretty profusely. Bailey began to fight shy, but Charles would not

321 As recorded in *The Cambrian,* 13 October 1827.

be denied, and after a few salutation, Bailey went down for shelter. 5 to 1 on Charles.

Round 4. Either distress or want of pluck was very visible in Bailey's countenance. Sparring. Here Charles convinced his man that he could stop (in his own method) clean, clever, and effectually. "Go it, Charles, it's all you own." To it they went. Sharp fighting; Bailey down, but without much punishment.

Round 5. Bailey gently and cautiously shifting towards his man; Charles firm and steady. Bailey put in a clean and pretty blow over the guard of his opponent, and recovered himself cleverly. Charles saw him coming it again, but it would not do; when within his reach he got the start, hit him a straight poke, threw him off balance, and put in a body blow, which grassed him.

Rounds 6, 7 and 8. Bailey shy. After the exchange of a few blows, Bailey went down each round, as if dreading further punishment; and at the end of the 8th cried "enough". Charles danced a hornpipe round the ring, amid the most deafening shouts.

REMARKS

Never were the knowing-ones taken in more completely than in this fight, which lasted but thirteen minutes. Bailey's confidence was such that he had actually stipulated with the stakeholder for the stakes and the purse. Nothing could be more disgusting than the taunting chaff he used before the fight; and we sincerely hope, if he goes further down the country, exhibiting the art of self-defence, that he may again and again pay for the insults he had offered to the Welsh.

* * * *

At the end of the battle between William Charles and Jem Bailey, a small purse was collected for John Keate, the 'Bristol Youth', to fight a sailor named Charles Stephens. The ring experience of Keate put paid to the hopes of Stephens, who was punished severely about the face for thirty four rounds and for over an hour before their supporters interfered and the men consented to split the purse and give in.

That evening, Jem Bailey, who had to be assisted into Newport following his battle with William Charles, made a surprise second appearance in the ring, against a rural opponent for a guinea a-side who was supposedly 'considered almost a match for W. Charles', and was deemed to be the 'champion of the parish' that he lived in. In the four rounds that followed, Bailey 'hit his man right and left, and peeled his face at pleasure, which soon obliged the Welshman to give in'.[322] According to the correspondent who sent his impression of the fight to *Bell's Life*, despite the Welshman being of superior weight and strength, Bailey's superiority was evident throughout, and Bailey 'cut him so much, that the flesh hung about his chops in slices', while Bailey was not hurt at all at the close of the contest.[323] The result of this second battle resulted in a great deal of heated discussion amongst the crowd, with many believing that Bailey might well have been party to a fix in his first battle against William Charles after having been beaten so soundly. Jem Bailey was quick to deny the rumour, stating that he considered Charles to be 'one of the best men he ever contended with.'[324]

Jem Bailey was eager to overturn his defeat at the hands of William Charles, so before the end of the month was out, he challenged Charles to a rematch for £20 a-side. The fight came off at Glascode Common, three miles from Pontypool on 29 October

322 As recorded in *The Cambrian,* 13 October 1827.

323 As recorded in *Bell's Life in London and Sporting Chronicle,* 14 October 1827.

324 The spectators may have had good reason to doubt Jem Bailey's sense of honour. Stephen Strong, known as 'Jack Cabbage', of Hanham in Gloucestershire, had fought such well-regarded men as Jack Martin and Jack Cooper, prior to having fought Bailey. It would appear that Bailey and his backers induced Cabbage to sign an agreement to lose to Bailey, although reports are contradictory as to whether this was as regards their first contest or a subsequent rematch. After agreeing to throw the fight, Jack Cabbage afterwards suffered a crisis of conscience and decided to give Bailey a sound beating according to *Bell's Life in London and Sporting Chronicle*, 7 November 1824. Cabbage confessed his wrongdoing to his backers, who consequently pressed for a bill of indictment for conspiracy at court in Bristol. Depressed by his damaged reputation, Cabbage turned to drink, and decided to drown himself in a canal at St Phillips's Marsh in Bristol on 29 July 1824. Jack Cabbage swam to the centre of the canal where he promptly sunk (*Hereford Journal*, 4 August 1824). His body was recovered twenty minutes later, by which time he was dead. *Bell's Life*, 1 August 1824 contradicts the later account slightly; believing that the agreement to fix the fight was on the occasion of a proposed re-match.

1827.[325] It was a tremendous fight lasting 117 hard rounds, fought over an astonishing three hours. The match, made in haste, was not confined to a ring, and was fought on open ground, surrounded by crowds of spectators. This time round, Jem Bailey had the best of it throughout, with his superior science coming to the fore, although William Charles would prove his capacity to endure 'more punishment than any ordinary men could give him' as the rounds wore on, and he was 'hideously marked' by the end of the fight. Bailey rattled the Welshman's head continually with one two blows, and the sounds of his fists connecting with Charles's cranium resounded throughout the crowd. Although William Charles scored the first knockdown blow, he quickly showed the marks of Jem Bailey's knuckles, and was bleeding profusely from the nose and mouth long before Bailey exhibited any signs of damage. Jem Bailey showed a great deal of judgement in his movements, and was forced to shift his position regularly and fought on the retreat, as Charles occupied the higher position on the inclined ground on which they battled, with Bailey fighting at a disadvantage due to the sun shining into his eyes.

Near the end of the fight, William Charles was very weak and nearly blind, and following another one-two peppering from Jem Bailey, Charles attempted to pay him back in kind, although the Bristol pugilist evaded his blows by falling. Charles deemed the strategy unfair, and called upon the umpires to intervene, but they merely held up their watches and called 'Time'. At the start of the 118th round, William Charles, suffering from 'complete exhaustion and dreadful punishment' sat still on his second's knee, and was unable to come up to the scratch, so the victory was awarded to Jem Bailey. The backers of William Charles were greatly disappointed with the defeat, and expressed the opinion that had the fight been confined to an enclosed 24ft ring, the tremendous hitting powers of Charles would have ensured that Bailey would have been quickly cornered and dropped.

Inevitably, with a win a-piece, a third match was quickly made for 50 sovereigns a-side in the new year. Jem Bailey won the toss to decide the battle ground, on the date of the second deposit at

325 As recorded in *Bell's Life in London and Sporting Chronicle*, 4 November 1827.

the George and Dragon public house, in Redcliffe Street, Bristol. Bailey chose Lansdown racecourse near Bath as his preferred venue, with the fight to come off on 29 January 1828.[326] By this time, the fame of William Charles, now widely consider to be the 'Welch Champion', had spread considerably, and he was said to be 'an immense favourite of his countrymen, who land and acknowledge him as their champion.'[327] Some idea of the level of Welsh support enjoyed by William Charles might be gleaned by his comparison to the heroic Prince of Wales, Owain Glyndwr, with it being said that the Welsh considered him 'another Glendower'.[328]

Perhaps fearing the interference of the authorities as a result of this public interest, the fight was moved to Kingswood Hill near Bristol and rescheduled for 28 January. On the day of the battle, a vast number of 'Taffylanders' took to the road in the hope of reaching the battleground before noon, the time appointed for the showdown between William Charles and Jem Bailey. Unfortunately, the police had already been alerted to the fight, and the venue was changed to Sodbury, a further eight miles away. The news was met with groans and moans by the Fancy, who had ridden their horses, driven their carriages, and in many cases trudged endless miles to the location. Most walked wearily on; some fell out along the road, adding to the takings of the inns along the way by drowning their disappointment with drink.

By two o'clock a rudely formed ring was put up in a field near Sodbury, and the two men stripped for battle. William Charles was attended by Bob Watson and his son, while Jem Bailey had A. Newton and Job Bath as his seconds. The fight would prove to be a supreme disappointment, mostly due to the unwillingness of Bailey to bring the fight to Charles, and he continually crept backwards, and would only fight on the retreat. Reaching the ropes, Jem Bailey fell continually without a blow in order to get out of harm's way, and his actions brought loud criticism from the Welsh spectators. Bailey's followers proved their willingness to try to defend the interests of their man by continually breaking into the ring, causing a number of delays between the rounds, and

326 As recorded in *Bell's Life in London and Sporting Chronicle,* 13 January 1828.

327 As recorded in the *Morning Advertiser,* 2 February 1828.

328 As recorded in *Bell's Life in London and Sporting Chronicle,* 3 February 1828.

allowing Bailey as much as 15 minutes recovery time inbetween. It was only by grim perseverance that the fight was finally brought to a conclusion, after 100 rounds and two hours of tedium, when Bailey, seeing that 'he had no chance by fighting, and his friends found that they had no chance by breaking the ring', finally gave in, and William Charles was declared the winner.

Jem Bailey's unwillingness to engage in a stand-up fight had resulted in a exceptionally poor match, with the *Morning Advertiser* commenting that 'the fight was altogether as bad as possible – pulling, hauling, and rolling about – and whatever may be said of Bailey's bad fighting and his dropping down, Charles could not be exceedingly clever when he took two hours to beat him'.[329]

Despite the disappointing nature of his third fight against Jem Bailey, William Charles's reputation was sufficiently enhanced by the victory to attract another challenge from one John (or Pat) Jennings, described as a 'Hibernian miller a few months later, after Charles had expressed a willingness to fight him.'[330] Jennings issued a challenge through the pages of *Bell's Life*, wishing to meet the 'new Welch Champion, Bill Charles' for £25 to £50 a-side.[331] Intriguingly, William Charles appears to have travelled to London at this time, and was eager to make the match, having mistakenly pitched up at the Castle Tavern in Holborn on the night appointed to meet Jennings, who was patiently waiting for the Charles at Peter Crawley's public house, the Queen's Head and French Horn, in Duke Street, Smithfield.[332] Charles had issued a response to the challenge of Jennings through the pages of the *Morning Advertiser*, but his response apparently went unread:

---

329 Jem Bailey retained an active dislike of Welsh pugilists in the years to come. A challenge to Bailey was printed in *Bell's Life in London and Sporting Chronicle,* 10 April 1831, from 'John Davies' which reads as follows, 'SIR – In consequence of the chaff of Jem Bailey, at Bristol, on Friday last, when he said he could lick any Welchman of his weight I beg leave to offer myself to him as a customer. I am a Welchman, under his weight, but will fight him, in two months, for 25*l.* or 50*l.*, not being particular to 10*l.* My money is ready at Reuben Marten's, City of London, Berwick-street, Soho, and the match can be made off hand by his sending the ready to that house. April 6, 1830 [*sic*]. JOHN DAVIES.'

330 As recorded in the *Morning Chronicle,* 18 June 1828.

331 As recorded in *Bell's Life in London and Sporting Chronicle,* 8 June1828.

332 As recorded in *Bell's Life in London and Sporting Chronicle,* 22 June 1828.

> To the EDITOR of the MORNING ADVERTISER.
> SIR, – To put an end to the chaff of Pat Jennings, I will meet him on Thursday evening next at Mr. Belcher's, Castle Tavern, Holborn, with my money ready to make a match with him for 25*l.* or 50*l.* a-side. I cannot leave my business to run after him, so if he means fighting me I hope to meet him at the above house with my money ready. Sir, by inserting the above you will oblige,
>
> Your humble Servant,
>
> WILLIAM CHARLES The Welch Champion.[333]

Having been disappointed in his attempts to make the match, John Jennings invited Charles to attend his benefit event to make a match for £25 the following week. William Charles was a no-show, and Jennings afterwards wrote of his disappointment to *Bell's Life*, requesting that 'if Taffy means fighting, and has any blood of the Ancient Britons in his veins,' he would feel inclined to call on Jennings to make the match.[334] Attempts to organise a meeting seem to have failed, although Jennings would not be the only one wishing to topple William Charles's crown.

In October, William Morgan, known as 'Josh Hudson's Black' stepped forward, stating that he was residing at Hereford, and wished to make a match against William Charles for £100 a-side, being willing to fight in Wales or London.[335] Morgan's call also went unanswered. Nothing more was heard of in relation to William Charles until the following year, when he issued a challenge to William Hicks of Sunninghill, Berkshire, to fight for between £10 and £25 a-side, with neither man to exceed 13st. In this instance, Charles would appear to have been eager to secure a match against Hicks, having left money to cover his deposit at the Castle Tavern in Holborn, but nothing appears to have come of it.[336]

In fact, William Charles would not be recorded as having fought again in the organised prize ring until 1832, over four

333 As recorded in the *Morning Advertiser,* 18 June 1828.

334 As recorded in *Bell's Life in London and Sporting Chronicle*, 29 June 1828.

335 As recorded in *Bell's Life in London and Sporting Chronicle*, 19 October 1828.

336 As recorded in *Bell's Life in London and Sporting Chronicle*, 22 November 1829.

years after having fought Jem Bailey for the third time, although it seems likely that he may have continued to fight further contests on his native turf. In January of 1832, the offices of *Bell's Life* received a scrawled challenge to William Charles which they deciphered as having come from a 'J. Trevor' who had heard that Charles had issued a challenge to fight any Irishman in Wales, and as a 'Patlander' himself, 'Trevor' wished to fight him for £50 between Hereford and Newport.[337] The writer of the challenge soon afterwards revealed himself to be a travelling hawker of silks named Stephen Trainer.

William Charles was willing to do battle with the Irishman, so both men laid a £5 deposit to seal the match at Newport in April, with the fight to come off on Monday, 4 June. Bets were apparently equal on the combatants due to their similarity in weight, with William Charles tipping the scale at 12st 13lbs to Stephen Trainer's 12st 10lbs.[338] In spite of it having initially been recorded that Trainer was 'well known in the ring', Trainer himself poured cold water on this claim soon afterwards, stating that he had 'never entered the London or Provincial Ring in his life.'[339]

In the weeks prior to the fight, there were some concerns about skulduggery among the Irish camp from the Welsh supporters of Willian Charles, and a letter was sent to Charles stating that his intended seconds, Harry Jones the 'Sailor Boy', and one 'Donovan', had been seen at Newport in the company of Bill Neat and Stephen Trainer. *Bell's Life* was forced to make a statement that the allegation was unfounded, and that both men were in 'tip top condition' and that the 'Potatoe's' were favoured over the 'Leek'.[340] Despite the confidence of his countrymen, given his complete lack of experience in the ring, it would appear to have been a rather risky decision on the part of Stephen Trainer to decide to face the 'tremendous' hitting powers of William Charles within a 24ft ring.

337 As recorded in *Bell's Life in London and Sporting Chronicle,* 1 January 1832.

338 As recorded in *Bell's Life in London and Sporting Chronicle,* 29 April x1832.

339 As recorded in *Bell's Life in London and Sporting Chronicle,* 6 May 1832.

340 As recorded in *Bell's Life in London and Sporting Chronicle,* 3 June 1832.

Chapter 25

The Patlander and the Old Horse

The fame of William Charles ensured that news of the outcome of his impending fight against Stephen Trainer was eagerly awaited by the Welsh Fancy. Following the earlier rumours that William Charles's Irish second, 'Donovan', might be biased in favour of Trainer, a blacksmith named Powell was substituted, who agreed to stand in the Welshman's corner, alongside Harry Jones.[341]

Recognising the keen interest of its readers, the *Monmouthshire Merlin* reported on the fight at greater length than was common in the Welsh newspapers at this time. A detailed account of the return of the 'Welch Champion' to the prize ring to fight Trainer was published on the Saturday after the contest on 9 June 1832:

THE MONMOUTHSHIRE MERLIN
PROVINCIAL MILLING
FIGHT BETWEEN STEPHEN TRAINER, AN IRISHMAN,
AND WILL CHARLES OF NEWPORT.

This match, which was for £50 a-side, came off on Monday last, at Monmouth Cap, a most eligible spot for the purpose, about equidistant from Monmouth, Hereford and Abergavenny. A good

341 It appears plausible that this may have been the same blacksmith named Powell of Broad Oak, Herefordshire, who fought Bob Parry, the Monmouthshire quarryman, on 2 August 1824. See *Chapter 22, The Game Welchmen*.

deal of interest had been excited in the affair and liberal betting took place, Charles being rather the favourite, but without odds, till a day or two previous to the fight, when rumours of the fine condition of Trainer, his activity and reported *stomach*, effected a change in his favour, and he was freely backed at even, and in some instances at trifling odds. Trainer is a hawker of silks, and in his line a very respectable man. All the potato-eaters travelling in the same way of business, congregated to the scene of action from many parts of the kingdom, all sanguine as to the result of the battle.

Large sales of Irish cloth and silks were made by them at considerably reduced prices, to enable them to put money in their pockets to back their *darling boy*. Some even put their pack in *pawn* to raise the blunt, which they sported to the last penny upon their *counthreman*.

Meanwhile, the friends of Charles were not shy. Some anxiety was felt by a few that he had made too free with the *exhilarating drops*, but those who knew him better averred that his constitution was that of a horse, and it was not *a drop* that would hurt him. It is said, we don't know with what truth, that on the morning of the fight he drank two quarts of strong beer, and sundry glasses of brandy and water and negus.[342] The ring was formed close to the Monmouth Cap Inn, in the same piece of ground where Young Gas and Yorkshire Robinson fought a few years since. The scene of the battle was delightfully picturesque, and those who were disappointed with the fight, were amply repaid for their ride by the beautiful, varied, and commanding scenery which the country presented.

At an early hour the different roads leading to the scene of action, were thronged with *toddlers*, and soon afterwards came the equestrians, mounted on all sorts of steeds, from the lame dog's-meat animal to the prancing hunter; carts, gigs, chaises, carriages, &c., followed, and by twelve o'clock there was a strong muster on the ground. The company was of a very motley description: there was the dark-featured collier, the robust peasant, the wily prig,

342 *Negus* – a drink made with wine, usually port, mixed with hot water, oranges or lemons and spices and sugar.

the exquisite, and the beggar. There was also a good sprinkling of the fair sex.

The arrangement was under the superintendence of one of the Fancy, named Cooke, and reflected great credit upon him. A most admirable ring was formed some distance from the 24ft roped ring, where the combatants were to exhibit their prowess. An outer ring of waggons was also formed, from which many hundred spectators were accommodated with a fine view of the *mill*. Some amusement was afforded to the assemblage during the suspense of waiting for Trainer and his opponent. While Cooke was clearing the ring, and compelling the front row to sit down, a countryman named Bolter, who, although *a yokel*, has obtained some celebrity in Herefordshire by his summary method of polishing-off his adversaries at wakes and fairs, was obstreperous, refused to comply with the order and stand back, and actually "shewed fight." Cooke accepted the offer and both put themselves in attitude for administering punishment. Just as Bolter was about making a hit, which appeared to be intended to settle the matter at once, Cooke came between his guard with his left, and met him like lightning on his box of ivories. The countryman's masticators rattled like dice in a box; his head flew back on his shoulders and he looked the picture of astonishment. Some of Bolter's friends then came round him, and by their intercessions succeeded for the time in moderating his choler. Everything then went on peaceably.

At 14 minutes past one, Monmouth time, Trainer entered the ring, attended by Deaf Burke and Old Watson, of Bristol. Charles followed immediately, accompanied by Harry Jones and Powell, the blacksmith. The company at this moment, we think, may be calculated to amount to about 4,000 persons. The spectators now began to scrutinise the appearance of the men, and the result of their observations was that the friends of Trainer began to look a little down in the mouth. Will Charles appeared confident, firm, cheerful and perfectly at his ease. Trainer, on the contrary, was pale, nervous and did not seem willing to look his adversary in the face. Still, it was hoped that he would recover himself and be more at home when he came to the scratch. On stripping, a great difference was observed in the men, decidedly in favour of Charles. The toss for side was won by Trainer.

THE FIGHT

Round 1. At 27 minutes past one, the combatants were placed at the scratch, the seconds retired to the corners of the ring and the fight commenced. After a feint from Trainer, Charles made a hit, in doing which he slipped and fell on his hand and knee. This chance was not taken advantage of by Trainer, either from want of tact, or spirit to go in, or from a proper feeling not to take what might be considered an undue advantage. They again came to the scratch, and after an exchange of blows, which did not tell, they closed, and Trainer adroitly threw his man. Notwithstanding the fall, the round was considered in favour of Charles, upon whom bets were freely offered, but few takers.

Round 2. On being placed in contact with his adversary, Trainer already shewed symptoms of exhaustion, and evident want of nerve. A rally commenced, in which no blow creditable to a scientific fighter was exchanged, and Trainer was almost immediately thrown down; – 2 to 1 on Charles.

Round 3. At the commencement of this round, Trainer made one or two pretty hits, but not effective. He was evidently afraid to follow it up. In a close, he endeavoured to *hide his head* under his arm to avoid the blows. Being hard pressed, he actually seized hold of Charles' arm with his mouth.

Rounds 4, 5 and 6. Charles beat his man all round the ring, but in such a manner that shewed he knew as much about scientific fighting as pig does of piano-forte playing. In the 4th round Trainer was knocked, or rather pushed, over the lower rope, and fell heavily on his back. In the 6th, after a rally, he fell from weakness without receiving a blow.

Round 7. All in favour of Charles, but at the conclusion Trainer threw him well.

Round 8. Trainer knocked through the ropes. No chance. A guinea to a potatoe.

Round 9. This was the concluding round of the fight. On coming to the scratch, Trainer was knocked down immediately and was not able again to rise when time was declared.

The fight lasted 13½ minutes, during which time Trainer had not the shadow of a chance. He betrayed throughout evident symptoms of a most dastardly white feather. The countenances of his countrymen underwent a considerable *elongation*, many whom were by no means sparing of very harsh epithets upon the man whom on the same morning they had been lauding to the skies as a *second Langan*. Immediately on the result of the fight being proclaimed by Harry Jones, the friends of Charles rent the air with deafening shouts, and a simultaneous rush was made to the ring to view the men. Trainer was lying on the ground in a pitiable state of exhaustion, but the visible marks of punishment were very slight. A respectable surgeon on the ground was asked to bleed him, but he replied, "No; I'll see the cowardly rascal d__d first." After a little time, he was conveyed into the Monmouth Cap public-house, and put to bed. Charles left the ring, hoisted triumphantly upon men's shoulders, amidst the huzzas of his Welsh friends. He was not marked, nor was he in the least distressed. We must, however, say that he gained few laurels by his victory. He had nothing to fight against. Had he been capable of hitting with any effect, the battle must have been decided in half the brief time it occupied. Trainer's fears had paralysed his exertions, and he was completely at the mercy of his antagonist.

After the conclusion of this fight, a great number of spectators left the ground and turned their nags' heads towards home, cursing the folly that prompted them to undertake such a foolish journey. Afterwards a purse was collected, and Bolter, the countryman, was easily persuaded to try his luck against Cooke. We are unable to give a detailed description of this battle, having departed from the scene of action before it was broached. The following, however, is as correct a description as from every inquiry we are enabled to give:- Bolter is considerably longer and heavier than Cooke, and proportionally strong. He is besides an excellent country fighter, and of most determined bottom. On the commencement of the set-to it was, however, easily observed that the only chance he had was, that his superior strength might ultimately overcome his antagonist. For the first 20 or 30 rounds, Cooke hit him just where he pleased, and adroitly got away without receiving any punishment. By the time poor Bolter's ogles were completely bunged up; bit a severe blow upon one of them cut open the swelling, and enabled him to see what he was about. Still it was evident that the more he procrastinated the battle, the less chance he had of winning; but nothing could induce him to cry "hold, enough." The spectators, the principal part of whom were fellow-countrymen to the poor fellow, now rushed to the ring, and by enclosing the combatants in a very limited pace, endeavoured to give Bolter an opportunity of grappling with his adversary. This he was fortunate in doing for several rounds; and Cooke, seeing how matters were going on, took the precaution of falling after he had succeeded in planting two or three good blows. It was at one time supposed that the fight, through this unfair interference of the mob, would have ended in the defeat of Cooke; but the latter, in the last few rounds, adopted the expedient of holding by the ropes with one hand, while with the other and the use of his legs, he succeeded in inflicting some severe falls upon his adversary. After fighting for upwards of an hour, Bolter's friends would not allow the battle to proceed, although he was himself willing to go on. The belligerents were accordingly separated. A glorious scene of confusion now ensued.

The mob claimed part of the purse for Bolter. This was refused; and it was feared the countrymen, by their numbers, would have overpowered the "Fancy" and half-murdered them. Harry Jones, the Sailor Boy, who officiated as second to Cooke, was actually thrown over the hedge of the field into a ditch, but he fortunately escaped without serious injury, only the loss of sundry portions of his toggery. An arrangement was effected by Cooke's friends refunding 30s – half of the blunt. A collection was also made for the beaten man, who presented a frightful spectacle – his head being as big as a bushel; his neck, face and body terribly bruised, covered with blood, and presenting all the varied colours of the rainbow. Cooke escaped with a slight scratch on the cheek.'

* * * *

Despite the statement that visible signs of Stephen Trainer's injuries were 'very slight', it was afterwards found that the Irishman had broken three ribs in the course of the battle. In contrast to the rather disparaging remarks made by the *Monmouthshire Merlin* about Trainer's performance, *Bell's Life* would state that Trainer was 'a courageous fellow, but wants experience and skill'.[343]

343 As recorded in *Bell's Life in London and Sporting Chronicle,* 10 June 1832.

Trainer's principal second, the legendary James Burke, or 'Deaf' Burke, had watched the fight with a great deal of interest and challenged William Charles to fight the day after the contest, with both men staking £1 a-side to make a match for £100 at the White Horse public house in Abergavenny, although the agreement to fight fell apart soon afterwards. *Pugilistica* states that this was principally due to the concern of William Charles's main backer that their champion might well be beaten by the 'Deaf 'un', and records the following details in its pages recounting the career of James Burke:

> Another of Burke's challengers at this time, a Welshman of the name of Bill Charles, "loomed large" in the Principality and the West of England. He had twice beaten Jem Bailey, of Bristol, and polished off several rural commoners, and recently (June 4th, 1832) conquered a local favourite, Tom Trainer (much under his own weight).
>
> From this triumph, the *soi disant* champion's bounce became so intolerable that Trainer's friends clubbed their resources, and resolved to back the Deaf 'un, as a fit and proper man, a very *Orlando* to floor this braggart *Charles*; but unfortunately this portion of *As You Like It* was not rehearsed in Taffy-land, the "Lunnon Cove" not being to the liking of Charles's friends. Burke went down to Newport (Monmouthshire) to make the match; but the Welshman's backers (like Aminadab's servant when he opened the door, on the chain, to the bailiff) seems to have taken alarm at the formidable appearance of the Deaf 'un, and Mr. Charles replied, on behalf on his patron, "Master hath seen thee and he doth not like thee;" preferring to forfeit a small deposit. Burke offered to fight "the Welsh Champion" half-way between Abergavenny and Newport, or near Bristol, or at Monmouth Gap, for £50 or £100 a side, but the affair went off, and Burke returned to London-matchless.

Bell's Life was exceedingly disgusted at the refusal of the backers of William Charles to meet Burke, informing its readers that the match had been cancelled at the start of July 1832:

> 'DEAF BURKE AND CHARLES – This match is off, the friends of Charles wishing to have it all their own way. Not only must they have all the deposits at their own house, but also have the naming of the place. Burke offered to fight half way between Abergavenny and Newport, but nothing would suit but to have the match decided within five miles of their own dunghill. Burke retired in disgust, and has arrived in town ready to fight any man weighing twelve stone and a half. He is prepared to make a match to fight near Bristol or Monmouth Gap with Charles, for 50*l.* or 100*l.*[344]'

After reading the critical account of his fight against William Charles that had been printed in the *Monmouthshire Merlin*, Stephen Trainer suffered a great deal of abuse from his supporters and countrymen. Trainer felt sufficiently hurt by the cruel tone of the newspaper's account to write a letter to the editor, which was published the following week on 16 June 183:[345]

> **THE MONMOUTHSHIRE MERLIN**
>
> *To the Editor of the Monmouthshire Merlin,*
>
> SIR, – As the first duty of a public Journalist should be impartiality, and to insert incidents as they occur, I beg to call your attention to a few particulars in the account given in your paper of Saturday last of the fight between William Charles and myself. You say, on entering the ring my appearance was pale and nervous: this I readily admit; but that it was the effect of fear or want of courage I flatly deny. It was from quite a different feeling; for, being the first time that I had ever entered a prize ring on such an occasion, and being surrounded by so many respectable inhabitants of this county with whom I had the honour

344 *Bell's Life in London and Sporting Chronicle*, 1 June 1832.

345 The comments in the account published in the *Monmouthshire Merlin*, 9 June 1932, to which Stephen Trainer most strongly objected to, namely that he hid 'his head under his arm to avoid the blows' and 'seized hold of Charles's arm with his mouth' in the third round, are not recorded in the account of the fight between William Charles and Stephen Trainer published in *Bell's Life in London and Sporting Chronicle*, 10 June 1832.

of being acquainted, I felt ashamed of my situation – a situation into which I was involuntarily drawn by the emissaries of both parties. This can be verified by my conduct in this county, which I have travelled the last seven years. You say, in the first round, when Charles fell on his knee, from want of tact or from fear, I did not avail myself of the advantage, which would have been decidedly fair. I assure you it was from neither of those feelings: it was from a feeling of generous forbearance, of which pugilists should not be devoid when they enter the ring. You say, in one round, to avoid punishment, I sheltered my head under my arm, and that I literally caught hold of Charles's arm in my mouth. This is most erroneous and unjust; for the truth of which I appeal to Charles, his seconds, and to the thousands of spectators, whether any such thing occurred, or any other unfair act on my part. The truth to a vanquished man is wounding enough to his feelings without the addition of a libel; of this I have received sufficient from my own countrymen, who, I must own, are never very sparing in the invectives when their hopes are frustrated.

Now, sir, from the injury I received on my side by falling on the ropes, in the fourth round, it was impossible for me to prolong the fight for any great time, and for which I have the authority of a medical gentleman to state; for every exertion on my part was but hastening my defeat. That there should be a partiality to Charles in his native county, I freely admit; but to misrepresent and slander a stranger is an act unworthy the liberal press of this country. Perhaps you may decline inserting this, by considering the subject not worth notice; but, remember you have already devoted your columns to the subject, and I appeal to you, as a man of feeling, if you stood in the same situation as myself, would not you plead for the same indulgence?

I write this letter without aid or dictation, therefore it is my own sentiments, neither studied nor composed. I hope you will, therefore, insert it all, without altering or curtailing it; and I hope you will pardon me for troubling you with so long an epistle, but it is of vital importance to me in a country where my character is my fortune, and where it has never before been sullied. I hope, as a lover of justice, you will give it a place in your valuable paper; and you will oblige,

Yours most respectfully,
Abergavenny, 13 June 1832. S. TRAINER.

* * * *

THE MERLIN

MONMOUTH

BOXING.—A pugilistic encounter will take place on Friday se'nnight, between Wm. Gardiner, alias "The Old Horse," and Wm. Charles, the Welsh Champion. The match is for 25 guineas a-side, and the scene of action is expected to be fixed about midway between Abergavenny and Ross.

An announcement of the fight between William Charles and Bill Gardiner published in the Monmouthshire Merlin, *16 March 1833.*

After the proposed fight against Deaf Burke had fallen apart, a new challenger quickly made himself known. Bill Gardner (Gardiner), who came from Ross in Herefordshire, and was known by the cognomen of 'the Old Horse', announced himself as willing to fight William Charles for £25 a-side through the pages of *Bell's Life*.[346]

The fight would not be finalised for a long period of time and it wasn't until the following year, in March of 1833, that Charles and Gardiner would finally do battle in the ring. On Friday, 29 March, as early as six o'clock in the morning, large numbers of pedestrians took to the Chepstow Road and were followed by every kind of vehicle from donkey carts to carriages, and scores of horse riders all heading for a field on the left-hand side of the road, about half a mile from 'Ragland' (Raglan). It would be estimated that about

346 As recorded in *Bell's Life in London and Sporting Chronicle*, 15 July 1832.

3,000 people descended upon the field, eager to witness William Charles meet Bill Gardiner in battle, many of them said to be well-respected people from Ross, Monmouth, Abergavenny and Newport.

Bill Gardiner made his way to the battleground in a coach from the Swan Hotel in Ross, and was lucky to get there in one piece. James Watkins, the head ostler, wasn't so fortunate, having become entangled between the rear wheel of the coach and a step on the journey to Raglan. Despite having had medical assistance, he afterwards slipped into a state of delirium, and it was thought that his injuries might well prove fatal.[347]

Despite this tragedy, at one o' clock, the 'Old Horse', entered the ring and tossed his hat in the air, and was loudly cheered by the Herefordshire men. Shortly afterwards, William Charles joined him and was repeatedly hailed by his Welsh supporters. James Woodward of Tewkesbury seconded Bill Gardiner, aided by J. Reading of Ross, who served as Gardiner's bottle holder, while William Charles was assisted by Long of Abergavenny and another. Both men appeared in admirable condition, although after stripping for battle, Gardiner had the advantage of both size and weight. After shaking hands, both men came up to the scratch, and were eager to settle down to business.

After some cautious sparring, it was Gardiner who launched the first significant assault, to the Welshman's head, but was sent back by the well-directed blows of Charles to his ribs. Gardiner continued to target his opponent's face but he was sent down after some tremendous returns. In the fourth, Charles was floored by the first knockdown blow, amidst cheers from the Herefordshire spectators. Not to be outdone, Charles launched into his man, throwing punches at the head and under the ribs of Gardiner, and soon sent him to earth. As the rounds continued, the Welch Champion was caught with greater frequency, but landed a number of punishing blows of his own. By the tenth, the betting favoured Charles, with 3/1 being repeatedly offered. Things changed abruptly in the following rounds, when Gardiner succeeded in landing powerful blows about the Welshman's head and face, spilling copious amounts of blood. Gardiner, showing

---

347 As recorded in the *Monmouthshire Merlin,* 6 April 1833.

his cleverness, repeatedly pummelled Charles about the face, and escaped any return blows by falling to the turf. The Old Horse continued these tactics as the fight progressed, and in doing so was seen to land a number of solid punches, and from the 26th round pressed his advantage. Hard and severe hitting on the part of Gardiner continued until the 32nd round, although in almost every round he slipped to the grass to avoid the punches of Charles. It was evident that William Charles was fast on the road to failure, and after the 38th round, the Welch Champion extended his hand to the Old Horse and acknowledged his defeat. Elated by the victory, Bill Gardiner leaped over the ropes to loud cheering from the Herefordshire men.

The fight proved to be a 'severely contested trial of strength between two decidedly good men',[348] although William Charles complained of Gardiner's continual falling to avoid punishment, which had hampered his ability to do his best. Charles believed that he would have beaten Gardiner in a fair 'stand-up fight'. While Gardiner had perhaps been guilty of 'seeking the grass', he was not deemed to have broken the laws of the ring, so Charles was unable to challenge the defeat. The Welsh supporters of William Charles lost a considerable amount of money, while the 'Men of Ross went home with money in both pockets'. Although the supporters of Charles had lost money on their man, the Welsh took the defeat in good spirits, as their champion was thought to have 'stood up to his antagonist to the last, and exhibited repeated proofs of a most gluttonous appetite'. Charles had proven himself to be a courageous stand-up fighter, and 'though vanquished, he was thorough game'.

It would prove to be the last recorded fight of the 'Welch Champion', William Charles. His fondness for drink, which had been so much in evidence prior to his fight with Stephen Trainer, had hastened his decline. His supporters would read of his sudden death less than four years later, on 1 January 1837, at his hometown of Newport, with it being reported in *The Cambrian* newspaper a fortnight later that 'William Charles, commonly called the

348 As recorded in the *Monmouthshire Merlin*, 30 March 1833. This account was afterwards reproduced with minor editing in *The Cambrian*, 6 April 1833, as well as having been reprinted in edited form in *Bell's Life in London and Sporting Chronicle,* 7 April 1833.

> **The Cambrian.**
>
> **DIED.**
>
> **On the 1st inst., at Newport, William Charles, commonly called the "Welsh Champion," from his fistic prowess and victories. The deceased, who was a man of fine proportions and Herculean strength, fell a victim, in the prime of life, to those habits of intemperance in which pugilists too frequently indulge.**

The obituary of William Charles of Newport, known as the 'Welsh Champion', published in The Cambrian, *14 January 1837.*

"Welsh Champion," from his fistic prowess and victories' had died. The famous pugilist had been a 'man of fine proportions and Herculean strength', but had fallen 'victim, in the prime of life, to those habits of intemperance in which pugilists too frequently indulge'.[349]

349 As recorded in *The Cambrian*, 14 January 1837. The death of William Charles was also recorded in the *Bristol Mercury*, 14 January 1837.

Afterword

This book has sought to explore the story of Welsh boxing from its earliest recorded days. One of the first recorded Welsh pugilists, Edward Morgan, the 'Welch Boy', made a name for himself following his victory over the famous Thomas Smallwood, while the 'Terrible Welchman', James Francis, earned sufficient fame to challenge the celebrated Prince Boswell. There are likely to have been other 'Welch' prize fighters of lesser renown, both before and after their time. As pugilistic contests from this early period were mostly recorded in the newspapers of London, there appears to be little further printed information that can tell us about the development of boxing within Wales itself.

That there were Welsh fighters of notable reputation by the mid-1780s is made apparent by the fact that 'Bloody', the butcher of Montgomery, had earned enough fame within Wales as to be recorded in the London press as having fought 'another noted bruiser' in 1784.

It seems highly likely that Bloody would have met other skilled opposition following this contest by virtue of having been matched to fight William Warr (Ward) in 1790. Welsh prize fighting had already developed to the point where it attracted a sizeable public following by this time. It would appear plausible that locally recognised Welsh 'champions' were almost certainly contesting against established rivals on a regular basis, as Ellis Pannwr was widely viewed as having been the 'Champion of Wales' for several years by 1791, when he fought and beat Roderick Lewis. With organised gambling on the outcome of the contest against Lewis taking place, and entrance money having been charged, it is clear that Welsh prize fighting was already fairly well established as a commercial activity.

It can also be seen that Ellis Pannwr's battle against Roderick Lewis at Dolgelly was merely the latest important contest in a Welsh pugilistic tradition that extended back before living memory, with *The Star* newspaper having commented that this contest was 'the hardest-fought battle ever remembered in that part of Wales'. Of these early native Welsh fighters who were fighting for local acclaim or even national recognition in their homeland, it seems fairly likely that little further detailed information will be uncovered. We will probably never know the name of the earlier 'esteemed Champion of Wales' from Denbighshire, who is said to have travelled to Caernarfon to challenge the Herculean strength of the youthful Foulke Jones when he was in his physical prime. The stories that might have been told in 1811 by an elderly John Williams, once known by the cognomen of 'Jack of the Wern', of the days of his youth when he had defeated the 'renowned Glan Brace' and several other 'Cambrian heroes' of the early Welsh prize ring are now forever lost to us.

By the time that Welsh pugilists had started making a name for themselves in the London Prize Ring, starting with Tom 'Paddington' Jones in the 1790s, Ned Davis, the 'Wrexham Champion', had already achieved such local pugilistic fame that despite having never contested in the official prize ring, his merits as a fighter would mean he was later deemed worthy of inclusion in Pierce Egan's *Boxiana*. Ned Turner, the 'Out-and-Outer', was the first Welsh prize fighter to have achieved widespread national recognition, due to the skill and science that he had demonstrated within the prize ring.

Turner's victories over the previously unconquerable Jack Scroggins propelled him to a lofty position amongst the lightweights, and his courageous stand against Jack Randall was afterwards celebrated in verse and song. Ned Turner was aligned more closely with Wales than any other pugilist of the period, and crowned as the 'Pugilistic Prince of Wales' by the London newspapers. Lesser pugilistic lights of Welsh origin, such as Jack Rasher, known as 'Ironface', and the notorious fighting 'Welsh Savages', Ned and Bill Savage, had also contended within the ropes and stakes of the London Prize Ring and through having frequently sparred on the stage of the Fives and Tennis Courts, were familiar faces to the Fancy throughout London.

In the years that followed, the taste for pugilism continued to spread in Wales throughout the 1820s. Welsh prize fighters, likely to have been inspired by the example set by Ned Turner, raised their fists in increasing numbers and continued to fight for the recognition of their fellow countrymen of their skill and 'science' in combat. William Charles of Newport would appear to be the first amongst them to have gained the widespread support of the local population and been viewed as having been the 'Champion of Wales' by popular consent since the days of Ellis Pannwr. Sporting newspapers such as *Bell's Life* were now being studied by a larger section of the general public in Wales, who found little representation of their interest in prize fighting reflected in the limited reporting found within the pages of the Welsh press. Welsh prize fighters also now began to write to the editor of *Bell's Life* in London to alert local rivals of their readiness to meet them in battle, or to throw out challenges to established pugilists on the other side of the border. Further afield, 'Game Welchmen' of varying ability contended in prize fights throughout England, some of them having decided to highlight their native origins and success in minor contests by awarding themselves the title of 'Welch Champion' to differentiate themselves from their English rivals.

Some years later, a rugged little scrapper of the 'good old stone wall type' from the town of Newbridge, now known as Pontypridd, whitened his fists and started engaging other Welsh knuckle fighters on the hills of South Wales.

Young 'Dan Bach' probably had no idea where his decision to do so would one day lead.

Lawrence Davies

Appendix 1

THE FIGHT AT CRAWLEY
BETWEEN
THE NONPAREIL
AND
THE OUT-AND-OUTER

Written by BOB GREGSON
And sung at the Daffy Club, held at the Castle Tavern, Holborn,
by TOM OWEN, with the MOST *spirited* applause.

Come, won't you list unto my lay,
About the fight at Crawley, O!
Where RANDALL, full of spunk, so gay,
Made good use of his *morleys*, O!
What's it to me, but the best d'ye see,
TO TURNER it means no scandal, O!
But the favourite boy, they all agree,
And his name it is JACK RANDALL, O!
With his fillaloo, trillaloo, Whack, fall al de dal di de do!

When from head quarters came the news
That the day was fix'd for fighting, O!
The bets ran high among the coves,
Who *milling* takes delight in, O!
The roads display'd a motley group,
While on their *prads* to handle, O!
But the sporting lads of *St. Giles's* troop,
To be sure we're for JACK RANDALL, O!
With his fillaloo, trillaloo, Whack, fall al de dal di de do!

When RANDALL leap'd into the ring,
He threw up his hat so gaily, O!
And taking TURNER by the hand,
He shook it frank and freely, O!
Each man then stripp'd and took their view,
Which was the best for to handle, O!
When the lads sung out from *St. Giles's* troop,
What a *"broth of a boy"* is JACK RANDALL, O!
With his fillaloo, trillaloo, Whack, fall al de dal di de do!

The *weaving* system went to work,
RANDALL made TURNER stagger, O!
But, like a *good one*, he scorn'd to *lurk*,
Taking all off with a swagger, O!
Exchequer'd soon his NOB appear'd,
The *claret* from his *handle* flow'd,
While the sporting lads all loudly cheer'd
The battle's your own, JACK RANDALL, O!
With his fillaloo, trillaloo, Whack, fall al de dal di de do!

When four and thirty rounds they'd fought,
With HEARTS just like two lions, O!
When *Baxter*[350] own'd *enough* he'd got,
My word you may rely on, O!
It's true that each man did his part;
Then the sparkling glass let's handle, O!
And drink success to the fistic art
And long life to Paddy Randall, O!
With his fillaloo, trillaloo, Whack, fall al de dal di de do!

---

350 The footnote to this song in *Boxiana* states that 'Baxter' was the brother of Ned Turner, who, 'perceiving that the latter hero had no chance whatever, and that he was only stand up to be slaughtered, (Although he had a great stake upon TURNER,) with the true feelings of humanity, insisted upon his second, TOM OLIVER, taking him out of the ring. This request was immediately complied with; but TURNER wished to continue the battle. The monosyllable NO! Does not belong to TURNER'S vocabulary'. Other sources claim that Baxter was Turner's uncle, or his brother-in-law.

Appendix 2

LINES ON THE FIGHT BETWEEN RANDALL AND TURNER[351]

Reproduced from *Jack Randall's Diary of Proceedings at the House of Call for Genius*, by Thomas Moore

All hail to the *Cove*, see his doxies have crowned him,
With gin-dripping shamrocks just pluck'd from the plain,
See the *Captain* and *Caleb*[352] are chuckling around him,
As he offers to *scuttle a nob* o'er again.

Ah! Erin, be proud of the boy you have got,
And toast his sweet name in the *water of life;*[353]
Drink joy to his *double-ups*, strength to his shot,[354]
And a laurel each time he embarks in the strife.

---

351 Stated in *Boxiana* as taken from a 'Literary Journal'. This poem was reproduced from *Jack Randall's Diary of Proceedings at the House of Call for Genius*, by Thomas Moore, (London: W. Simpkin and R. Marshall, 1820).

352 Captain Barclay and Caleb Baldwin, trainers and betters on *Randall* – (the author must excuse us in observing that he is not quite FLASH in this respect, as neither *Captain Barclay* nor *Old Caleb* had anything to do with the *training of Randall*. If he had stated that the worthy GENERAL BARTON had had a *hand* in it, he would have been nearer the *mark*) – ED. (Source: *Boxiana*)

353 Gin.

354 A peculiar blow that Randall has the power of giving, and denominated among the Fancy, "*Randall's shot*". (Source: *Boxiana*)

Oh, the leek that beam'd gaily on *Turner's* clear brow,
Glitters still in the wind both purely and bright;
Though the fast springing buds are close clipp'd round it now,
Yet the leek is but robbed of the glare of its light.

Say, thou *Shakespeare of Fancy men*, who could resist
The *Fibber*, the *Touter*, the *light Bit of Stuff*,
The man who knew *head-work,* and whose mutton fist
Could have tipp'd e'en a young rampant bullock enough.

Let feather-bed whelps, without any discerning,
In fashion's gay rounds pass the best of their days;
Let students and poets, in bowers of learning,
Drawl out their existence, and sing their soft lays:

Be ours the wild pleasure, be ours the bright hopes,
Which e'en when devoid of our *day-lights* we see,
The chance but of *flinging* our man on the ropes,
Or of *boring a customer* down on the knee.

We're just like the flowers that bloom in that clime,
Where all sorts of sun-shining sweetmeats are eaten,
Blushing on, blooming on, through the whole summer time,
And whose value's not known till *most soundly they're beaten.*

'Tis then that their soft rosy fragrance glows,
And expands with delight as their strength dies away,
And we, when the *claret* bright, torrent-like flows,
Prove our worth by our *nobs* being board-like and gay.[355]

355 This poem is reproduced from *Boxiana* by Pierce Egan, with the original footnotes. Thomas Moore was a spectator at the fight between Turner and Randall, along with the poet John Keats.

Appendix 3

Elegiac Stanzas on the Death of Ned Turner
(By Frosty-Faced Fogo, P.L. of the Ring)

Alas, poor Ned! –
He's floor'd-he's dead;
His fighting days are ended.
The *Champion* DEATH
Has stopp'd his breath;
His *bellows* can't be *mended*.

Death is a foe,
Who deals a blow,
That cannot well be guarded:
At him to aim
Our fists would lame:
He has a mortal *hard head*.

A blow ne'er miss'd
From his dry fist;
He measures well his distance:
One blow, for all
Makes strong men sprawl,
And *seconds* no assistance.

If *to he sets*,
And since but gets
His foeman to advance awry;
He either *fibs*

Him in the ribs,
Or gets his head in *Chancery*.[356]

In this we see
Grim DEATH agree,
With ELDON; who gets few in
His dreadful Court;
But he, in *sport*,
Is their most *certain ruin*.

Joe Hume, averse,
Call'd him a *curse*,
And Peel objected to it:
We all curse Death,
Yet no Peel saith
We've not a right to do it.

Death cannot die,
And therefore I
Maintain the likeness stronger;
For ancient *Bags*,
The more he tags,
He only *lasts the longer.*

But this 'tis true,
Has nought to do
With him we've been to bury;
But I'm so sad,
I'm really glad
To say one word that's merry.

Poor Ned is gone;
And now has done
His *fist-work* and his *mouth-work.*
The boast of Wales,

356 To get an opponent in 'Chancery' was to use a pugilistic strategy whereby the opponent's head was held in a headlock under one arm, allowing the prize fighter to restrain his opponent while continuing to punch him with the other.

"*Odds splutter a' nails*,"
And glory of all Southwark.

The *tanner's* trade
He always made
His business, and took pride in
A desperate fight,
Because he might,
By *trade* give folks a *hiding*.

And, reader, mark,
Though with oak *bark*
He work'd to tan his leather,
His heart, now broke,
Was *heart of oak*,
Yet light as any feather.

Too light, alas!
Since *flesh is grass*,
Because he was light-hearted;
The best *blue ruin*[357]
Was his undoing,
And so he soon *departed*.

'Twas *Deady's best*
Laid him to rest;
He *died*, alas! thro *Deady*
With *full proof gin*
He fill'd his skin,
And soon for Death was ready.

At thirty-four
(He was no more),
This noble-minded Tanner
Into a *pit*
Was put, to fit
His corpse in proper manner.

---

357 Blue ruin – a slang phrase for gin.

Now weep all you, Who ought to do,
Well-scienc'd man, or *learner*;
And freely join
Your tears with mine
To mourn for poor Ned Turner!

If honest worth
Less priz'd on earth,
In heavenly choir should seat him;
To join him there,
Let all prepare
For *I should like to meet him.*

(Published in *Bell's Life in London and Sporting Chronicle*,
30 April 1826)

Appendix 4

Young Bloody
'A Prize Fight Poem'

Come all you gallant boxers
In boxing take delight,
Draw near and I will tell you
Of a famous noble fight.
It was as hard a battle, boys,
As ever yet was seen.
And now, for it was fought, my boys,
On Ludlow Castle Green.

Chorus

Success unto Young Bloody,
Let every hearty sing,
He is the conquering hero,
And the champion of the ring.

The match was made between two gentlemen
Of courage stout and bold,
The money stake was entered down
Five hundred pounds in gold.

Each man to find a champion
As good as e'er was seen,
The conqueror for the money, boys,
On Ludlow Castle Green.

The one was a prize fighter
Brought up unto the stage;
The other was a Montgomery lad,
Not twenty years of age.
The betts they went so handy,
The money went so free,
It was ten to five and five to one,
Bri[s]tol Jack will win the day.

Then spoke a clothier from Newtown,
His money he had laid,
This young man as to bribery
Indeed I am afraid.
O then, replied a gentleman,
Squire Harrison by name,
Saying I'll be bound for all your gold
If bribery there is ta'en.

Then up spoke young Bloody,
Saying it never shall be told
That I would sell my country
For silver or for gold.
So make sure of your betts, me men,
To flinch I'll ne'er be seen,
Before your money shall be lost,
I'll die upon the green.

Then up steps a butcher lad,
Hearing what young Bloody said.
He pulled out twenty guineas,
And on this Welch boy laid.
The champion pulled out twenty more,
And this to him replied,
Before I leave this country
I'll tan thy greecy hide.

The ring was clear at one o'clock,
The men went on the ground,
And in the midst of thousands stood
As you may dare go bound.
So now the battle as begun,
As you may well suppose,
The very first blow young Bloody struck
He fairly split his nose.

The third round young Bloody rose
Just like a lion stout,
And with his bunch of fives
He made his man to reel about.
The seventh round young Bloody gave
A hard blow on the ear,
Which 'most took it from his head,
So plainly doth appear.

He panned him on the knowledge box
Which made the claric [*claret*] fly.
The streams of blood came down his cheeks,
Poor Jack began to cry
My head it is so mangled,
My body is so sore,
I must give in, kind gentlemen,
I cannot fight no more.

So now the battle it is o'er,
And Bloody as won the day.
And now let him fight when he will
I hope he alway may.
The element did roar like thunder
With the echo of their noise
Hosaw! Hosaw! was all their cry,
Hosaw! Montgomery boys!

(*Historical & Archaeological Collections Relating to Montgomeryshire and its Borders*, Vol. XLV., Issued by the Powys-Land Club, (Welshpool: David Rowlands Ltd., 1938.)[358]

358 This undated and unattributed song, 'Young Bloody', was copied from a manuscript owned by John Davies, Parish Clerk of Montgomery since 1891. The 'Squire Harrison' mentioned in the poem is likely to be Major Robert J. Harrison (born approx. 1780), who was the father of the Reverend R.J. Harrison, Vicar of Forden, and the grandfather of Major R.J. Harrison, the first Mayor of Montgomery. John Davies believed that the Squire wagered his carriage and horses on the contest.

Appendix 5

Pugilistic Terminology

Phrases frequently used in connection with the early Prize Ring[359]

It should be noted that many pugilistic terms have been retained and are still used in the modern English language. To come up to the scratch, to throw in the towel, to throw one's hat in the ring, or to be deemed a 'glutton for punishment', are all terms that derive from the days of the prize ring.

AMATEUR – Applied to frequenters and backers of pugilistic contests; most of whom spar a bit, if they be not proficients.

BANKRUPTCY LIST – To be put on the, signifies, in pugilism – to be completely finished. Randall, in his poetic *Farewell to the Prize Ring*, says:

> Oh sad is the heart that can say 'the deuce take her,'
> To fame, when she's backing a blade of the fist;
> But Turner I've *clean'd out*; and Martin the *Baker*,
> I'd very near put on the *Bankruptcy list*.
>
> *Jack Randall's Diary of Proceedings at the House of Call for Genius*.[360]

BATTLE ROYAL – A battle or bout at cudgels or fisticuffs, wherein more than two persons are engaged: perhaps from its resemblance, in that particular, to more serious engagements fought to settle royal disputes.

BEAK – A justice of peace or magistrate. Also a judge or chairman who presides in court.

BELCHER – A yellow silk handkerchief, intermixed with white and a little black. *The kiddy flashes his Belcher*: the young fellow wears a silk handkerchief round his neck. First introduced by the celebrated Jem Belcher, according to Pierce Egan (Jon Bee disputes this point – see *Yellow-man*).

BELLIGERENT – A fighting party, or crowd at a boxing match.

BELLOWS – The lungs.

---

359 The majority of these entries are taken from Francis Grose's *Classical Dictionary of the Vulgar Tongue*, Revised by Pierce Egan, (London: Sherwood, Neely and Jones, 1823), and *Sportsman's Slang: A New Dictionary of Terms Used in the Affairs of the Turf, the Ring, the Chase and the Cock-pit*, etc., by Jon Bee, (London: W. Lewis, 1825) with some additions by the author.

360 *Jack Randall's Diary of Proceedings at the House of Call for Genius*, by Thomas Moore, (London: W. Simpkin and R. Marshall, 1820).

BELL SWAGGER – A noisy bullying fellow.

BELLYFUL – A hearty beating, sufficient to make a man yield or give out.

BENEFIT – An event held to honour a recently defeated or retired pugilist, who would *benefit* from the ticket sales to spectators to watch a number of exhibition, or sparring bouts between well-known fighters.

BLUE RUIN – Gin; and so is *blue tape.*

BLUNT – Post the – To lay money down,

> 'When old Jack Wiggins counts for my score
> I'll bid him *post the blunt* for me no more.'
> *Jack Randall's Diary of Proceedings at the House of Call for Genius.*

BLUSTER – To talk big, to hector or bully.

BONE BOX – The mouth.

BORING – See below, also see *Fibbing.*

BORING IN – (Ring) When one man hammers away at another, pressing forward – *a-la*-Scroggins.

BOTTOM – Among bruisers it is used to express a hardy fellow, who will bear a good beating – courage and fortitude. He was of sound *game* and *bottom.*

BOUGHTONIAN – A boxer, a disciple of Broughton, who was ... *once* the best boxer of his day.

BOUNCE – To bully, threaten, talk loud, or affect great consequence; to bounce a person out of anything is to use threatening or high words, in order to intimidate him, and attain the object you are intent upon.

BOXIANA – The name of a work, which contains the lives and battles of all the prize pugilists. A complete history of boxing, from the days of Figg and Broughton to Cribb and the Nonpareil.

BREAD-BASKET – The stomach, a term used by boxers. I took him a punch in his *bread-basket*; i.e. I gave him a blow in the stomach.

A BREATHING – Running at half-speed. (Turf and Ring) Used in training a horse or a man.

BRUISER – A boxer; one skilled in the art of boxing; also an inferior workman among chasers.

BUFFER – One that steals and kills horses and dogs for their skins; also an innkeeper: it signifies also a boxer.

> 'And the first words the *Buffer* said,
> Were, – By the living Jingo, Ned,' &c.
> *Jack Randall's Diary of Proceedings at the House of Call for Genius.*

> 'And whips waved high, and fists flew out,
> For Belcher leapt the ring without,
> And peeled the *Buffers* dextrously.'
> *Jack Randall's Diary of Proceedings at the House of Call for Genius.*

BUNCH OF FIVES – The fist.

BYE-BATTLE – A contest of minor importance.

CANISTER – The head. To mill his canister; to break his head.

CASTOR – A hat – castor is the old name for the beaver, from whose felt most hats are covered.

CATOLLER – A noisy, prating fool; one who annoys the company with proposals for betting, and ultimately never makes a bet. 'Few evenings pass over at the Castle-Tavern, Holborn, without meeting with a *Catoller*: in fact, the pass word is, at this celebrated sporting house, that TOM BELCHER would be in danger of losing his *licence*, if he did not often have a fool or *Catoller* exhibit himself for the amusement of his visitors.'

CHAFF-CUTTER – A knowing person, one whose tongue is of great use to him, in order to silence an antagonist, whether right or wrong.

CHAFFING – To blow up, to talk aloud.

CHANCERY – Getting your head *in chauncery*, among pugilists, is when your *nob* is completely at the mercy of your opponent; or, in other words, you cannot protect it. Receiving blow after blow. Randall, termed the Nonpareil of the prize ring, was distinguished for this peculiar trait among the boxers.

CHATTERERS – The teeth.

CHOPPER – A *chopper* is a blow struck on the face with the back of the hand. Mendoza claims the honour of its invention, but unjustly; he certainly revived, and considerably improved it. It was practised long before our time – Broughton occasionally used it; and Slack, it also appears, struck the *chopper* in giving the return in many of his battles.

CLARET – Blood; he spilled his opponent's *claret*. Also *'clarified'* – he *clarified* his opponent's head.

COCK HOIST – A cross buttock.

COGNOMEN – A surname, travelling name, or fighting name. The 'Out-and Outer' (Ned Turner), 'The Nonpareil' (Jack Randall), 'The Phenomenon' (Peace Inglis), etc.

COMMANDER-IN-CHIEF – (Ring) 'Gentleman' John Jackson, to whom is often confided the arrangements towards pugilistic fighting.

COMMISSARY-GENERAL – Bill Gibbons, in whom 'centres the news as to where fights are to take place, he having the care of the P.C. ropes, stakes and whips for making a ring. His pay, three quid.'

COMMONER – In the ring, 'Commoners' are ordinary boxers; *bye commoners* are those who mistakenly presume they know how to fight and try it on, when they can get a customer.

CONK – The nose.

CORINTHIANS – The highest order of swells.

> 'If this Corinthian were the sun,
> And we could not well do without him,
> Why then, &c.'
>
> *Jack Randall's Diary of Proceedings at the House of Call for Genius.*
>
> 'Twas diverting to see, as one ogled around,
> How Corinthians and commoners mix'd on the ground.'
>
> *Tom Cribb's Memorial to Congress.*[361]

361 *Tom Cribb's Memorial to Congress*, by 'One of the Fancy', Thomas Moore, (London: Longman, Hurst, Rees, Orme & Brown, 1819).

CORK – A man's *cork* is said to be drawn, when he had received a bloody nose. 'Draw his *cork*'.

COSTARD – The head. I'll smite your *costard*, I'll give you a knock on the head.

COUNTER-HIT – (Ring) – when both hit from the same side, as a left-hander for a right. See *Return blow*.

COVE – Fellow.

CRAG – The neck.

CRASHING CHEATS – Teeth.

CROSS (X) – A fixed or 'thrown' contest, that which is not fair.

CROSS BUTTOCK – A particular lock or fall in the Broughtonian art, which conveyed more pleasant sensations to the spectators than the patient.

DAFFY – Gin.

DAFFY CLUB – This original society was founded by Mr. James Soares, at the Castle Tavern, Holborn, and who is the perpetual president of it. 'The sporting world is its *hobby*; and, respecting original anecdotes of the turf; the incidents of the prize-ring, and promoting scientific pugilism; the merits of the swift pedestrians of the day; a knowledge of the first-rate TROTTERS; an acquaintance with the best *shots*; good cockers; great cricketers; distinguished anglers; and thoroughbred cattle, dogs, &c. most of the members of the club can prize themselves not deficient riders, whenever necessity requires them to mount. It is also conspicuous for its *accommodation* to *story* tellers. The spirituous liquor drank by the club is DAFFY, (i.e. *gin*,) but in small quantities: as, the *third* of a quarter is the allowance for each member, at one time. It has obtained much notoriety from its good *chaunting*, every Friday night during the season.'

DART – A straight-armed blow in boxing.

DAY-LIGHTS – Eyes. To darken his day-lights, or sow up his sees; to close up a man's eyes in boxing.

DEW BEATERS – Feet.

DISTRESSED – In boxing, when a man is *distressed*, he is out.

DOSE – A man is supposed to have 'Got his *dose*' when he has been well thrashed. Thence probably comes 'a *douse* in the chops' and '*douse*, or *dust* his jacket well.'

DRAWING THE CORK – To give a man a bloody nose: i.e. I have drawn his *cork*.

FACER – A straight, violent blow to the face.

FALL – In ring affairs, a fall is a throw upon the ground which one boxer gives another at in-fighting.

FANCY – One of the Fancy means a sporting character, that is either attached to pigeons, dog-fighting, boxing, &c.

FEINT – A blow aimed at the head (say) but not sent home, while the other hand alights on *the mark*.

FIBBING – In bruising, signifies the getting of an adversary's head under the arm and punching it. 'RANDALL is more celebrated for the dexterity with which he administers a *fibbing* than any in the prize-ring, either hand equally effective, as in the case of West Country Dick, whom, after having *fibbed*, till he was tired, with the right hand, he flung on the right arm, holding him all the time *with his feet off the ground*, and rendered him, in a few seconds, a perfect spectacle.' See also *Chancery*.

FIBBING CLOAK – A boxer professed, who misapplies his talents.

FISTIANA – A record book, containing details of the fights undertaken by the leading pugilists of the prize ring. Originally compiled by Vincent Dowling, the editor of *Bell's Life*, and afterwards continued by his son, Francis. The full title of the work is *Fistiana: or The Oracle of the Ring*.

FISZOG – or Physiog; the face.

FIVES COURT – A place distinguished (in addition to the game of *fives*) for sparring matches between the pugilists. 'The combatants belonging to the prize-ring exhibit the art of self-defence at the Fives-Court with the gloves; and it is frequently at this Court where public challenges are given and accepted by the boxers. The most refined and fastidious person may attend these exhibitions of sparring with pleasure; as they are conducted with all the neatness, elegance and science, of FENCING. Admission, 3s. each person. It is situated in St Martin's Street, Leicester-fields. A few boxers in like manner exhibit at the Tennis-Court, Windmill-street.'

FLOORED – Knocked down.

FLOORER – A finishing blow that hits hard enough to send an opponent to the turf.

FOGLE – A handkerchief used as 'colours' by a pugilist.

GAME – Among pugilists, courage of the highest order. 'He is a *game* man; he will not give up the contest, until nature forsakes him. He will not say, NO!'

GAMMON – A deceit or a lie. 'The pugilist dismissed his opponent's recollections as gammon.'

GINGLING-CART – (Ring) The commissary-general's tumbrel, in which he carries down the P.C. traps – arbitrary.

GIVER – A good boxer.

GLOVES – Used by pugilists to communicate the art of self-defence to their pupils.

GLUTTON – A term used by bruisers to signify a man who will bear a great deal of beating.

GRASSED NEATLY – (Ring) A prettier expression than floored, used when the act is performed on turf.

GUARD – A posture of defence. A man is 'on guard' when he is prepared for the blows of his assailant. He 'hit over his *guard*' – meaning that the opponents defensive posture was ineffectual.

HAMMER – (Ring) When a man hits very hard, chiefly with a favourite hand, his blows are said to 'fall like those of a *sledge-hammer*.' Such boxers are '*hammering* fighters, that do not *defend* their own *vitals*, cannot make sure of a blow', and are termed *hammerers* and *hammermen*. They are not *Pugilists*, which see, also *Miller*.

HAMMERING BOXERS – Are great country loobies, who possess no one quality for the exercise but strength, the consciousness whereof gives them pluck. 'These hammer away for an hour or two, hearken not to the call of 'time,' and turn a deaf ear to 'enough,' always act most unfairly in other respects, and sometimes commit murder! – for which they deserve the halter.'

HEAD – 'Gave away his head,' (Ring) – said of a boxer, who to place a favourite body-blow exposes his head as the sacrifice; e.g. Dutch Sam and Scroggins; 'Nosworthy felt for the head of Sam as Turner did for Scroggins'.

HITTITES – An assembly of boxers and ring-goers.

IVORIES – The teeth. A pugilist who has broken his opponent's teeth is said to have 'cabbaged his ivories'.

IVORY CASE – The mouth.

KNIGHT OF THE CLEAVER – A term used to denote that a pugilist was employed as a butcher outside the prize ring.

KNIGHT OF THE LEEK – A term used to denote that a pugilist was of Welsh origin. Occasionally also used to describe his supporters: 'the benefit was well attended by the *knights of the leek*'.

KNOWLEDGE-BOX – The head.

LIGHT WEIGHTS – A pugilistic expression for gentlemen under 12 stone. If under nine stone, they receive the appellation of *little-ones*.

LISTENER – The ear. 'Gas now planted his favourite hit under the left *listener* of his antagonist, which sent him to *dorse*.' Vide *Fancy Gazette*.

LOVE – Nothing; to fight for love, or play for it, is to do so without payment.

L.P.R. – The 'London Prize Ring'. A pugilist was thought of little consequence until he had featured in the L.P.R.

MARK – To hit to the mark (Ring). The pit of the stomach is termed '*the mark*,' and 'Broughton's mark'. It was Bill Warr's favourite hit; also, had been Dick Humphries'.

MASTER OF THE CEREMONIES – (Ring) He who at the Fives' Court, or other sparring exhibition, shows up and announces the combatants, and ties on the gloves. 'Joe Norton was the long time MC and died *in office*; his pay, *8s. 6d.* per diem. *The Colonel* (Lennox) was occasionally vice ould Joe, as he is also, of Paddington Jones – the actual Master of the Ceremonies.'

MASTER OF THE NOBLE ART OF SELF-DEFENCE – This was a title with official status that was awarded to a scholar who had studied the use of weaponry and achieved a high level of skill. The original 'prize-fighters' were weapons exponents who took part in stage fights known as 'trials of skill', meaning that they were armed with weapons as opposed to being engaged in a 'trial of manhood' (using the fists). Although James Figg is generally known as England's first pugilistic champion, he was better known in his time for his skill with weapons. There is some evidence to suggest that boxing or fist fighting was looked upon as a lesser art by the weapons exponents. Also see *Trial of Manhood*, *Trial of Skill*.

MAWLEY – The hand or fist. 'He pounded his opponent with his *mawleys*.' Sometimes written as 'morleys'.

MAZZARD – The face, or sometimes the whole head.

MILL – A fight.

MILLER – A prize fighter (specifically fists and not weapons). Usually a second-rate boxer, whose arms run round in rapid succession, not always falling very hard, or with determinate object; and they seldom win against equal strength in a scientific opponent, but by accident. 'Gas was a *miller*; the Hudsons *were* nothing else – but Josh improves. Shelton is a reformed miller: Scroggins, an incorrigible one.'

MILLING – The act of boxing. 'Good *milling* was seen on both sides.'

MILLING COVE – A boxer. 'How the milling cove served the cull out'; how the boxer beat the fellow.

MILVADERING – Boxing (Scottish).

MOULDER – A lumbering boxer, one who fights as if he were moulding clay. 'Go along, *moulder*,' i.e. fight on.

MUFFLERS – Boxing gloves, used in sparring, with knuckles padded by wool.

MUZZLER – (Ring) A blow, slanting upwards, placed on the upper tip of the nose; the 'latter is most effectualy conducive towards victory of any blow whatever, – 'tis a puzzler too.'

NAP – Nap it – to get the worst of a contest – 'at fistycuffs' is understood. 'To *nap toco* for yam,' to get more beating than is given.

NOB – The head. 'His *nob* was *pinked* all over,' i.e. marked in sundry places.

NOBBER – A blow launched at the head. 'He hit him with *nobbers*, left and right.'

NONPAREIL CLUB – This club was established at the house of John Randall, the celebrated pugilist, at the Hole-in-the-Wall, Chancery Lane, in 1819 and named after him, from his being termed the Nonpareil of the boxers. 'It is held every Monday evening during the season; and it is *free* and *easy*.'

NOSEGAY – A blow on the nose.

NOUS-BOX – The head.

NOVICE – (Ring) A new or untried boxer.

NOZZLE – The nose.

NULLING COVE – A fighting man.

OGLES – Eyes.

ONE-TWO – In boxing, two blows rapidly put in after each other with alternate hands. Jem Belcher was distinguished for his one-two. Also see *Tapping*.

OUT-AND-OUTER – Complete, up to everything. He who engages in any matter, and sticks to it like a trump, is an *out-and-outer*. Ned Turner was for a long time 'nothing but an *out-and-outer*.'

PARRY – (Ring) To prevent blows descending on the body, whereupon the receiver should return with the same hand. See *Stop*, *Guard*, *Counter-hit*.

PATLANDER – An Irishman.

PAY-AWAY – (Ring) When one man gets disabled by a stunning blow or otherwise, the other '*sarves* (serves) him out,' fast and quick, by paying away at his nob, ribs and bread-basket.

PEEPERS – Eyes. Single peeper; a one-eyed man.

TO PICK – (Wrestling) Provincial phrase used in the North of England, meaning to throw a man.

PINK – One deemed to be above the common herd in his chosen pursuit/ pastime, is a *pink*. 'Such *a pink* at skittles is Jem Bunn, he is *the pink* of all Bow,' i.e. the best player at skittles in the town of Bow. 'My bitch beat the best among them tonight; she is *the pink* of the pit so far.' 'Now, be *a pink* for once,' said to a combatant to keep up his spirits. 'I felt myself suddenly *pinked* all over, like the man in the almanack; no blow of finishing importance to be sure, but all conducing toward victory' – vide Jack Furby's account of his battle with Belcher. 'Meddle with my affairs and I'll *pink* your eye out; a common place rebuff. 'In this round, the baker's eye showed *pinky*.'

POMMEL – To beat; originally confined to beating with the hilt of a sword, the knob being, from its similarity to a small apple, called *pomelle*; in Spain it is still called the apple of the sword. As the clenched fist likewise somewhat resembles an apple, perhaps that might occasion the term pomelling to be applied to fisticuffs.

POTATOE-TRAP – The mouth.

PUG – A shortened term for pugilist.

PUGILISM – The art and practice of manual defence. Derived from *pugiles* – the fists, and *pugnandum* – fighting. 'Straight hitting from the shoulder; to parry and counter-hit; to *throw* the adversary when *in*, to *get out* from his clutches, or drop from his grasp out of a chancery-suit – are characteristics of the Bristol, or native school of *pugilism*.'

PUGILISTIC CLUB, P.C. – A society of gentlemen, founded in 1814, expressly for the purpose of keeping alive the 'principles of courage and hardihood which have distinguished the British character, and to check the progress of that effeminacy which wealth is apt to produce. Men of rank, associating together, learn to prize the native and acquire powers of human nature. The incitement which they produce to noble deeds of hardihood and bravery, and the high respectability which they confer by the patronage of their rank and fortune, is of inestimable benefit.' This club consists of about 120 subscribers.

PULLY-HAWLEY – Abbreviated from 'pull-away, haul-away,' – apparently the action and cheering at finishing a first-rate cable. In ring affairs, two novices getting hold of each other, *pully-hawley* for the throw.

PURR – (Ring) The rushing-in Lancashire fashion, with head against an opponent's guts: inefficacious. See *Rush*.

PURRING – Shin-kicking in an attempt to wrestle an opponent to the ground.

RAW 'UNS – A term used to denote a fight held with bare knuckles rather than boxing gloves. He had won 30 fights with the *raw 'uns*.

RETURN-BLOW – (Ring) When one combatant, having planted a hit, receives a blow from his adversary with the same hand ('within a *colon-pause*').

THE RING.

***The Ring*, is the roped space within which pugilists and boxers display their science or their hardihood. It is usually 24 feet each way, though liable to alteration. These two men, attended by seconds and bottle-holders are within a roped space on the turf. The mode of setting to is that of Abra. Belasco and Jack Martin, the latter standing *square*, the former drawing up the right mawley for a hit—if possible. Ould Joe Norton and Tom Owen, intheir lilly shallows, show they have the sun in their eyes, the others (Belcher and Jones) having won the *toss*.**

THE RING – The roped space within which pugilists display their science or their hardihood; usually about 24 feet each way, and by an easy transition, applied to those who look on, or take delight in the manly contests there exhibited. 'I leave it to the ring.' 'Not a voice was heard all round the ring'. They are divided into *amateurs* (persons of property) and 'the men,' or boxers, part of whom only are *pugilists*. The word is derived from a certain circular space enclosed with rails in Hyde Park, by command of George II, having a large oak in the middle; the area is now planted with young limes and the railing is decayed; going straight up from Grosvenor Gate, *the ring* lies about 550 steps into the park.[362]

ROLLS – Dough-baked small bread, eaten by low-bred cockneys for the most part. By a poor pun, 'Master of the *Rolls*' – is any baker, 'if he can box any.' Jack Martin is the actual Master of the Rolls.

ROUNDS – (Ring) When boxers set-to, they fight till down, and that is *a round*; the next *round* begins not until *half a minute*, at least, has expired. Any deviation, attended with fatal consequences, is an act constituting manslaughter, on the part of the assistants.

RUFFIAN – In the pugilistic *cant*, is a fellow regardless of knowledge of the science; one who hits away right or wrong, so that he can only obtain conquest.

RUSH – (Ring) When a milling-cove runs in at his opponent, hitting away hard and sharp, his head is more or less low. (see *Purr*). 'Such must be received

362 The featured illustration for this term is taken from *Sportsman's Slang: A New Dictionary of Terms Used in the Affairs of the Turf, the Ring, the Chase and the Cock-pit, etc.*, by Jon Bee, (London: W. Lewis, 1825).

by sharp right and left nobbers, continuing to retreat; and tis fair and safe to tumble over the ropes, to drop, as if from the blows.'

SARVICE, SARVE OUT – (Ring) See *pay-away*, which being done effectually, is a *sarvice*, i.e. of some service towards victory.

SATISFACTION – To demand of any man satisfaction, is an invitation to fight. Used in both duelling with weapons and fighting using the fists.

SAWNY – A general nickname for a 'Scotchman', as Paddy is for an Irishman, or Taffy for a Welshman. Sometimes misspelt as Sawney, which is a term for a flitch of bacon.

SCRATCH – (Ring) 'The *scratch*,' is a mark made in the middle of a stage, room, or ring, in which men may be fighting, and up to which, as to a centre, the men are to be brought at the commencement of each round; if one cannot come to this mark (real or 'supposed, for 'tis not always distinct') in *time*, he is pronounced the loser.

SCIENCE, (*the*) – The art and practice of boxing, according to rule. 'Conductive to success herein, amateurs reckon mainly upon quantity, but admit other requisites, which may augment or diminish the chances in favour of either party, as these may be possessed in a greater or less degree of perfection – these are, 1. Weight. 2. Strength. 3. Activity. 4. Skill (or Science.) 5. Bottom.'

SECOND – (Ring) – (seldom performed completely) He who aids with advice the actual pugilist, or, indeed, boxer; who, when his principal is down, 'raises him up, bodily, supports him on his knee, gives advice as to the opponent's weak points, admonishes him if neglectful – cheers him up – moistens his lips with water or orange, and, as the contest is protracted, with brandy diluted, who, if an accident happens, takes prompt means of alleviation. He must be furnished with a lancet, to let out the extravasated blood *below* the puff; and never desert his man on account of reverse of luck.'

SEEKING THE GRASS – The strategy of throwing oneself down in a prize fight, either at the lightest contact, or sometimes without contact at all, bringing about the end of a round, and enabling a second-rate pugilist to take a rest. The practice is also sometimes referred to as 'Seeking the turf', and much frowned upon in the London Prize Ring.

SHIVER – '*Shiver* his fist' (Ring) When a boxer means mischief and 'nothing else,' he shakes his hand and generally lets fly with it. This happens early in the battle, usually; 'but 'tis a symptom of gayness that leaves a man, as the contest approaches the end.'

SLAP-BANG – A blow from each hand. See *One-Two*.

SLASHING FIGHTER – He who throws about his arms without judgement, but heavily.

STAKES – Money put down to be contended for at a horse race, boxing match, etc.

STINGER – A sharp and rapid hit, generally understood to be placed upon the 'upper works', is described as – 'My eyes, what a *stinger*!'

STINKER – A black eye.

STOP A BLOW – (Ring) To prevent its alighting on the part intended, by means of *the guard*, or position of defence, i.e. the forearm or elbow. But this was effected differently by the several schools: the Broughtonian caught the coming blow on the perpendicular arm, which enabled them to make a quick return, cutting downwards. Mendoza's consisted of throwing up the arm from the elbow, catching the adversary at the wrist or higher, which disabled the muscle, and spoiled that arm awhile, when he chopped. The Bristolian *tactic* is to hit past the intended blow, length-wise, inside the arm (if possible), when the arm must be thrown away, and the man stopping be well in; but he gets himself to off-fighting again, if desirable, by hitting the ribs with the other hand – this springs him back, though he has the option of in-fighting, if, instead thereof, he lets fly at the neck, throat and upper-works. Harmer's guard (a square one) for the head, or rather his eyes, would inevitably cost him a broken arm (when fighting) were he a shorter man. The sloping guard, against an antagonist's main arm, who ruffians in, is a good one and effectual, as exemplified in the celebrated battle of Neat and Hickman. We said, "If Neat can be induced to fight upon the retreating system, knocking away at the nob of his antagonist, as he comes on, with an almost straight left-handed guard, while hitting away with the right, he may pockets the brads, and realise the odds that are now so freely laid upon the invincible gas-man." Vide *(Old) Fancy*, for 4 November 1821.

STOTER – A great blow. 'Tip him a stoter in the haltering place'; give him a blow under the left ear.

SUIT OF MOURNING – A pair of black eyes.

SWELL – A gentleman; but any well-dressed person is emphatically termed a swell, or a rank swell, a family man who appears to have plenty of money, and makes a genteel figure, is said, by his associates, to be in 'Swell-street'. Sometimes, in alluding to a particular gentleman, whose name is not requisite, he is styled *the swell*, meaning the person who is the object of your discourse or attention.

TAPP'D – (Ring) 'He tapp'd his claret,' – gave him a bloody nose.

TAPPING – When an opponent is repeatedly hit with the one-two. See *One-Two*.

TEAZER – A hit on some queer point, as on the tip of the nose.

THING – 'A *thing* of a man' is he who has not much sense or spunk in him. A poor, weak, but pretending mortal, is a *thing*, whether his defect be of mind or body. After punishing Tom Spring, Jack Randall said he had never been beaten by a '*thing*' – alluding to Spring's fight against Ned Painter, who Randall perceived to be an inferior fighter.

THROW – (Ring) When boxers are tired at 'in-fighting,' they struggle to get each other down, and *the throw* is sometimes rendered so hard as to win the battle, especially when an adroit tumble upon the opponent's wind is added thereto. See *Full*, *Floorer*, &c. A *throw* over the knee is effected similarly to a cross-buttock, but is not half as effectual, unless the thrower punishes him as his adversary is going down.

TIE UP *in the wind* – (Ring) A blow on the *mark* will do it for anyone. '*Tie yourself up*' – to bind oneself negatively, either not to *play*, to *fight*, to *lay bets*, &c. for a certain period, usually to the end of time; but seldom kept. 'My opinion is Tom Cribb may safely tie-up from this time.' Vide *Soares's speech*.

TOM OWEN'S STOP – (Ring) Left hand open, crawling over the antagonist's face, service with the right – a poor strategy.

TOPPER – A violent blow on the head: also, a hat.

TOSS FOR SIDES – A custom adopted in the prize ring, to decide which man shall face the sun. The seconds '*shy a copper*'.

TRIAL OF MANHOOD – A phrase employed in the early days of prize fighting to denote a fight was to be a pugilistic contest (using fists), rather than a 'trial of skill' (using weapons). It was not uncommon for boxing, cudgelling and wrestling to feature as 'diversions' prior to a trial of skill, although trials of manhood and trials of skill very rarely appeared on the same billing.

TRIAL OF SKILL – A phrase employed to denote that a contest fought between early prize fighters was using weaponry, and not a 'trial of manhood' (using fists). A number of weapons were employed in a contest of this kind, including the backsword, sword and dagger, sword and buckler, single falchion, a case of falchions (a pair), and the quarter staff.

TURN-UP – A fight produced from a hasty quarrel. A casual boxing match. It is also to desist from, or relinquish, any particular habit or mode of life. To quit a person suddenly in the street is termed, *turning him up*.

TWO-HANDED – Great. A two-handed fellow or wench; a great strapping man or woman.

WALLUP – A random hit, anywhere. 'A walloping bout', a fight without skill.

WAP – A species of slap, resounding, as if imparted by a wet dishclout. So, a man may tumble down, *wap*, in battle, when he gets grassed by the *first intention*.

WHIP OUT THE RING – To 'whip out the ring', 10 or 12 pugilists, with whips, clear a large space round the *roped ring*; and the spectators then form the personal ring, or outer ring; the whippers' pay is 5s. each.

WRANGLE – (Ring) Is that state of a battle, wherein the spectators, losers, try to make a drawn battle by jawbation, as in the case of Warren and Curtis.

X – The sign of cheatery, see *Cross*.

YELLOW-MAN – The silk *fogle* or canary, tied round the neat squeeze of our pugilists. John Gully introduced the *yellow-man* (according to Jon Bee).

Bibliography

Books

Beck, Rev Thomas, *The Age of Frivolity: a Poem Addressed to the Fashionable, the Busy and the Religious World,* Third Edition, Revised and Enlarged (London: Maxwell and Wilson, 1809).

Bee, Jon, (pseud.) [John Badcock] *Fancy-Ana; or A History of Pugilism, From Figg and Broughton's Time to Spring and Langan's; Including Every Transaction in the Prize-Ring, And Every Incident Worthy Notice (whether of Spree, Turn-Up, Boxing-Match, or Prize-Fight,) From 1719 to 1824 Inclusive.* (London: W. Lewis, 1824).

Bee, Jon, (pseud.) [John Badcock] *Sportsman's Slang: A New Dictionary of Terms Used in the Affairs of the Turf, the Ring, the Chase and the Cock-pit, etc.* (London: W. Lewis, 1825).

Besant, Sir Walter, *London in the Time of the Stuarts,* Volume 6, (London: A & C. Black, 1903).

Bingley, Rev. William, *North Wales: Including Its Scenery, Antiquities, Customs, and Some Sketches of Its Natural History, etc., Volume 1* (London: T. N. Longman and O. Rees, 1804).

Castle, Egerton, *Schools and Masters of Fencing From the Middle Ages to the Eighteenth Century,* (London: George Bell and Sons, 1885).

Dowling, Francis, *Fistiana: or The Oracle of the Ring* (London: Offices of Bell's Life, 1868).

Dowling, Vincent, *Fistiana: or The Oracle of the Ring* (London: William Clement, 1841).

Dowling, Vincent, *Fistiana: or The Oracle of the Ring* (London: William Clement, 1845).

Dowling, Vincent, *Fistiana: or The Oracle of the Ring* (London: William Clement, 1846).

Egan, Pierce, *Boxiana; or, Sketches of Ancient and Modern Pugilism,* Vol 1-5 (London: 1812 – 1829).

Egan, Pierce, *Pierce Egan's Book of Sports, and Mirror of Life: Embracing the Turf, the Chase, the Ring and the Stage Interspersed with Original Memoirs of Sporting Men, etc,* (London: Thomas Tegg and Son, 1836).

Erskine (trans), *The Memoirs and Adventures of the Marquis de Bretagne and Duc D'Harcourt, etc. Vol 2.* (London: T. Cooper, 1743).

Evans, Rev. John, *A Tour Through Part of North Wales: In the Year 1798, Principally Undertaken with a View to Botanical Researches In that Alpine Country, etc.,* (London: J. White, 1800).

Evans, Rev. John, *The Beauties of England and Wales: Or Delineations, Topographical, Historical, and Descriptive, of Each County* (London: Longman and Co., 1812).

Ford, John, *Prizefighting, The Age of Regency Boxiamania* (Newton Abbott: David and Charles, 1971).

Gee, Tony, *Up To Scratch, Bareknuckle Fighting and Heroes of the Prize-ring* (Harpenden: Queen Anne Press, 1998).

Godfrey, Capt. John, *A Treatise upon the Useful Science of Defence* (London: Robinson and Milton's, 1747).

Grose, Francis, *Classical Dictionary of the Vulgar Tongue, Revised by Pierce Egan* (London: Sherwood, Neely, and Jones, 1823).

Henning, Fred, *Fights for the Championship, The Men and Their Times* (London: Licensed Victualler's Gazette, 1902).

Lucas, John, *The Memoranda Book of John Lucas* 1712–1750 (Leeds: The Thoresby Society, 2006).

Magriel, Paul (ed), *The Memoirs of the Life of Daniel Mendoza* (London: B.T. Batsford Ltd. 1951).

Malcom, James Peller, F.S.A, *Anecdotes of the Manners and Customs of London During the Eighteenth Century*, Volume 2 (London: Longman, Hurst, Rees and Orme, 1810).

McBane, Donald, *The Expert Sword-Man's Companion* (Glasgow: J. Duncan, 1728).

Miles, Henry Downes, *Pugilistica: The History of British Boxing, Vols. 1 & 2* (London: Weldona and Co., 1880-1881; reprint, Edinburgh: John Grant, 1906).

Miller, Captain James, *A Treatise on backsword, sword, buckler, sword and dagger, sword and great gauntlet, falchon, quarterstaff,* (London: 1738).

Moore, Thomas, *Jack Randall's Diary of Proceedings at the House of Call for Genius* (London: W. Simpkin and R. Marshall, 1820).

Oxberry, William, *Pancratia, or a History of Pugilism* (London: W. Oxberry, 1812).

Parry, Richard, *The History of Kington, by a member of the Mechanics institute of Kington,* (Kington: Charles Humphreys, 1845).

Pepys, Samuel, *Diary and Correspondence of Samuel Pepys, Vol. 2,* (Philadelphia: J.B. Lippincott & Co., 1866).

Pugnus, *History of the Prize Ring, Parts 1 & 2* (London: B.T. Gale, 1876-1877).

Rocheford, Lorevin de, *An Account of a Journey to the British Isles*' (Paris: 1672).

Articles, Journals and Periodicals

Gee, Tony, 'Broughton, John (*c*.1703–1789)', *Oxford Dictionary of National Biography*, (Oxford: Oxford University Press, 2004).

Gee, Tony, 'Figg, James (*b*. Before 1700, *d*. 1734)', *Oxford Dictionary of National Biography*, (Oxford: Oxford University Press, 2004).

The Gentleman's and London Magazine or Monthly Chronologer, 1741–1794 (Dublin: John Exshaw).

Historical & Archaeological Collections Relating to Montgomeryshire and its Borders, Vol. XLV., Issued by the Powys-Land Club (Welshpool: David Rowlands Ltd.,1938).

La Belle Assemblée Or, Bell's Court and Fashionable Magazine, Volume 5, (London: J. Bell, 1808).

Sporting Magazine: Or, Monthly Calendar of the Transactions of the Turf, the Chase and Every Other Diversion Interesting to the Man of Pleasure, Enterprize, and Spirit, Volume 6, (London: Rogerson & Tuxford, 1820).

Sporting Magazine: Or, Monthly Calendar of the Transactions of the Turf, the Chase and Every Other Diversion Interesting to the Man of Pleasure, Enterprize, and Spirit, Volume 8, (London: Rogerson & Tuxford, 1821).

Sporting Magazine: Or, Monthly Calendar of the Transactions of the Turf, the Chase and Every Other Diversion Interesting to the Man of Pleasure, Enterprize, and Spirit, Volume 11, (London: Rogerson & Tuxford, 1823).

Sporting Magazine: Or, Monthly Calendar of the Transactions of the Turf, the Chase and Every Other Diversion Interesting to the Man of Pleasure, Enterprize, and Spirit, Volume 25, (London: J. Wheble, 1805).

The Sportsman's Magazine & Life in London and the Country, Volume 1 – 'The History of British Boxing from Fig and Broughton to the Modern Time' (London: F. Dipple, 1845).

Newspapers

Annals of Sporting and Fancy Gazette

Bell's Life in London and Sporting Chronicle

Bristol Mercury

Bristol Mirror

The Cambrian

Cambridge Chronicle and Journal

Carmarthen Journal and South Wales Weekly Advertiser

Cheltenham Chronicle

Chester Chronicle

Cumberland Pacquet, and Ware's Whitehaven Advertiser

Daily Advertiser
Daily Courant
Diary; or Woodfall's Register
Dublin Correspondent
Dublin Evening Post
Famous Fights – Past and Present
The Globe
Hampshire Chronicle
Hereford Journal
Hull Packet
Ipswich Journal
Kentish Gazette
Kentish Weekly Post or Canterbury Journal
Liverpool Mercury
London Chronicle
Mist's Weekly Journal
Monmouthshire Merlin
Morning Advertiser
Morning Chronicle, and London Advertiser
Morning Post and Daily Advertiser
Morning Post and Gazetteer
North Wales Chronicle
North Wales Gazette
Penny London Post, or, the Morning Advertiser
The Post Boy
The Post Man
Public Advertiser
Public Ledger and Daily Advertiser
Salisbury and Winchester Journal
Saunders's News-Letter and Daily Advertiser
Sheffield Independent
St. James's Chronicle; or British Evening Post
The Star
Star Daily Evening Advertiser
Sussex Advertiser
The Times
True Protestant Mercury
Weekly Journal or the British Gazetteer
Whitehall Evening-Post
World, Fashionable Advertiser